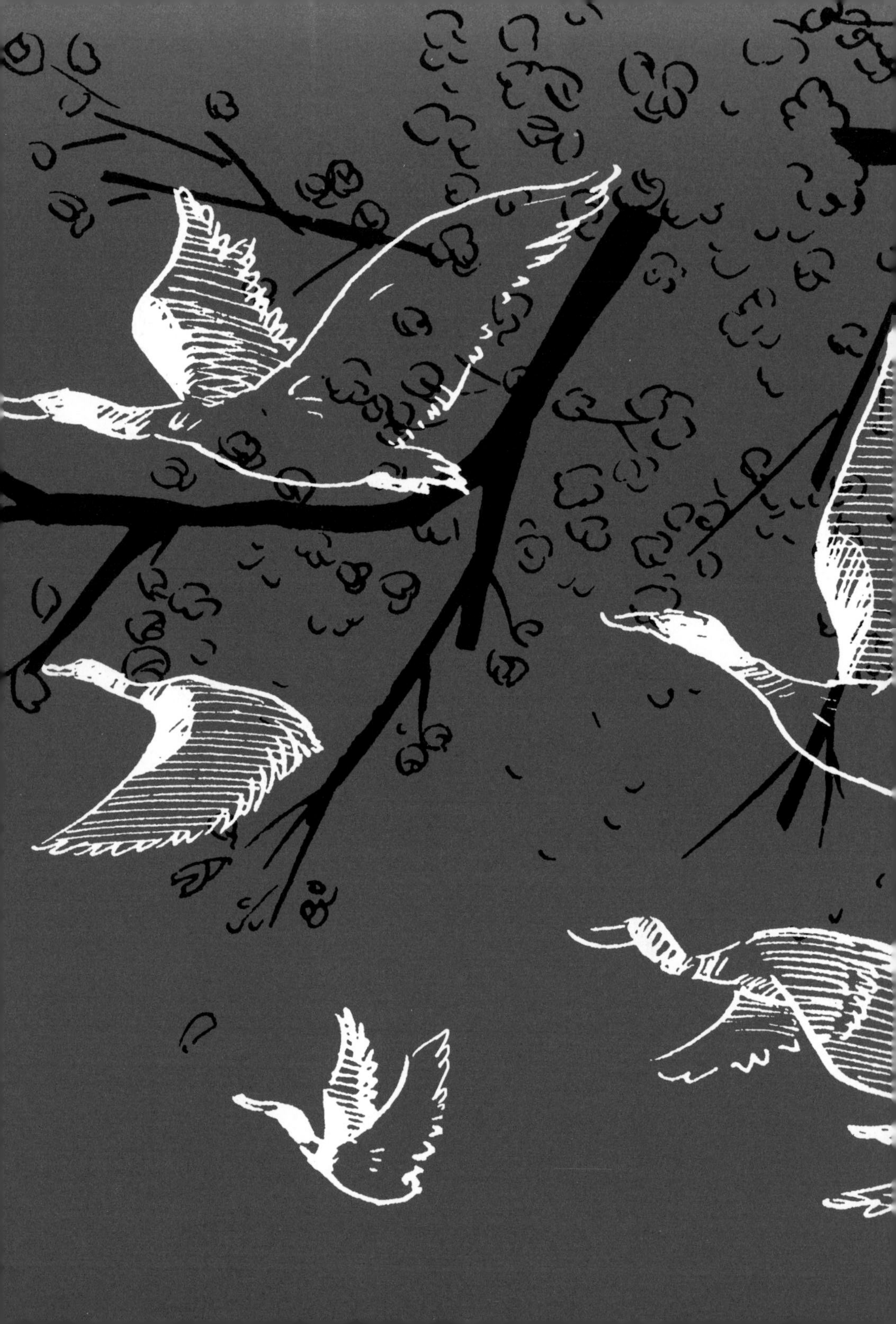

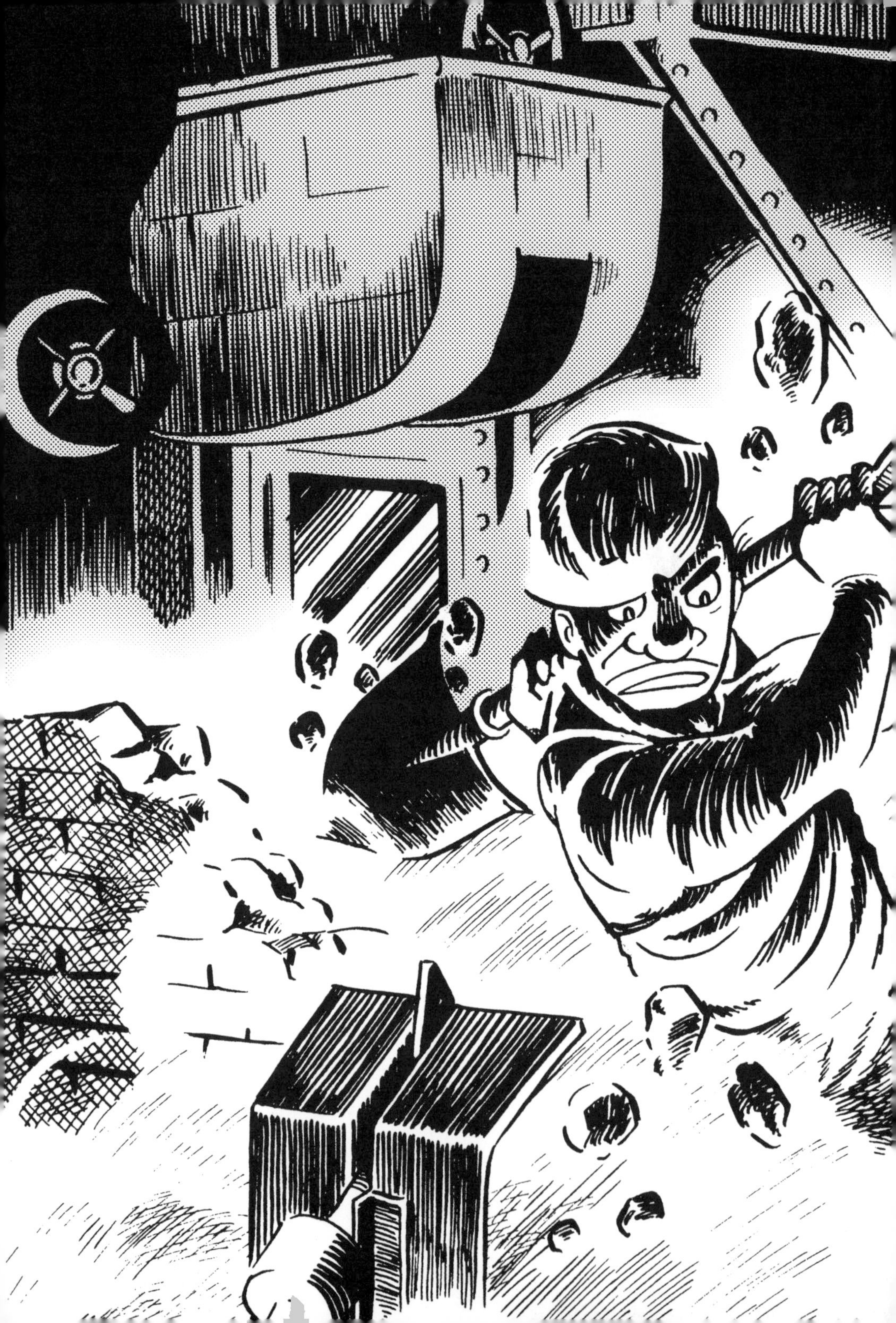

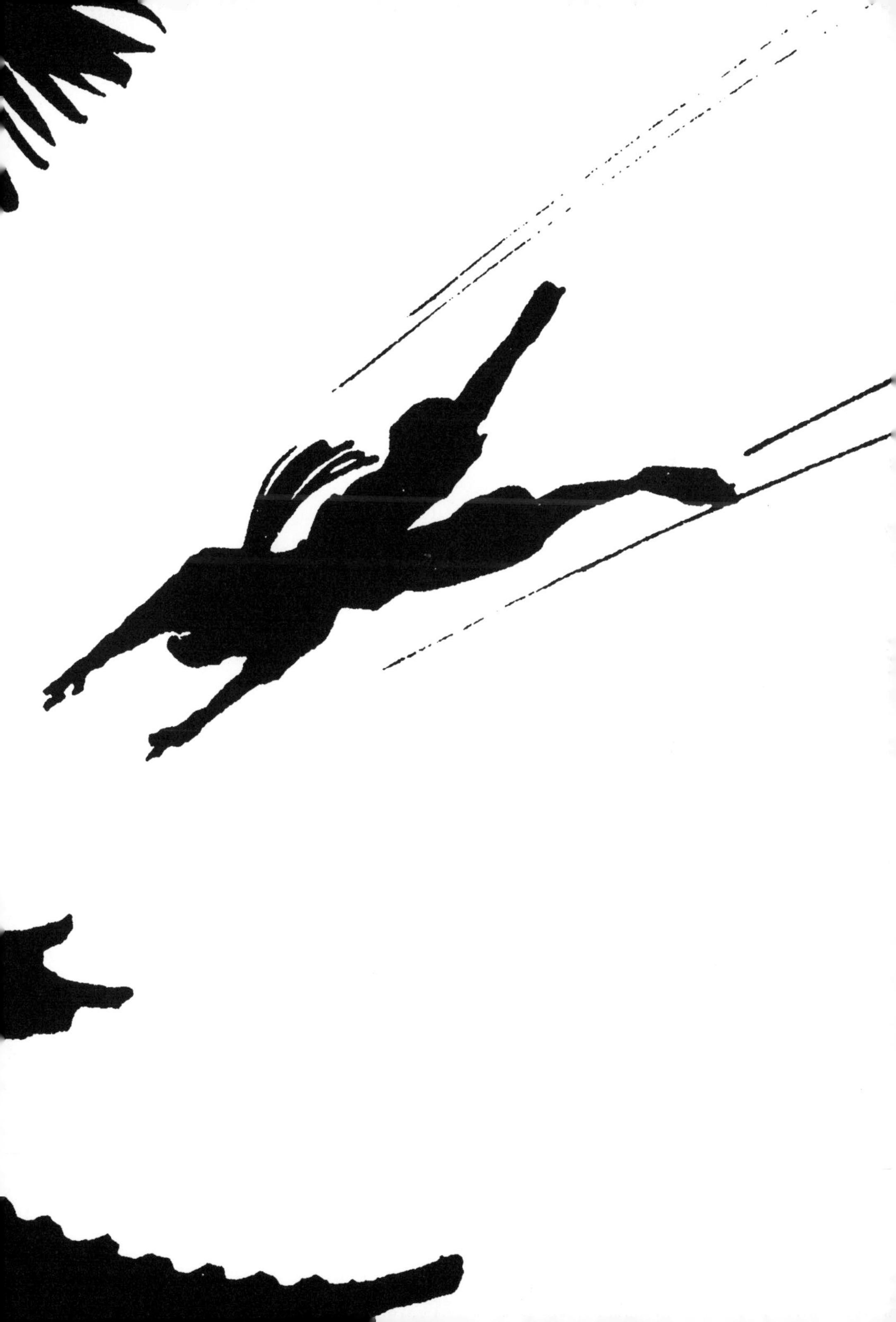

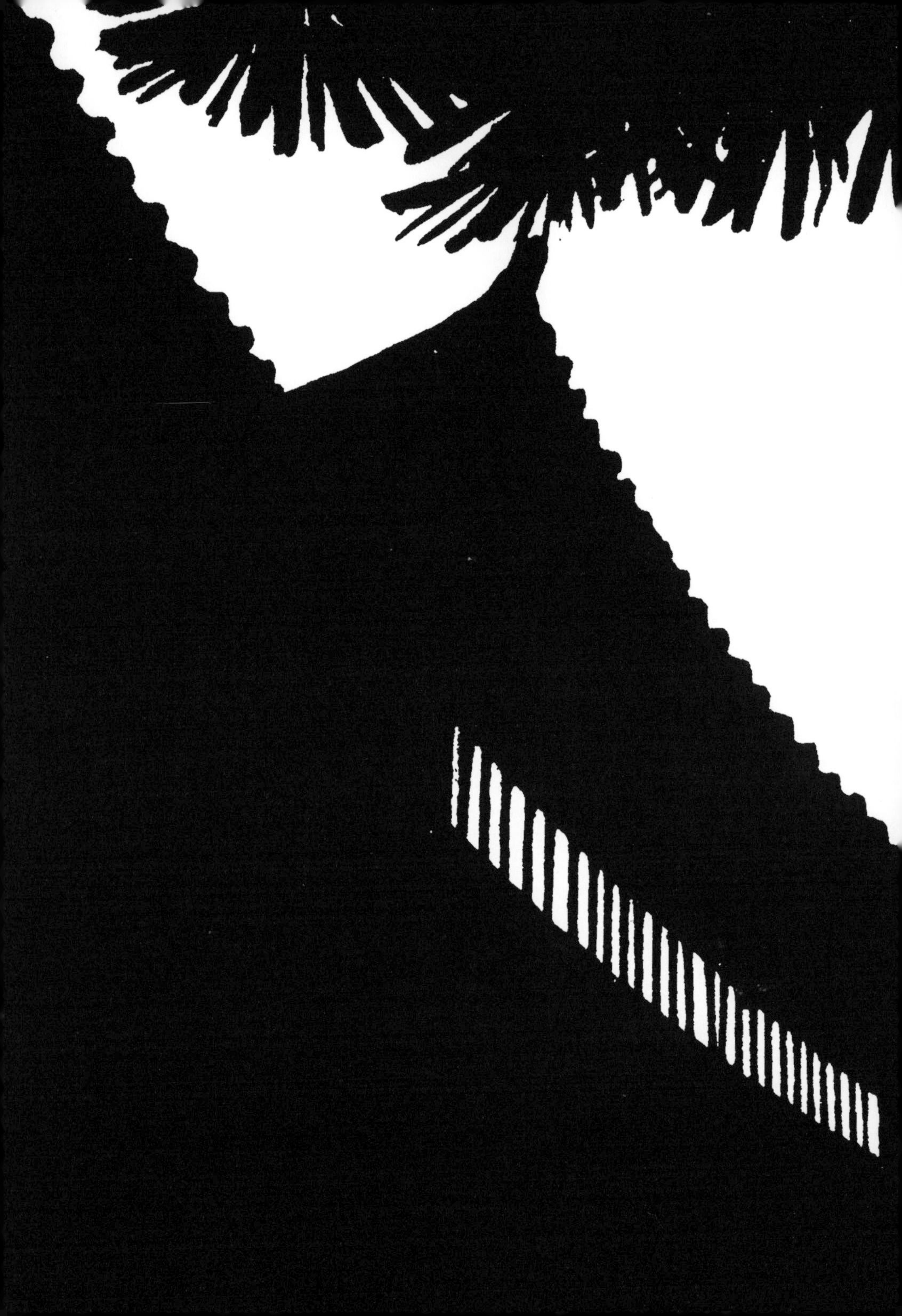

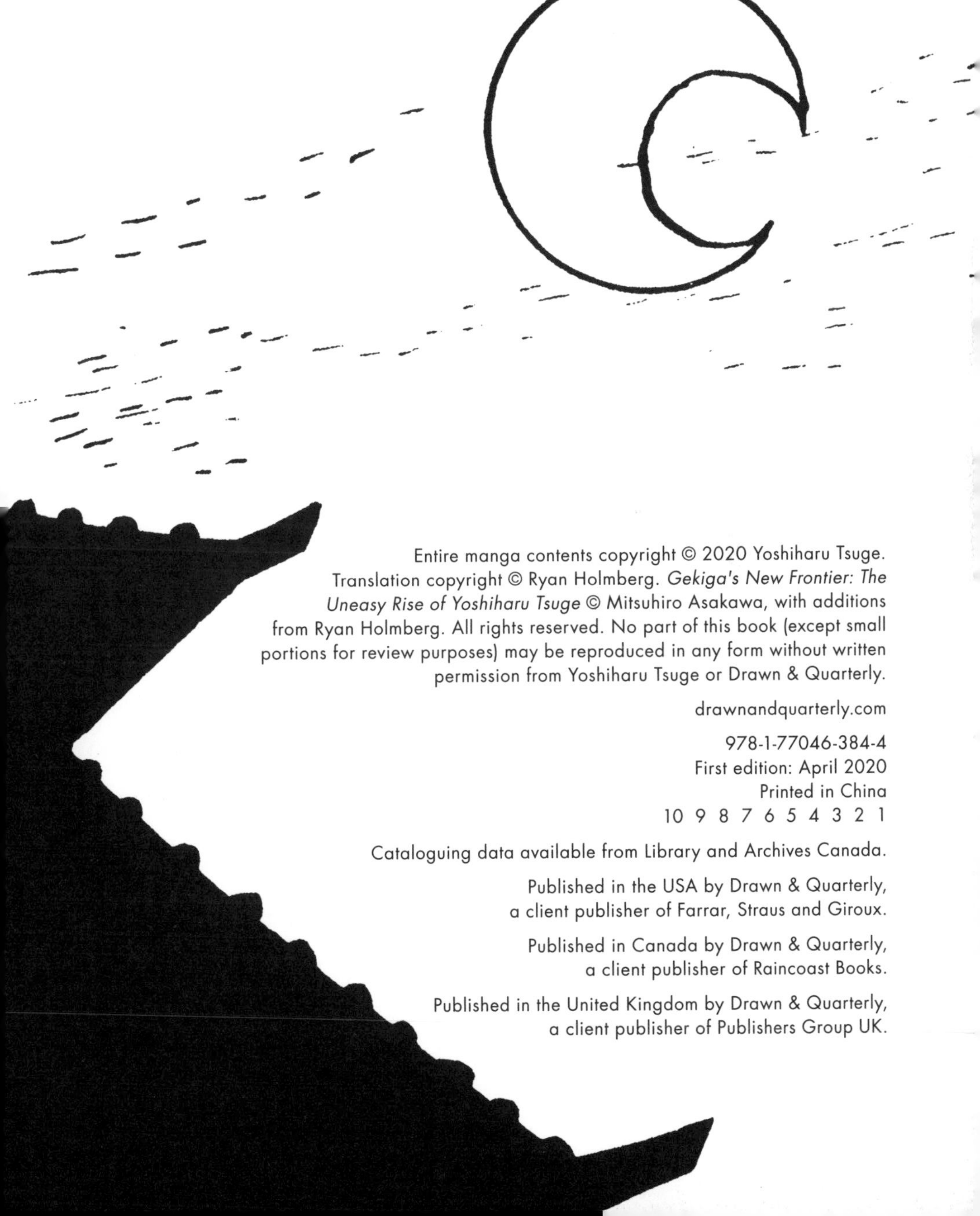

drawnandquarterly.com

978-1-77046-384-4
First edition: April 2020
Printed in China
10 9 8 7 6 5 4 3 2 1

Cataloguing data available from Library and Archives Canada.

Published in the USA by Drawn & Quarterly, a client publisher of Farrar, Straus and Giroux.

Published in Canada by Drawn & Quarterly, a client publisher of Raincoast Books.

Published in the United Kingdom by Drawn & Quarterly, a client publisher of Publishers Group UK.

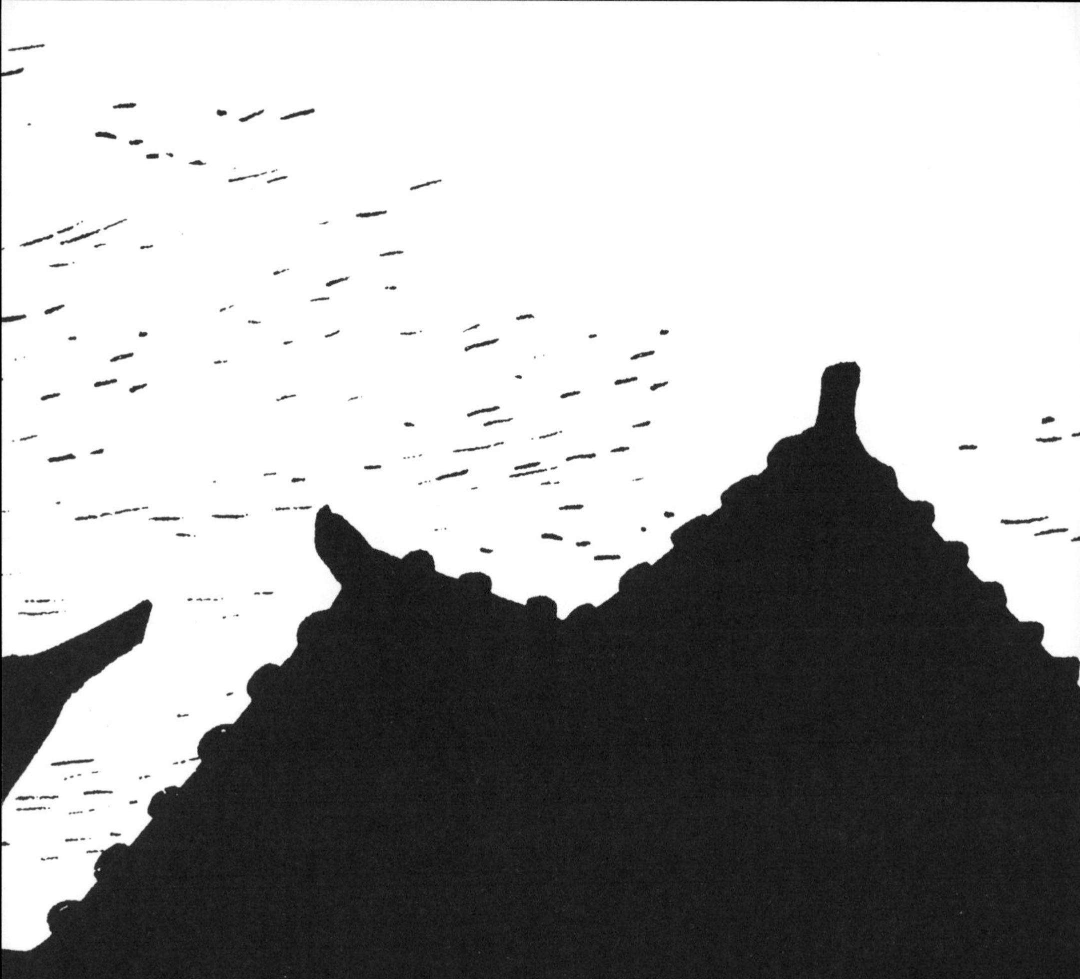

The Swamp

YOSHIHARU TSUGE

The Complete Mature Works of Yoshiharu Tsuge Volume 1

Series editor and essay, Mitsuhiro Asakawa
Co-editor and translation, Ryan Holmberg

DRAWN & QUARTERLY

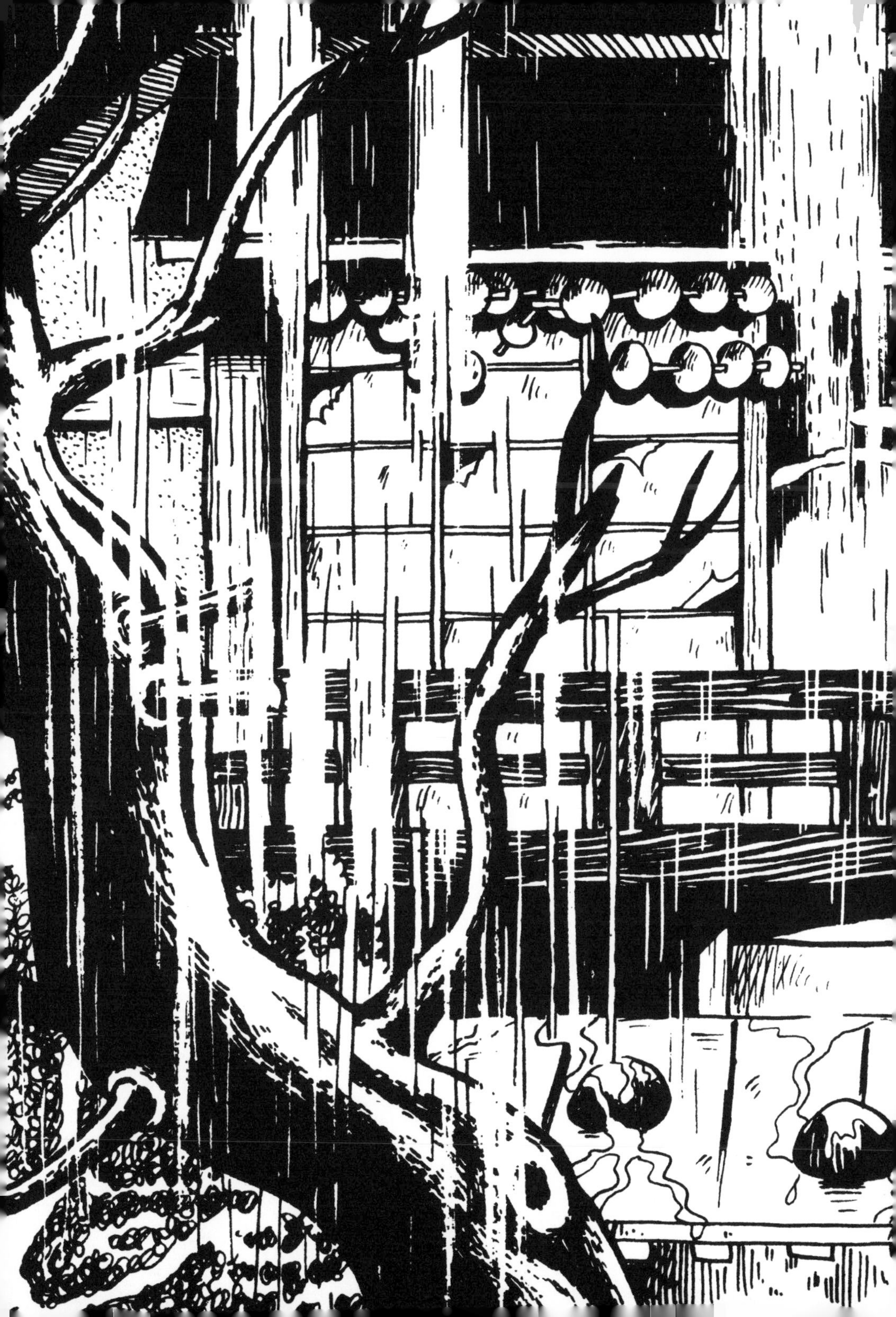

CONTENTS

THE PHONY WARRIOR

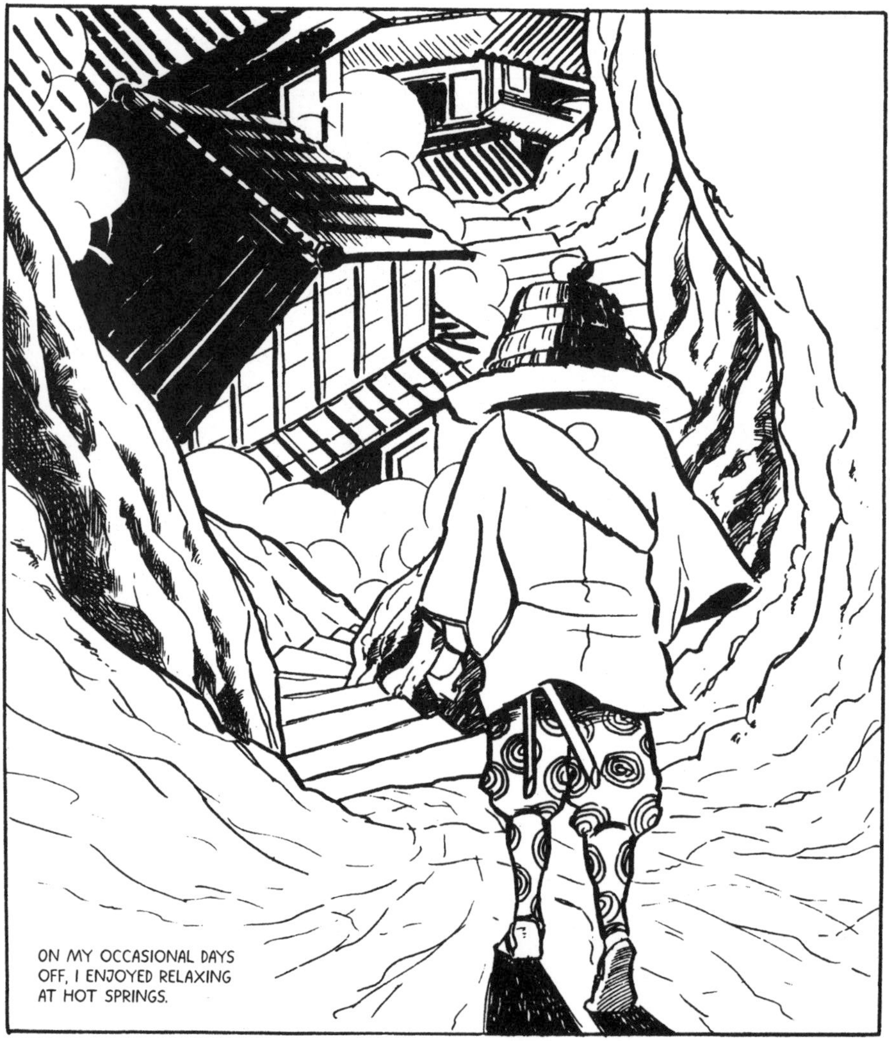
ON MY OCCASIONAL DAYS OFF, I ENJOYED RELAXING AT HOT SPRINGS.

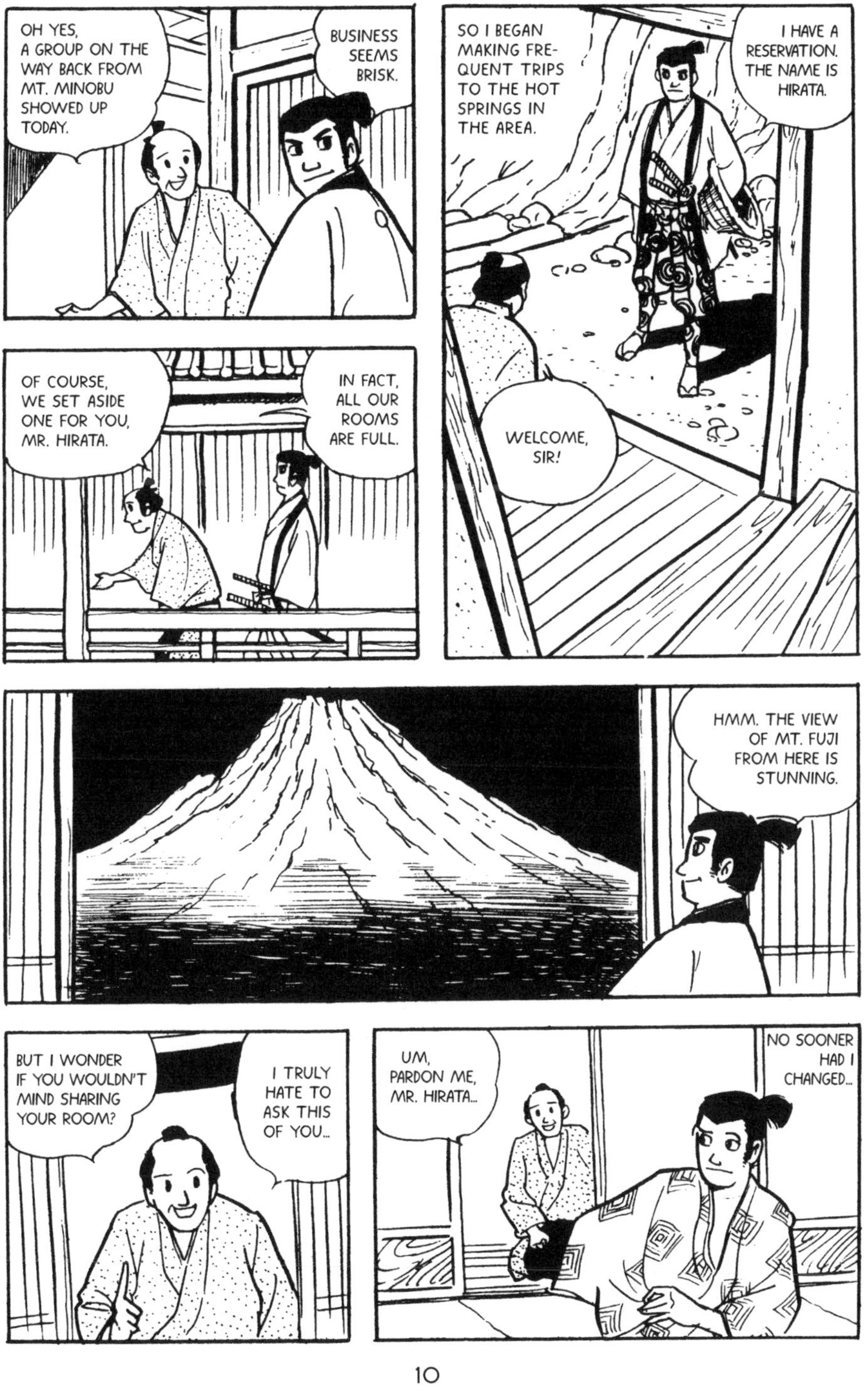
SO I BEGAN MAKING FRE-QUENT TRIPS TO THE HOT SPRINGS IN THE AREA.
I HAVE A RESERVATION. THE NAME IS HIRATA.
WELCOME, SIR!
BUSINESS SEEMS BRISK.
OH YES, A GROUP ON THE WAY BACK FROM MT. MINOBU SHOWED UP TODAY.
IN FACT, ALL OUR ROOMS ARE FULL.
OF COURSE, WE SET ASIDE ONE FOR YOU, MR. HIRATA.
HMM. THE VIEW OF MT. FUJI FROM HERE IS STUNNING.
NO SOONER HAD I CHANGED...
UM, PARDON ME, MR. HIRATA...
I TRULY HATE TO ASK THIS OF YOU...
BUT I WONDER IF YOU WOULDN'T MIND SHARING YOUR ROOM?

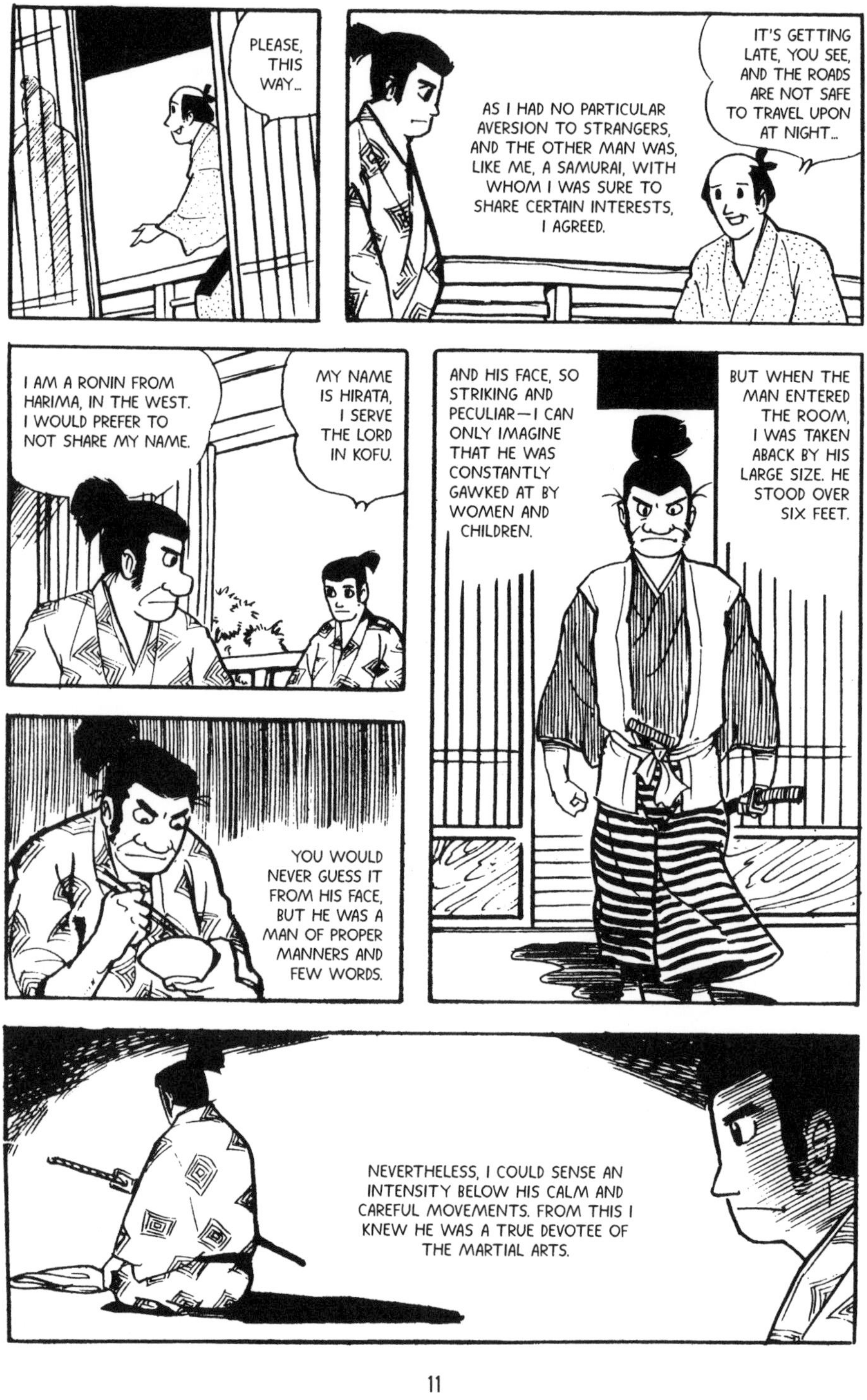
IT'S GETTING LATE, YOU SEE, AND THE ROADS ARE NOT SAFE TO TRAVEL UPON AT NIGHT...
AS I HAD NO PARTICULAR AVERSION TO STRANGERS, AND THE OTHER MAN WAS, LIKE ME, A SAMURAI, WITH WHOM I WAS SURE TO SHARE CERTAIN INTERESTS, I AGREED.
PLEASE, THIS WAY...
BUT WHEN THE MAN ENTERED THE ROOM, I WAS TAKEN ABACK BY HIS LARGE SIZE. HE STOOD OVER SIX FEET.
AND HIS FACE, SO STRIKING AND PECULIAR—I CAN ONLY IMAGINE THAT HE WAS CONSTANTLY GAWKED AT BY WOMEN AND CHILDREN.
MY NAME IS HIRATA, I SERVE THE LORD IN KOFU.
I AM A RONIN FROM HARIMA, IN THE WEST. I WOULD PREFER TO NOT SHARE MY NAME.
YOU WOULD NEVER GUESS IT FROM HIS FACE, BUT HE WAS A MAN OF PROPER MANNERS AND FEW WORDS.
NEVERTHELESS, I COULD SENSE AN INTENSITY BELOW HIS CALM AND CAREFUL MOVEMENTS. FROM THIS I KNEW HE WAS A TRUE DEVOTEE OF THE MARTIAL ARTS.

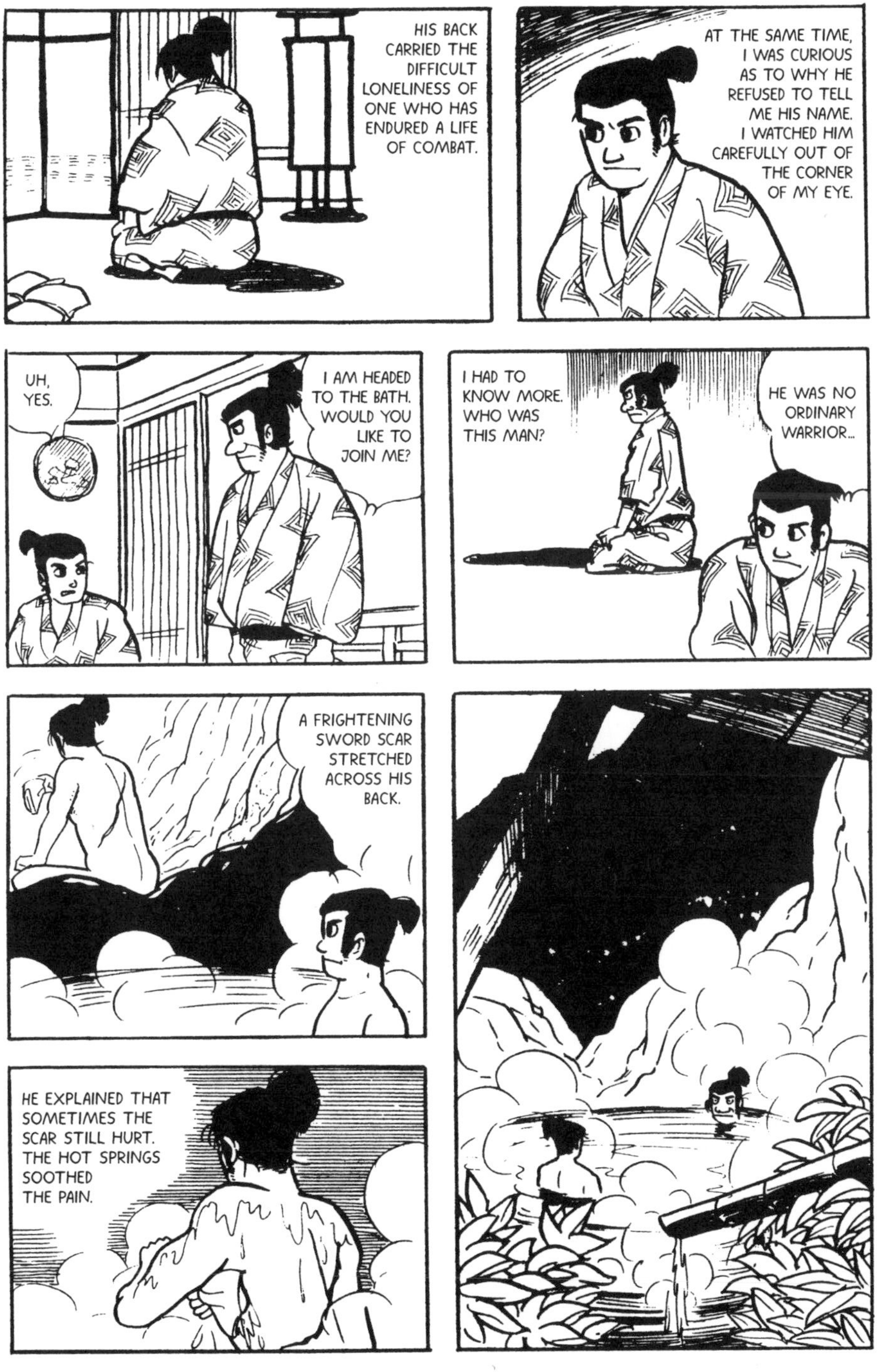
AT THE SAME TIME, I WAS CURIOUS AS TO WHY HE REFUSED TO TELL ME HIS NAME. I WATCHED HIM CAREFULLY OUT OF THE CORNER OF MY EYE.
HIS BACK CARRIED THE DIFFICULT LONELINESS OF ONE WHO HAS ENDURED A LIFE OF COMBAT.
HE WAS NO ORDINARY WARRIOR...
I HAD TO KNOW MORE. WHO WAS THIS MAN?
I AM HEADED TO THE BATH. WOULD YOU LIKE TO JOIN ME?
UH, YES.
A FRIGHTENING SWORD SCAR STRETCHED ACROSS HIS BACK.
HE EXPLAINED THAT SOMETIMES THE SCAR STILL HURT. THE HOT SPRINGS SOOTHED THE PAIN.

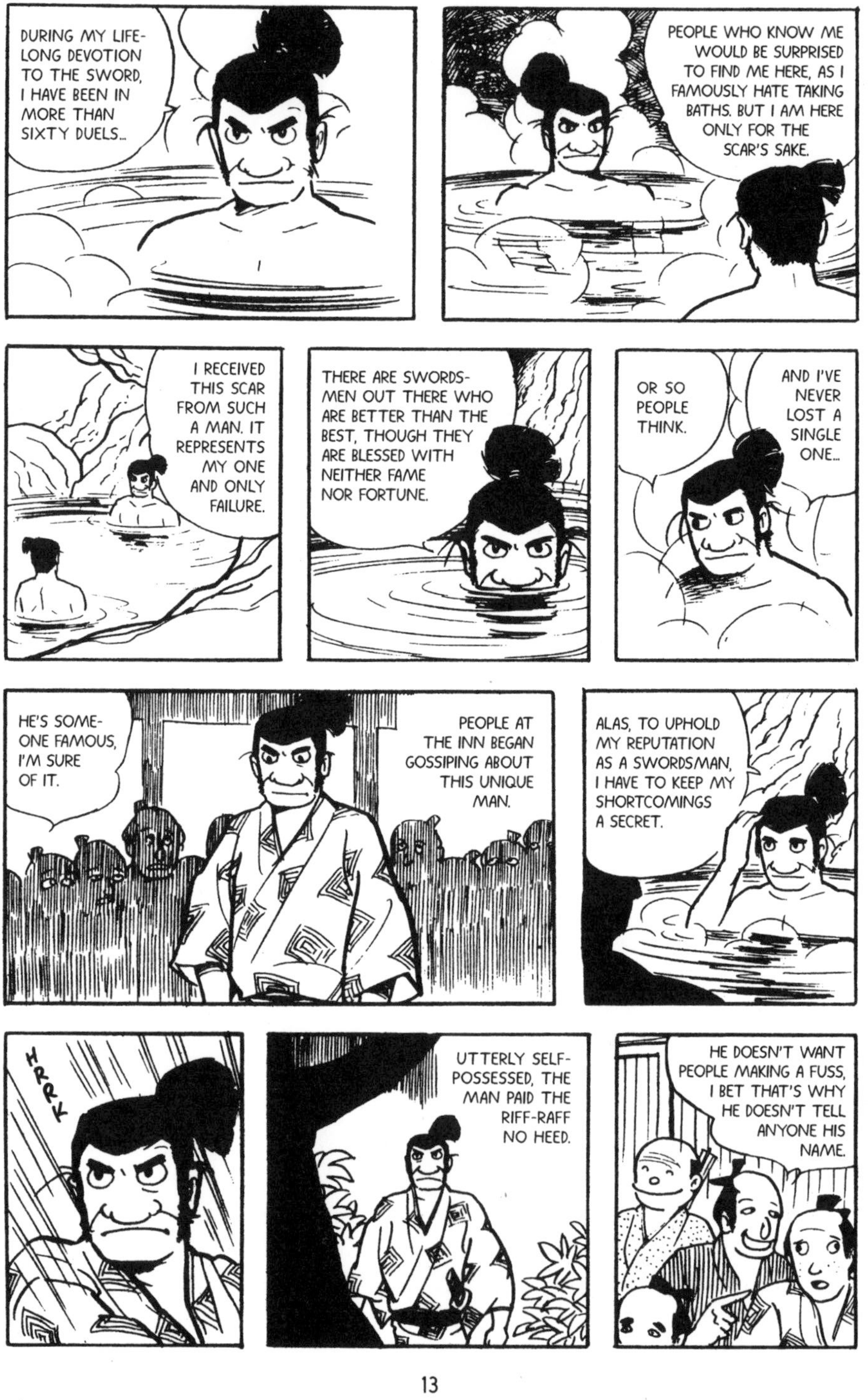

PEOPLE WHO KNOW ME WOULD BE SURPRISED TO FIND ME HERE, AS I FAMOUSLY HATE TAKING BATHS. BUT I AM HERE ONLY FOR THE SCAR'S SAKE.
DURING MY LIFE-LONG DEVOTION TO THE SWORD, I HAVE BEEN IN MORE THAN SIXTY DUELS...
AND I'VE NEVER LOST A SINGLE ONE...
OR SO PEOPLE THINK.
THERE ARE SWORDS-MEN OUT THERE WHO ARE BETTER THAN THE BEST, THOUGH THEY ARE BLESSED WITH NEITHER FAME NOR FORTUNE.
I RECEIVED THIS SCAR FROM SUCH A MAN. IT REPRESENTS MY ONE AND ONLY FAILURE.
ALAS, TO UPHOLD MY REPUTATION AS A SWORDSMAN, I HAVE TO KEEP MY SHORTCOMINGS A SECRET.
PEOPLE AT THE INN BEGAN GOSSIPING ABOUT THIS UNIQUE MAN.
HE'S SOME-ONE FAMOUS, I'M SURE OF IT.
HE DOESN'T WANT PEOPLE MAKING A FUSS, I BET THAT'S WHY HE DOESN'T TELL ANYONE HIS NAME.
UTTERLY SELF-POSSESSED, THE MAN PAID THE RIFF-RAFF NO HEED.
HRRK

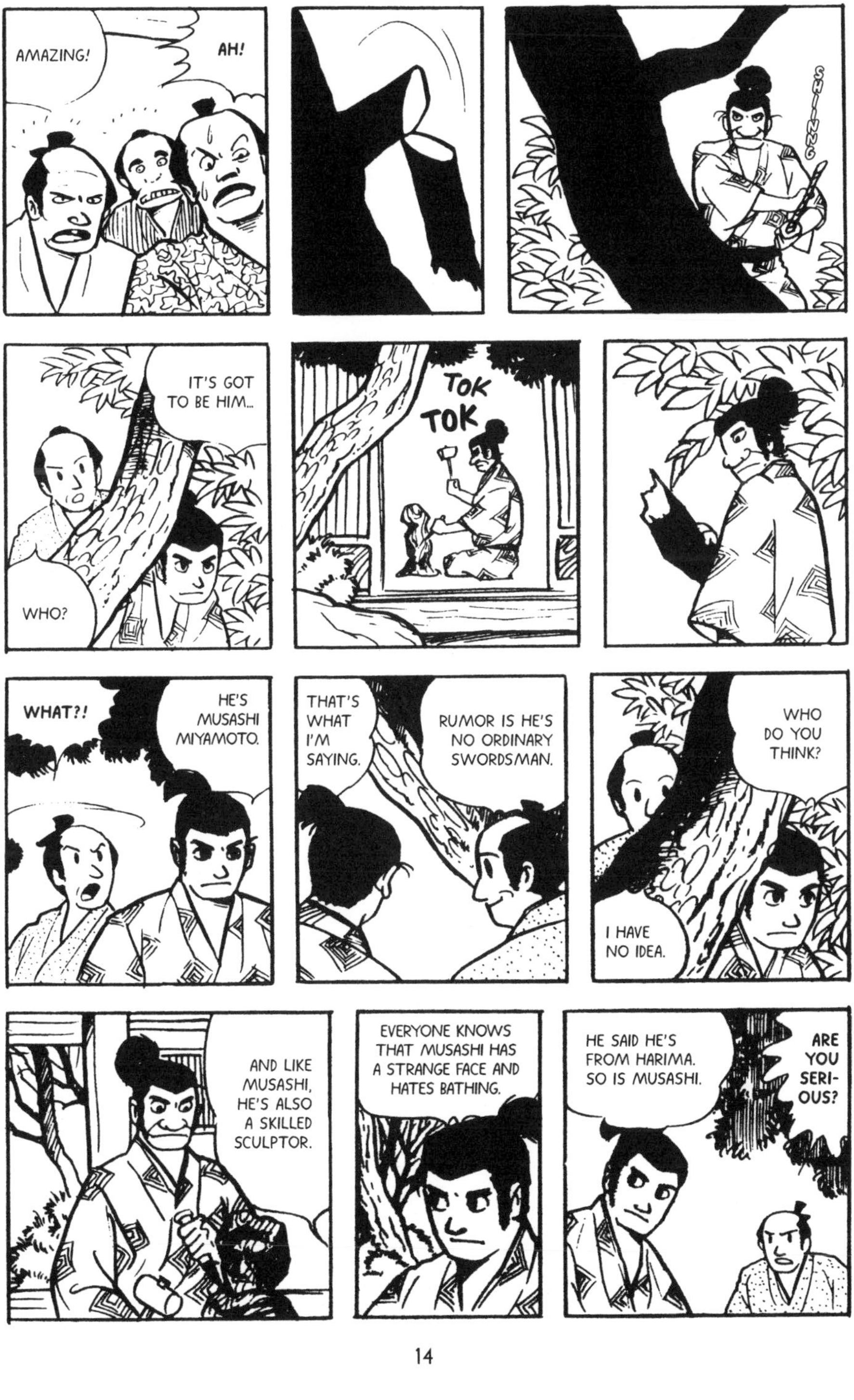

SHIING
AH!
AMAZING!
TOK
TOK
IT'S GOT TO BE HIM...
WHO?
WHO DO YOU THINK?
I HAVE NO IDEA.
RUMOR IS HE'S NO ORDINARY SWORDSMAN.
THAT'S WHAT I'M SAYING.
HE'S MUSASHI MIYAMOTO.
WHAT?!
ARE YOU SERI-OUS?
HE SAID HE'S FROM HARIMA. SO IS MUSASHI.
EVERYONE KNOWS THAT MUSASHI HAS A STRANGE FACE AND HATES BATHING.
AND LIKE MUSASHI, HE'S ALSO A SKILLED SCULPTOR.

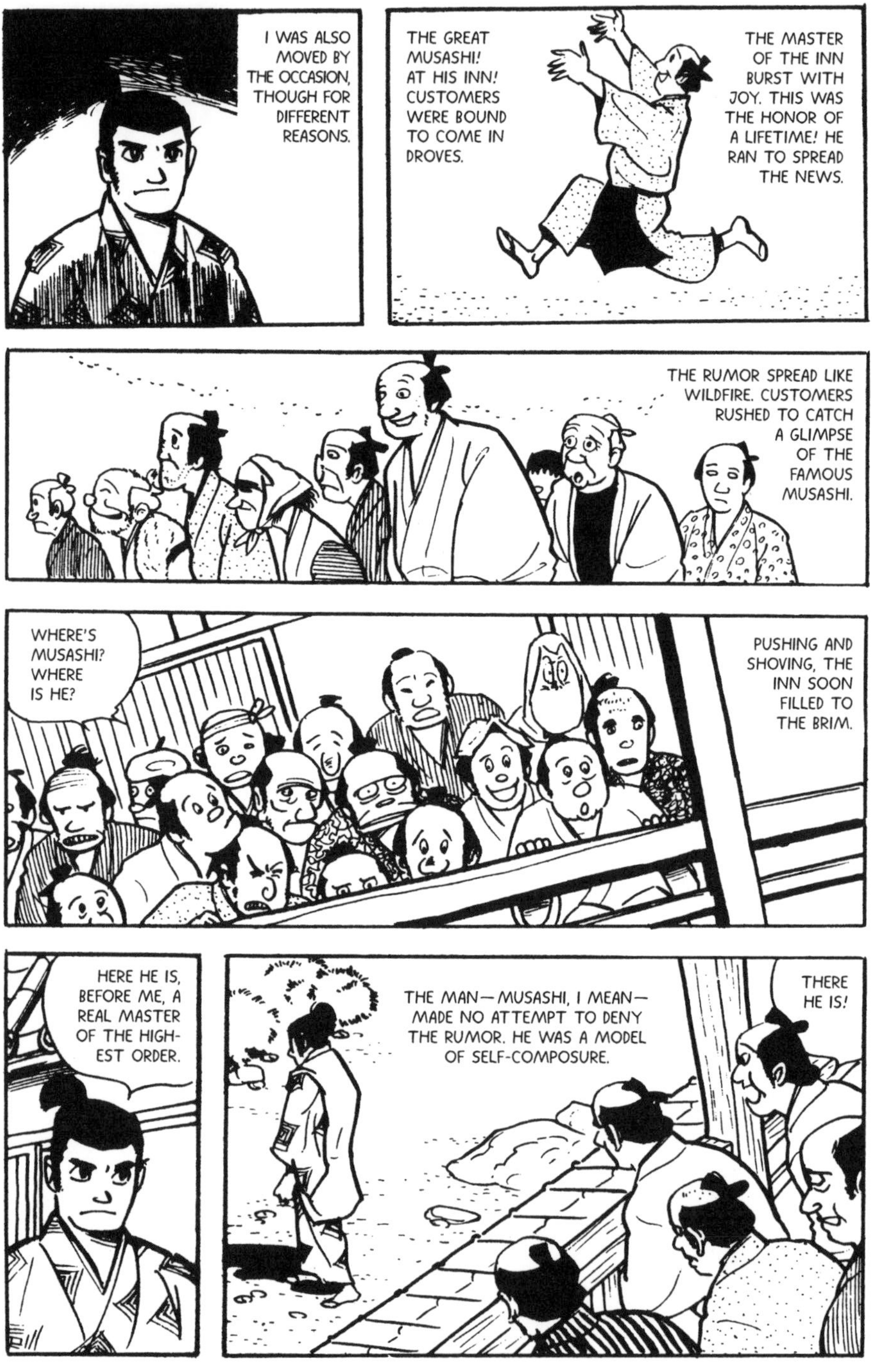
THE MASTER OF THE INN BURST WITH JOY. THIS WAS THE HONOR OF A LIFETIME! HE RAN TO SPREAD THE NEWS.
THE GREAT MUSASHI! AT HIS INN! CUSTOMERS WERE BOUND TO COME IN DROVES.
I WAS ALSO MOVED BY THE OCCASION, THOUGH FOR DIFFERENT REASONS.
THE RUMOR SPREAD LIKE WILDFIRE. CUSTOMERS RUSHED TO CATCH A GLIMPSE OF THE FAMOUS MUSASHI.
PUSHING AND SHOVING, THE INN SOON FILLED TO THE BRIM.
WHERE'S MUSASHI? WHERE IS HE?
THERE HE IS!
THE MAN—MUSASHI, I MEAN—MADE NO ATTEMPT TO DENY THE RUMOR. HE WAS A MODEL OF SELF-COMPOSURE.
HERE HE IS, BEFORE ME, A REAL MASTER OF THE HIGH-EST ORDER.

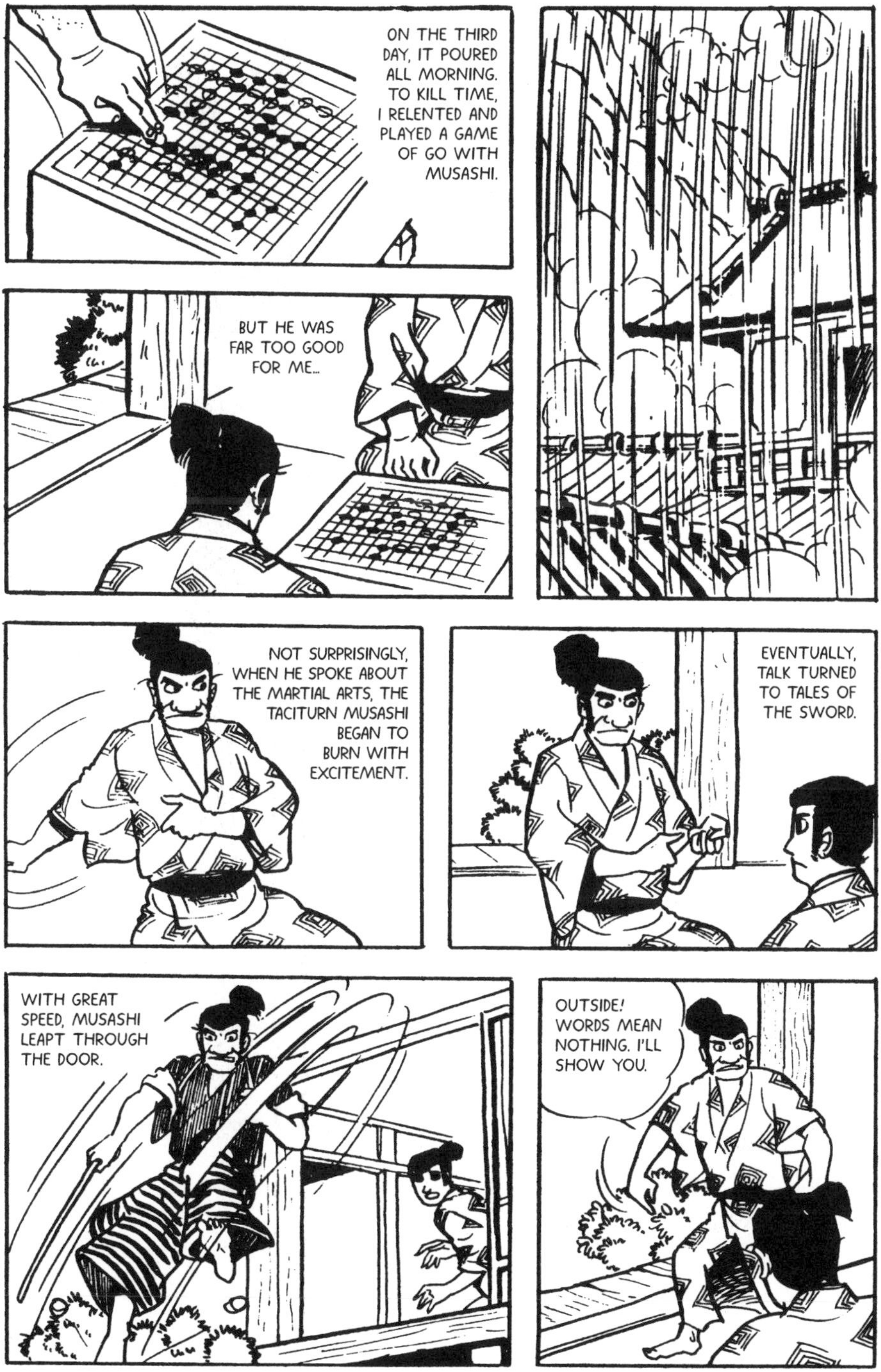
ON THE THIRD DAY, IT POURED ALL MORNING. TO KILL TIME, I RELENTED AND PLAYED A GAME OF GO WITH MUSASHI.
BUT HE WAS FAR TOO GOOD FOR ME...
EVENTUALLY, TALK TURNED TO TALES OF THE SWORD.
NOT SURPRISINGLY, WHEN HE SPOKE ABOUT THE MARTIAL ARTS, THE TACITURN MUSASHI BEGAN TO BURN WITH EXCITEMENT.
OUTSIDE! WORDS MEAN NOTHING. I'LL SHOW YOU.
WITH GREAT SPEED, MUSASHI LEAPT THROUGH THE DOOR.

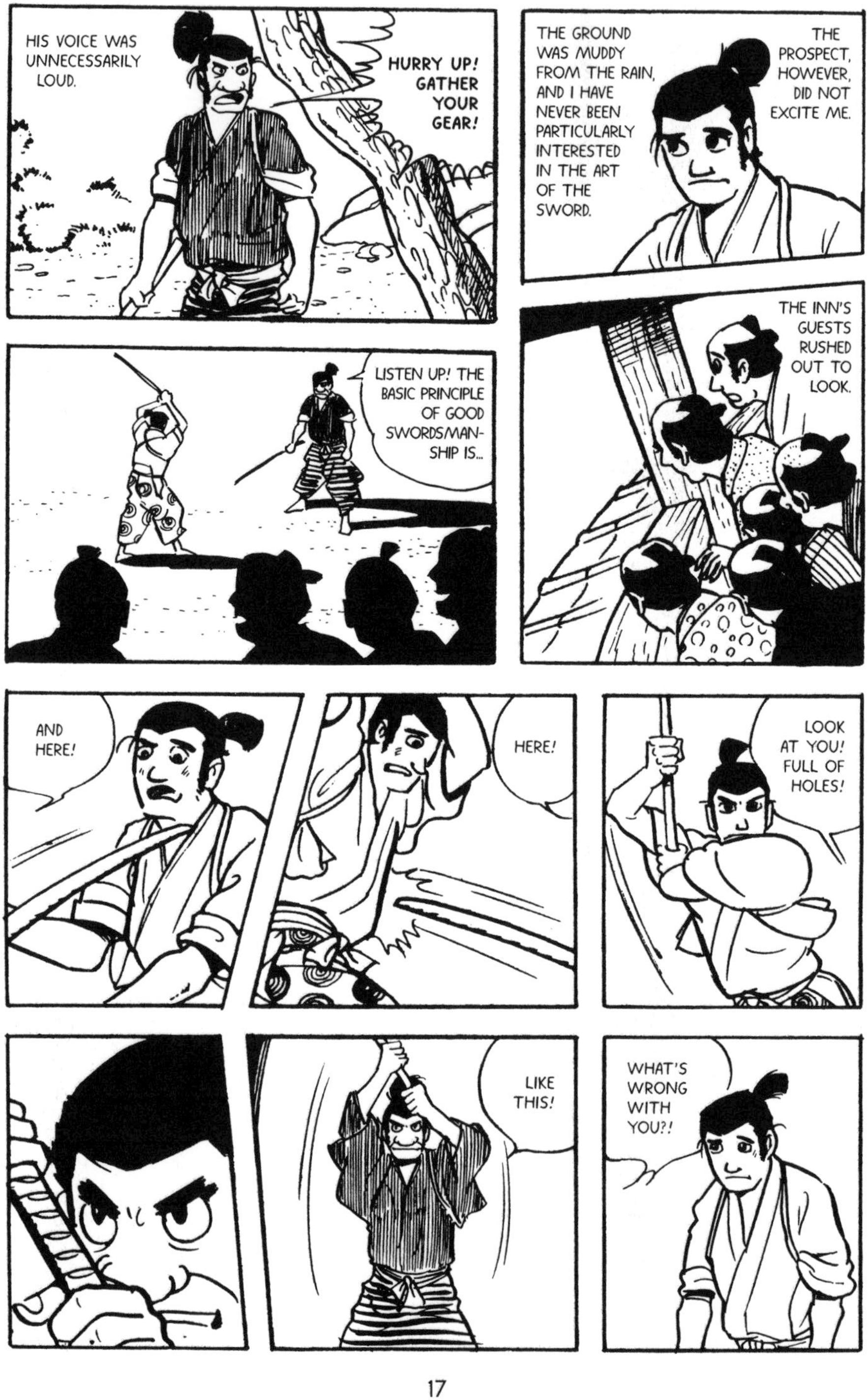
THE PROSPECT, HOWEVER, DID NOT EXCITE ME.
THE GROUND WAS MUDDY FROM THE RAIN, AND I HAVE NEVER BEEN PARTICULARLY INTERESTED IN THE ART OF THE SWORD.
HURRY UP! GATHER YOUR GEAR!
HIS VOICE WAS UNNECESSARILY LOUD.
THE INN'S GUESTS RUSHED OUT TO LOOK.
LISTEN UP! THE BASIC PRINCIPLE OF GOOD SWORDSMAN-SHIP IS...
LOOK AT YOU! FULL OF HOLES!
HERE!
AND HERE!
WHAT'S WRONG WITH YOU?!
LIKE THIS!

GIVE ME YOUR BEST SHOT.

NOW, COME AT ME.

PERFECT FORM, JUST AS YOU WOULD EXPECT FROM THE GREAT MUSASHI.

SLIIIP

RRRAH!

I COULDN'T BELIEVE IT. MUSASHI LOST HIS FOOTING IN THE MUD.

BDOOSH

AH

REMEMBER THIS DEFENSIVE TECHNIQUE.

MUSASHI QUICKLY COMPENSATED.

A MASTER AT HIS LEVEL CANNOT TOLERATE ANY FAILURES.

DISAPPOINTING HIS AUDIENCE IS ABSOLUTELY UNACCEPTABLE.

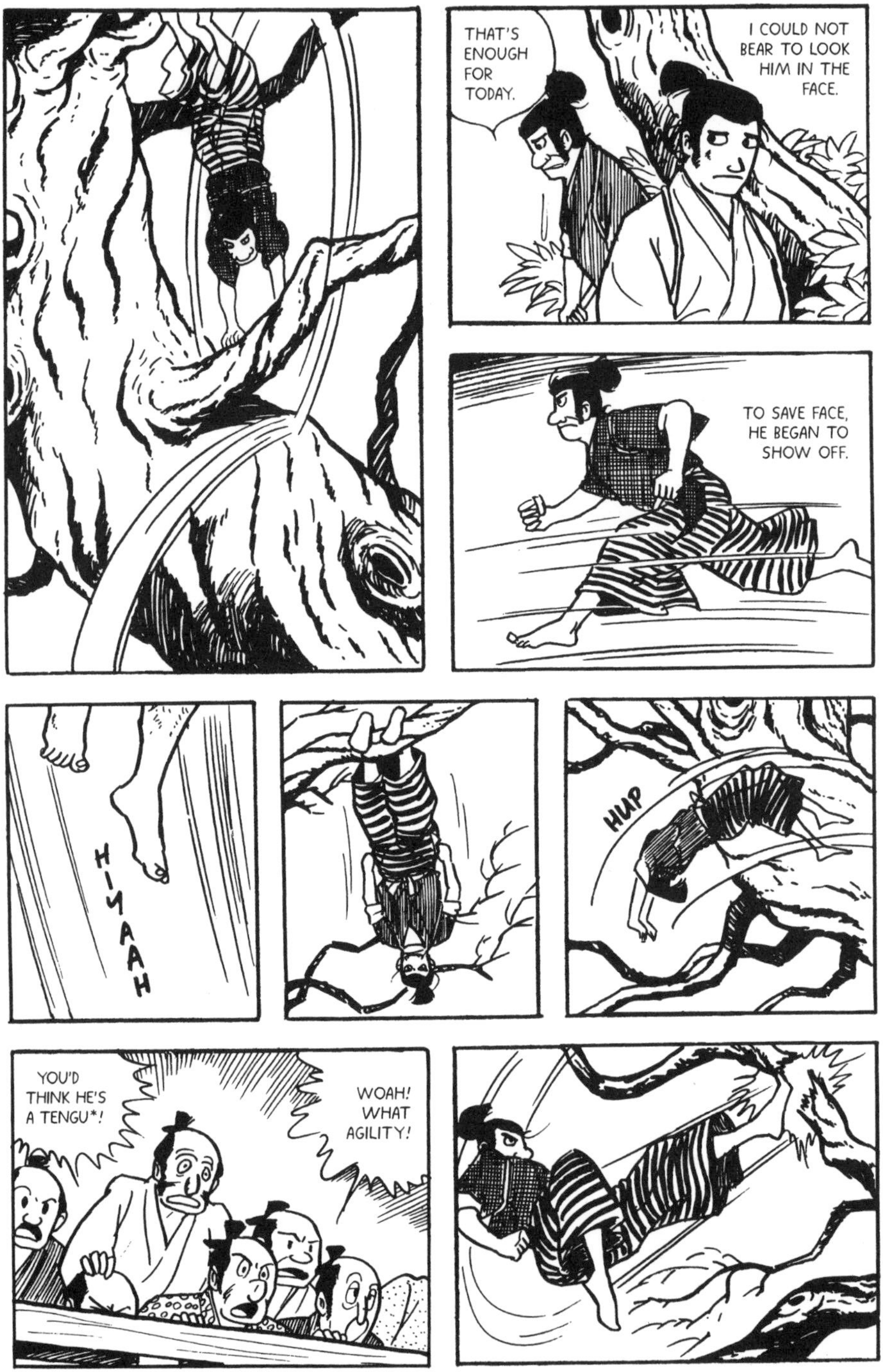
I COULD NOT BEAR TO LOOK HIM IN THE FACE.
THAT'S ENOUGH FOR TODAY.
TO SAVE FACE, HE BEGAN TO SHOW OFF.
HUP
HIYAAAH
WOAH! WHAT AGILITY!
YOU'D THINK HE'S A TENGU*!

*TENGU: A TYPE OF YOKAI AND BIRD-LIKE GOBLIN

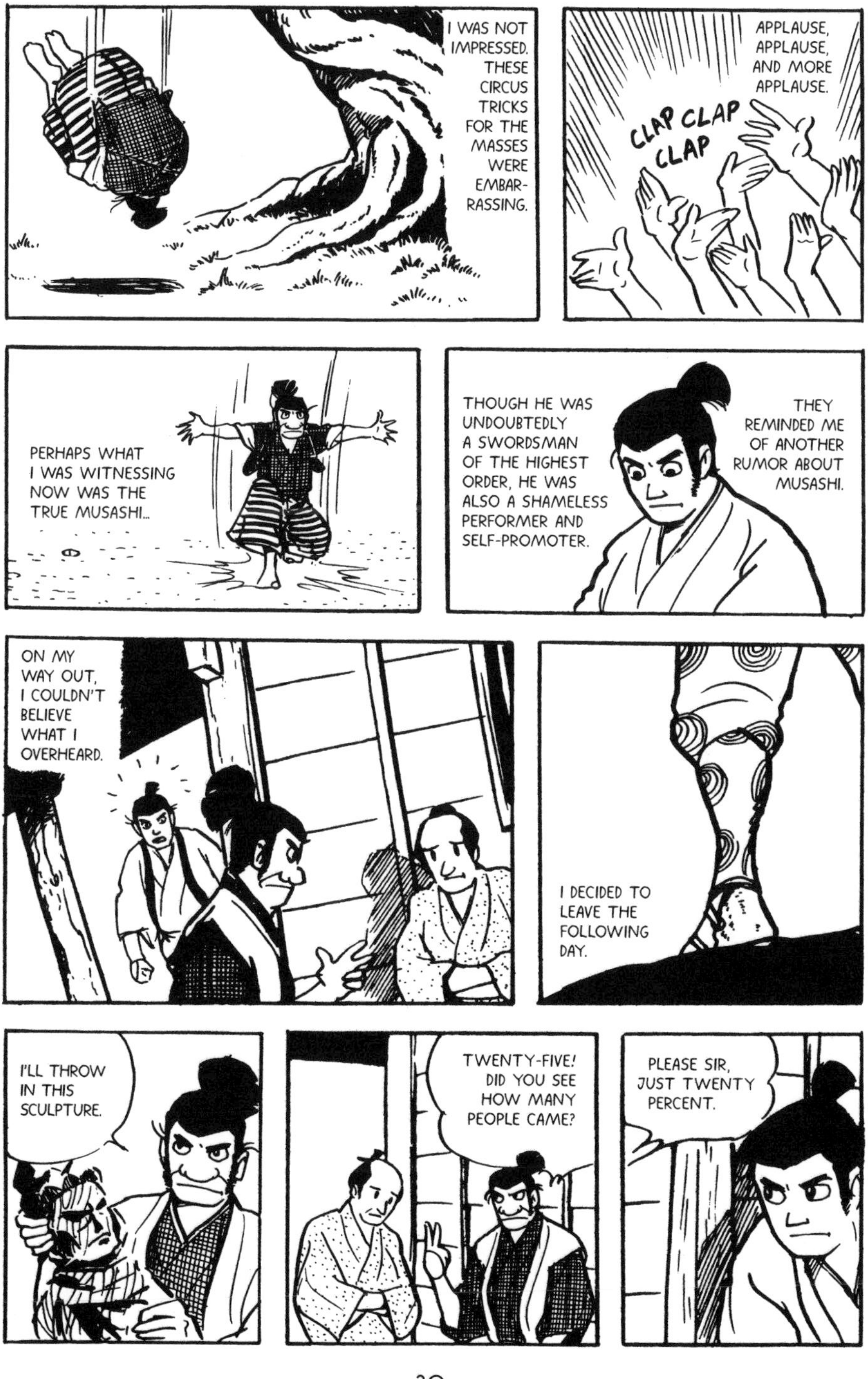

APPLAUSE, APPLAUSE, AND MORE APPLAUSE.
CLAP CLAP CLAP
I WAS NOT IMPRESSED. THESE CIRCUS TRICKS FOR THE MASSES WERE EMBAR-RASSING.
THEY REMINDED ME OF ANOTHER RUMOR ABOUT MUSASHI.
THOUGH HE WAS UNDOUBTEDLY A SWORDSMAN OF THE HIGHEST ORDER, HE WAS ALSO A SHAMELESS PERFORMER AND SELF-PROMOTER.
PERHAPS WHAT I WAS WITNESSING NOW WAS THE TRUE MUSASHI...
I DECIDED TO LEAVE THE FOLLOWING DAY.
ON MY WAY OUT, I COULDN'T BELIEVE WHAT I OVERHEARD.
PLEASE SIR, JUST TWENTY PERCENT.
TWENTY-FIVE! DID YOU SEE HOW MANY PEOPLE CAME?
I'LL THROW IN THIS SCULPTURE.

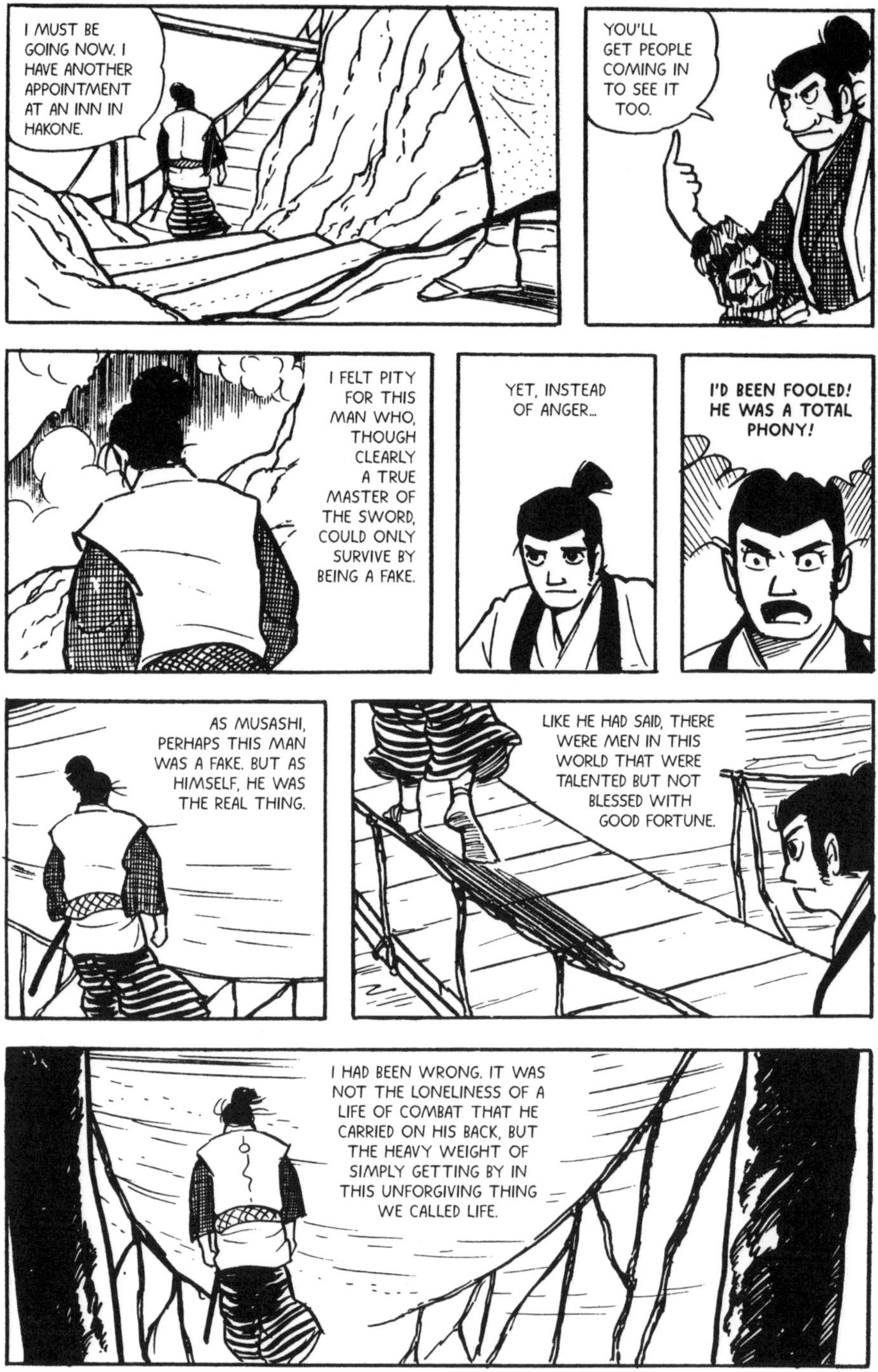
YOU'LL GET PEOPLE COMING IN TO SEE IT TOO.
I MUST BE GOING NOW. I HAVE ANOTHER APPOINTMENT AT AN INN IN HAKONE.
I'D BEEN FOOLED! HE WAS A TOTAL PHONY!
YET, INSTEAD OF ANGER...
I FELT PITY FOR THIS MAN WHO, THOUGH CLEARLY A TRUE MASTER OF THE SWORD, COULD ONLY SURVIVE BY BEING A FAKE.
LIKE HE HAD SAID, THERE WERE MEN IN THIS WORLD THAT WERE TALENTED BUT NOT BLESSED WITH GOOD FORTUNE.
AS MUSASHI, PERHAPS THIS MAN WAS A FAKE. BUT AS HIMSELF, HE WAS THE REAL THING.
I HAD BEEN WRONG. IT WAS NOT THE LONELINESS OF A LIFE OF COMBAT THAT HE CARRIED ON HIS BACK, BUT THE HEAVY WEIGHT OF SIMPLY GETTING BY IN THIS UNFORGIVING THING WE CALLED LIFE.

WATERMELON SAKE

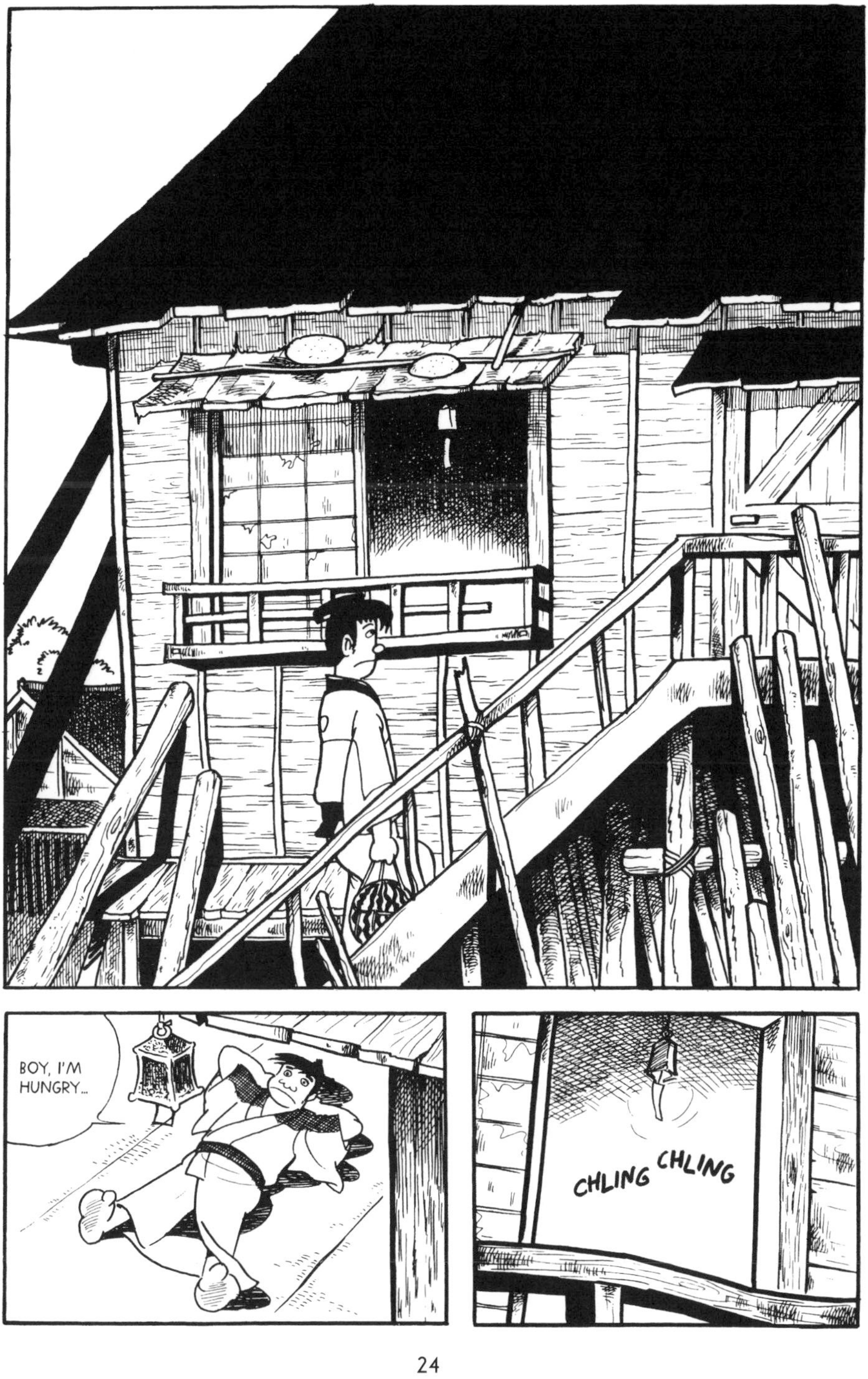
CHLING CHLING
BOY, I'M HUNGRY...

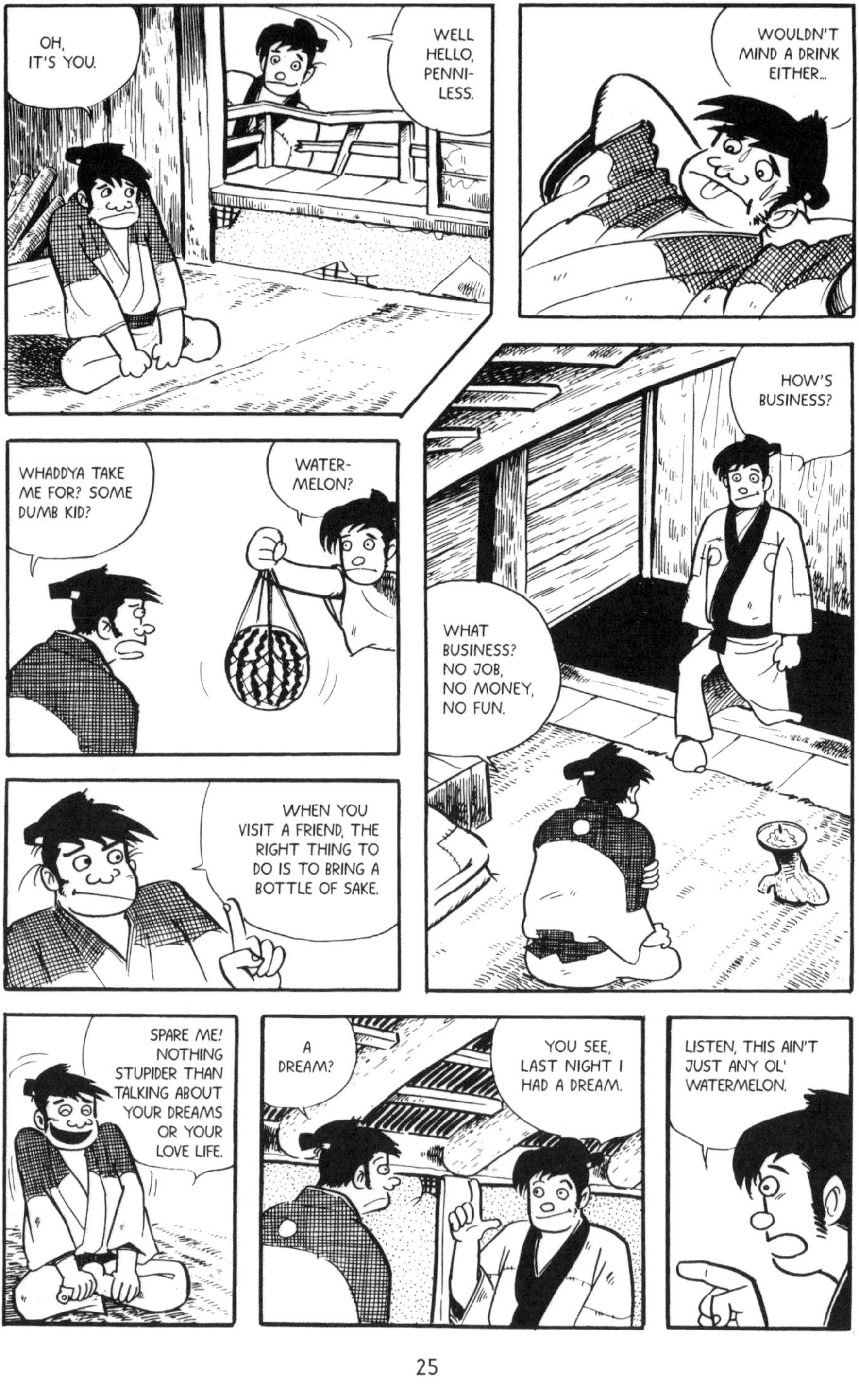
WOULDN'T MIND A DRINK EITHER...
WELL HELLO, PENNI-LESS.
OH, IT'S YOU.
HOW'S BUSINESS?
WHAT BUSINESS? NO JOB, NO MONEY, NO FUN.
WATER-MELON?
WHADDYA TAKE ME FOR? SOME DUMB KID?
WHEN YOU VISIT A FRIEND, THE RIGHT THING TO DO IS TO BRING A BOTTLE OF SAKE.
LISTEN, THIS AIN'T JUST ANY OL' WATERMELON.
YOU SEE, LAST NIGHT I HAD A DREAM.
A DREAM?
SPARE ME! NOTHING STUPIDER THAN TALKING ABOUT YOUR DREAMS OR YOUR LOVE LIFE.

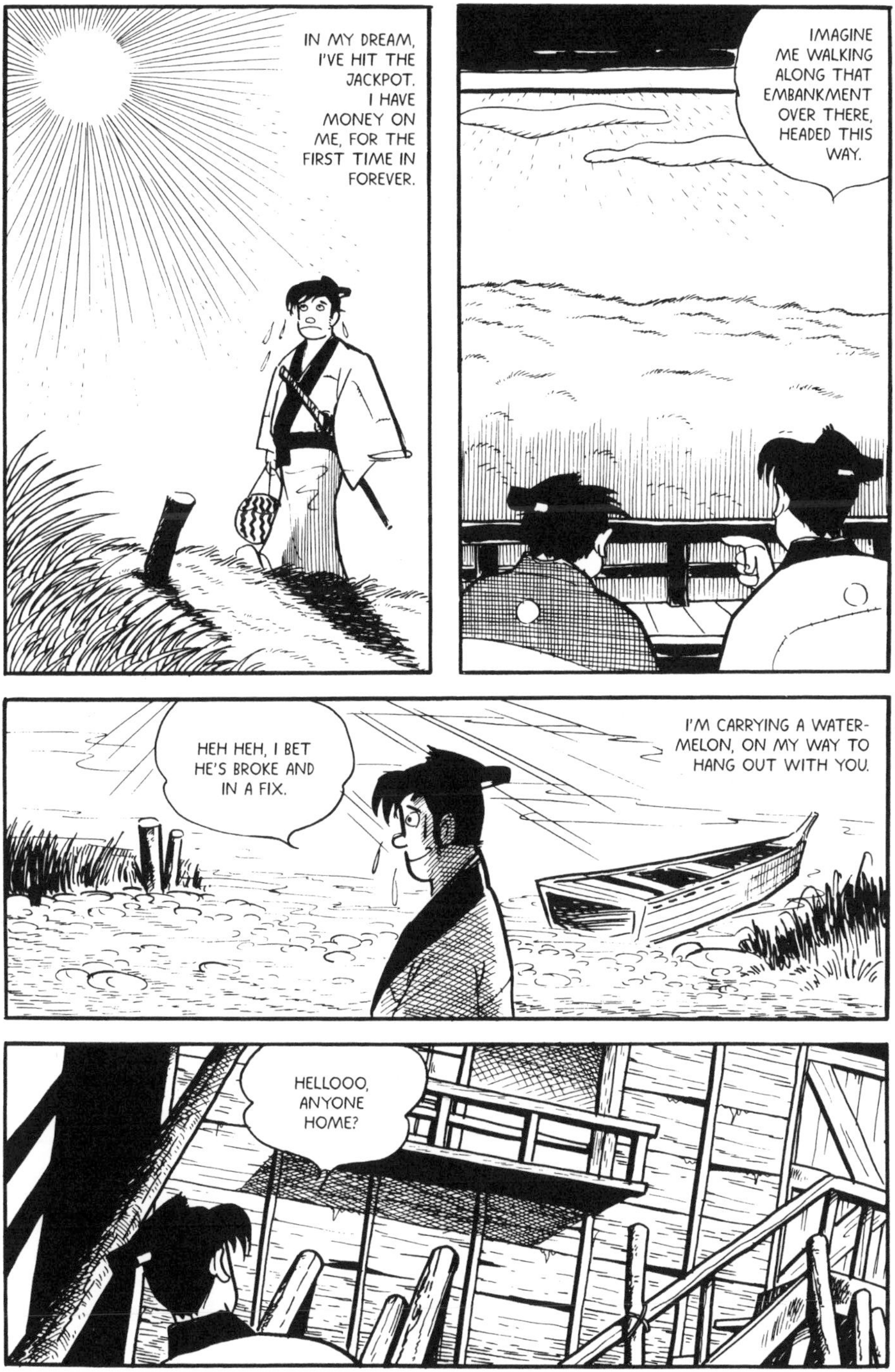
IMAGINE ME WALKING ALONG THAT EMBANKMENT OVER THERE, HEADED THIS WAY.
IN MY DREAM, I'VE HIT THE JACKPOT. I HAVE MONEY ON ME, FOR THE FIRST TIME IN FOREVER.
I'M CARRYING A WATER-MELON, ON MY WAY TO HANG OUT WITH YOU.
HEH HEH, I BET HE'S BROKE AND IN A FIX.
HELLOOO, ANYONE HOME?

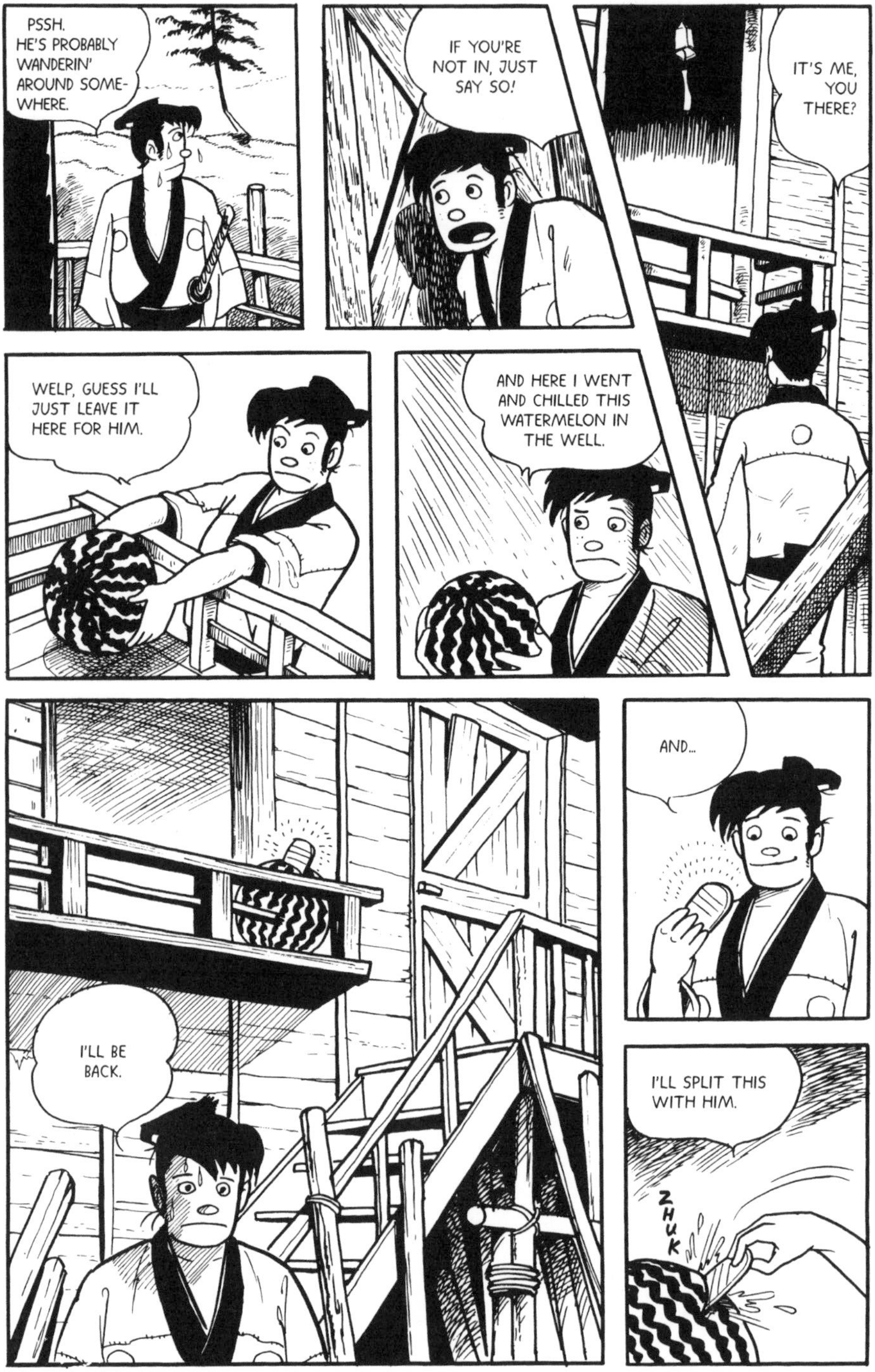
IT'S ME, YOU THERE?
IF YOU'RE NOT IN, JUST SAY SO!
PSSH. HE'S PROBABLY WANDERIN' AROUND SOME-WHERE.
AND HERE I WENT AND CHILLED THIS WATERMELON IN THE WELL.
WELP, GUESS I'LL JUST LEAVE IT HERE FOR HIM.
AND...
I'LL SPLIT THIS WITH HIM.
ZHUK
I'LL BE BACK.

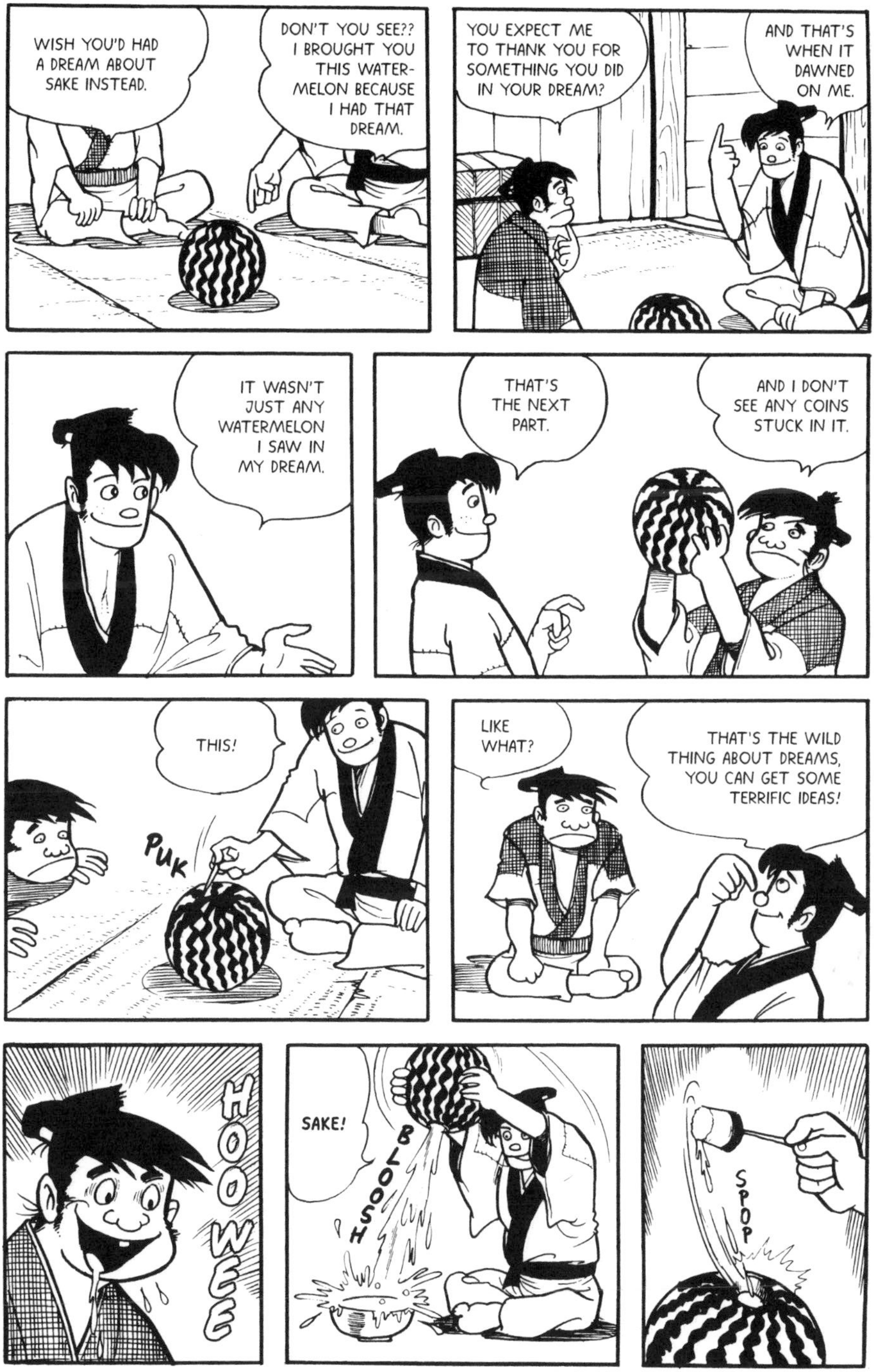
AND THAT'S WHEN IT DAWNED ON ME.
YOU EXPECT ME TO THANK YOU FOR SOMETHING YOU DID IN YOUR DREAM?
DON'T YOU SEE?? I BROUGHT YOU THIS WATER-MELON BECAUSE I HAD THAT DREAM.
WISH YOU'D HAD A DREAM ABOUT SAKE INSTEAD.
AND I DON'T SEE ANY COINS STUCK IN IT.
THAT'S THE NEXT PART.
IT WASN'T JUST ANY WATERMELON I SAW IN MY DREAM.
THAT'S THE WILD THING ABOUT DREAMS, YOU CAN GET SOME TERRIFIC IDEAS!
LIKE WHAT?
THIS!
PUK
SPOP
BLOOSH
SAKE!
HOOWEE

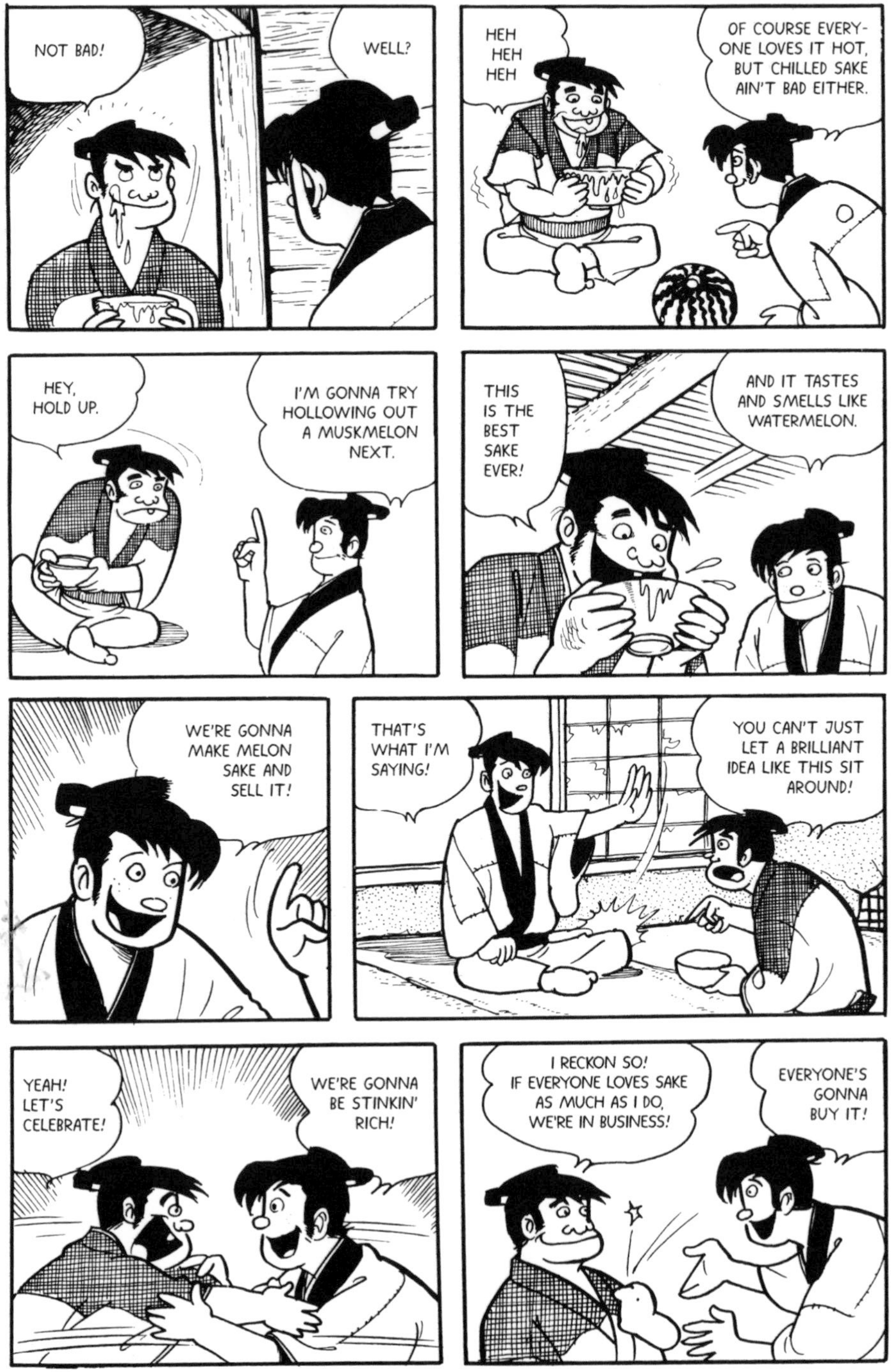
OF COURSE EVERYONE LOVES IT HOT, BUT CHILLED SAKE AIN'T BAD EITHER.
HEH HEH HEH
WELL?
NOT BAD!
AND IT TASTES AND SMELLS LIKE WATERMELON.
THIS IS THE BEST SAKE EVER!
I'M GONNA TRY HOLLOWING OUT A MUSKMELON NEXT.
HEY, HOLD UP.
YOU CAN'T JUST LET A BRILLIANT IDEA LIKE THIS SIT AROUND!
THAT'S WHAT I'M SAYING!
WE'RE GONNA MAKE MELON SAKE AND SELL IT!
EVERYONE'S GONNA BUY IT!
I RECKON SO! IF EVERYONE LOVES SAKE AS MUCH AS I DO, WE'RE IN BUSINESS!
WE'RE GONNA BE STINKIN' RICH!
YEAH! LET'S CELEBRATE!

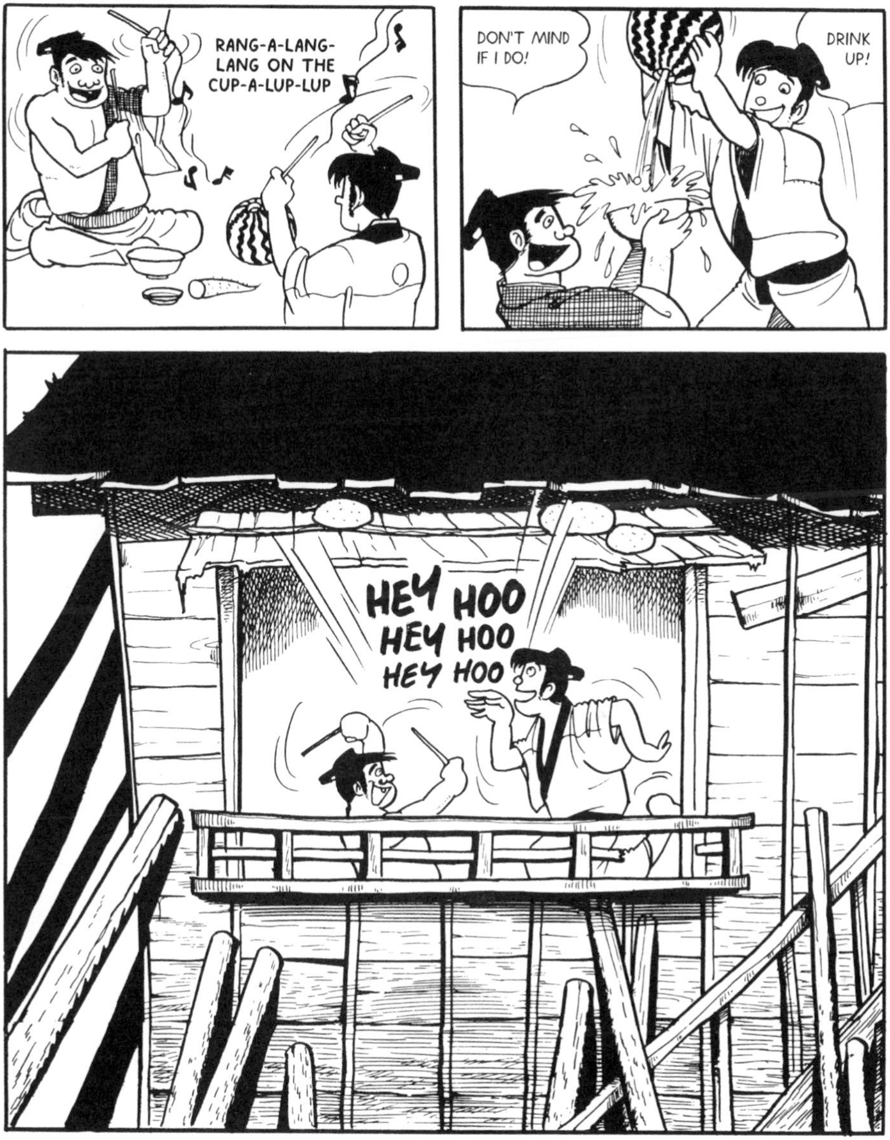
DRINK UP!
DON'T MIND IF I DO!
RANG-A-LANG-LANG ON THE CUP-A-LUP-LUP
HEY HOO
HEY HOO
HEY HOO

YET HISTORY PROVIDES NO RECORD OF
THESE TWO MEN GETTING RICH...
ALAS, WATERMELONS ONLY
GROW IN THE SUMMER.

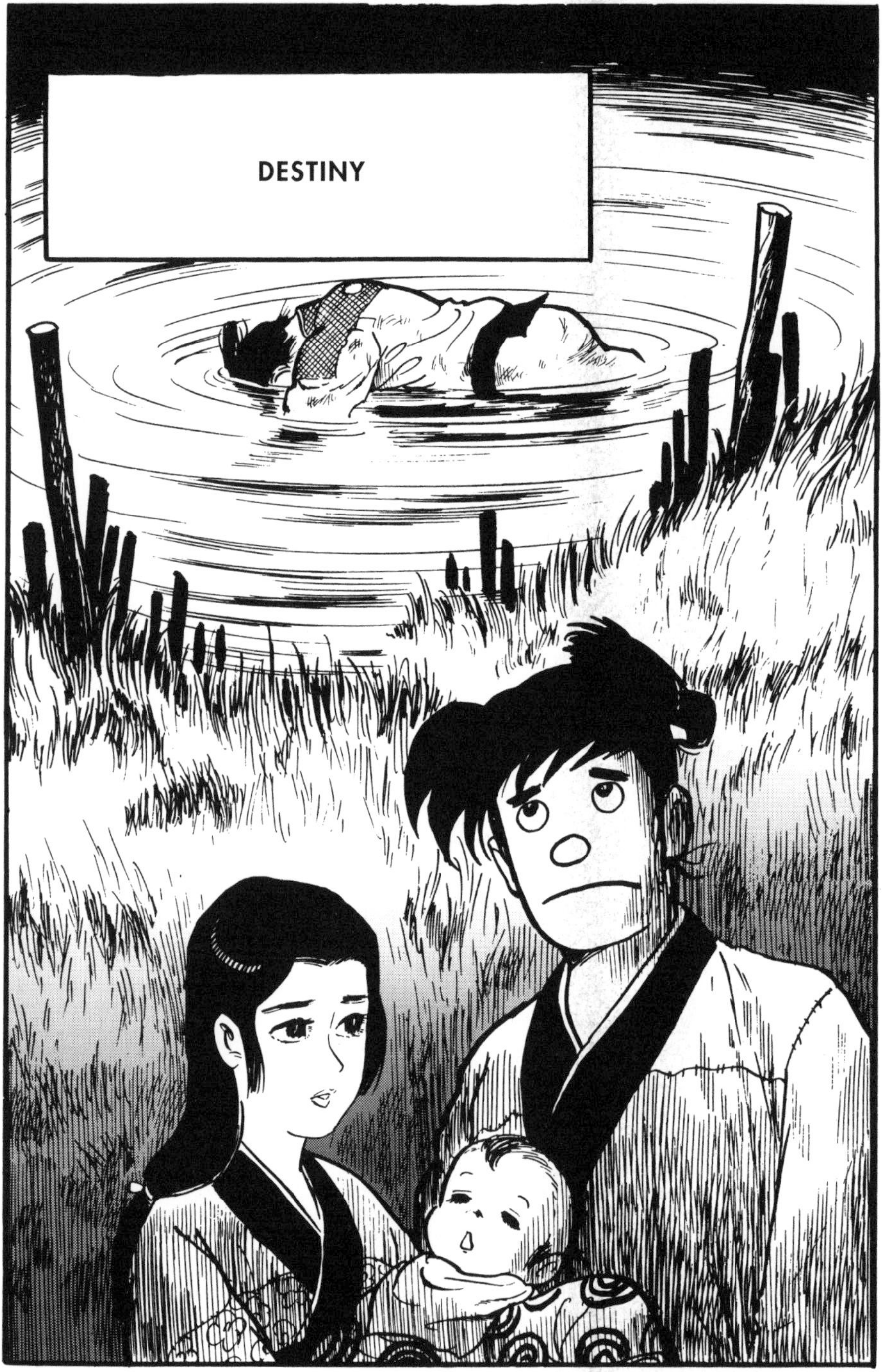
DESTINY

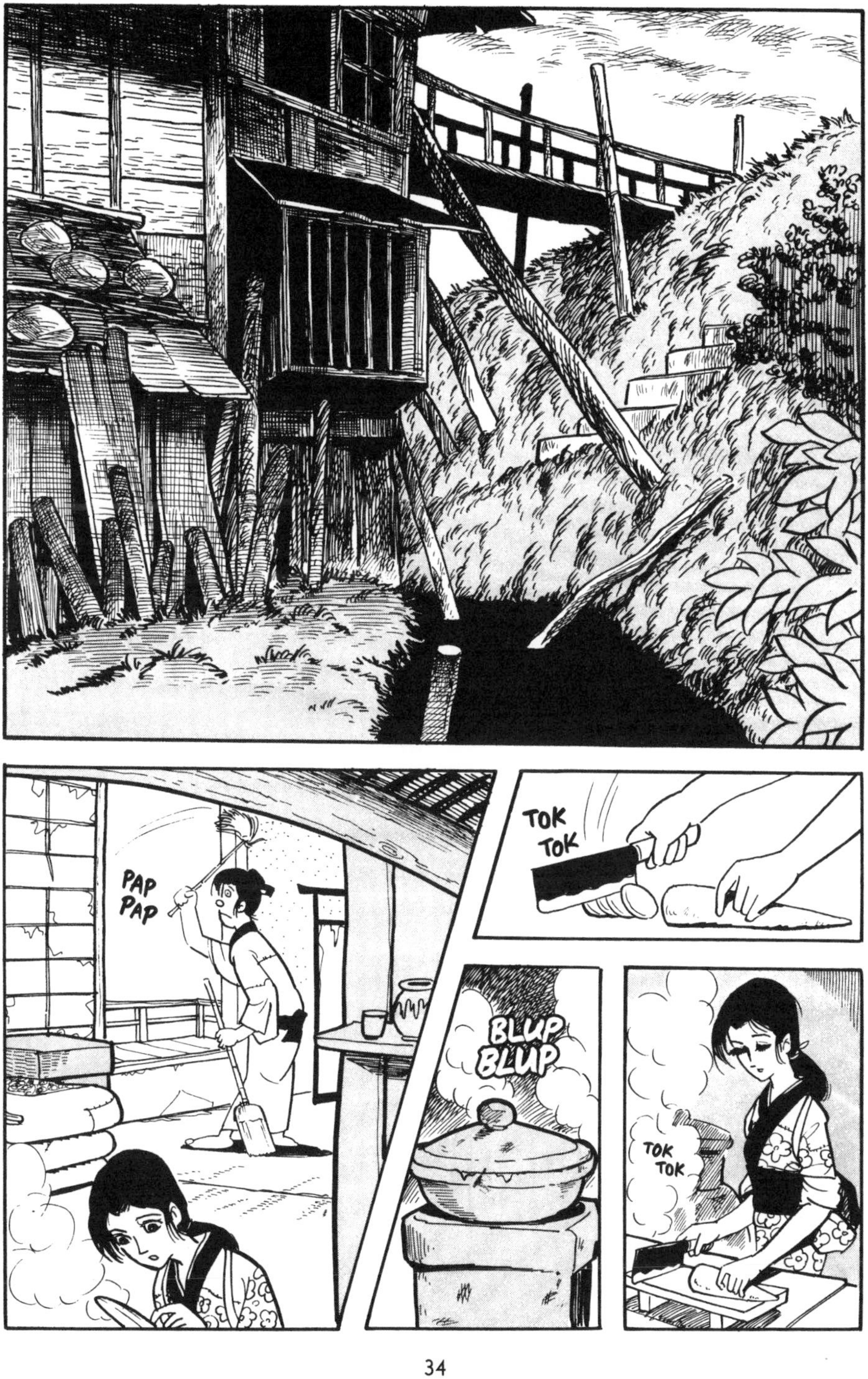
TOK TOK
TOK TOK
BLUP BLUP
PAP PAP

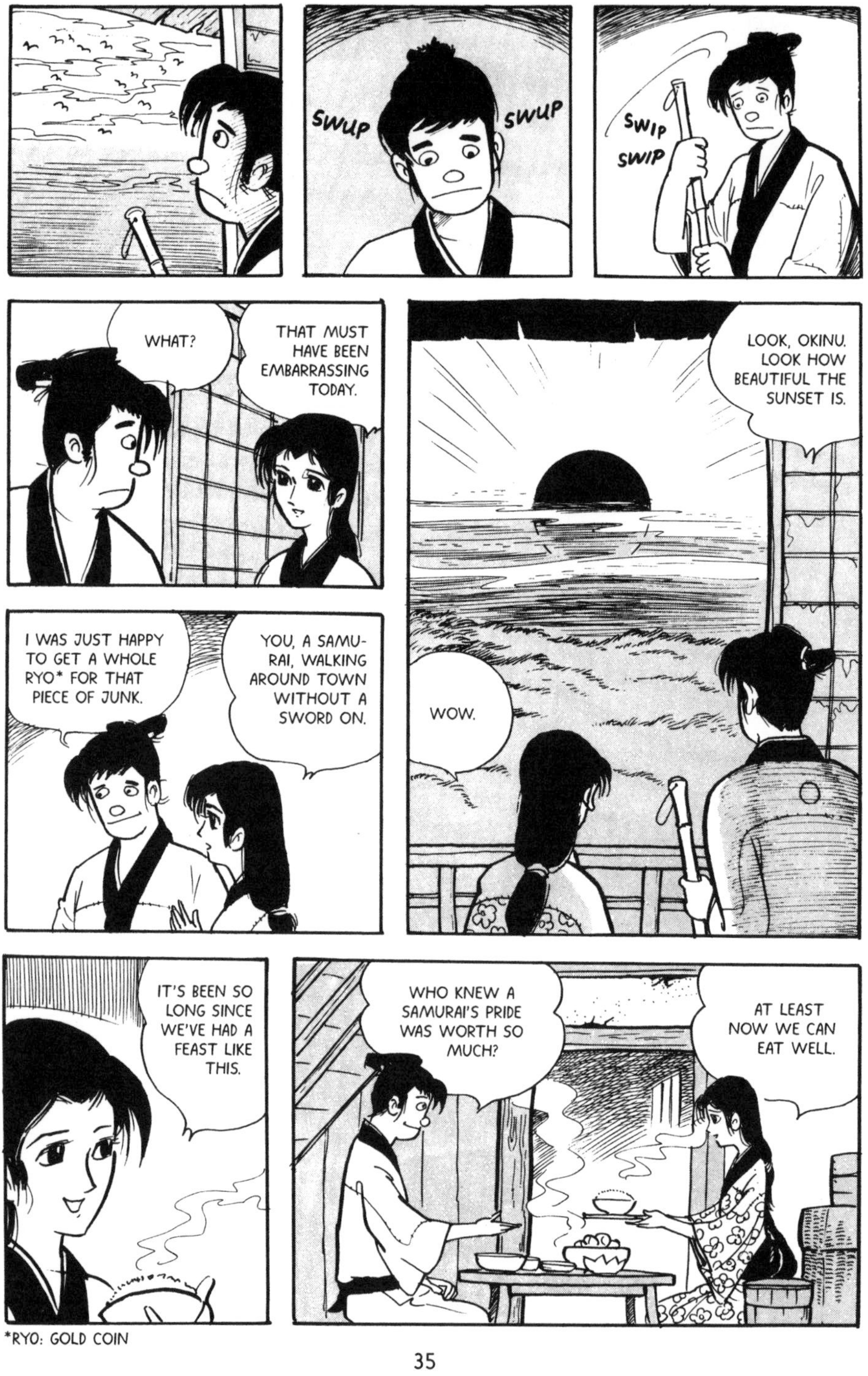

SWIP
SWIP
SWUP
SWUP
LOOK, OKINU. LOOK HOW BEAUTIFUL THE SUNSET IS.
WOW.
THAT MUST HAVE BEEN EMBARRASSING TODAY.
WHAT?
YOU, A SAMURAI, WALKING AROUND TOWN WITHOUT A SWORD ON.
I WAS JUST HAPPY TO GET A WHOLE RYO* FOR THAT PIECE OF JUNK.
AT LEAST NOW WE CAN EAT WELL.
WHO KNEW A SAMURAI'S PRIDE WAS WORTH SO MUCH?
IT'S BEEN SO LONG SINCE WE'VE HAD A FEAST LIKE THIS.

*RYO: GOLD COIN

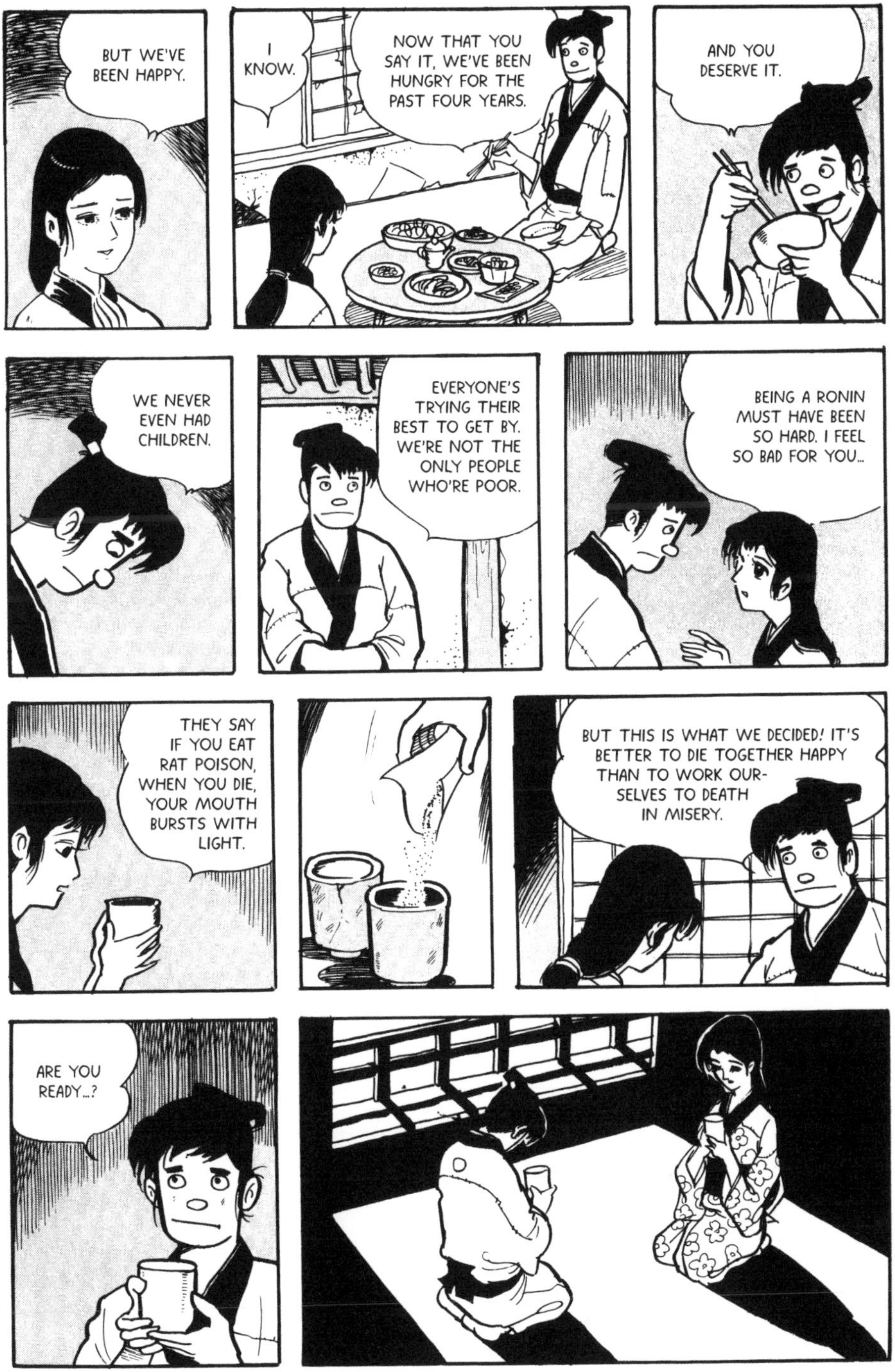
AND YOU DESERVE IT.
NOW THAT YOU SAY IT, WE'VE BEEN HUNGRY FOR THE PAST FOUR YEARS.
I KNOW.
BUT WE'VE BEEN HAPPY.
BEING A RONIN MUST HAVE BEEN SO HARD. I FEEL SO BAD FOR YOU...
EVERYONE'S TRYING THEIR BEST TO GET BY. WE'RE NOT THE ONLY PEOPLE WHO'RE POOR.
WE NEVER EVEN HAD CHILDREN.
BUT THIS IS WHAT WE DECIDED! IT'S BETTER TO DIE TOGETHER HAPPY THAN TO WORK OUR-SELVES TO DEATH IN MISERY.
THEY SAY IF YOU EAT RAT POISON, WHEN YOU DIE, YOUR MOUTH BURSTS WITH LIGHT.
ARE YOU READY...?

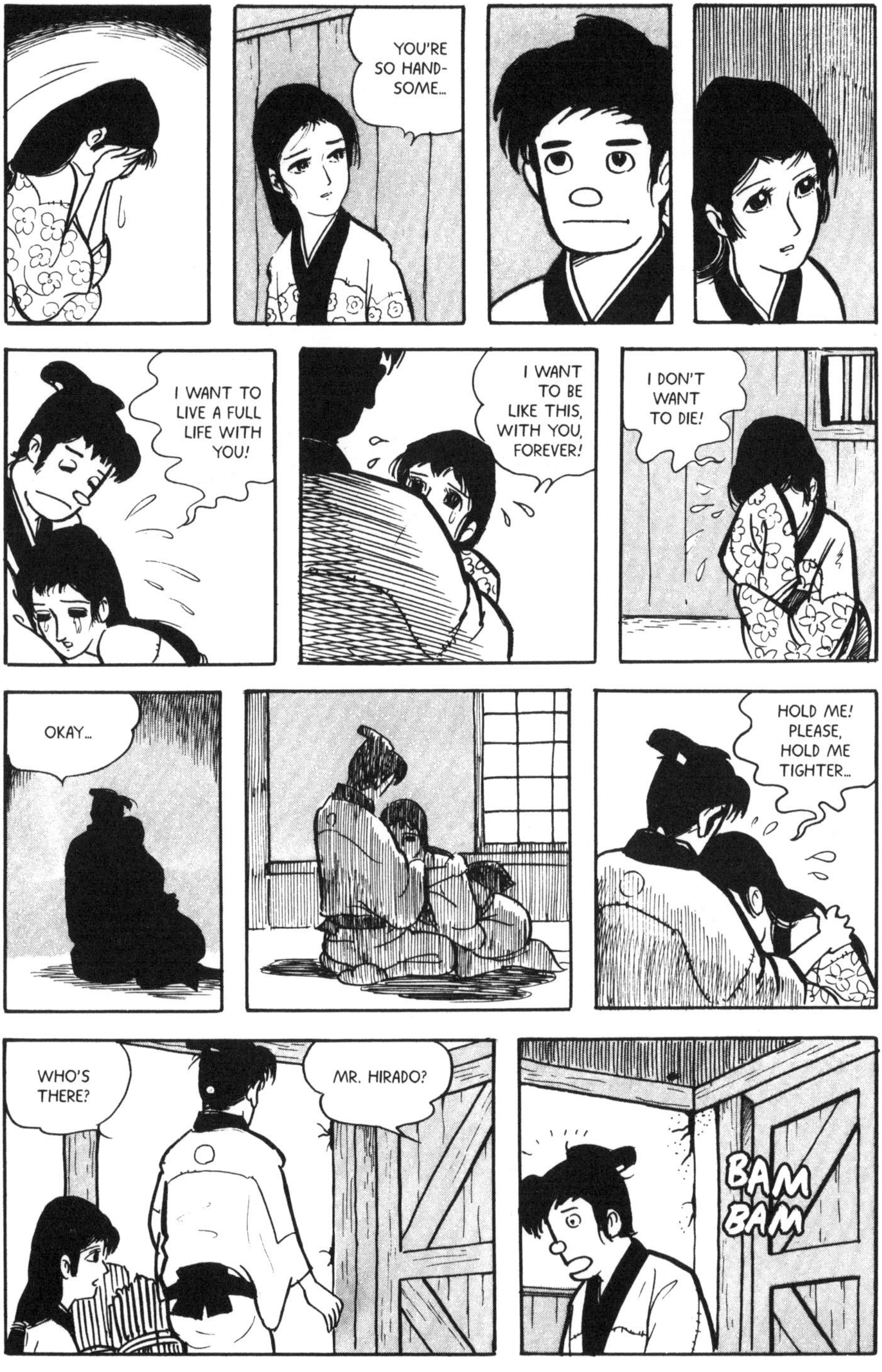
YOU'RE SO HAND-SOME...
I DON'T WANT TO DIE!
I WANT TO BE LIKE THIS, WITH YOU, FOREVER!
I WANT TO LIVE A FULL LIFE WITH YOU!
HOLD ME! PLEASE, HOLD ME TIGHTER...
OKAY...
BAM BAM
MR. HIRADO?
WHO'S THERE?

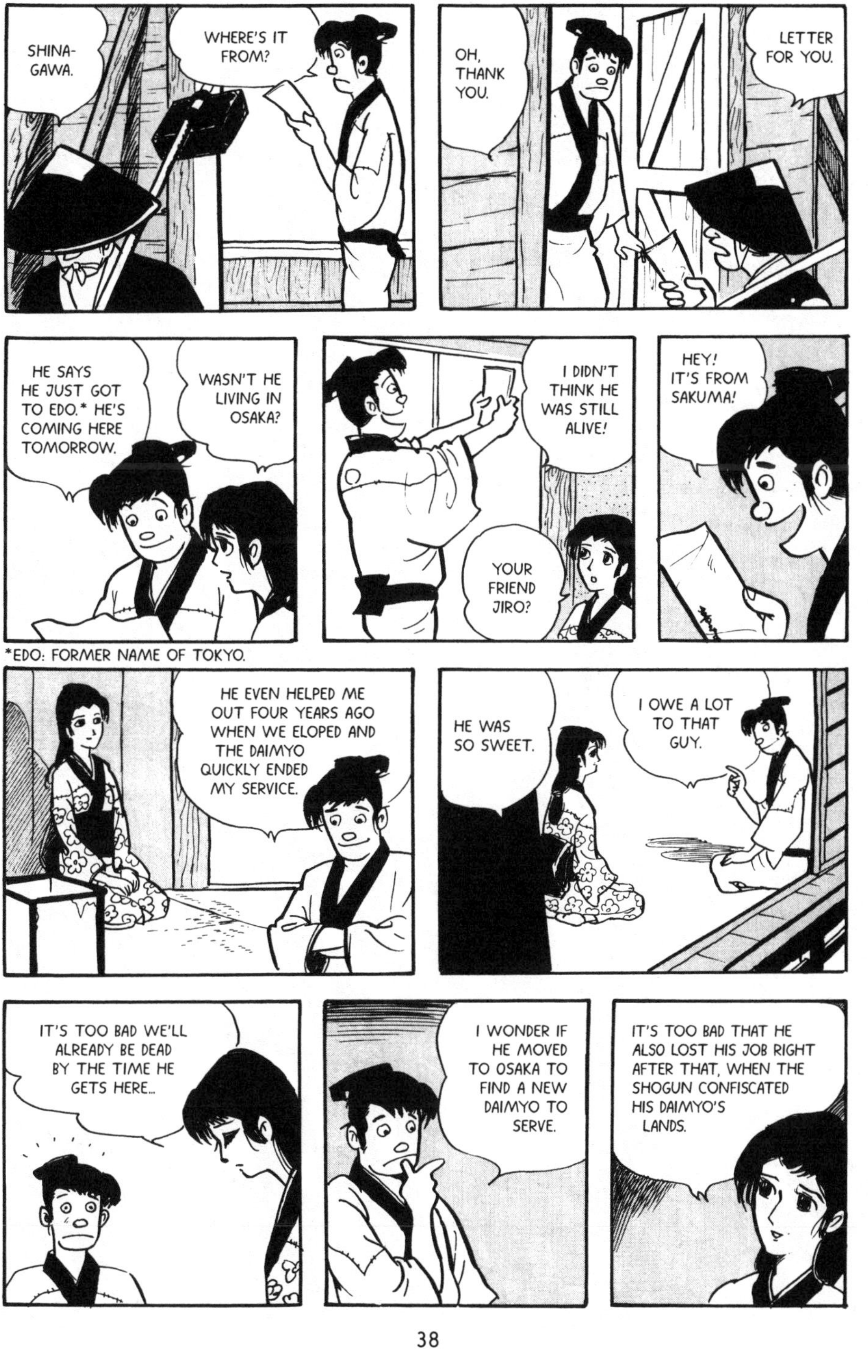
LETTER FOR YOU.
OH, THANK YOU.
WHERE'S IT FROM?
SHINA-GAWA.
HEY! IT'S FROM SAKUMA!
I DIDN'T THINK HE WAS STILL ALIVE!
YOUR FRIEND JIRO?
WASN'T HE LIVING IN OSAKA?
HE SAYS HE JUST GOT TO EDO.* HE'S COMING HERE TOMORROW.
I OWE A LOT TO THAT GUY.
HE WAS SO SWEET.
HE EVEN HELPED ME OUT FOUR YEARS AGO WHEN WE ELOPED AND THE DAIMYO QUICKLY ENDED MY SERVICE.
IT'S TOO BAD THAT HE ALSO LOST HIS JOB RIGHT AFTER THAT, WHEN THE SHOGUN CONFISCATED HIS DAIMYO'S LANDS.
I WONDER IF HE MOVED TO OSAKA TO FIND A NEW DAIMYO TO SERVE.
IT'S TOO BAD WE'LL ALREADY BE DEAD BY THE TIME HE GETS HERE...

*EDO: FORMER NAME OF TOKYO.

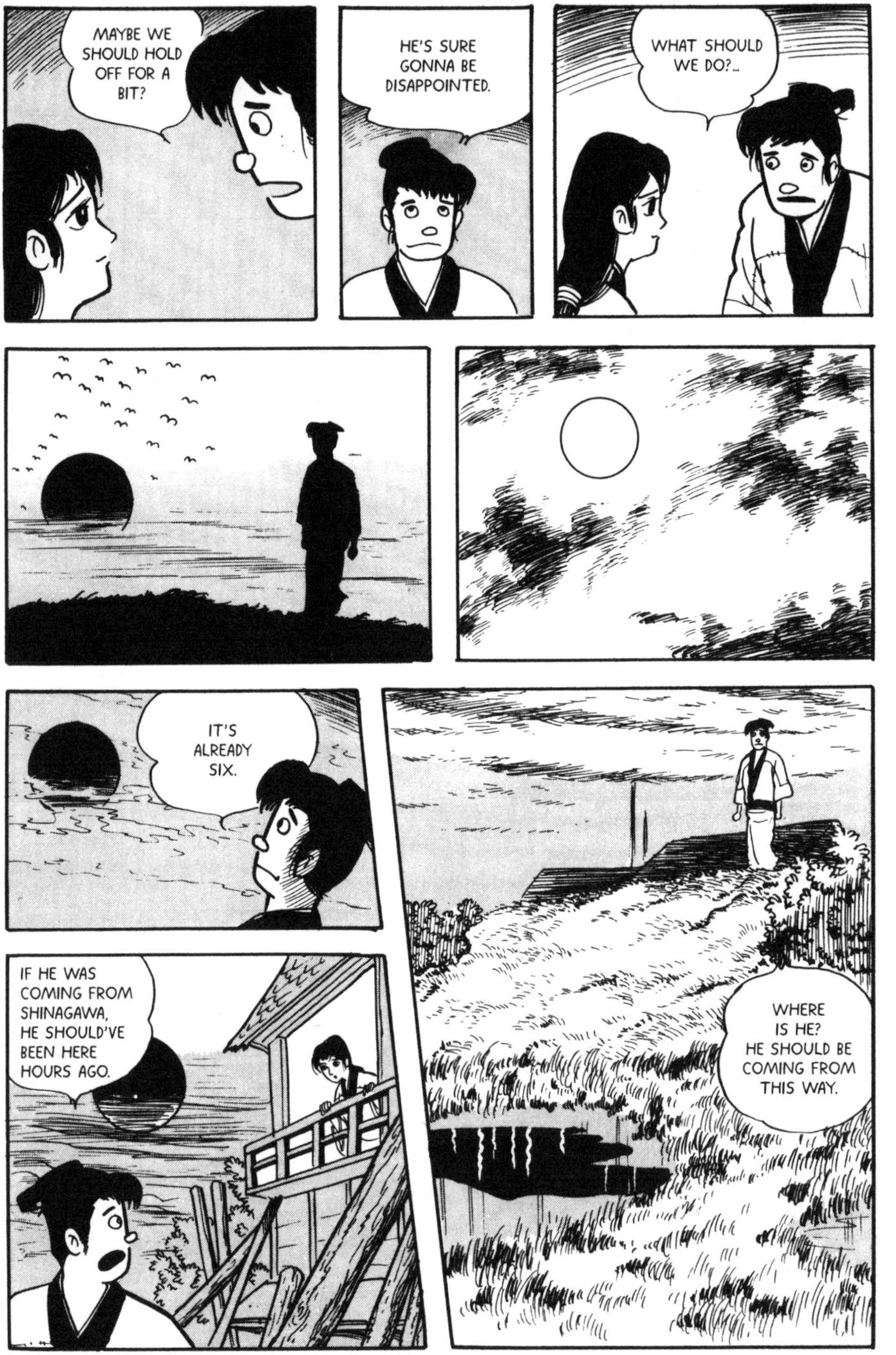
WHAT SHOULD WE DO?...
HE'S SURE GONNA BE DISAPPOINTED.
MAYBE WE SHOULD HOLD OFF FOR A BIT?
WHERE IS HE? HE SHOULD BE COMING FROM THIS WAY.
IT'S ALREADY SIX.
IF HE WAS COMING FROM SHINAGAWA, HE SHOULD'VE BEEN HERE HOURS AGO.

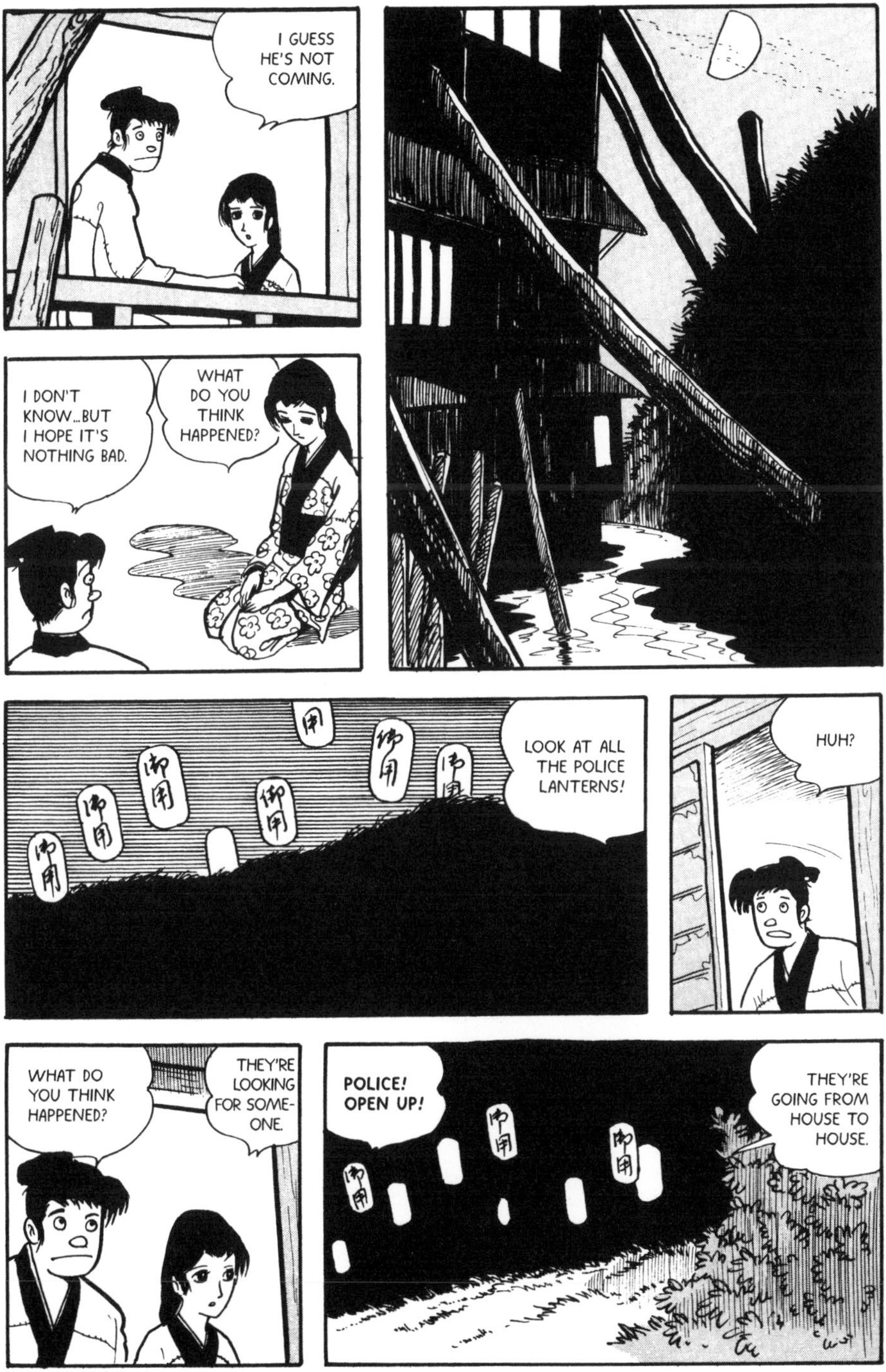
I GUESS HE'S NOT COMING.
WHAT DO YOU THINK HAPPENED?
I DON'T KNOW...BUT I HOPE IT'S NOTHING BAD.
HUH?
LOOK AT ALL THE POLICE LANTERNS!
THEY'RE GOING FROM HOUSE TO HOUSE.
POLICE! OPEN UP!
THEY'RE LOOKING FOR SOME-ONE.
WHAT DO YOU THINK HAPPENED?

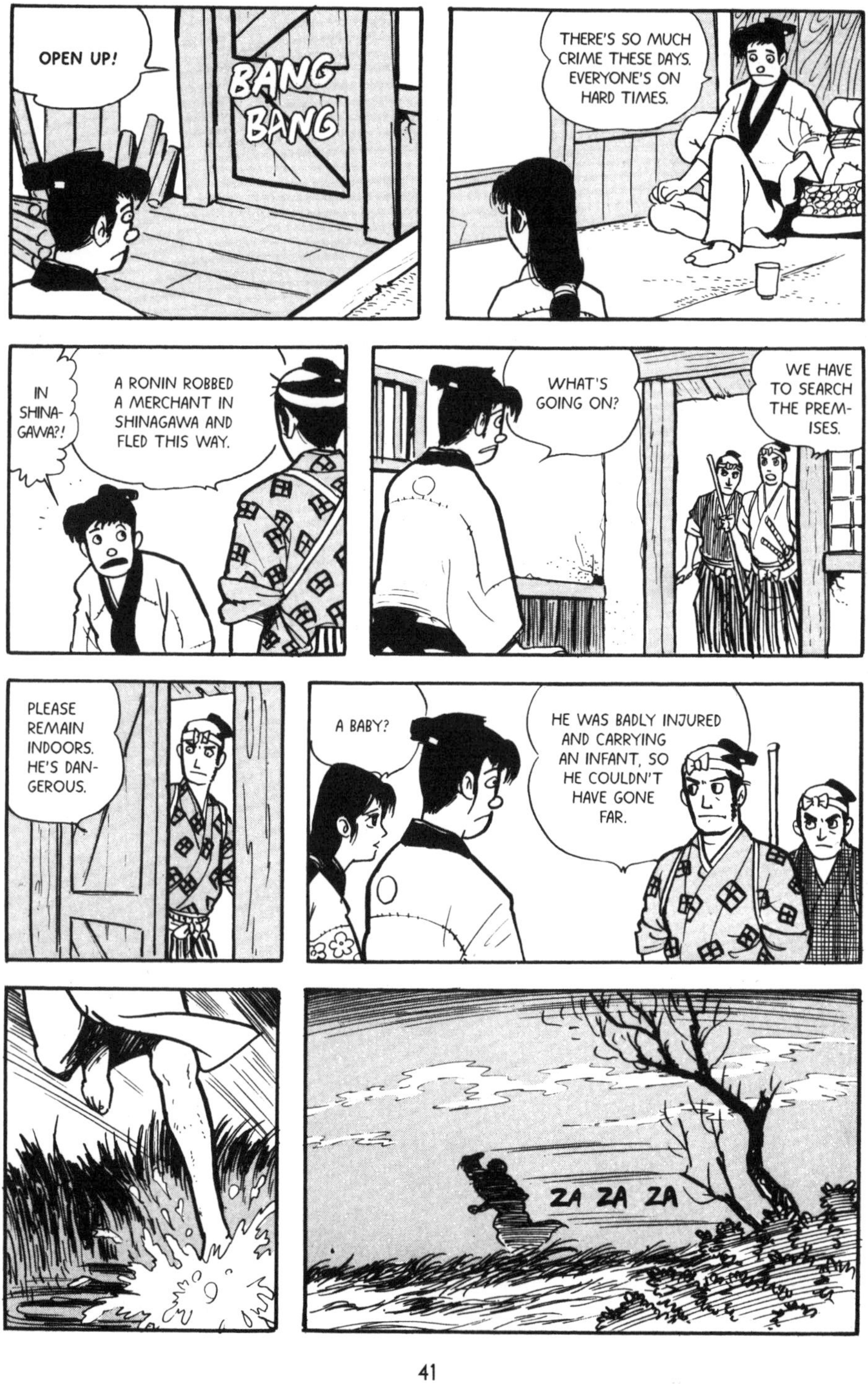
THERE'S SO MUCH CRIME THESE DAYS. EVERYONE'S ON HARD TIMES.
OPEN UP!
BANG BANG
WE HAVE TO SEARCH THE PREMISES.
WHAT'S GOING ON?
A RONIN ROBBED A MERCHANT IN SHINAGAWA AND FLED THIS WAY.
IN SHINAGAWA?!
HE WAS BADLY INJURED AND CARRYING AN INFANT, SO HE COULDN'T HAVE GONE FAR.
A BABY?
PLEASE REMAIN INDOORS. HE'S DANGEROUS.
ZA ZA ZA

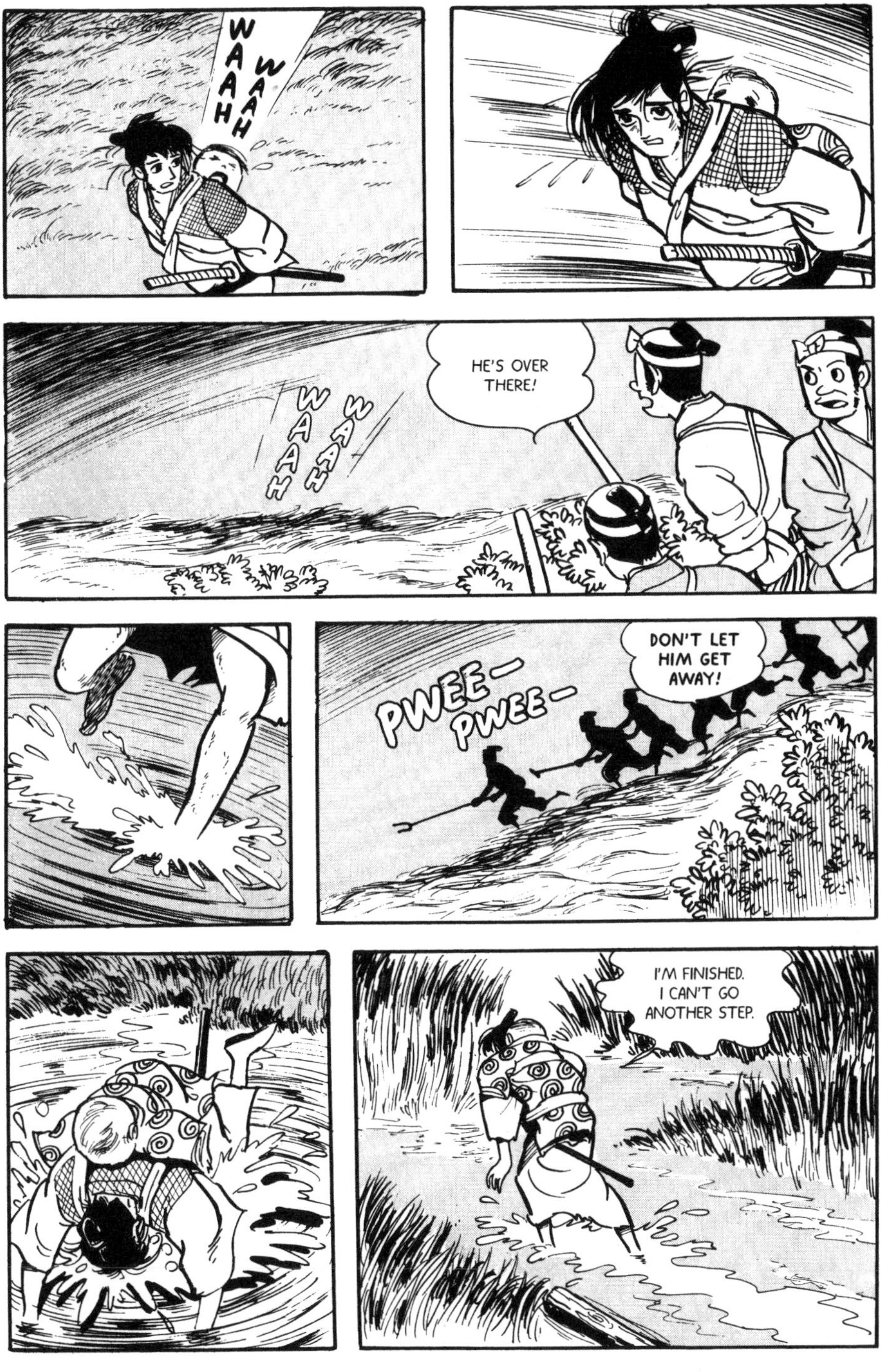
WAAH WAAH
HE'S OVER THERE!
WAAH WAAH
DON'T LET HIM GET AWAY!
PWEE— PWEE—
I'M FINISHED. I CAN'T GO ANOTHER STEP.

URH-MMM
PLEASE, DON'T CRY.
I BEG YOU...
WAAAAAAA
IF I COULD JUST GET ACROSS THE RIVER...
BUT IT'S TOO COLD. SHE'D FREEZE TO DEATH.
I DON'T HEAR THE BABY ANYMORE.
WHERE'D HE GO?
HE WON'T LAST LONG WITH THOSE WOUNDS.
LET'S TRY OVER HERE.

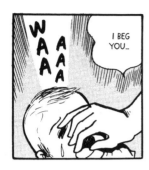

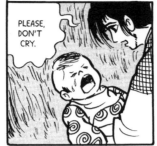

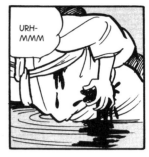

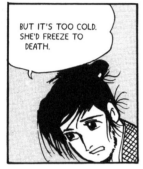

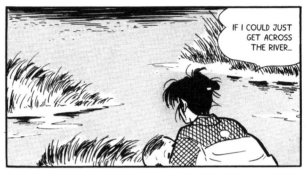

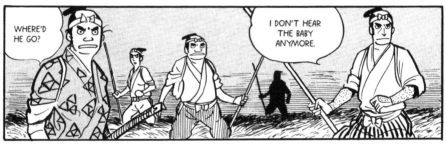

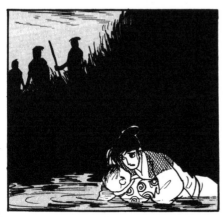

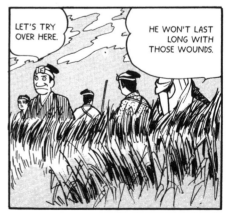

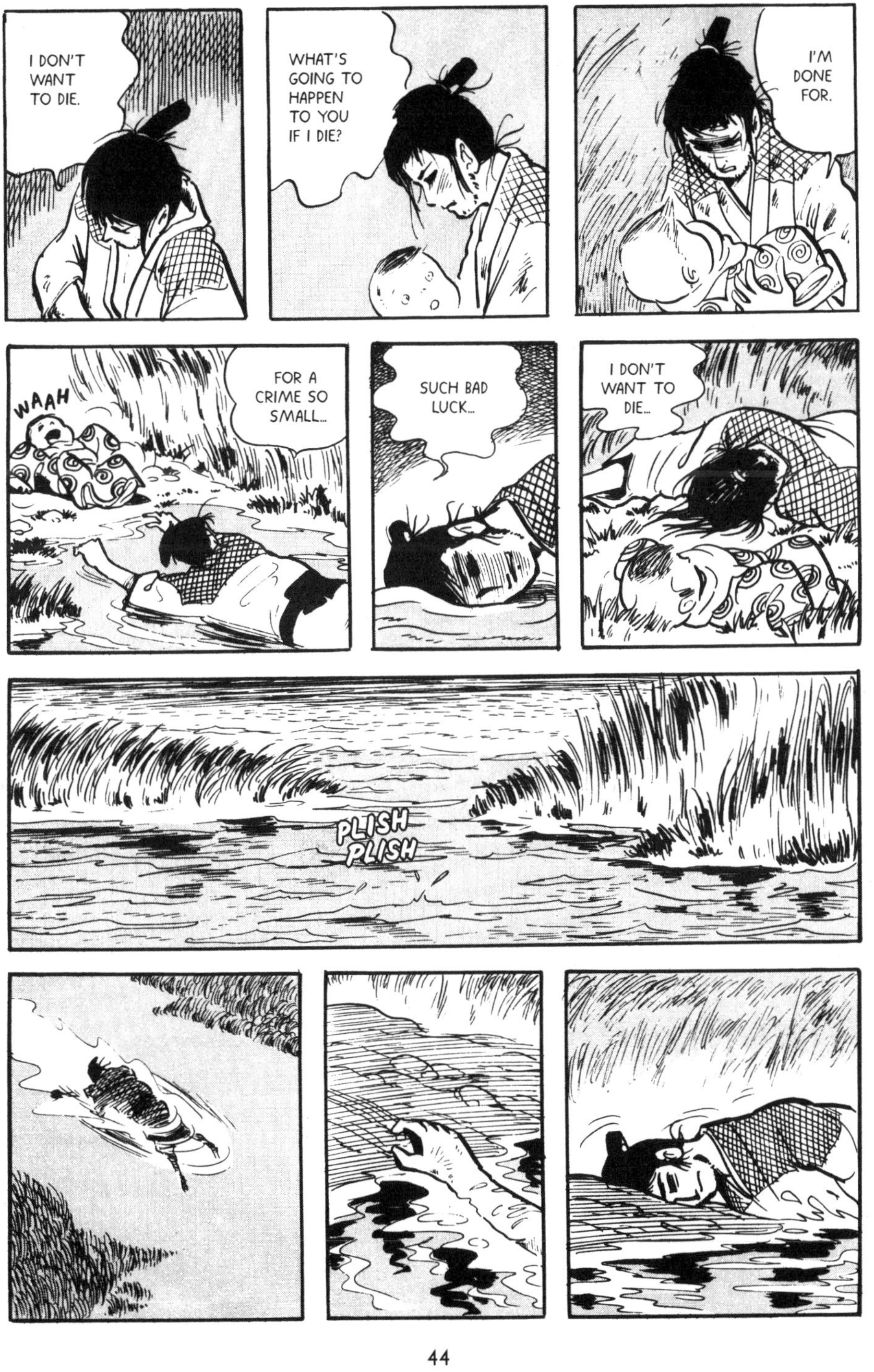
I'M DONE FOR.
WHAT'S GOING TO HAPPEN TO YOU IF I DIE?
I DON'T WANT TO DIE.
I DON'T WANT TO DIE...
SUCH BAD LUCK...
FOR A CRIME SO SMALL...
WAAH
PLISH PLISH

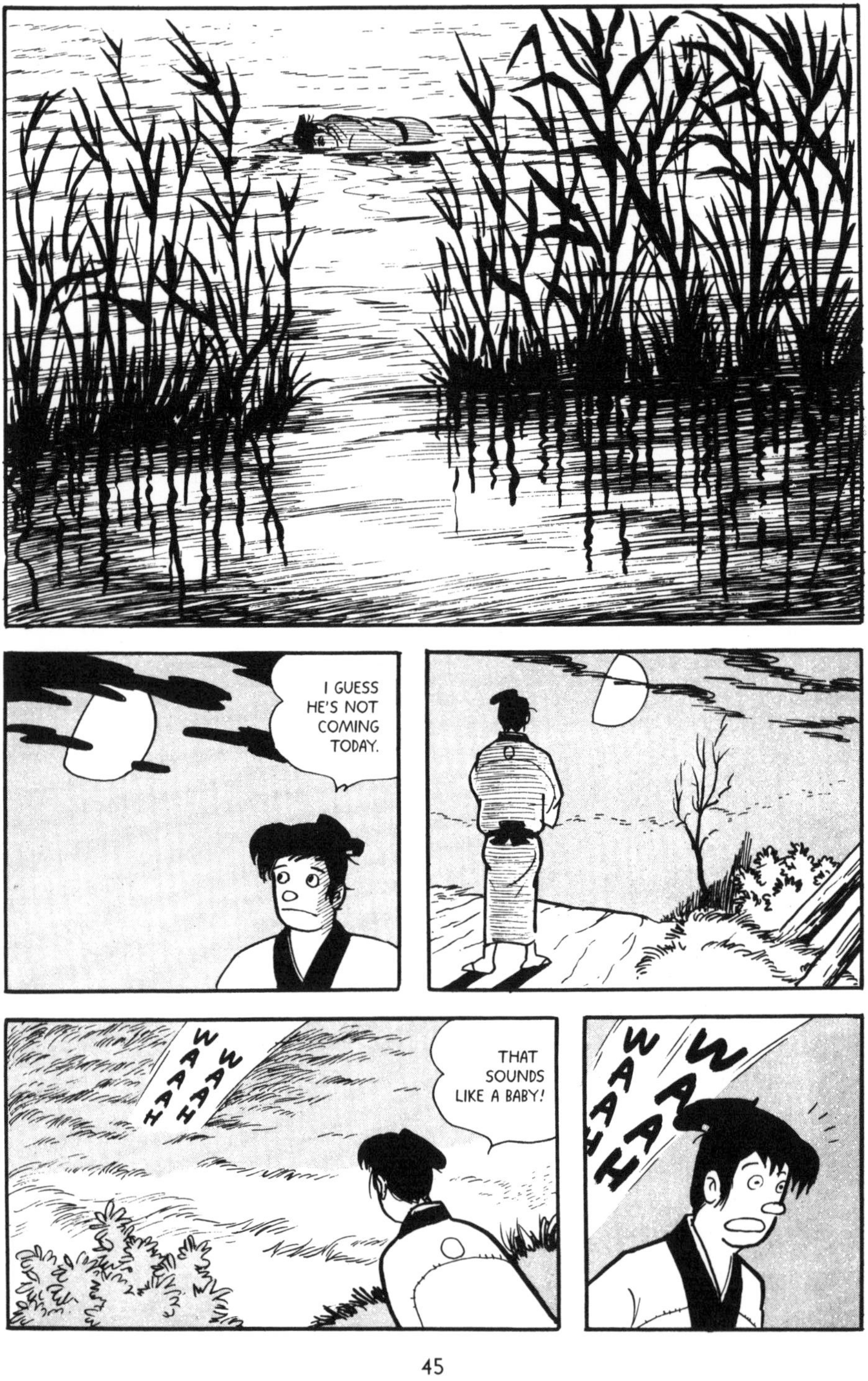
I GUESS HE'S NOT COMING TODAY.
WAAAH
WAAAH
THAT SOUNDS LIKE A BABY!
WAAAH
WAAAH

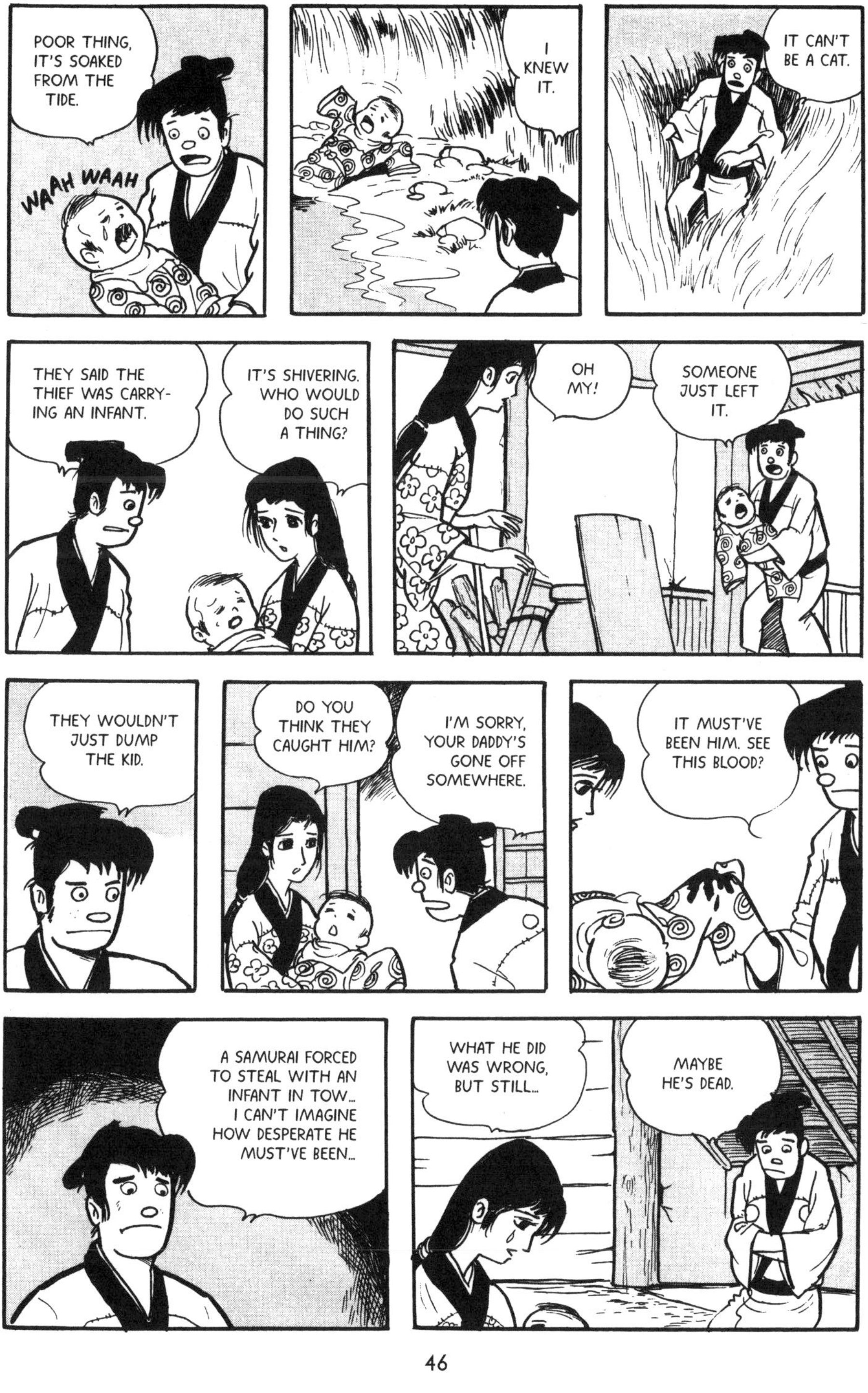
IT CAN'T BE A CAT.
I KNEW IT.
POOR THING, IT'S SOAKED FROM THE TIDE.
WAAH WAAH
SOMEONE JUST LEFT IT.
OH MY!
IT'S SHIVERING. WHO WOULD DO SUCH A THING?
THEY SAID THE THIEF WAS CARRY-ING AN INFANT.
IT MUST'VE BEEN HIM. SEE THIS BLOOD?
I'M SORRY, YOUR DADDY'S GONE OFF SOMEWHERE.
DO YOU THINK THEY CAUGHT HIM?
THEY WOULDN'T JUST DUMP THE KID.
MAYBE HE'S DEAD.
WHAT HE DID WAS WRONG, BUT STILL...
A SAMURAI FORCED TO STEAL WITH AN INFANT IN TOW... I CAN'T IMAGINE HOW DESPERATE HE MUST'VE BEEN...

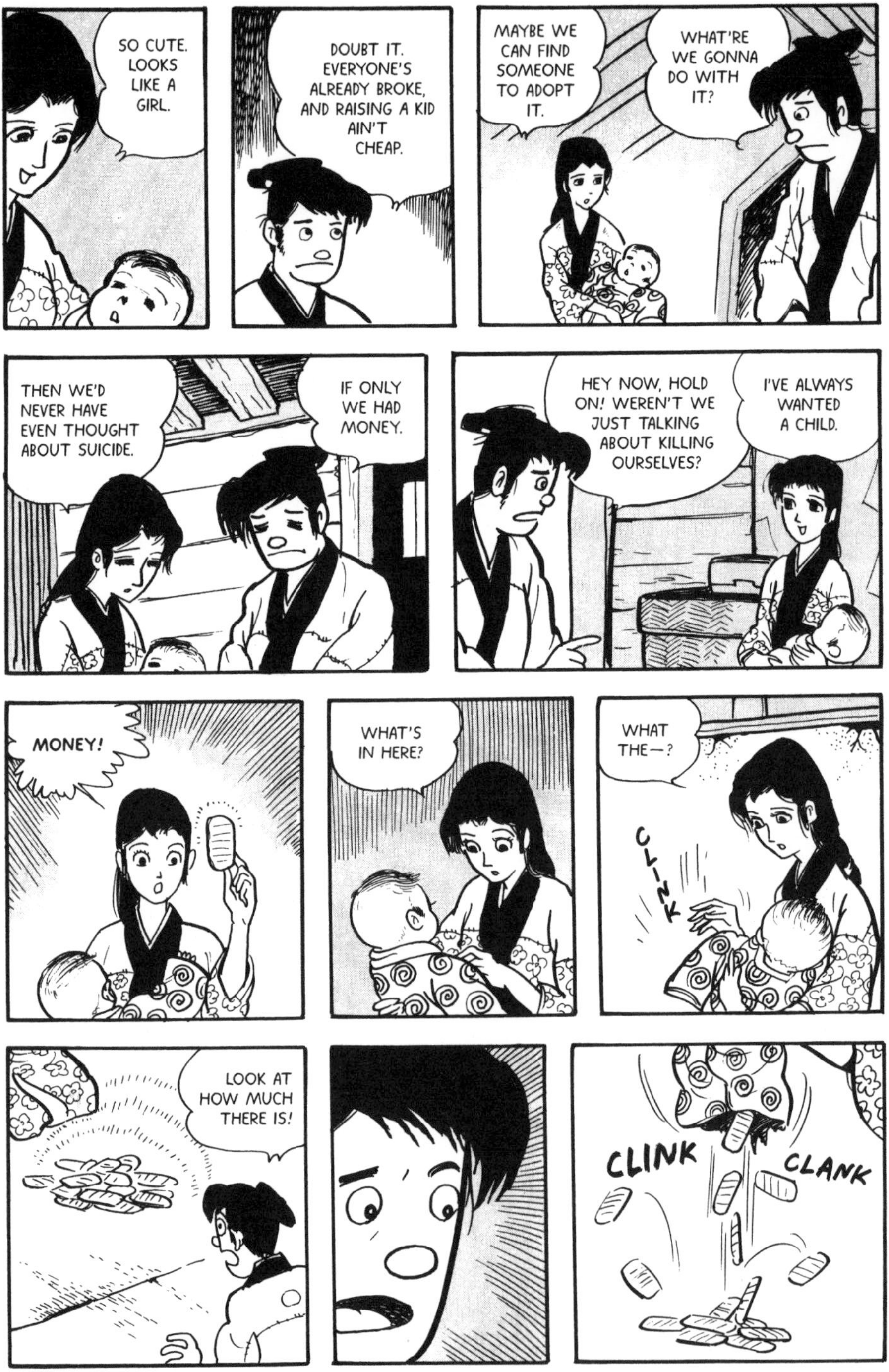
WHAT'RE WE GONNA DO WITH IT?
MAYBE WE CAN FIND SOMEONE TO ADOPT IT.
DOUBT IT. EVERYONE'S ALREADY BROKE, AND RAISING A KID AIN'T CHEAP.
SO CUTE. LOOKS LIKE A GIRL.
I'VE ALWAYS WANTED A CHILD.
HEY NOW, HOLD ON! WEREN'T WE JUST TALKING ABOUT KILLING OURSELVES?
IF ONLY WE HAD MONEY.
THEN WE'D NEVER HAVE EVEN THOUGHT ABOUT SUICIDE.
WHAT THE—?
CLINK
WHAT'S IN HERE?
MONEY!
CLINK
CLANK
LOOK AT HOW MUCH THERE IS!

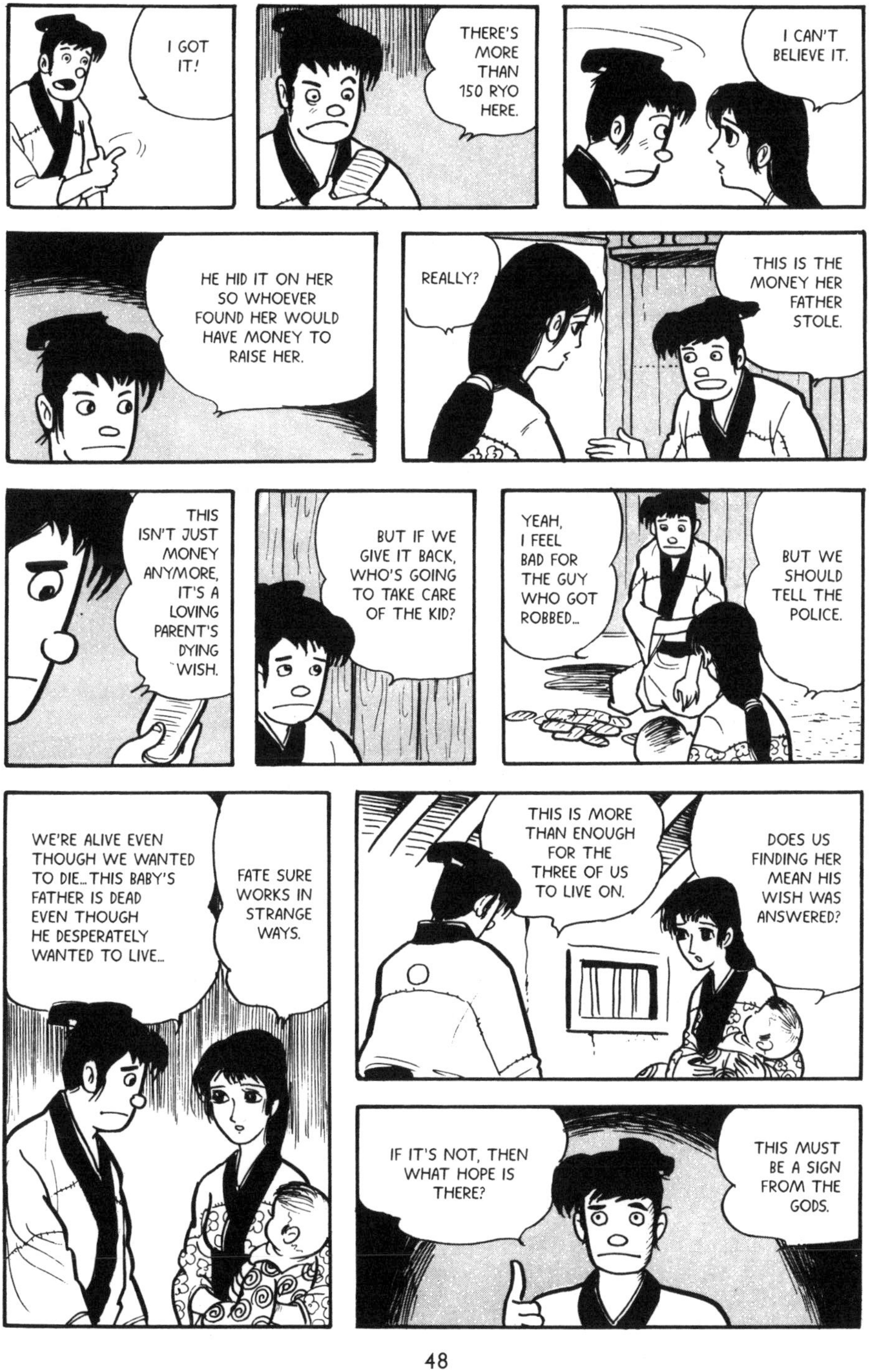
I CAN'T BELIEVE IT.
THERE'S MORE THAN 150 RYO HERE.
I GOT IT!
THIS IS THE MONEY HER FATHER STOLE.
REALLY?
HE HID IT ON HER SO WHOEVER FOUND HER WOULD HAVE MONEY TO RAISE HER.
BUT WE SHOULD TELL THE POLICE.
YEAH, I FEEL BAD FOR THE GUY WHO GOT ROBBED...
BUT IF WE GIVE IT BACK, WHO'S GOING TO TAKE CARE OF THE KID?
THIS ISN'T JUST MONEY ANYMORE, IT'S A LOVING PARENT'S DYING WISH.
DOES US FINDING HER MEAN HIS WISH WAS ANSWERED?
THIS IS MORE THAN ENOUGH FOR THE THREE OF US TO LIVE ON.
THIS MUST BE A SIGN FROM THE GODS.
IF IT'S NOT, THEN WHAT HOPE IS THERE?
FATE SURE WORKS IN STRANGE WAYS.
WE'RE ALIVE EVEN THOUGH WE WANTED TO DIE... THIS BABY'S FATHER IS DEAD EVEN THOUGH HE DESPERATELY WANTED TO LIVE...

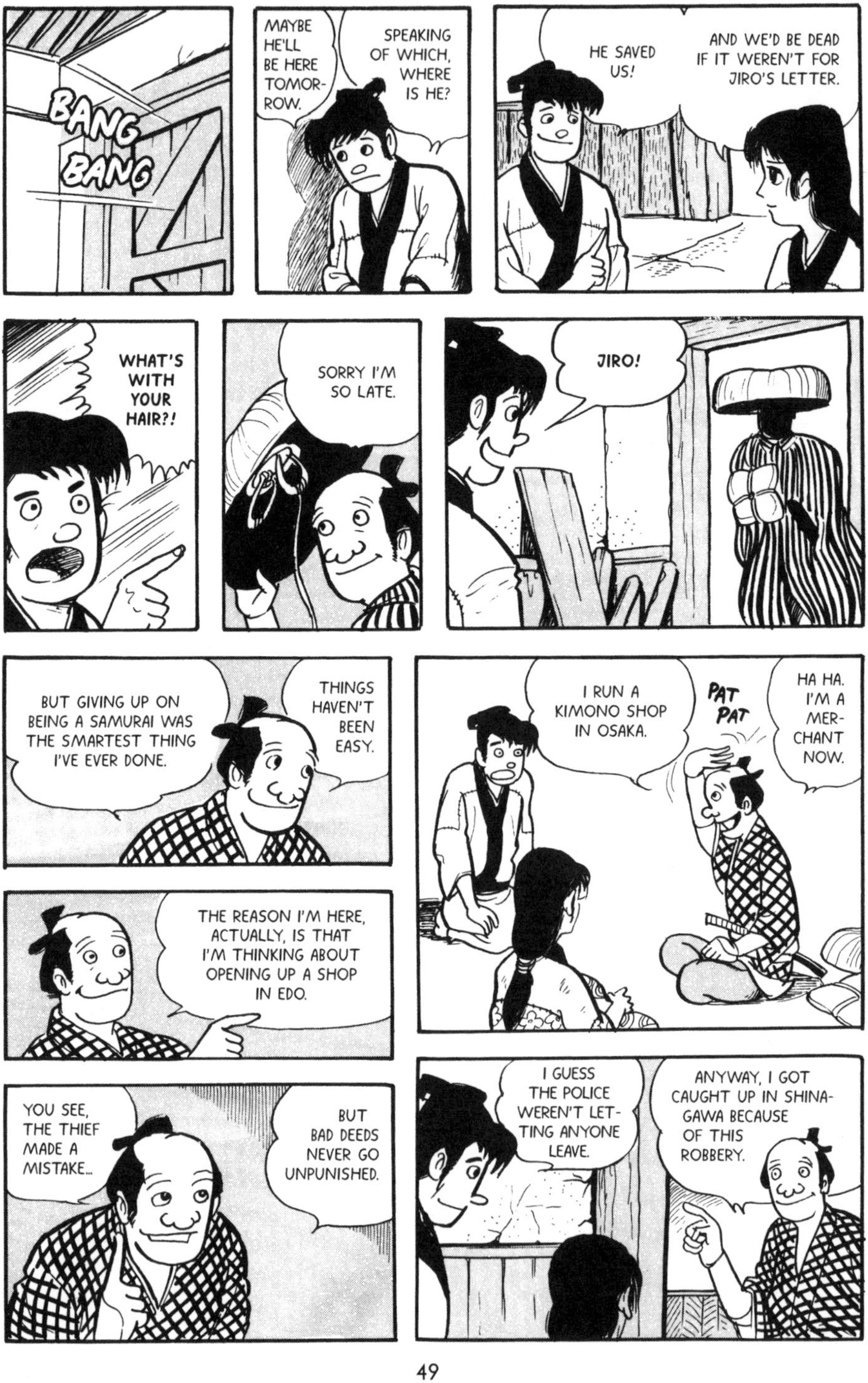
AND WE'D BE DEAD IF IT WEREN'T FOR JIRO'S LETTER.
HE SAVED US!
SPEAKING OF WHICH, WHERE IS HE?
MAYBE HE'LL BE HERE TOMORROW.
BANG BANG
JIRO!
SORRY I'M SO LATE.
WHAT'S WITH YOUR HAIR?!
HA HA. I'M A MERCHANT NOW.
PAT PAT
I RUN A KIMONO SHOP IN OSAKA.
THINGS HAVEN'T BEEN EASY.
BUT GIVING UP ON BEING A SAMURAI WAS THE SMARTEST THING I'VE EVER DONE.
THE REASON I'M HERE, ACTUALLY, IS THAT I'M THINKING ABOUT OPENING UP A SHOP IN EDO.
ANYWAY, I GOT CAUGHT UP IN SHINAGAWA BECAUSE OF THIS ROBBERY.
I GUESS THE POLICE WEREN'T LETTING ANYONE LEAVE.
BUT BAD DEEDS NEVER GO UNPUNISHED.
YOU SEE, THE THIEF MADE A MISTAKE...

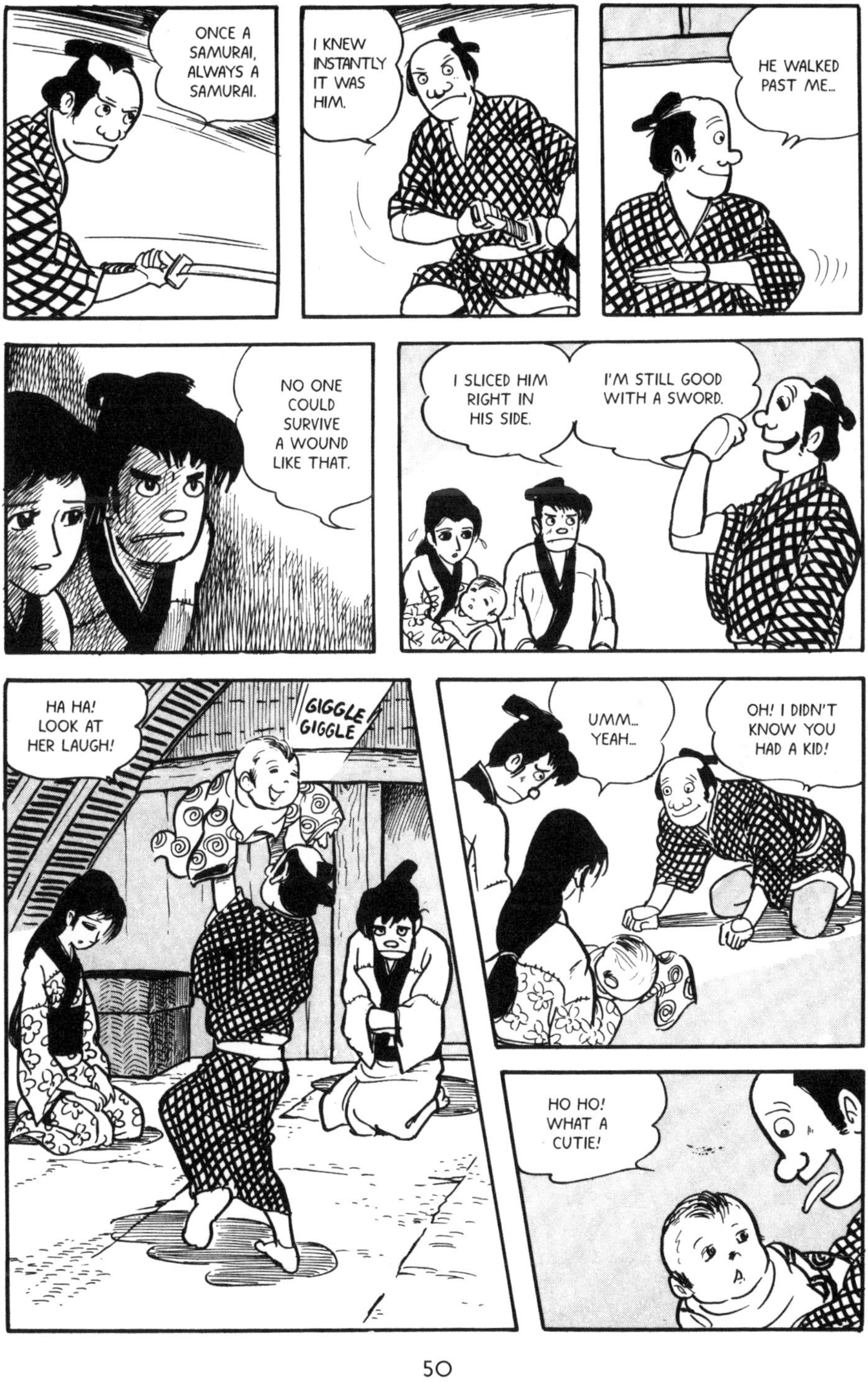
HE WALKED PAST ME...
I KNEW INSTANTLY IT WAS HIM.
ONCE A SAMURAI, ALWAYS A SAMURAI.
I'M STILL GOOD WITH A SWORD.
I SLICED HIM RIGHT IN HIS SIDE.
NO ONE COULD SURVIVE A WOUND LIKE THAT.
OH! I DIDN'T KNOW YOU HAD A KID!
UMM... YEAH...
HO HO! WHAT A CUTIE!
GIGGLE GIGGLE
HA HA! LOOK AT HER LAUGH!

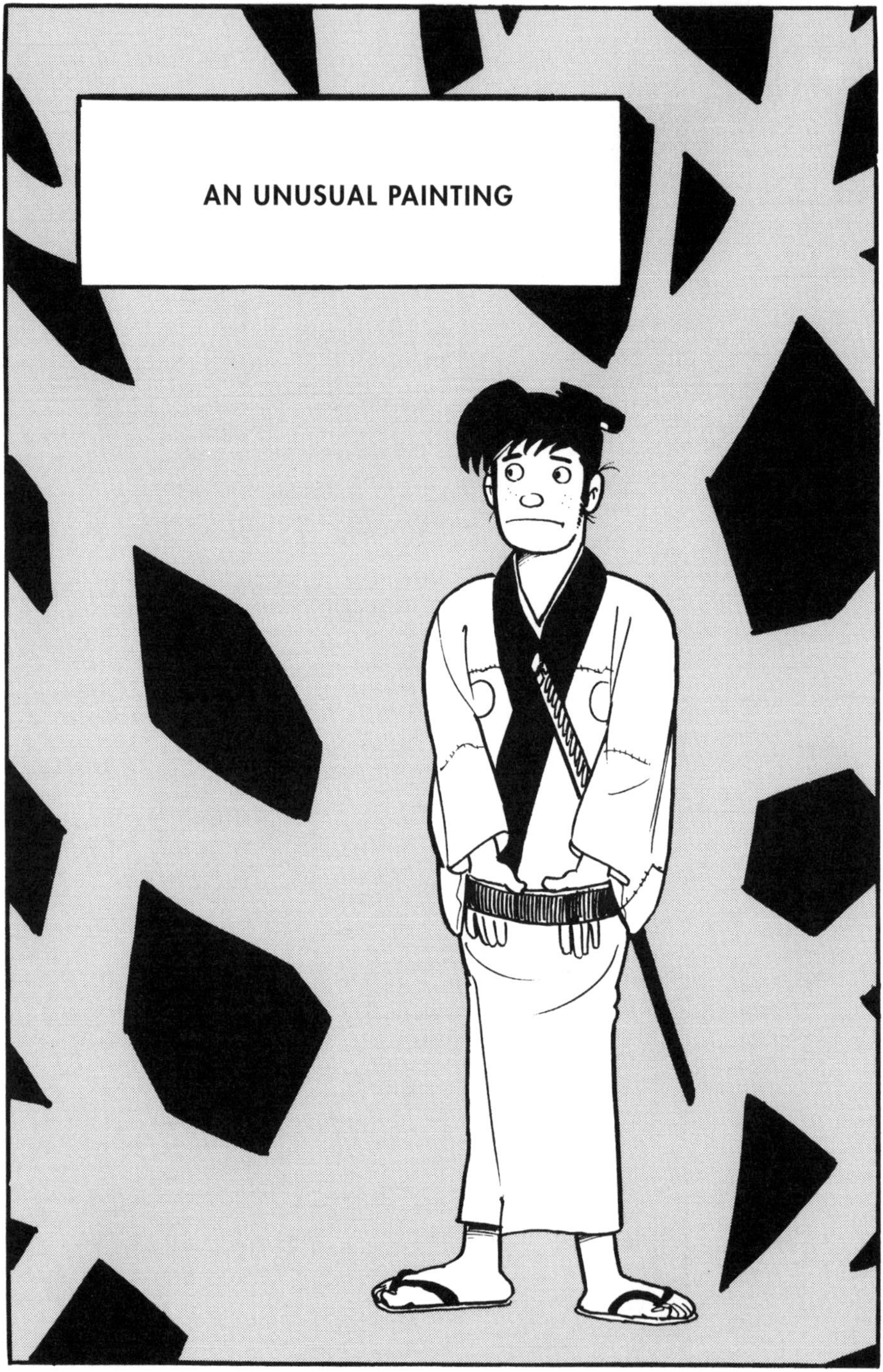
AN UNUSUAL PAINTING

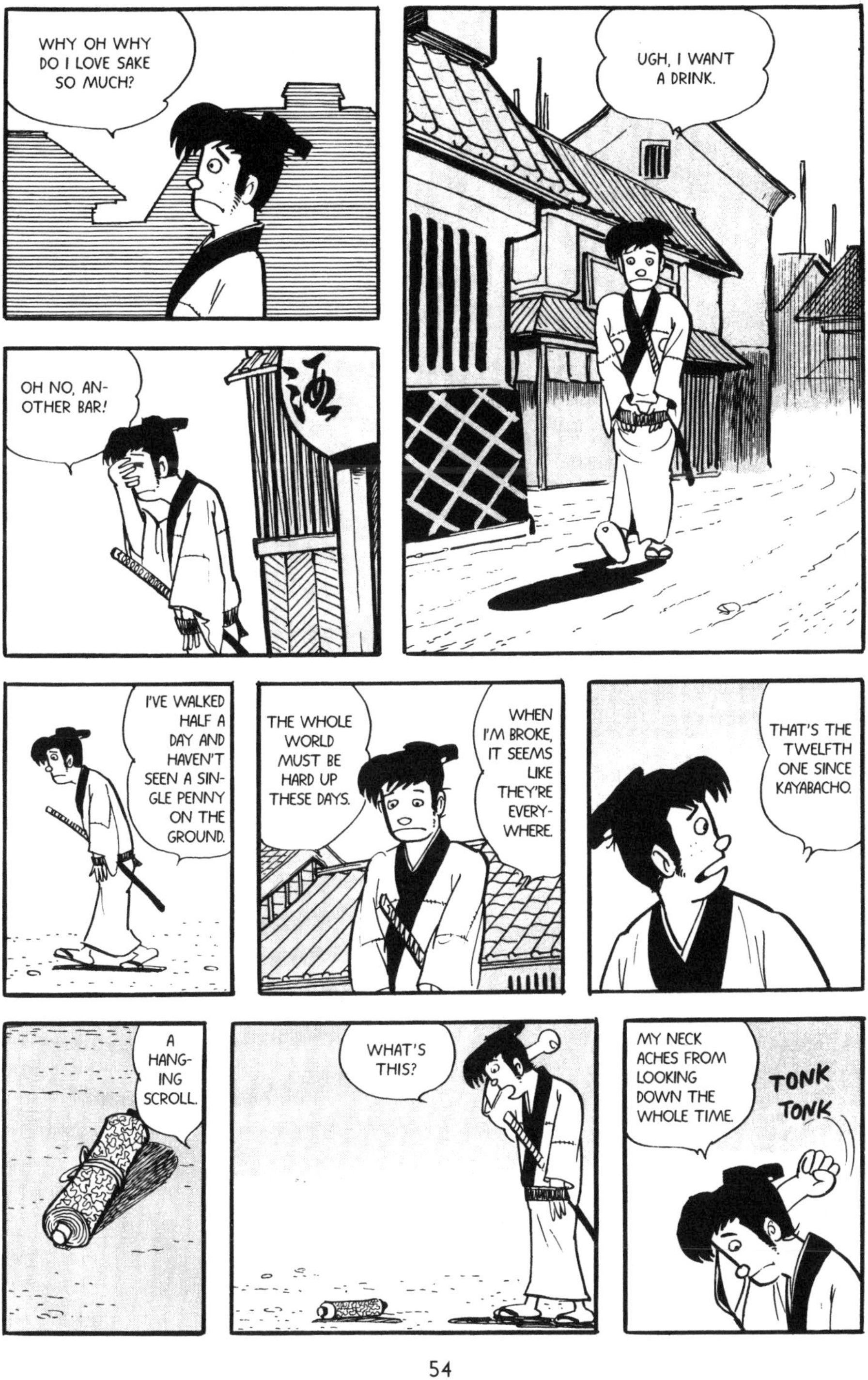
UGH, I WANT A DRINK.
WHY OH WHY DO I LOVE SAKE SO MUCH?
OH NO, AN-OTHER BAR!
THAT'S THE TWELFTH ONE SINCE KAYABACHO.
WHEN I'M BROKE, IT SEEMS LIKE THEY'RE EVERY-WHERE.
THE WHOLE WORLD MUST BE HARD UP THESE DAYS.
I'VE WALKED HALF A DAY AND HAVEN'T SEEN A SIN-GLE PENNY ON THE GROUND.
MY NECK ACHES FROM LOOKING DOWN THE WHOLE TIME.
TONK
TONK
WHAT'S THIS?
A HANG-ING SCROLL.

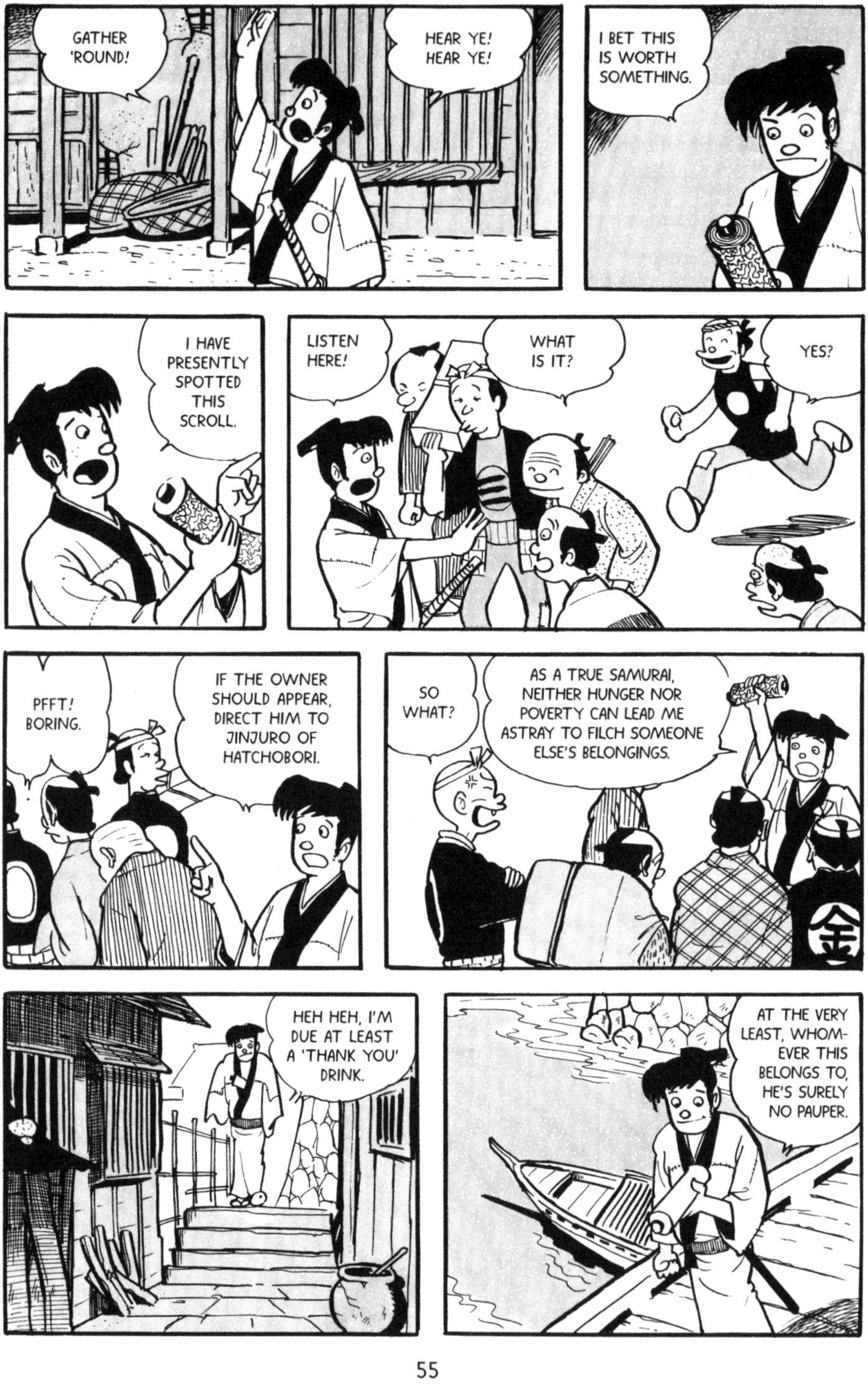
I BET THIS IS WORTH SOMETHING.
HEAR YE! HEAR YE!
GATHER 'ROUND!
YES?
WHAT IS IT?
LISTEN HERE!
I HAVE PRESENTLY SPOTTED THIS SCROLL.
AS A TRUE SAMURAI, NEITHER HUNGER NOR POVERTY CAN LEAD ME ASTRAY TO FILCH SOMEONE ELSE'S BELONGINGS.
SO WHAT?
IF THE OWNER SHOULD APPEAR, DIRECT HIM TO JINJURO OF HATCHOBORI.
PFFT! BORING.
AT THE VERY LEAST, WHOM-EVER THIS BELONGS TO, HE'S SURELY NO PAUPER.
HEH HEH, I'M DUE AT LEAST A 'THANK YOU' DRINK.

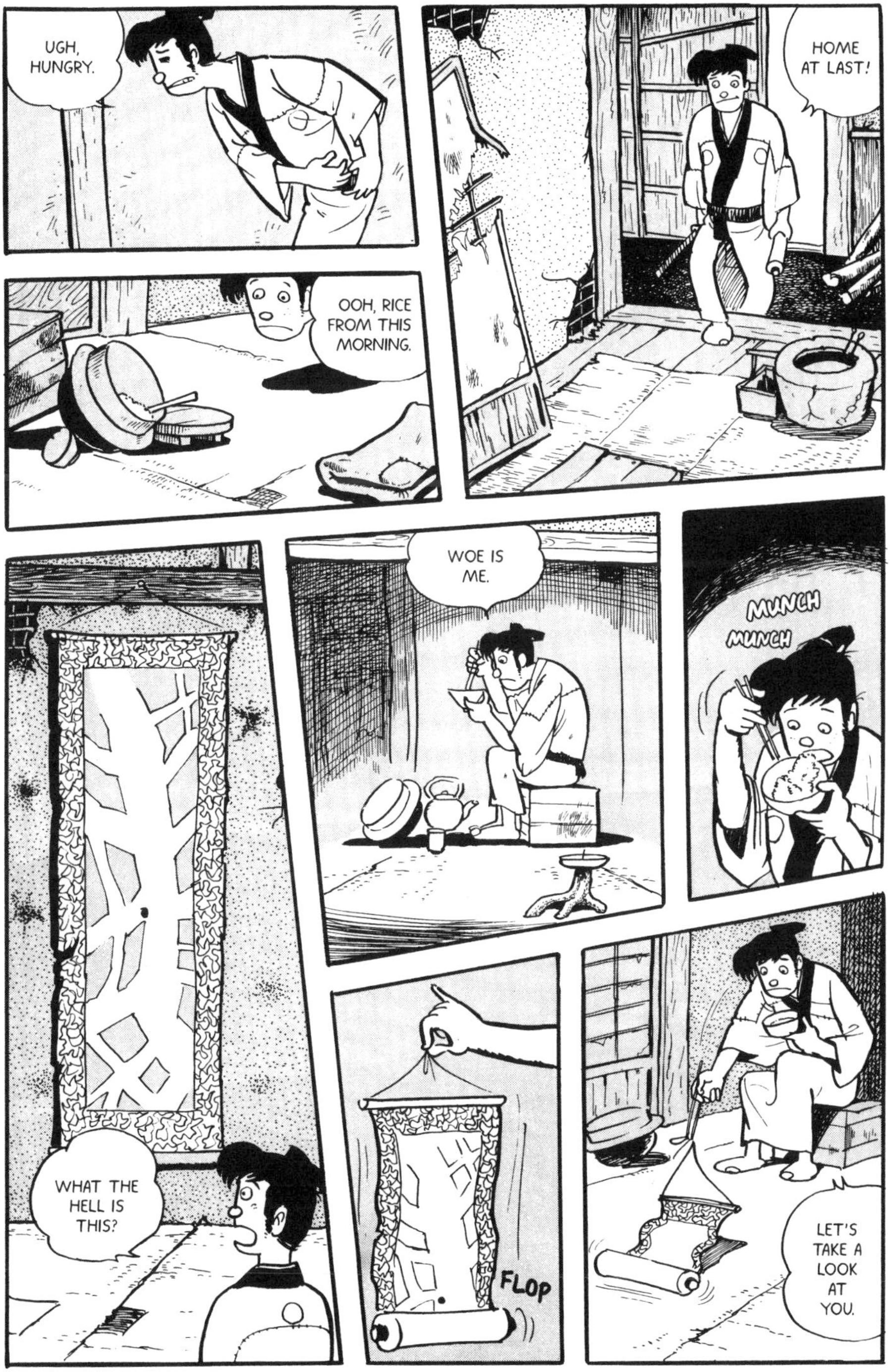
HOME AT LAST!
UGH, HUNGRY.
OOH, RICE FROM THIS MORNING.
MUNCH MUNCH
WOE IS ME.
LET'S TAKE A LOOK AT YOU.
FLOP
WHAT THE HELL IS THIS?

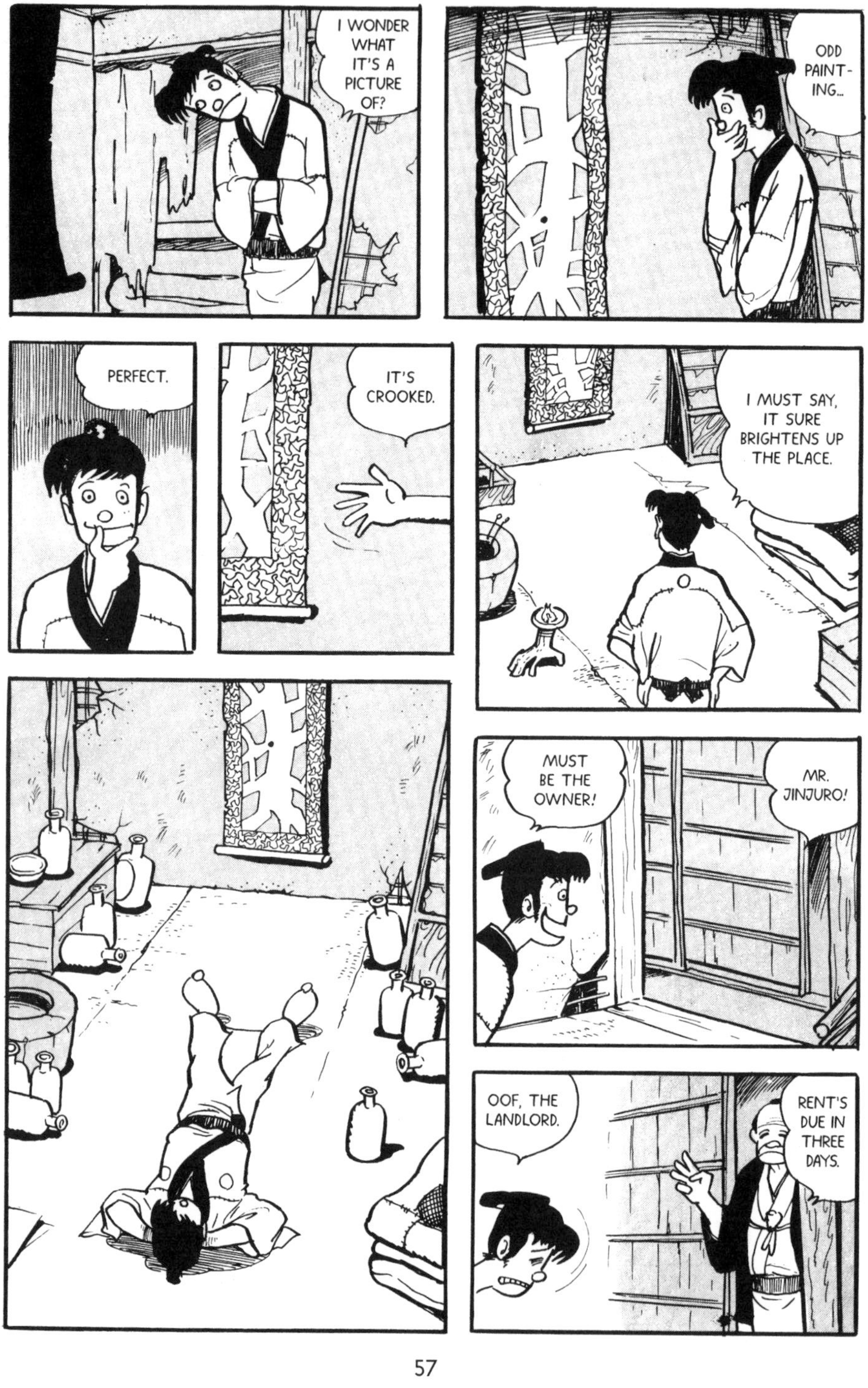
ODD PAINTING...
I WONDER WHAT IT'S A PICTURE OF?
I MUST SAY, IT SURE BRIGHTENS UP THE PLACE.
IT'S CROOKED.
PERFECT.
MR. JINJURO!
MUST BE THE OWNER!
RENT'S DUE IN THREE DAYS.
OOF, THE LANDLORD.

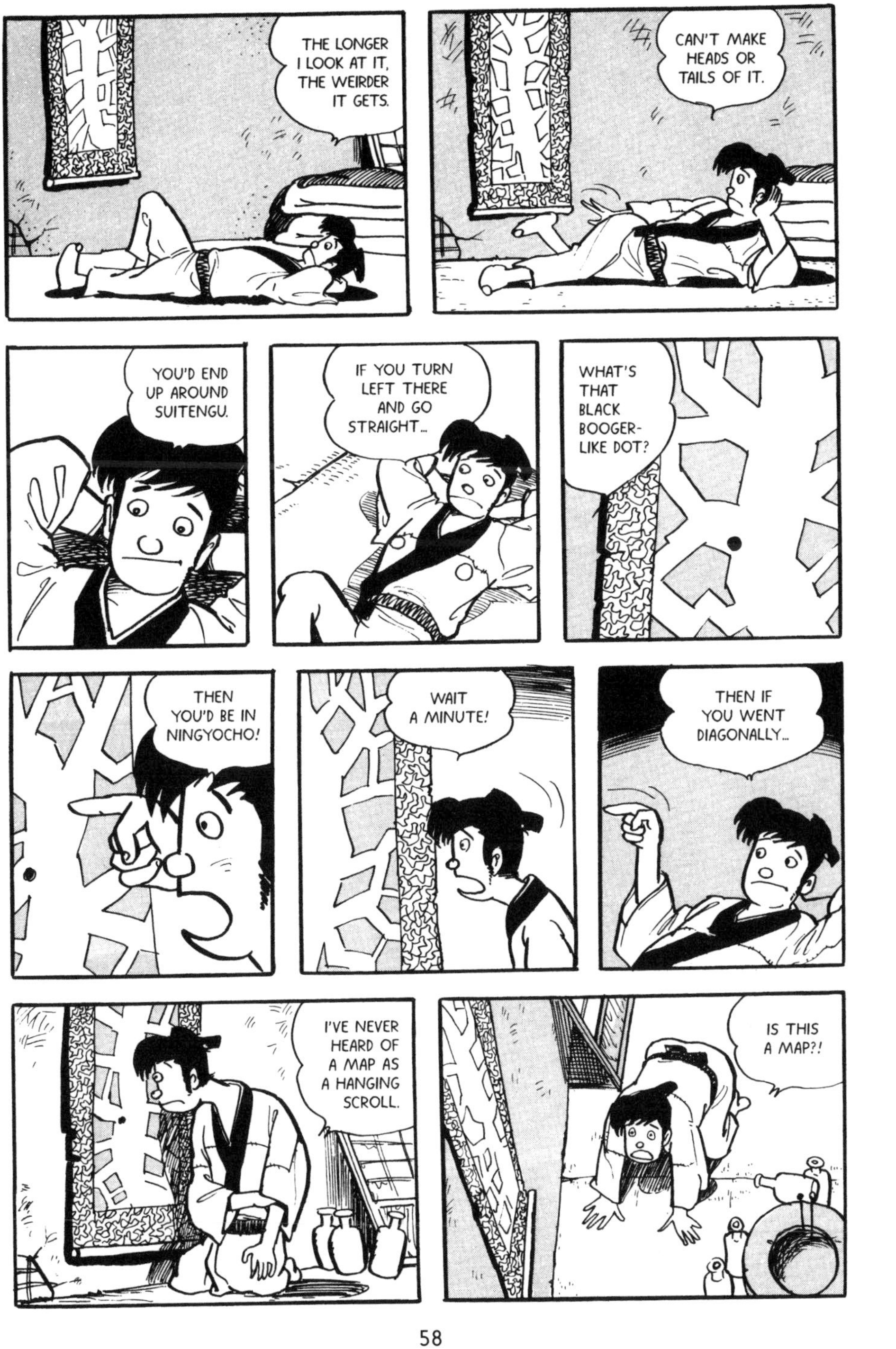
CAN'T MAKE HEADS OR TAILS OF IT.
THE LONGER I LOOK AT IT, THE WEIRDER IT GETS.
WHAT'S THAT BLACK BOOGER-LIKE DOT?
IF YOU TURN LEFT THERE AND GO STRAIGHT...
YOU'D END UP AROUND SUITENGU.
THEN IF YOU WENT DIAGONALLY...
WAIT A MINUTE!
THEN YOU'D BE IN NINGYOCHO!
IS THIS A MAP?!
I'VE NEVER HEARD OF A MAP AS A HANGING SCROLL.

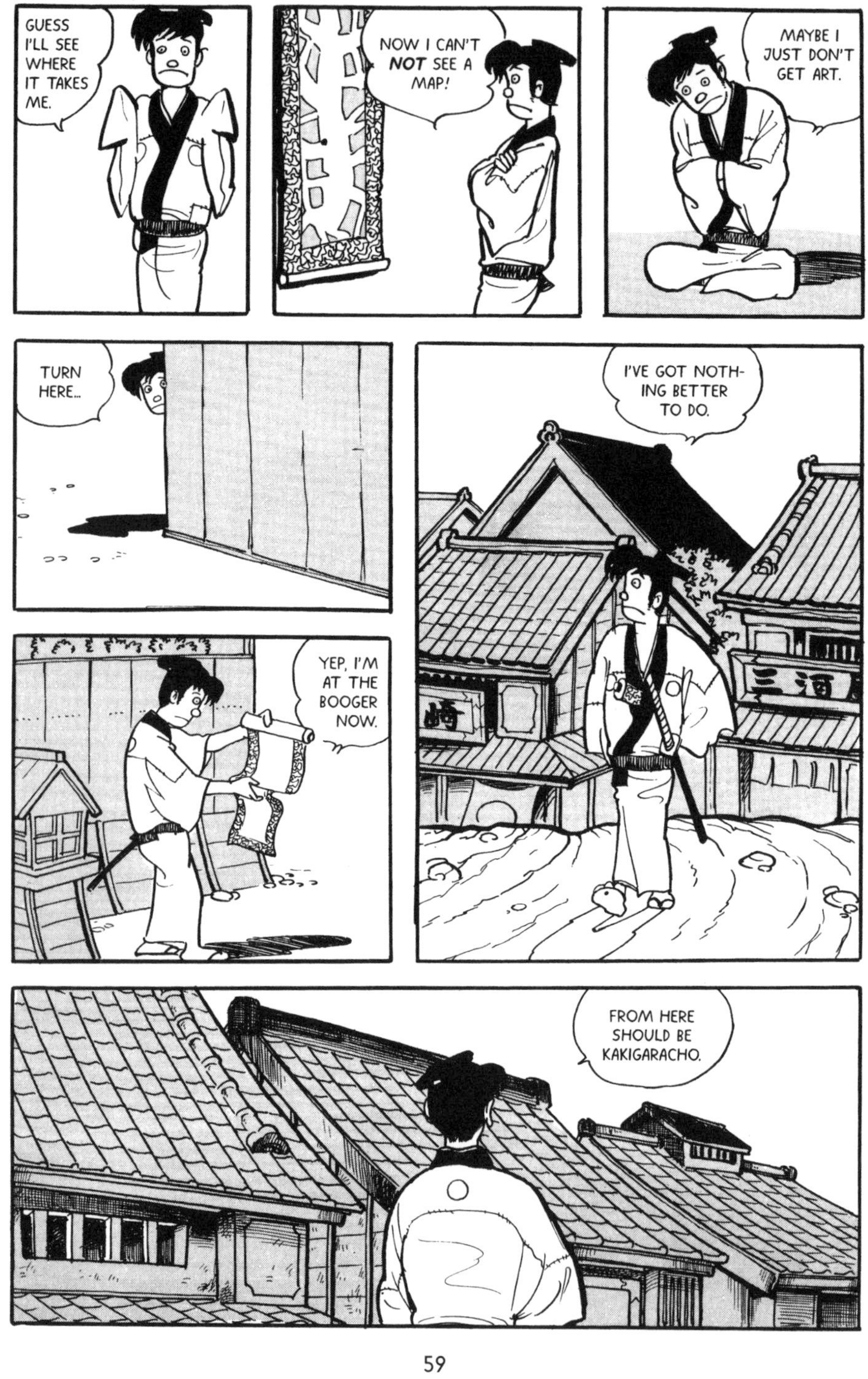
MAYBE I JUST DON'T GET ART.
NOW I CAN'T **NOT** SEE A MAP!
GUESS I'LL SEE WHERE IT TAKES ME.
I'VE GOT NOTHING BETTER TO DO.
三河
崎
TURN HERE...
YEP, I'M AT THE BOOGER NOW.
FROM HERE SHOULD BE KAKIGARACHO.

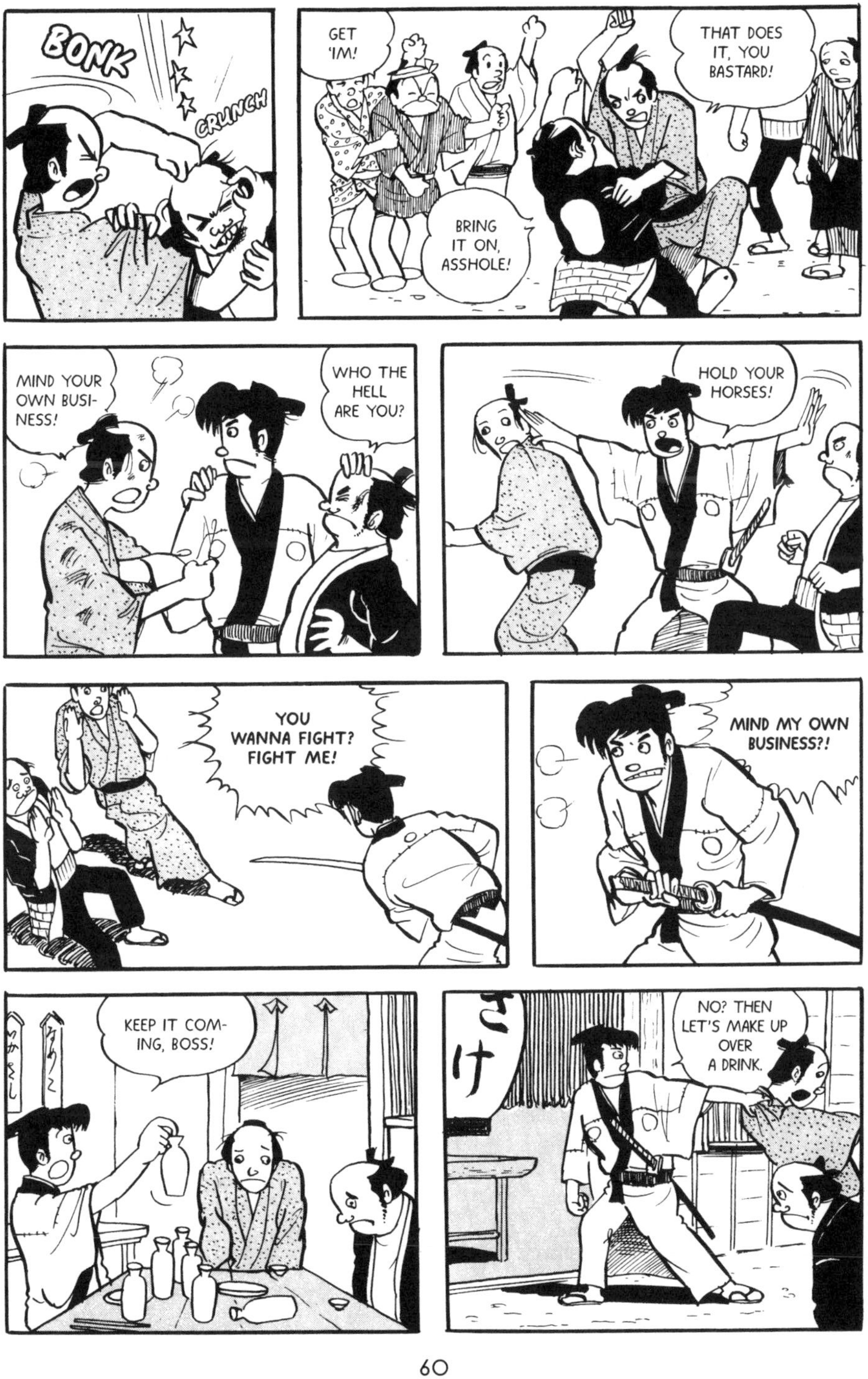
THAT DOES IT, YOU BASTARD!
GET 'IM!
BRING IT ON, ASSHOLE!
BONK
CRUNCH
HOLD YOUR HORSES!
WHO THE HELL ARE YOU?
MIND YOUR OWN BUSINESS!
MIND MY OWN BUSINESS?!
YOU WANNA FIGHT? FIGHT ME!
さけ
NO? THEN LET'S MAKE UP OVER A DRINK.
KEEP IT COMING, BOSS!

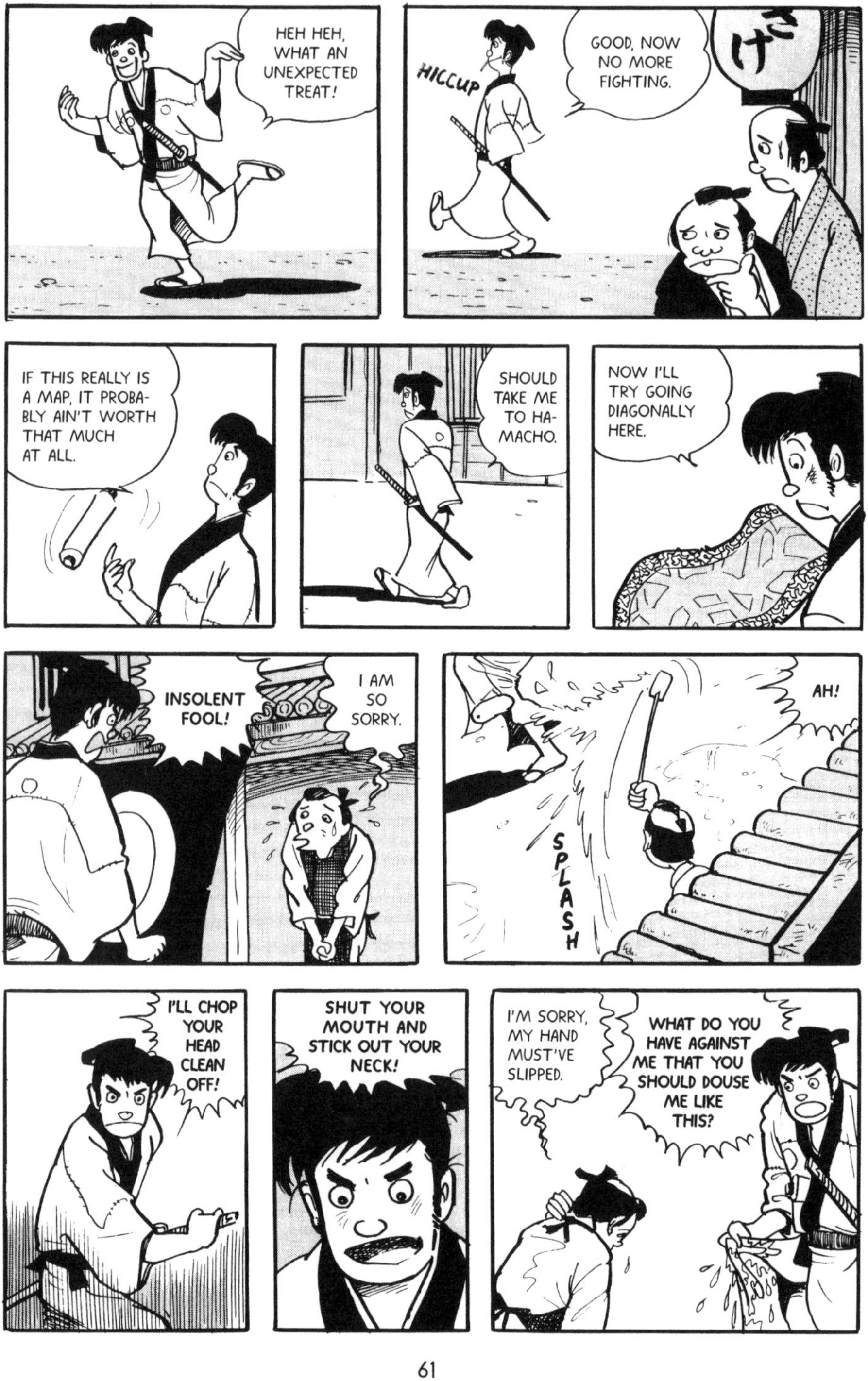
さけ
GOOD, NOW NO MORE FIGHTING.
HICCUP
HEH HEH, WHAT AN UNEXPECTED TREAT!
NOW I'LL TRY GOING DIAGONALLY HERE.
SHOULD TAKE ME TO HA-MACHO.
IF THIS REALLY IS A MAP, IT PROBA-BLY AIN'T WORTH THAT MUCH AT ALL.
AH!
SPLASH
I AM SO SORRY.
INSOLENT FOOL!
WHAT DO YOU HAVE AGAINST ME THAT YOU SHOULD DOUSE ME LIKE THIS?
I'M SORRY, MY HAND MUST'VE SLIPPED.
SHUT YOUR MOUTH AND STICK OUT YOUR NECK!
I'LL CHOP YOUR HEAD CLEAN OFF!

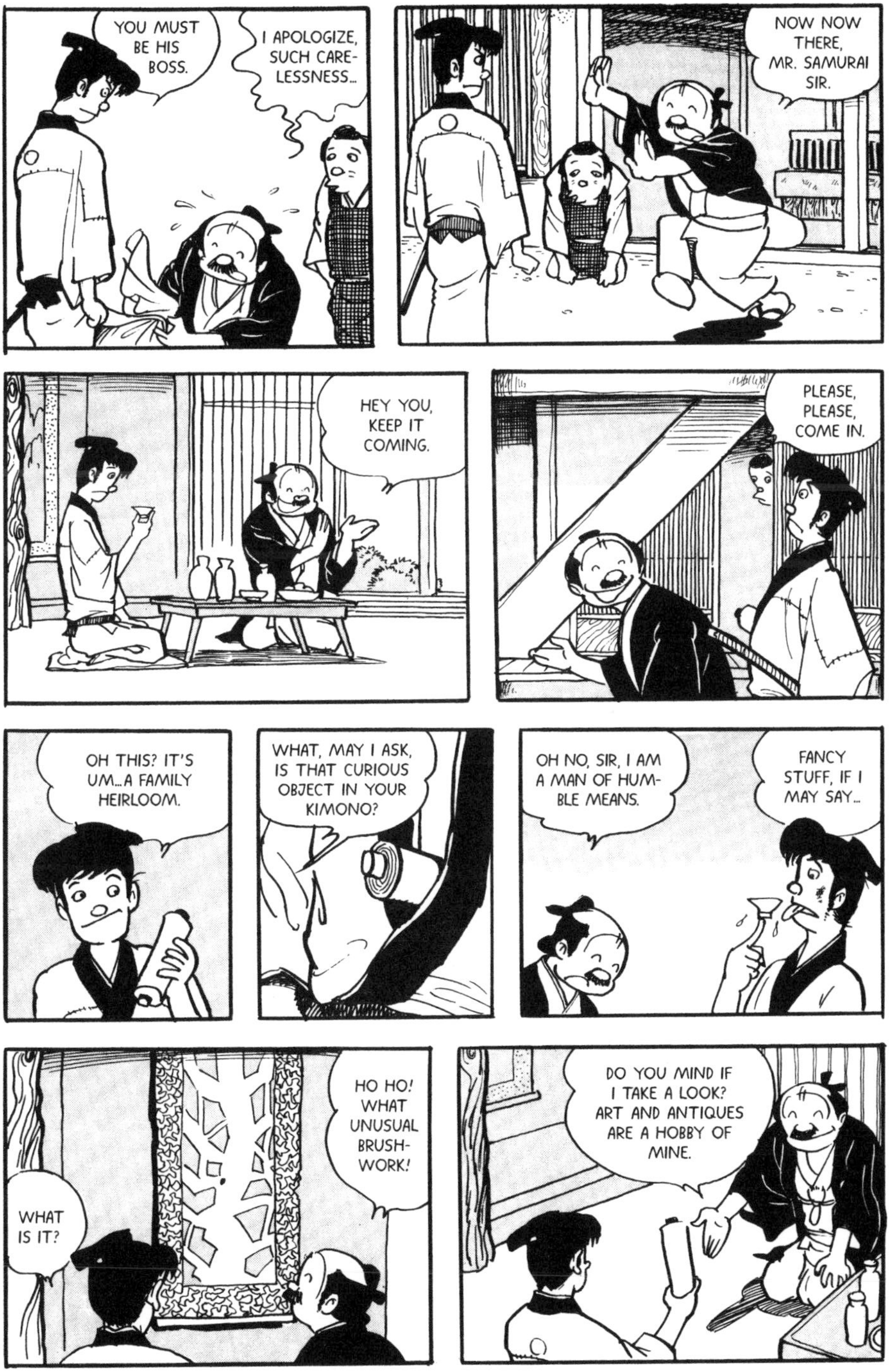
NOW NOW THERE, MR. SAMURAI SIR.
I APOLOGIZE, SUCH CARELESSNESS...
YOU MUST BE HIS BOSS.
PLEASE, PLEASE, COME IN.
HEY YOU, KEEP IT COMING.
FANCY STUFF, IF I MAY SAY...
OH NO, SIR, I AM A MAN OF HUMBLE MEANS.
WHAT, MAY I ASK, IS THAT CURIOUS OBJECT IN YOUR KIMONO?
OH THIS? IT'S UM...A FAMILY HEIRLOOM.
DO YOU MIND IF I TAKE A LOOK? ART AND ANTIQUES ARE A HOBBY OF MINE.
HO HO! WHAT UNUSUAL BRUSHWORK!
WHAT IS IT?

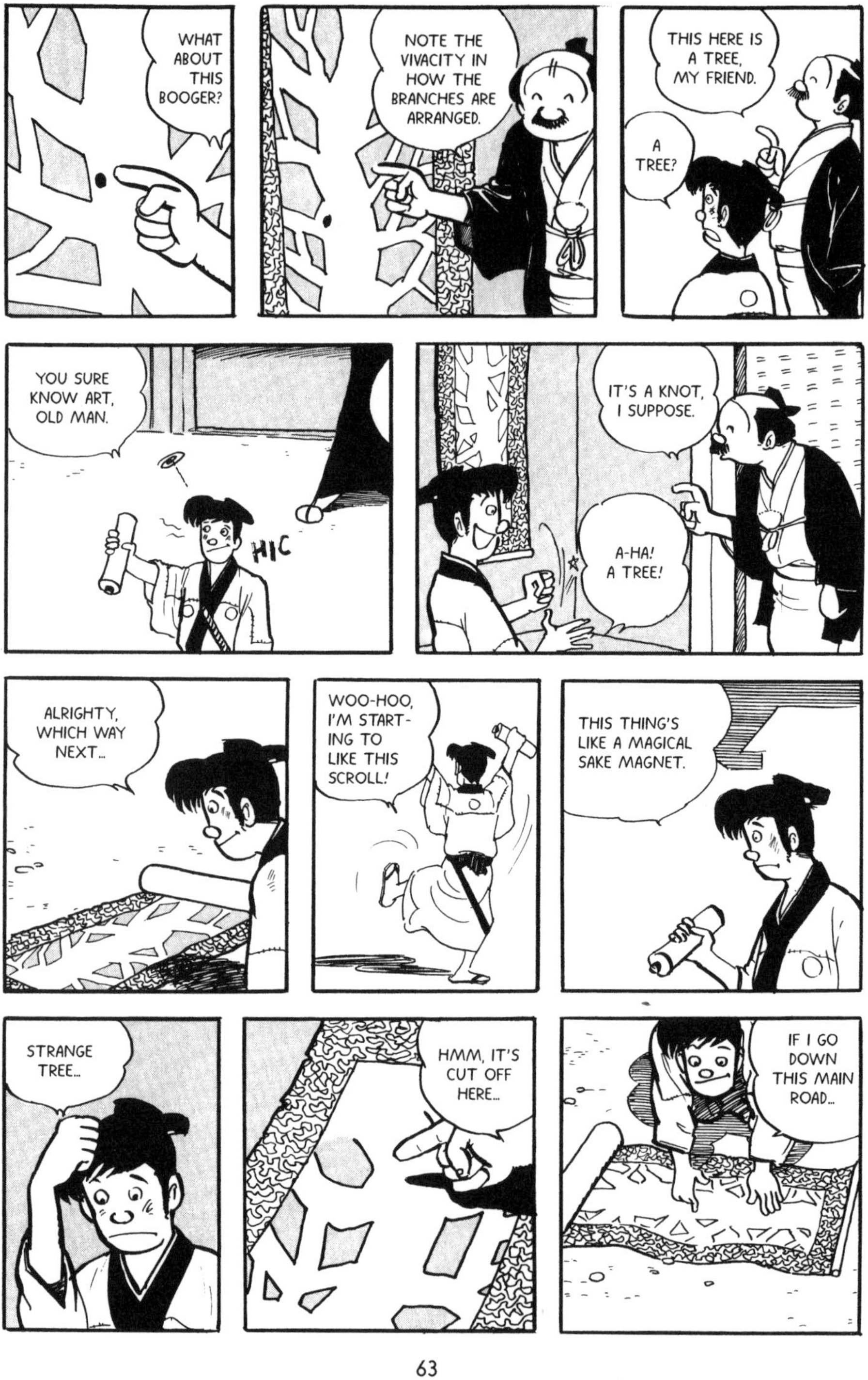
THIS HERE IS A TREE, MY FRIEND.
A TREE?
NOTE THE VIVACITY IN HOW THE BRANCHES ARE ARRANGED.
WHAT ABOUT THIS BOOGER?
IT'S A KNOT, I SUPPOSE.
A-HA! A TREE!
YOU SURE KNOW ART, OLD MAN.
HIC
THIS THING'S LIKE A MAGICAL SAKE MAGNET.
WOO-HOO, I'M START-ING TO LIKE THIS SCROLL!
ALRIGHTY, WHICH WAY NEXT...
IF I GO DOWN THIS MAIN ROAD...
HMM, IT'S CUT OFF HERE...
STRANGE TREE...

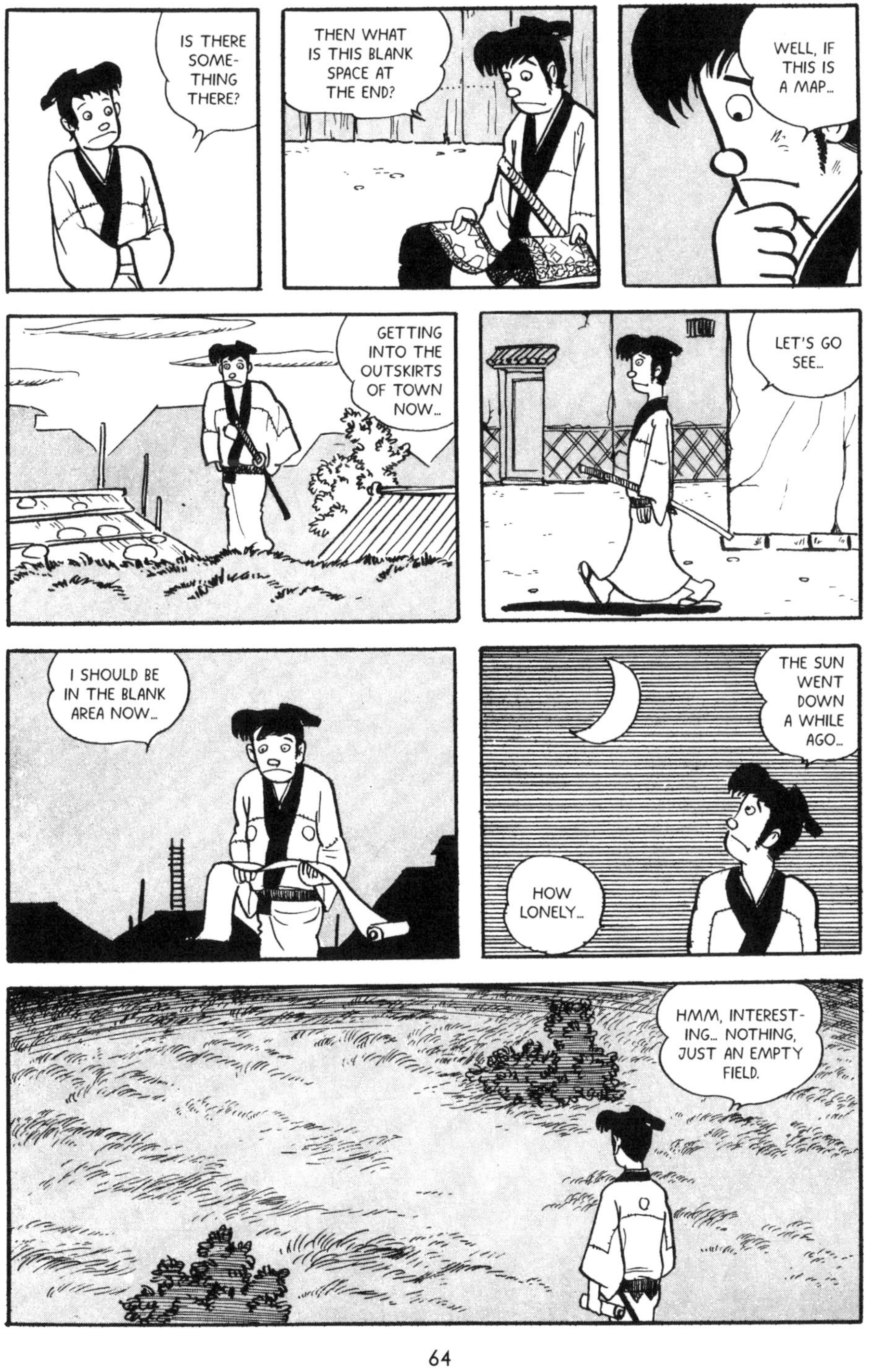

WELL, IF THIS IS A MAP...
THEN WHAT IS THIS BLANK SPACE AT THE END?
IS THERE SOME-THING THERE?
LET'S GO SEE...
GETTING INTO THE OUTSKIRTS OF TOWN NOW...
THE SUN WENT DOWN A WHILE AGO...
HOW LONELY...
I SHOULD BE IN THE BLANK AREA NOW...
HMM, INTEREST-ING... NOTHING, JUST AN EMPTY FIELD.

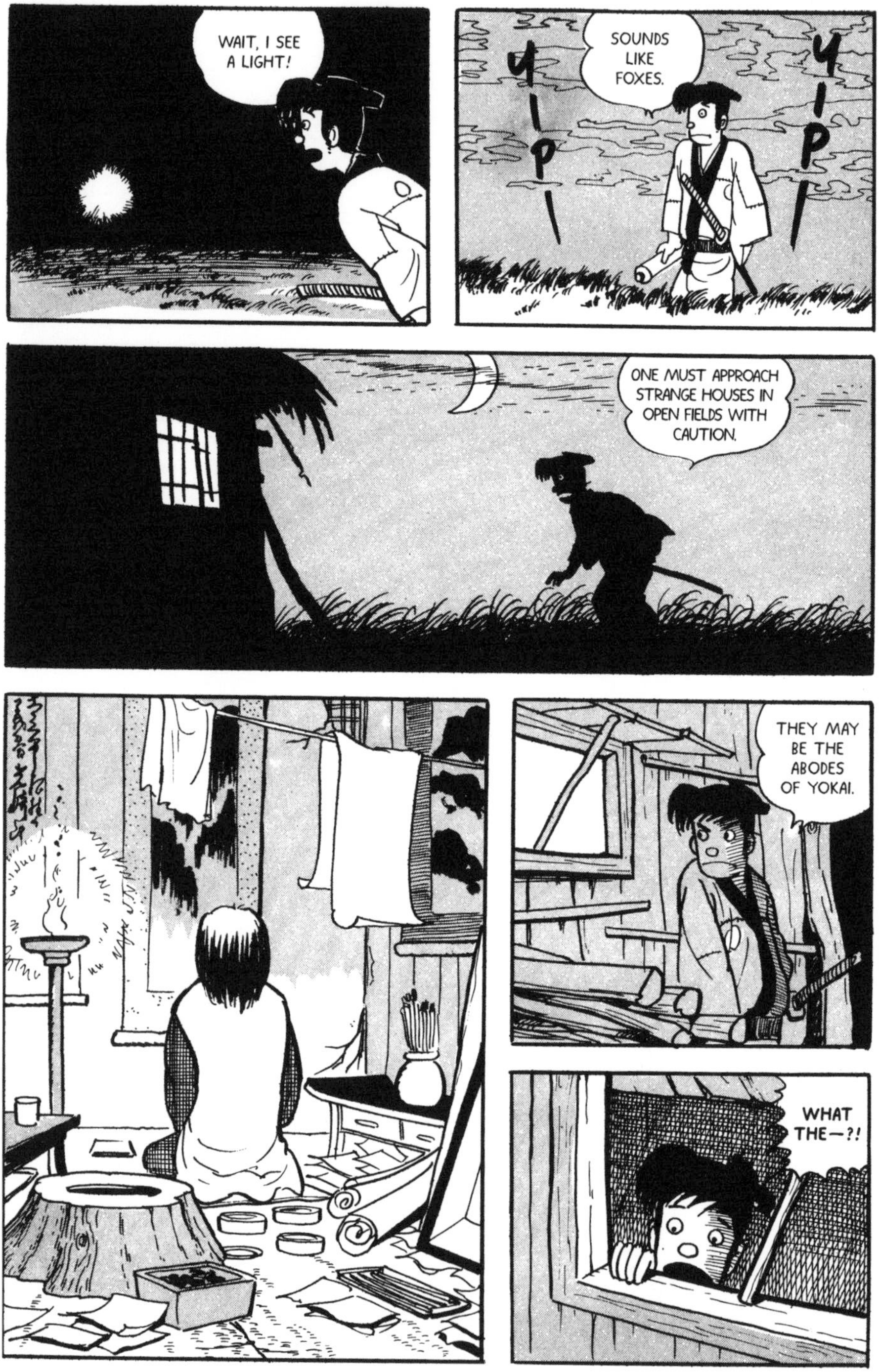
YIP
SOUNDS LIKE FOXES.
YIP
WAIT, I SEE A LIGHT!
ONE MUST APPROACH STRANGE HOUSES IN OPEN FIELDS WITH CAUTION.
THEY MAY BE THE ABODES OF YOKAI.
WHAT THE—?!

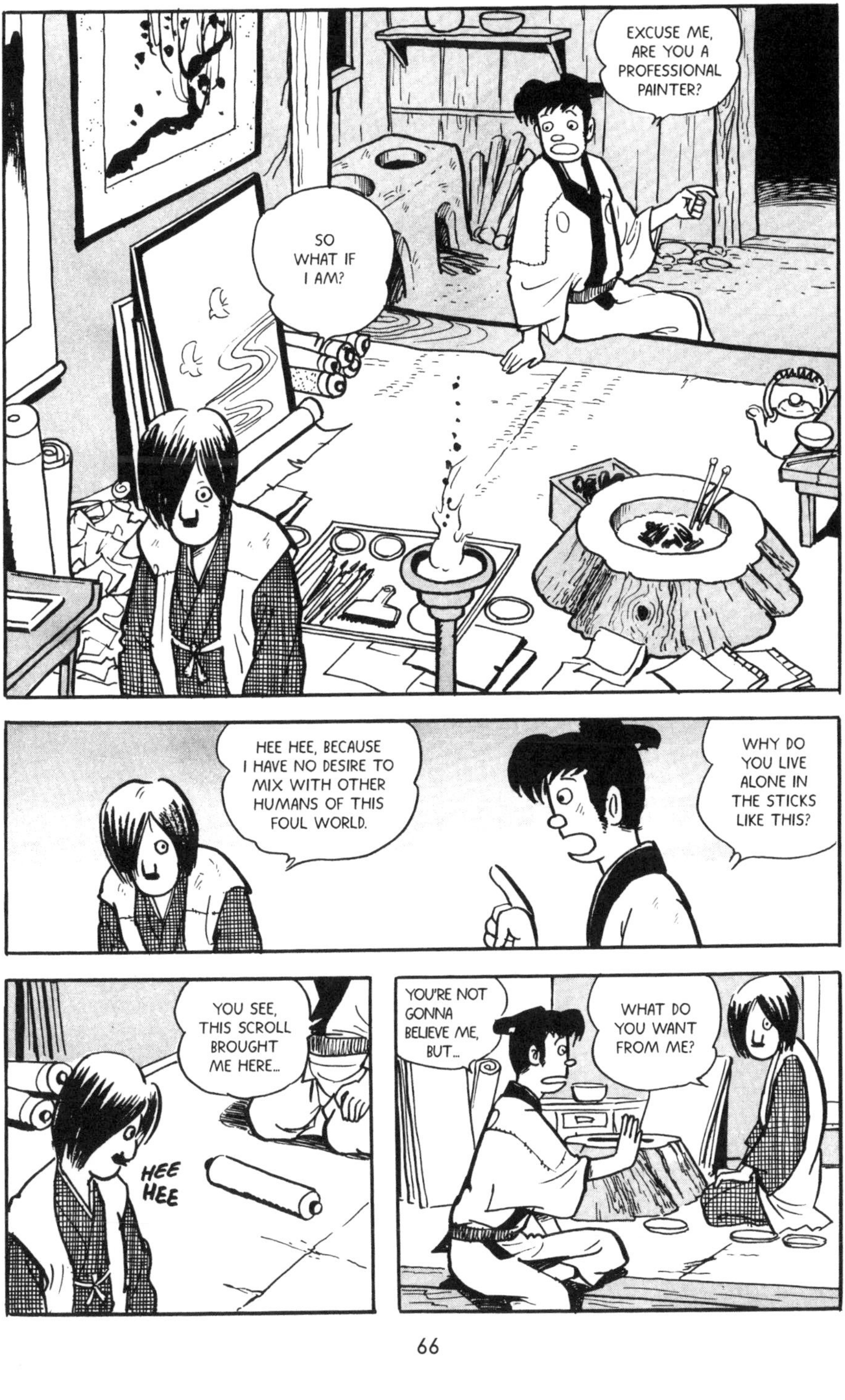
EXCUSE ME, ARE YOU A PROFESSIONAL PAINTER?
SO WHAT IF I AM?
WHY DO YOU LIVE ALONE IN THE STICKS LIKE THIS?
HEE HEE, BECAUSE I HAVE NO DESIRE TO MIX WITH OTHER HUMANS OF THIS FOUL WORLD.
WHAT DO YOU WANT FROM ME?
YOU'RE NOT GONNA BELIEVE ME, BUT...
YOU SEE, THIS SCROLL BROUGHT ME HERE...
HEE HEE

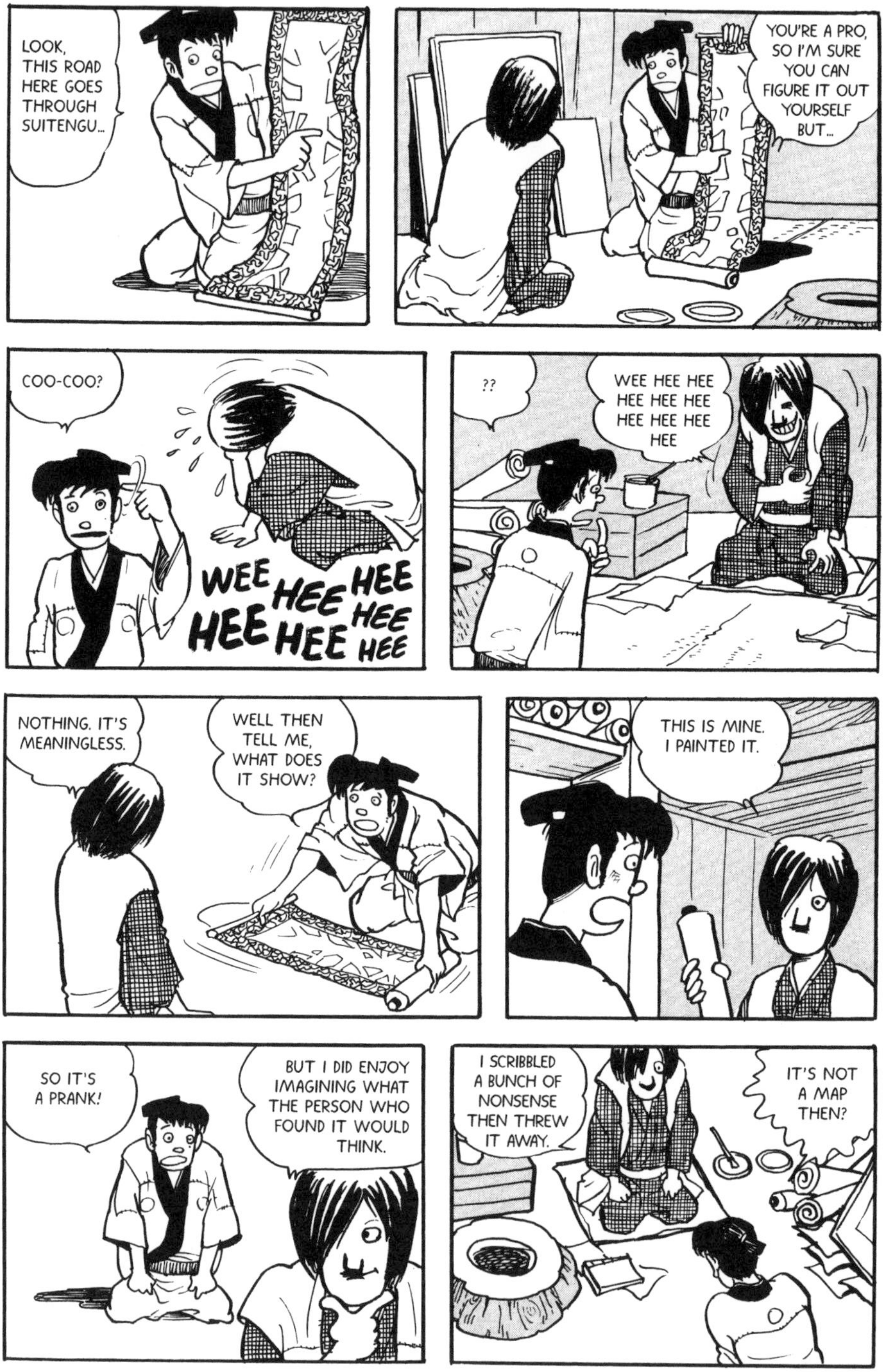

YOU'RE A PRO, SO I'M SURE YOU CAN FIGURE IT OUT YOURSELF BUT...
LOOK, THIS ROAD HERE GOES THROUGH SUITENGU...
WEE HEE HEE HEE HEE HEE HEE HEE HEE HEE
??
COO-COO?
WEE HEE HEE HEE HEE HEE HEE
THIS IS MINE. I PAINTED IT.
WELL THEN TELL ME, WHAT DOES IT SHOW?
NOTHING. IT'S MEANINGLESS.
IT'S NOT A MAP THEN?
I SCRIBBLED A BUNCH OF NONSENSE THEN THREW IT AWAY.
BUT I DID ENJOY IMAGINING WHAT THE PERSON WHO FOUND IT WOULD THINK.
SO IT'S A PRANK!

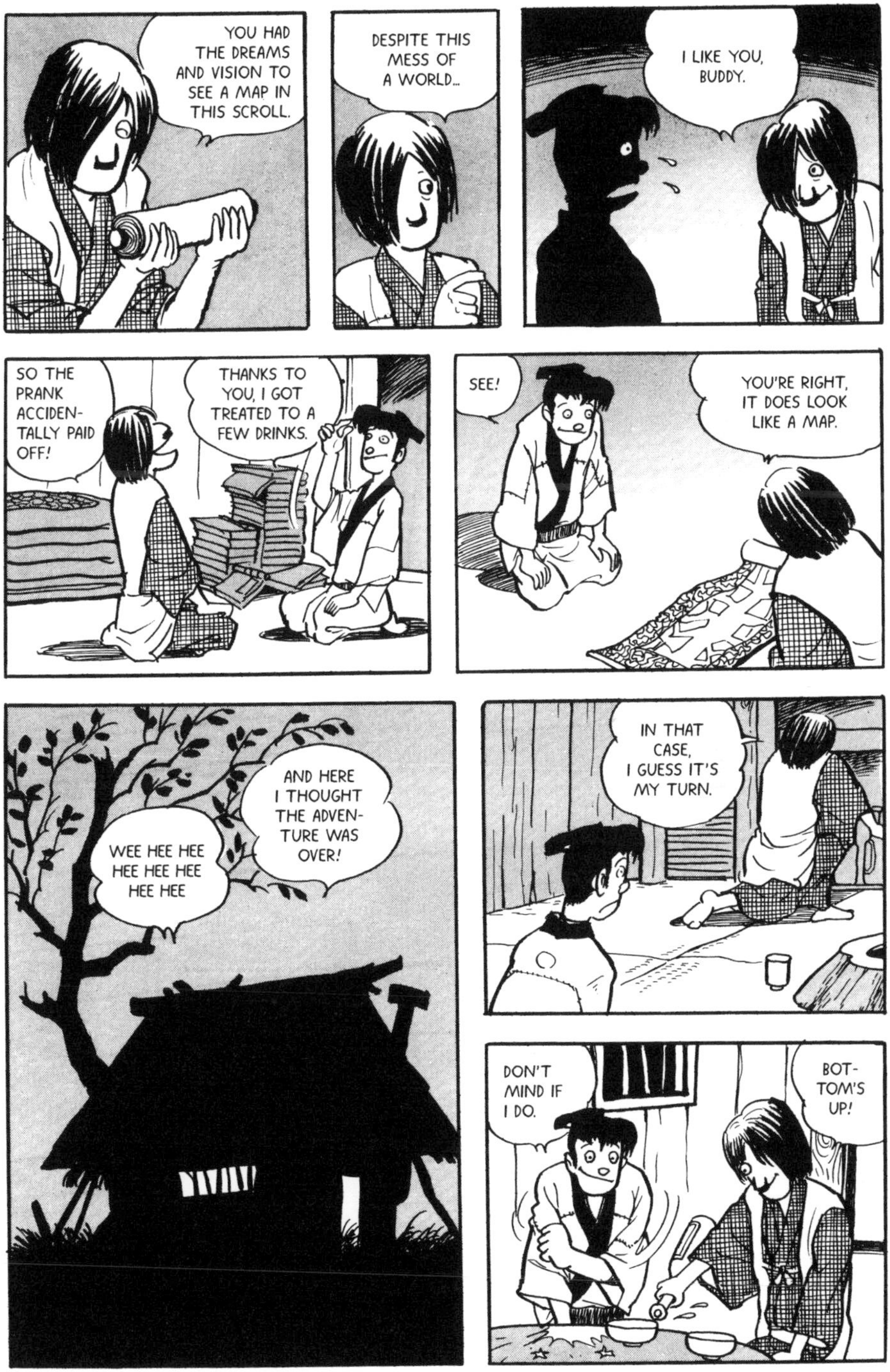
I LIKE YOU, BUDDY.
DESPITE THIS MESS OF A WORLD...
YOU HAD THE DREAMS AND VISION TO SEE A MAP IN THIS SCROLL.
YOU'RE RIGHT, IT DOES LOOK LIKE A MAP.
SEE!
THANKS TO YOU, I GOT TREATED TO A FEW DRINKS.
SO THE PRANK ACCIDEN-TALLY PAID OFF!
IN THAT CASE, I GUESS IT'S MY TURN.
BOT-TOM'S UP!
DON'T MIND IF I DO.
AND HERE I THOUGHT THE ADVEN-TURE WAS OVER!
WEE HEE HEE HEE HEE HEE HEE HEE

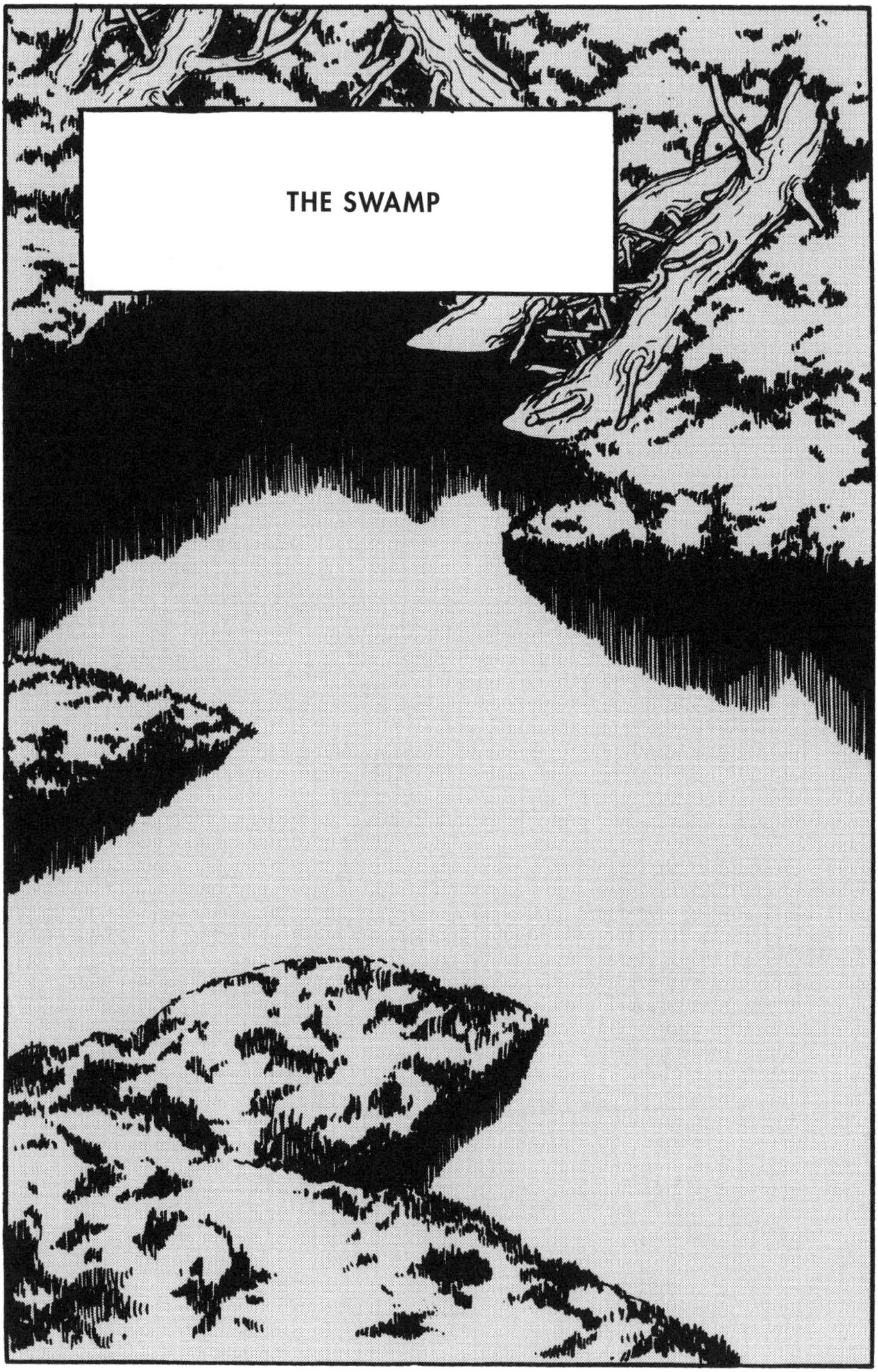
THE SWAMP

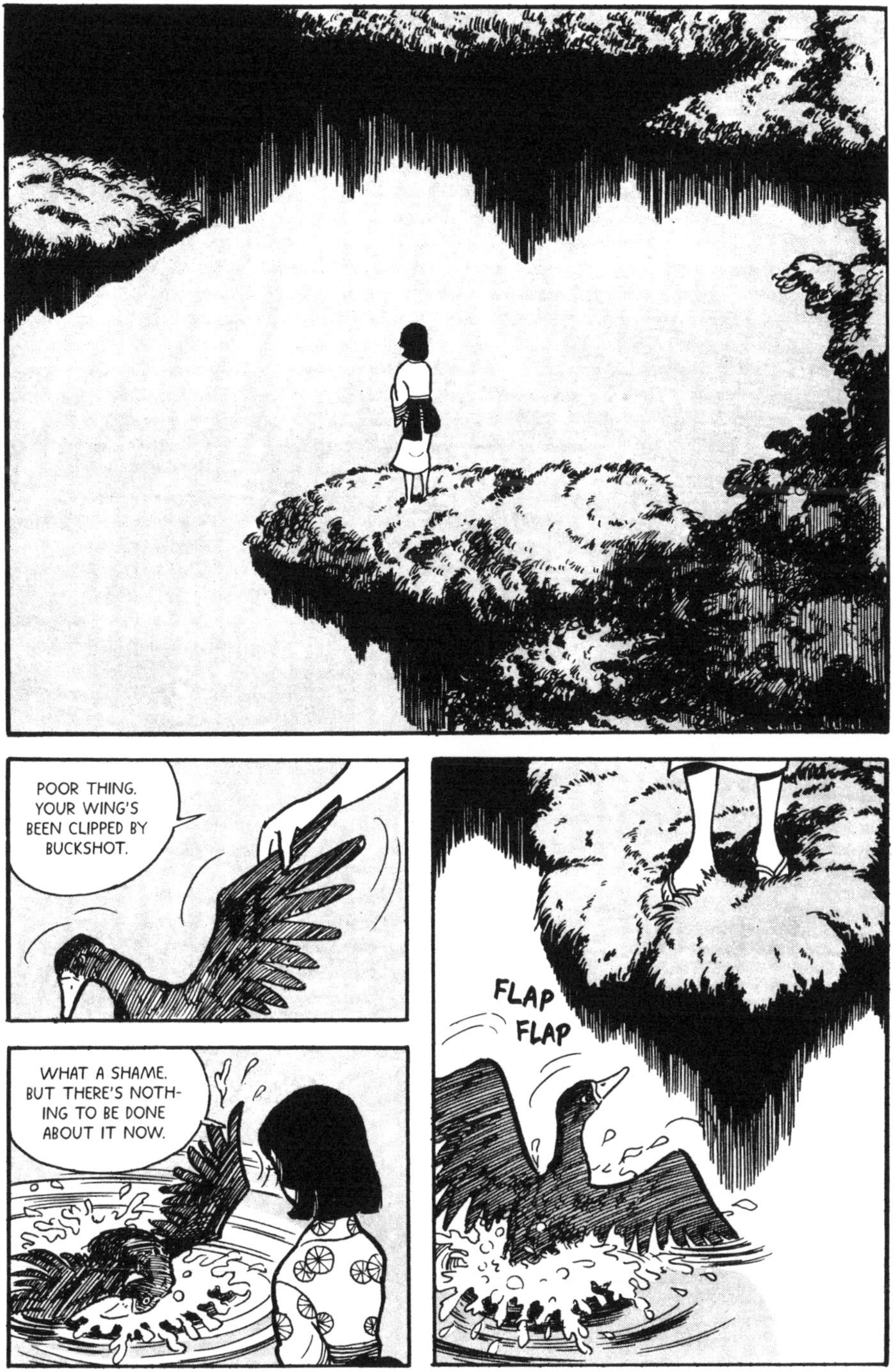
FLAP
FLAP
POOR THING. YOUR WING'S BEEN CLIPPED BY BUCKSHOT.
WHAT A SHAME. BUT THERE'S NOTHING TO BE DONE ABOUT IT NOW.

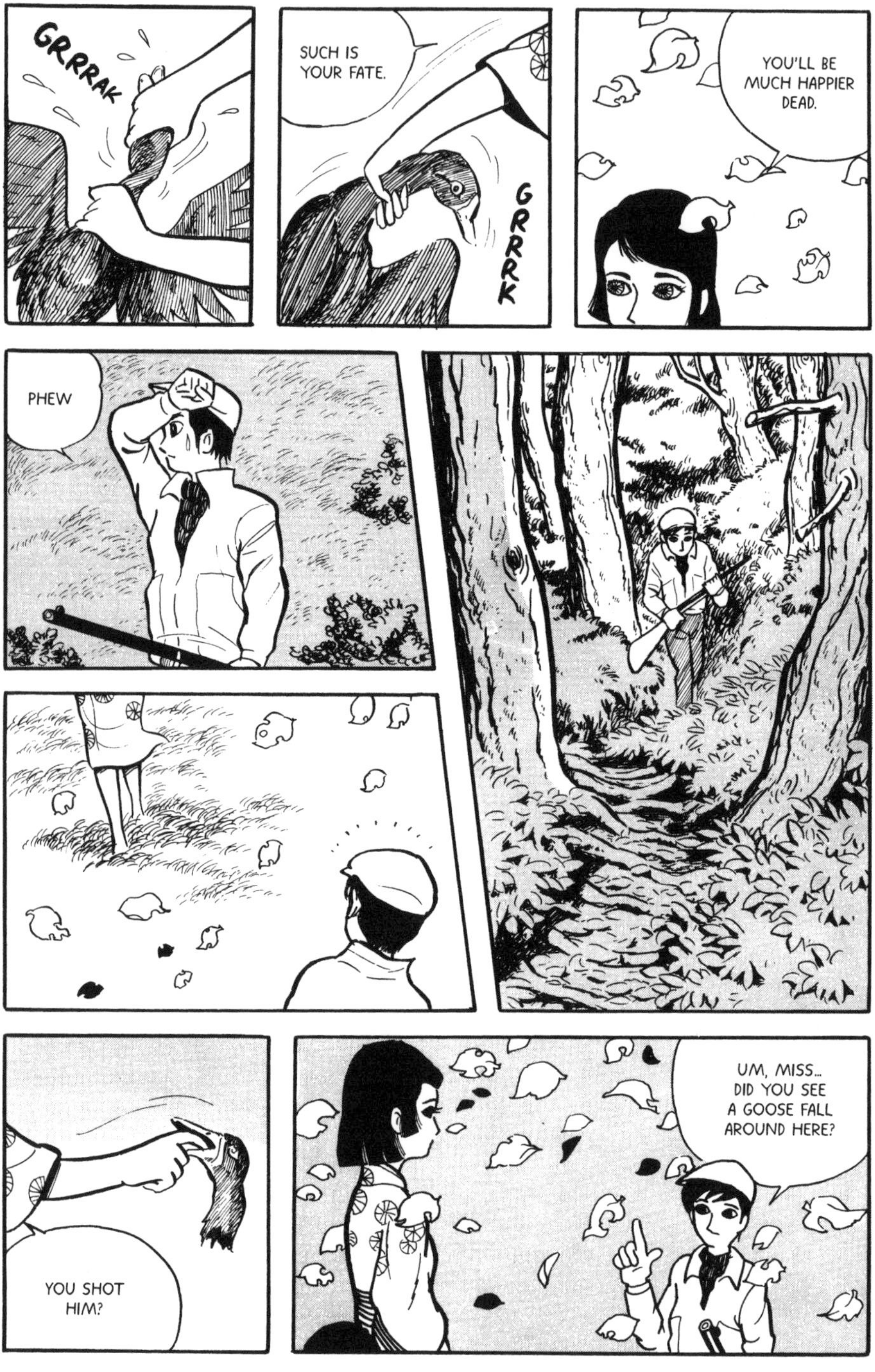
YOU'LL BE MUCH HAPPIER DEAD.
SUCH IS YOUR FATE.
GRRRK
GRRRAK
PHEW
UM, MISS... DID YOU SEE A GOOSE FALL AROUND HERE?
YOU SHOT HIM?

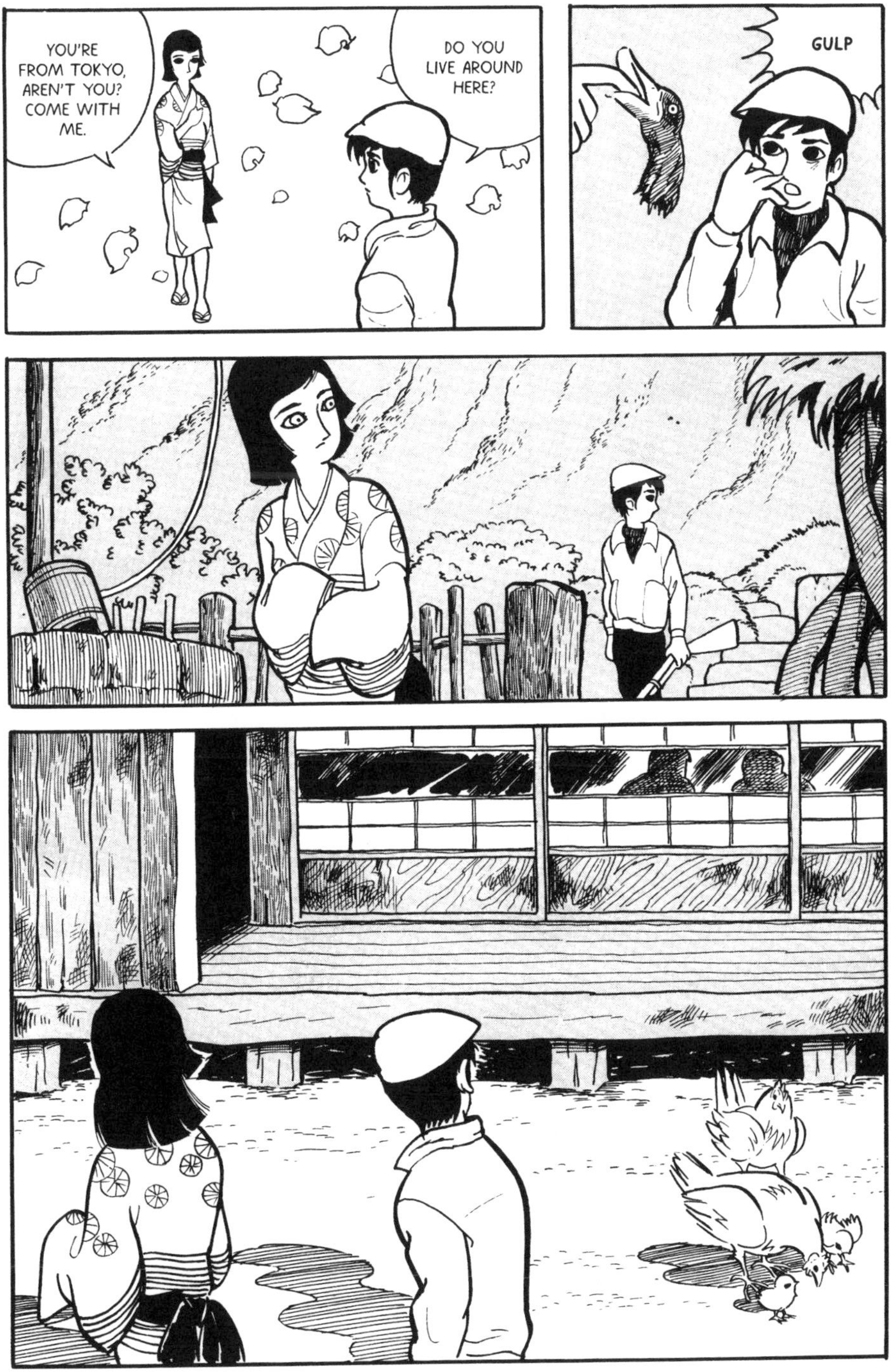
GULP
DO YOU LIVE AROUND HERE?
YOU'RE FROM TOKYO, AREN'T YOU? COME WITH ME.

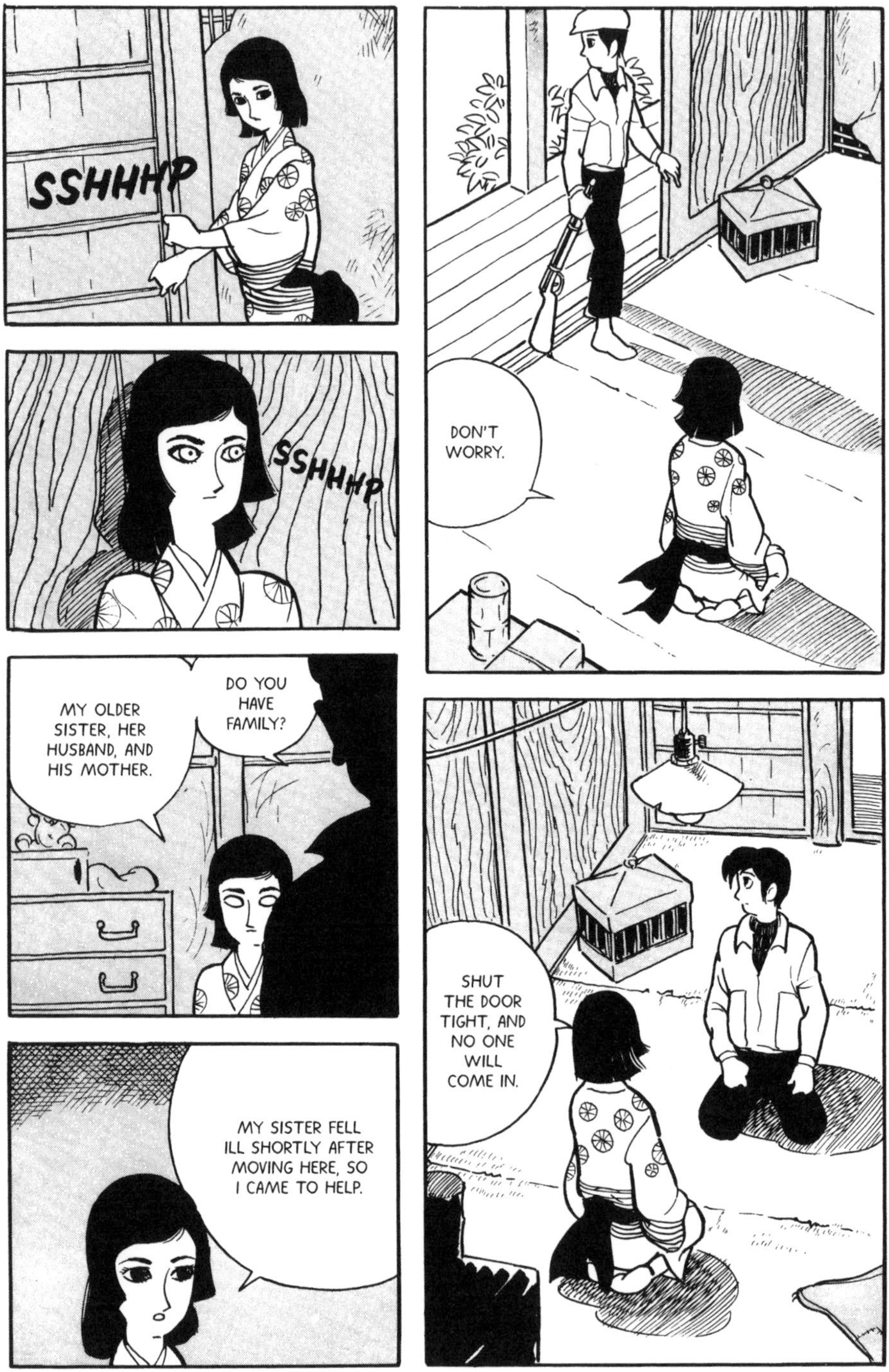
DON'T WORRY.
SSHHHP
SSHHHP
SHUT THE DOOR TIGHT, AND NO ONE WILL COME IN.
DO YOU HAVE FAMILY?
MY OLDER SISTER, HER HUSBAND, AND HIS MOTHER.
MY SISTER FELL ILL SHORTLY AFTER MOVING HERE, SO I CAME TO HELP.

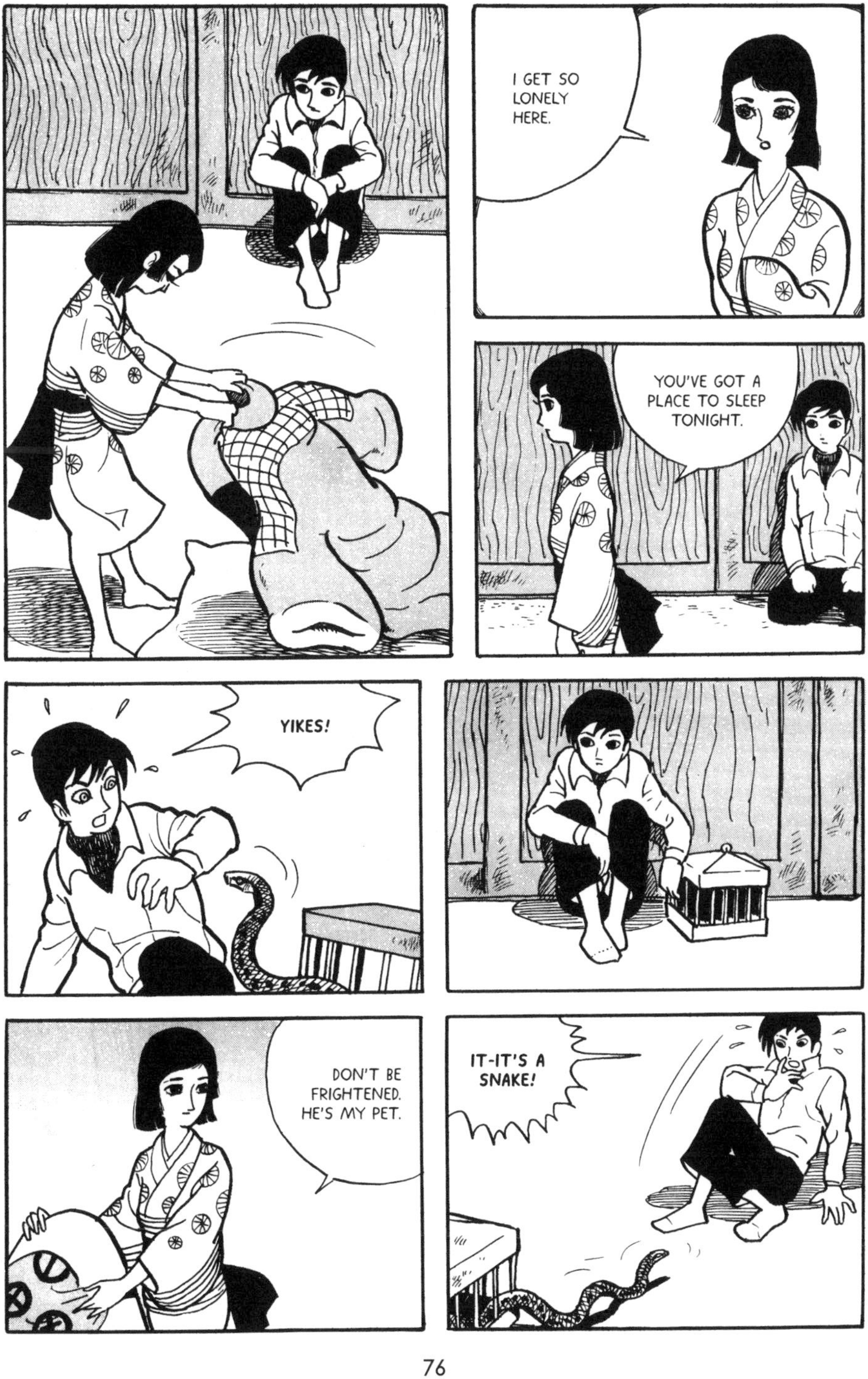
I GET SO LONELY HERE.
YOU'VE GOT A PLACE TO SLEEP TONIGHT.
YIKES!
IT-IT'S A SNAKE!
DON'T BE FRIGHTENED. HE'S MY PET.

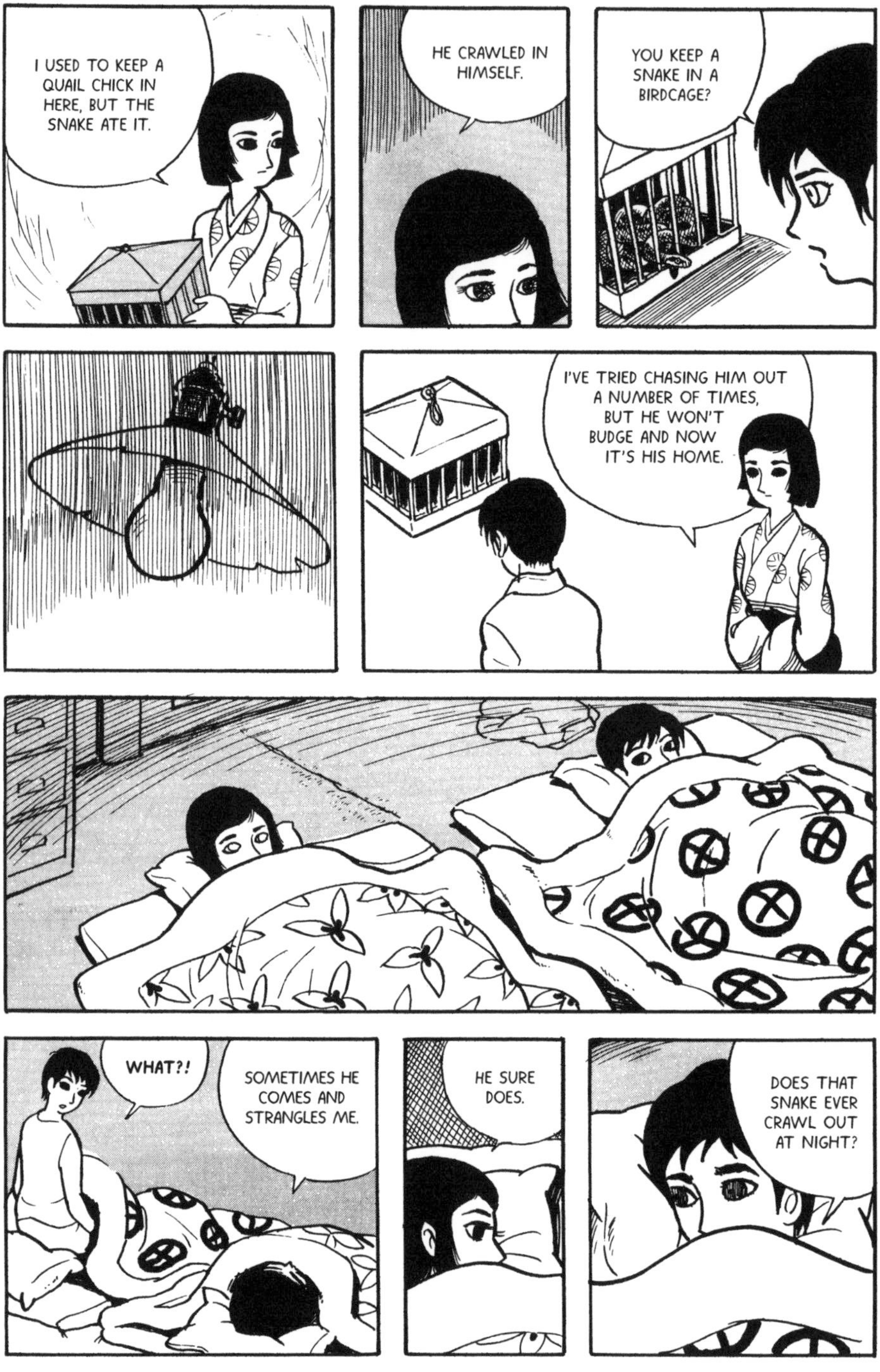
YOU KEEP A SNAKE IN A BIRDCAGE?
HE CRAWLED IN HIMSELF.
I USED TO KEEP A QUAIL CHICK IN HERE, BUT THE SNAKE ATE IT.
I'VE TRIED CHASING HIM OUT A NUMBER OF TIMES, BUT HE WON'T BUDGE AND NOW IT'S HIS HOME.
DOES THAT SNAKE EVER CRAWL OUT AT NIGHT?
HE SURE DOES.
SOMETIMES HE COMES AND STRANGLES ME.
WHAT?!

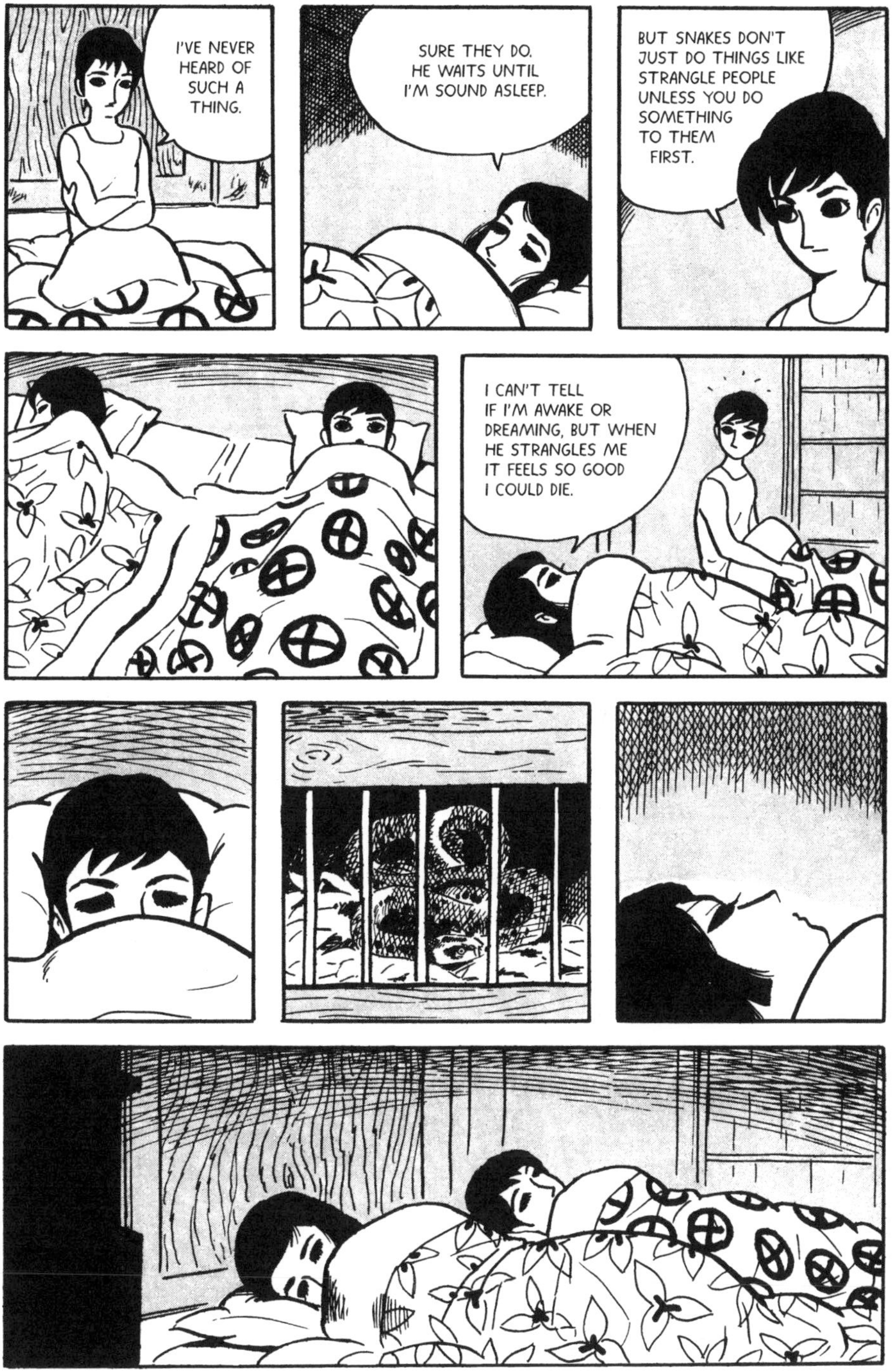

BUT SNAKES DON'T JUST DO THINGS LIKE STRANGLE PEOPLE UNLESS YOU DO SOMETHING TO THEM FIRST.
SURE THEY DO. HE WAITS UNTIL I'M SOUND ASLEEP.
I'VE NEVER HEARD OF SUCH A THING.
I CAN'T TELL IF I'M AWAKE OR DREAMING, BUT WHEN HE STRANGLES ME IT FEELS SO GOOD I COULD DIE.

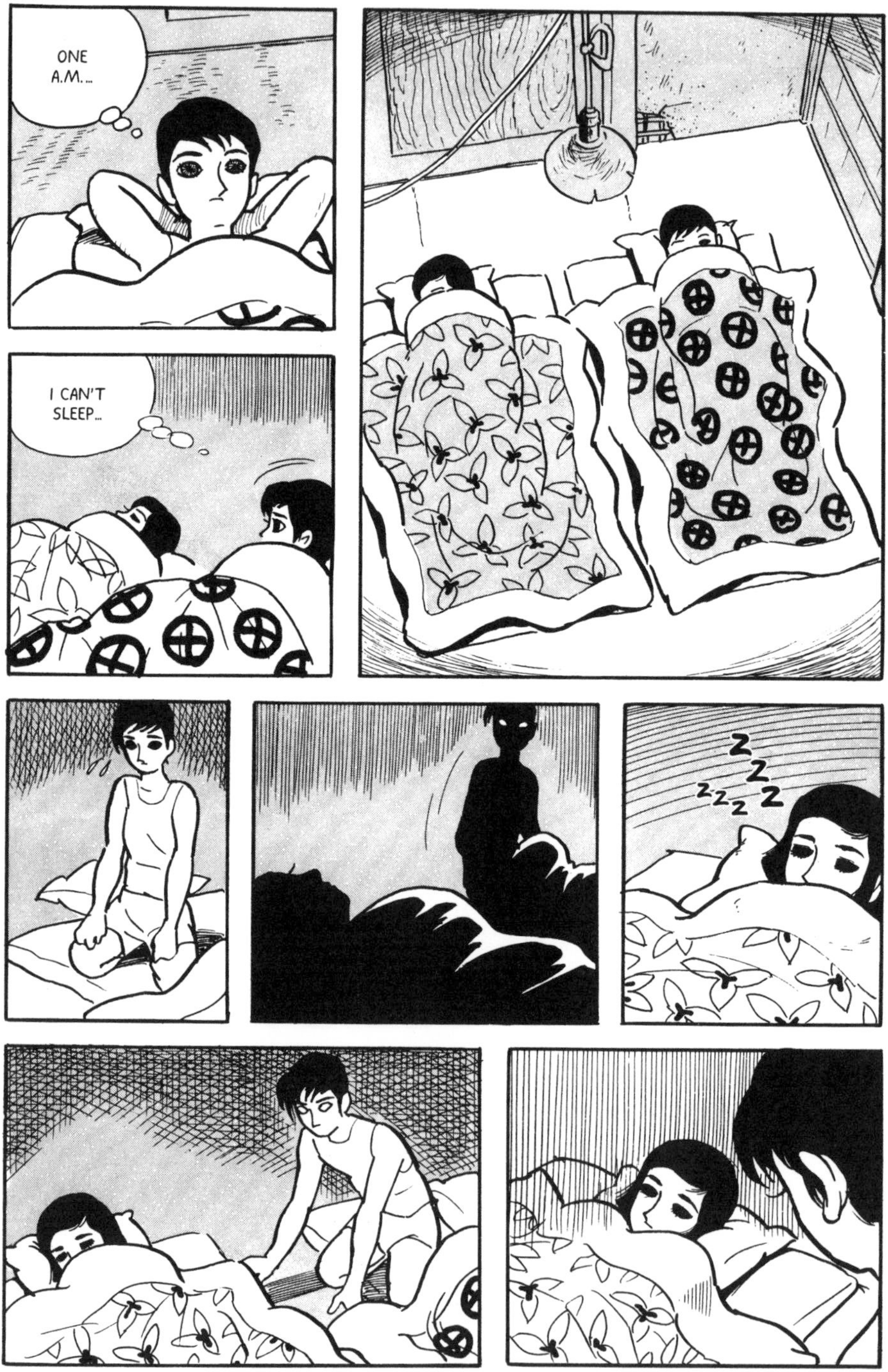
ONE A.M....
I CAN'T SLEEP...
Z Z Z z z z Z

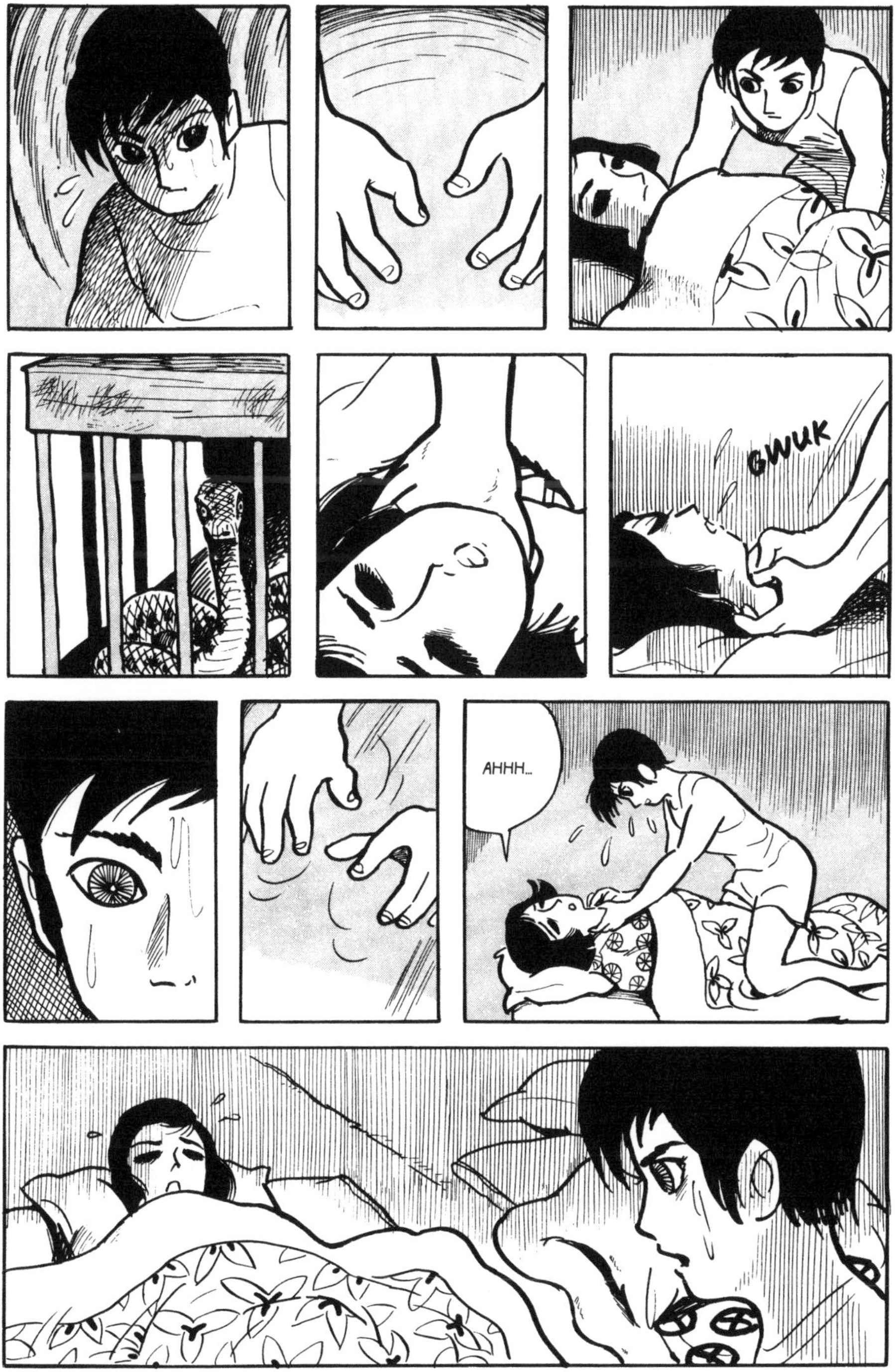
GWUK
AHHH...

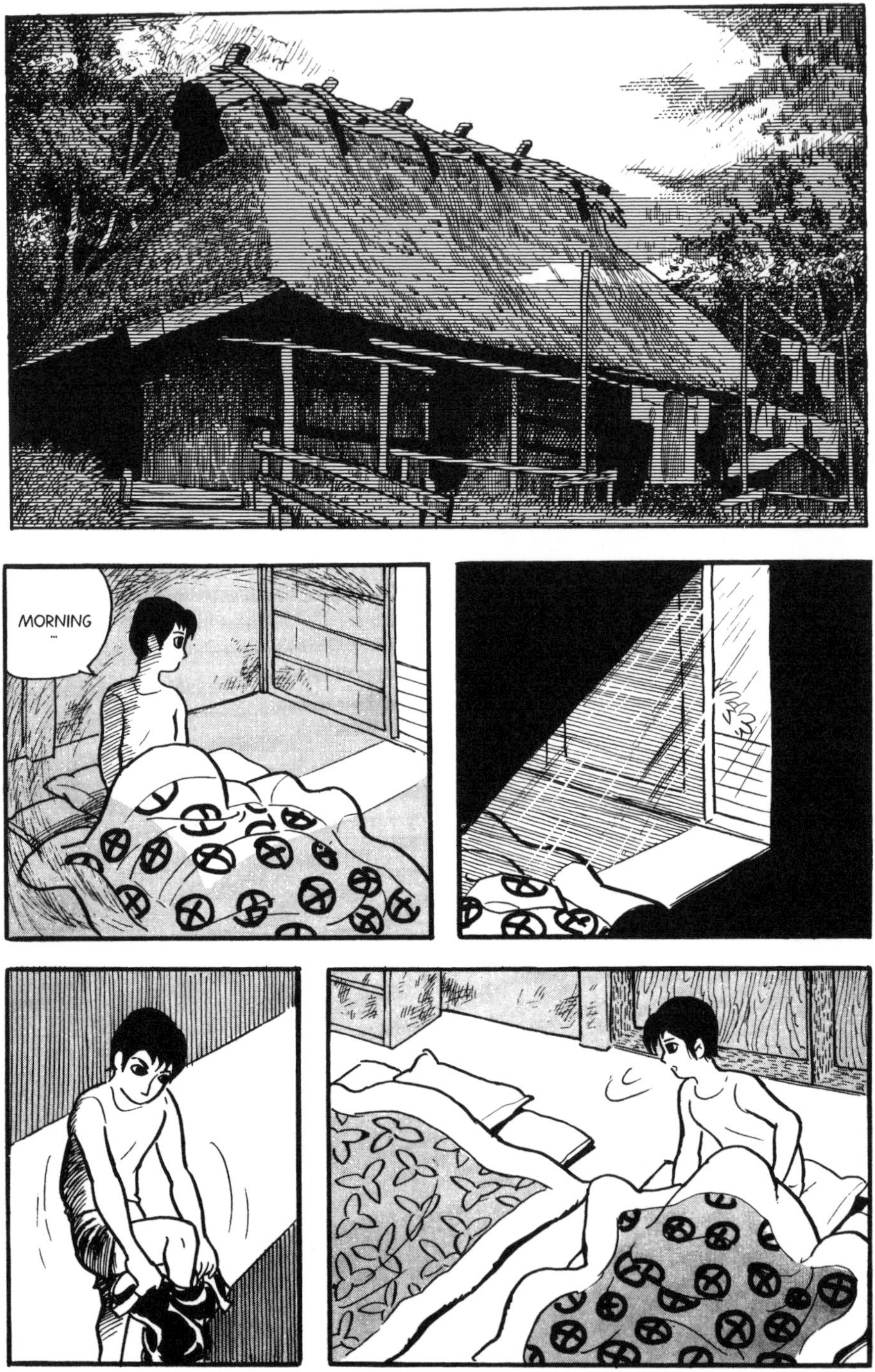
MORNING
...

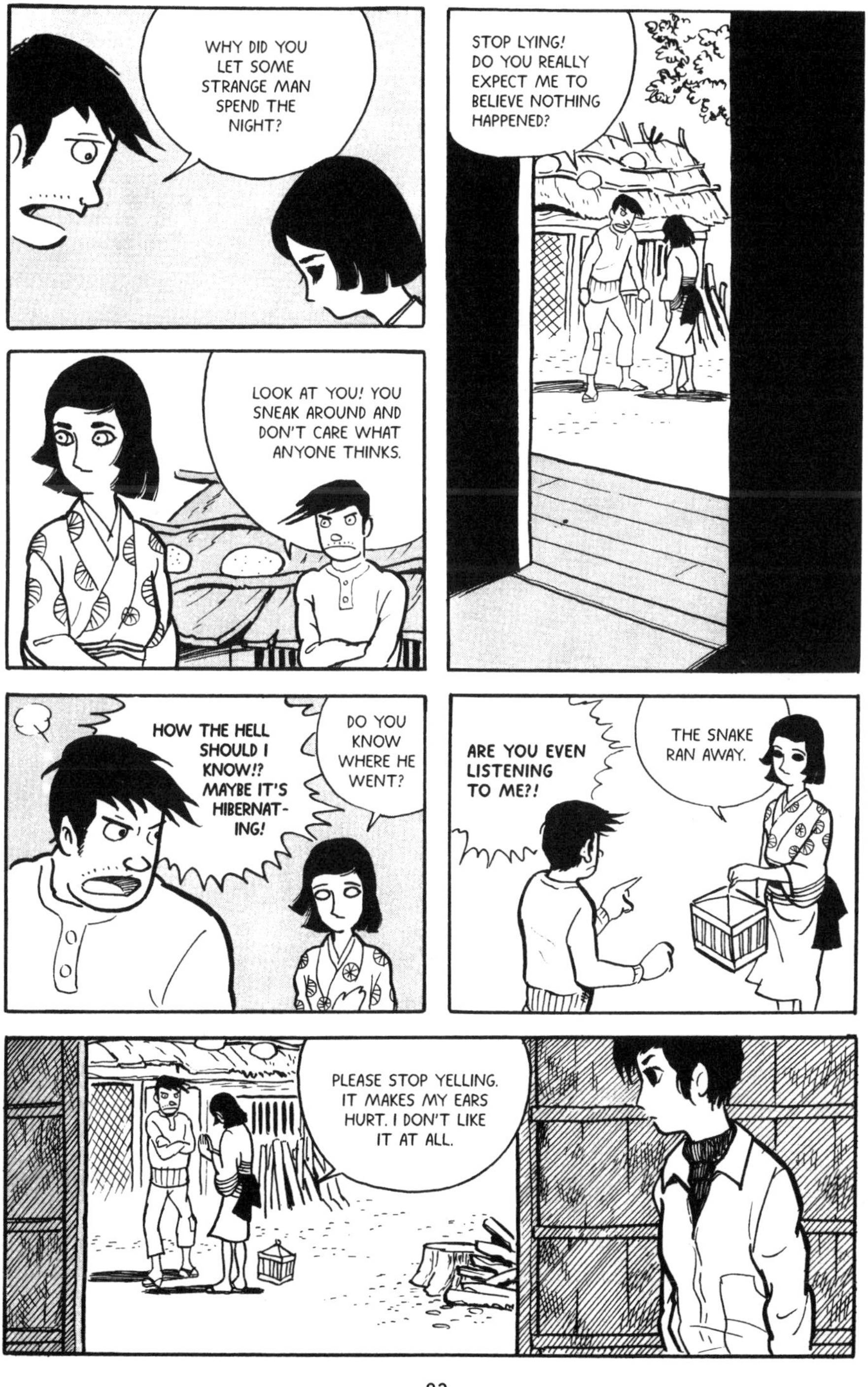
STOP LYING! DO YOU REALLY EXPECT ME TO BELIEVE NOTHING HAPPENED?
WHY DID YOU LET SOME STRANGE MAN SPEND THE NIGHT?
LOOK AT YOU! YOU SNEAK AROUND AND DON'T CARE WHAT ANYONE THINKS.
THE SNAKE RAN AWAY.
ARE YOU EVEN LISTENING TO ME?!
DO YOU KNOW WHERE HE WENT?
HOW THE HELL SHOULD I KNOW!? MAYBE IT'S HIBERNAT-ING!
PLEASE STOP YELLING. IT MAKES MY EARS HURT. I DON'T LIKE IT AT ALL.

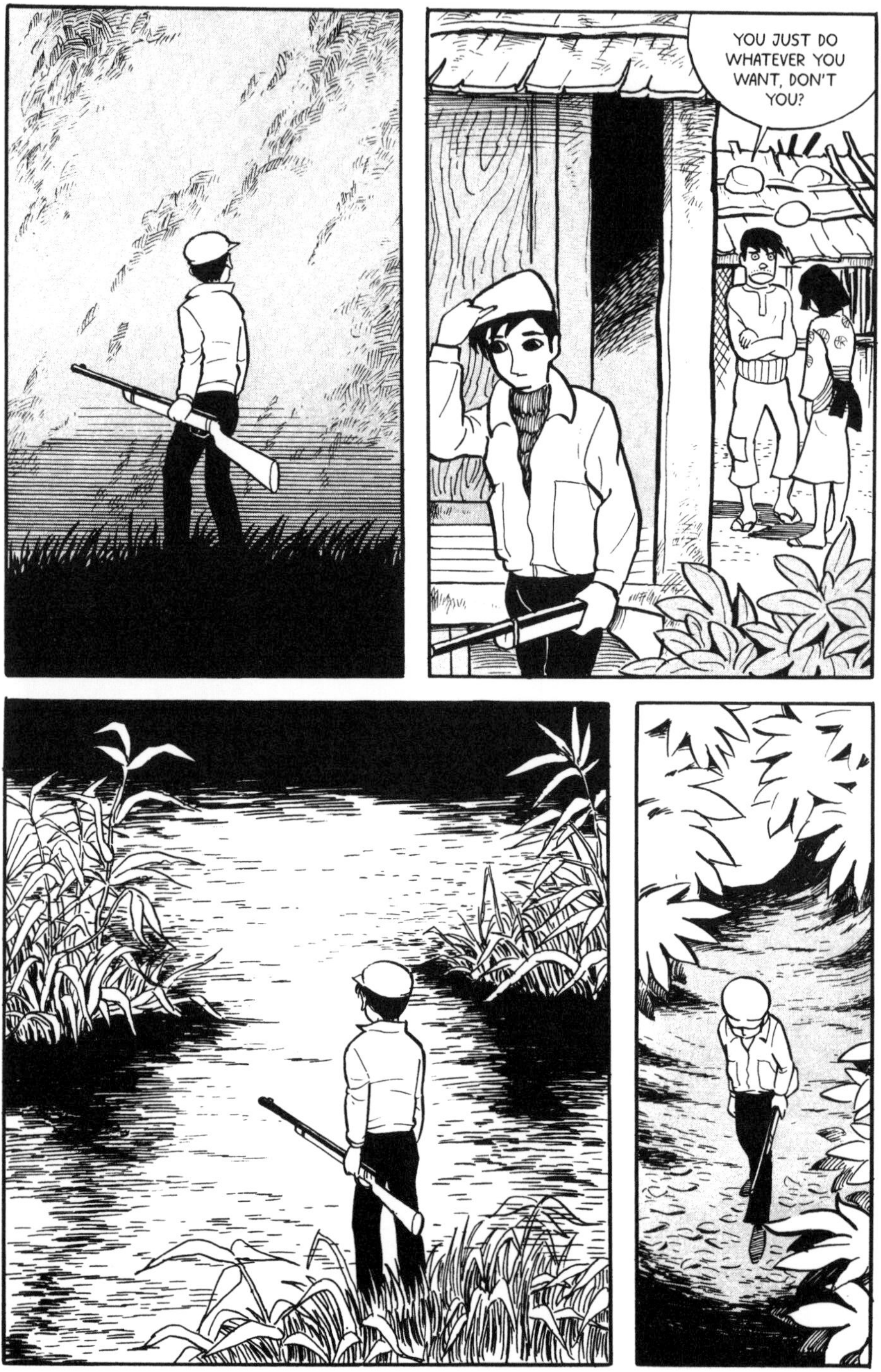
YOU JUST DO WHATEVER YOU WANT, DON'T YOU?

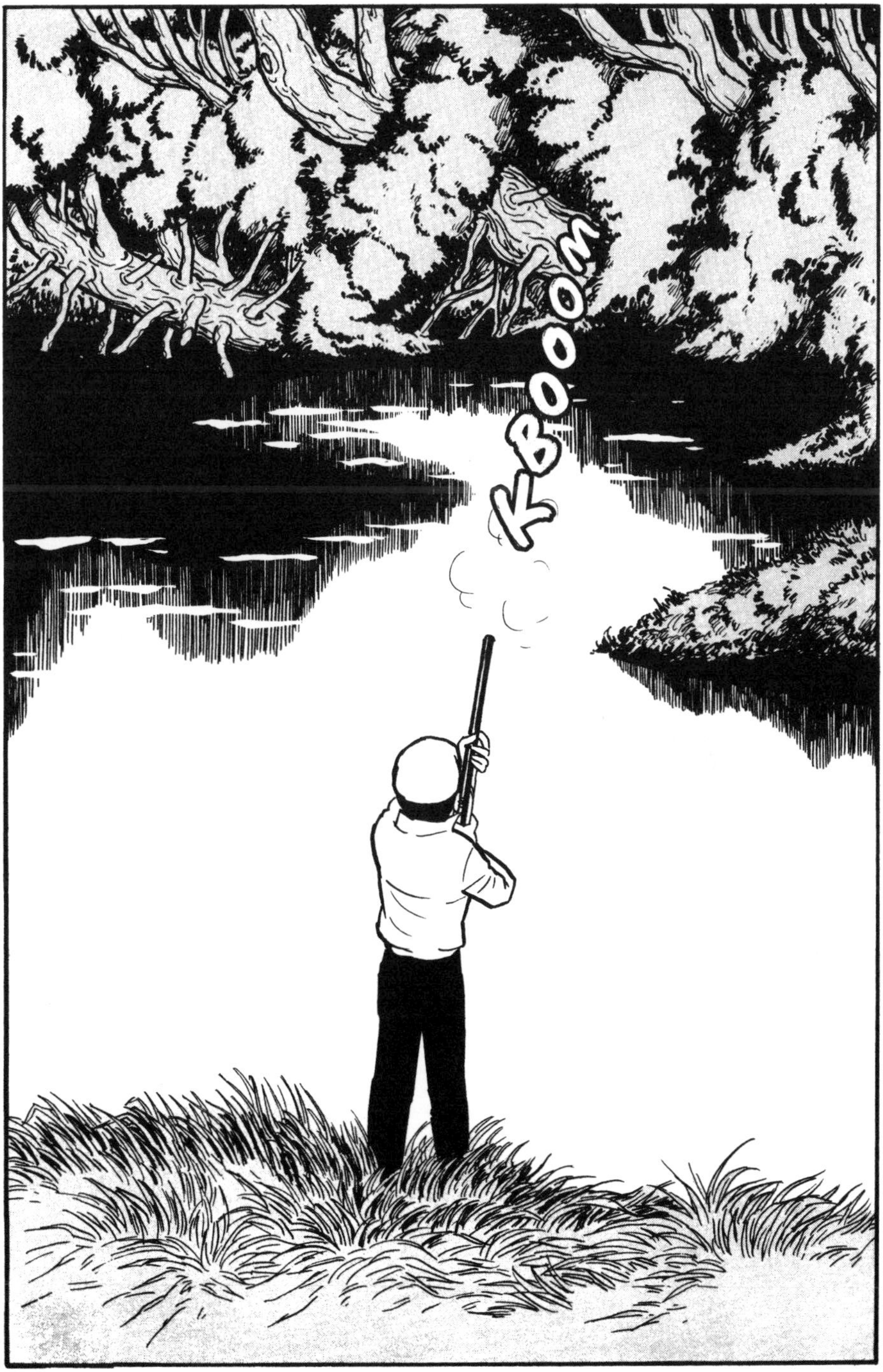
KBOOM

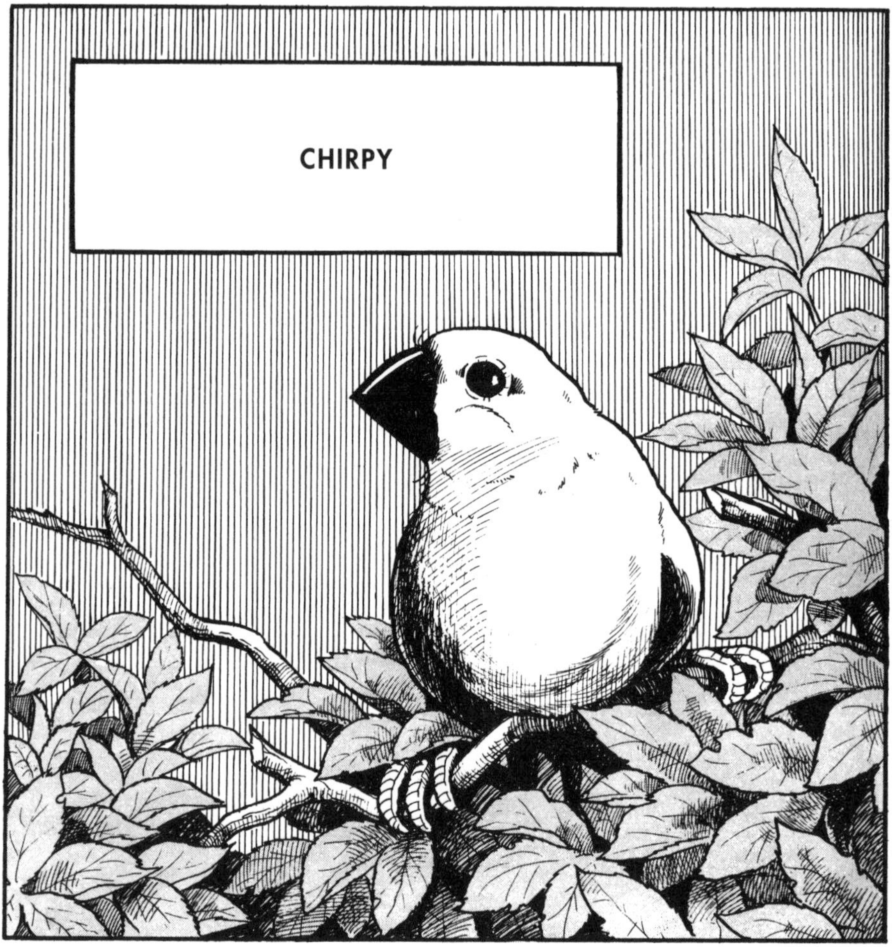
CHIRPY

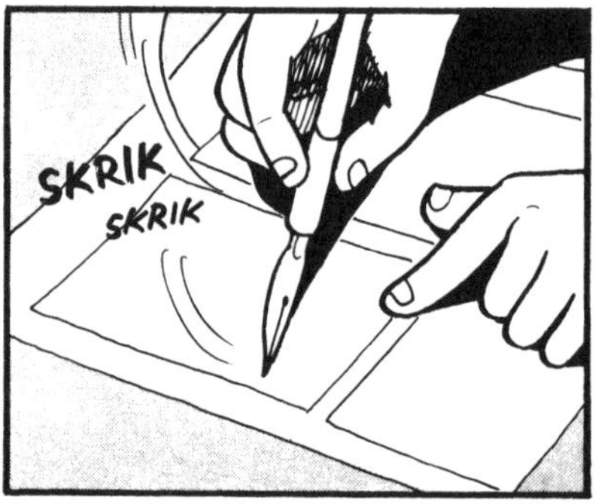
SKRIK
SKRIK

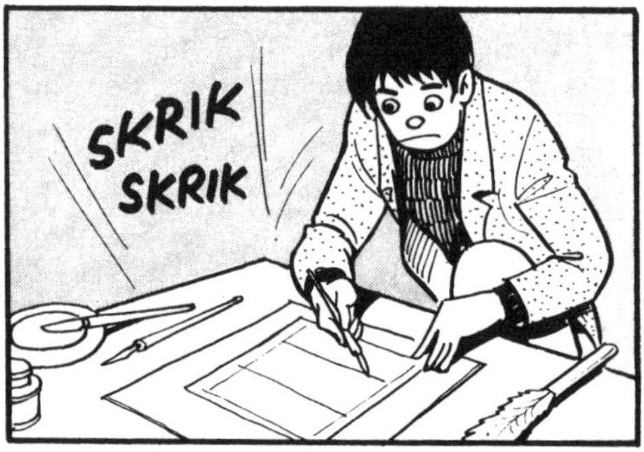
SKRIK
SKRIK

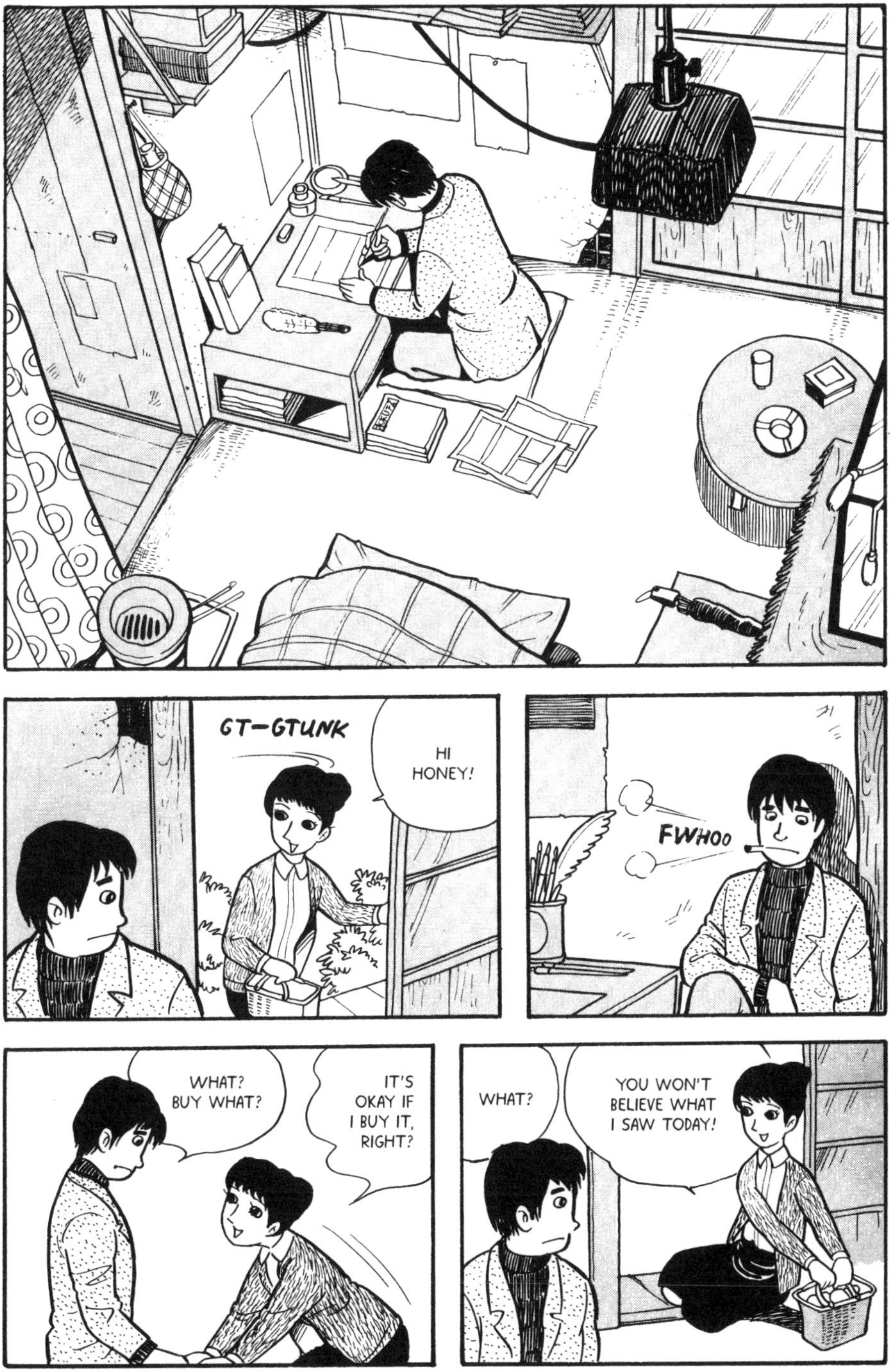
FWHOO
GT-GTUNK
HI HONEY!
YOU WON'T BELIEVE WHAT I SAW TODAY!
WHAT?
IT'S OKAY IF I BUY IT, RIGHT?
WHAT? BUY WHAT?

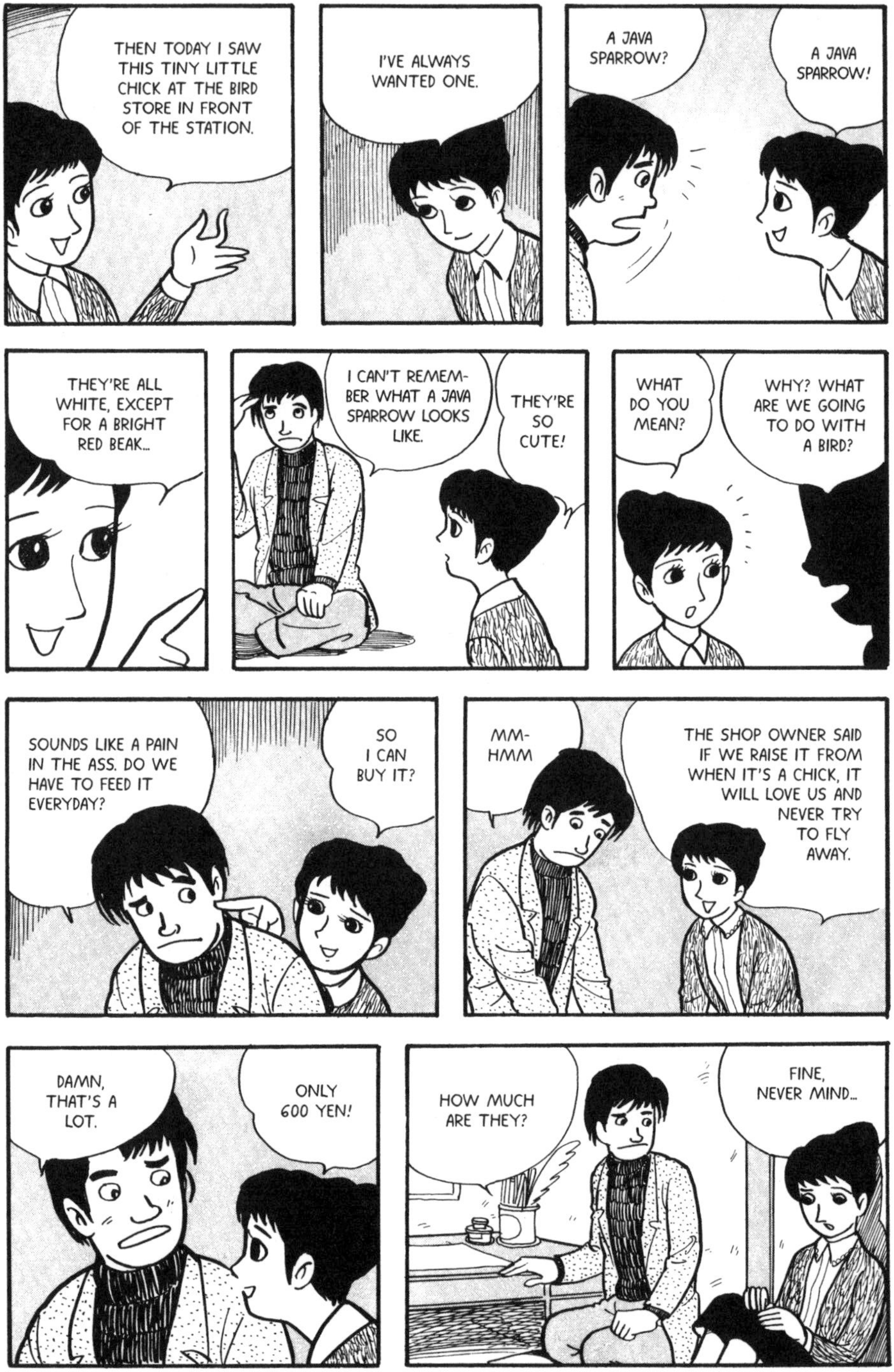
THEN TODAY I SAW THIS TINY LITTLE CHICK AT THE BIRD STORE IN FRONT OF THE STATION.
I'VE ALWAYS WANTED ONE.
A JAVA SPARROW?
A JAVA SPARROW!
THEY'RE ALL WHITE, EXCEPT FOR A BRIGHT RED BEAK...
I CAN'T REMEMBER WHAT A JAVA SPARROW LOOKS LIKE.
THEY'RE SO CUTE!
WHAT DO YOU MEAN?
WHY? WHAT ARE WE GOING TO DO WITH A BIRD?
SOUNDS LIKE A PAIN IN THE ASS. DO WE HAVE TO FEED IT EVERYDAY?
SO I CAN BUY IT?
MM-HMM
THE SHOP OWNER SAID IF WE RAISE IT FROM WHEN IT'S A CHICK, IT WILL LOVE US AND NEVER TRY TO FLY AWAY.
DAMN, THAT'S A LOT.
ONLY 600 YEN!
HOW MUCH ARE THEY?
FINE, NEVER MIND...

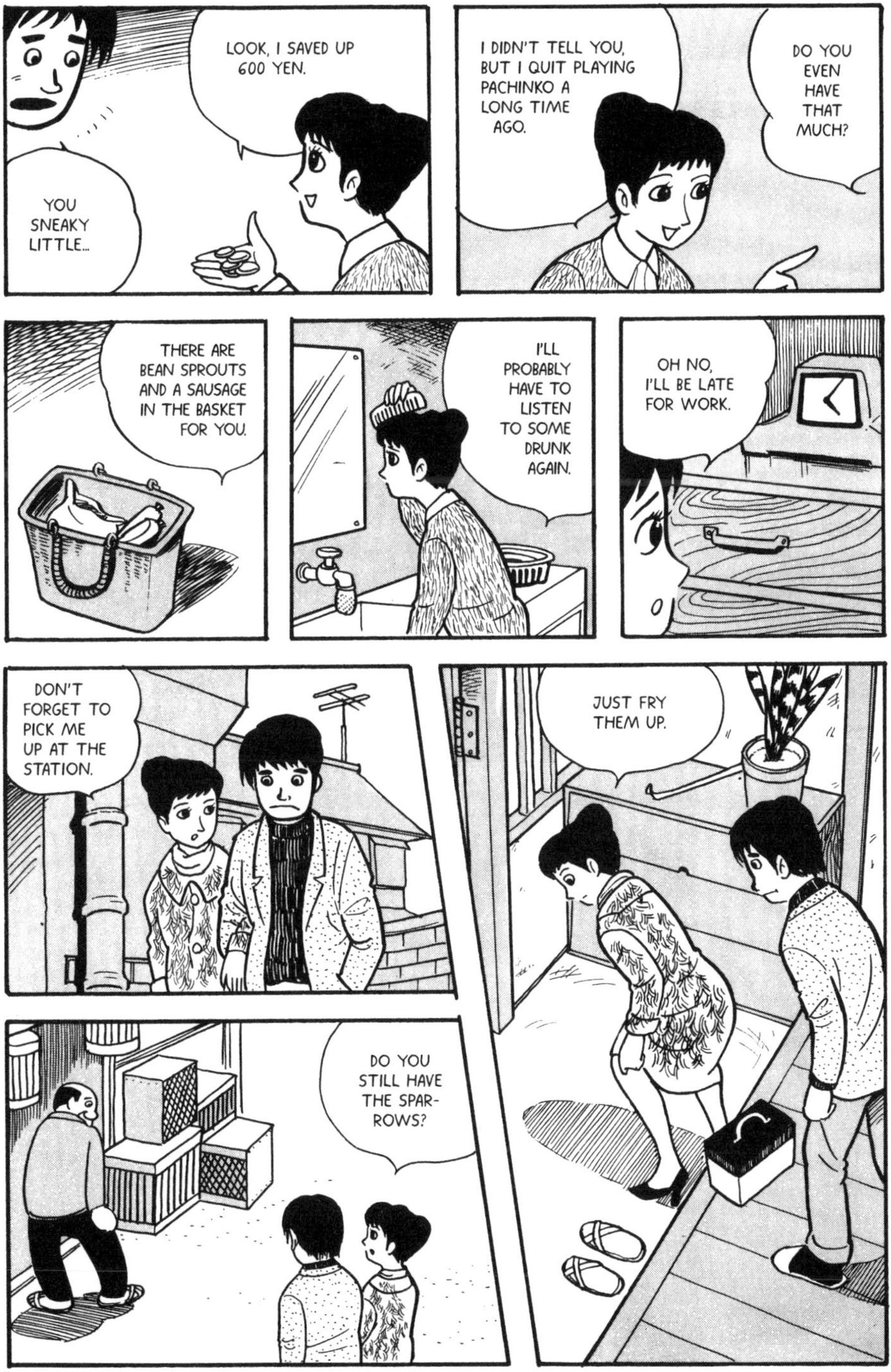
DO YOU EVEN HAVE THAT MUCH?
I DIDN'T TELL YOU, BUT I QUIT PLAYING PACHINKO A LONG TIME AGO.
LOOK, I SAVED UP 600 YEN.
YOU SNEAKY LITTLE...
OH NO, I'LL BE LATE FOR WORK.
I'LL PROBABLY HAVE TO LISTEN TO SOME DRUNK AGAIN.
THERE ARE BEAN SPROUTS AND A SAUSAGE IN THE BASKET FOR YOU.
JUST FRY THEM UP.
DON'T FORGET TO PICK ME UP AT THE STATION.
DO YOU STILL HAVE THE SPARROWS?

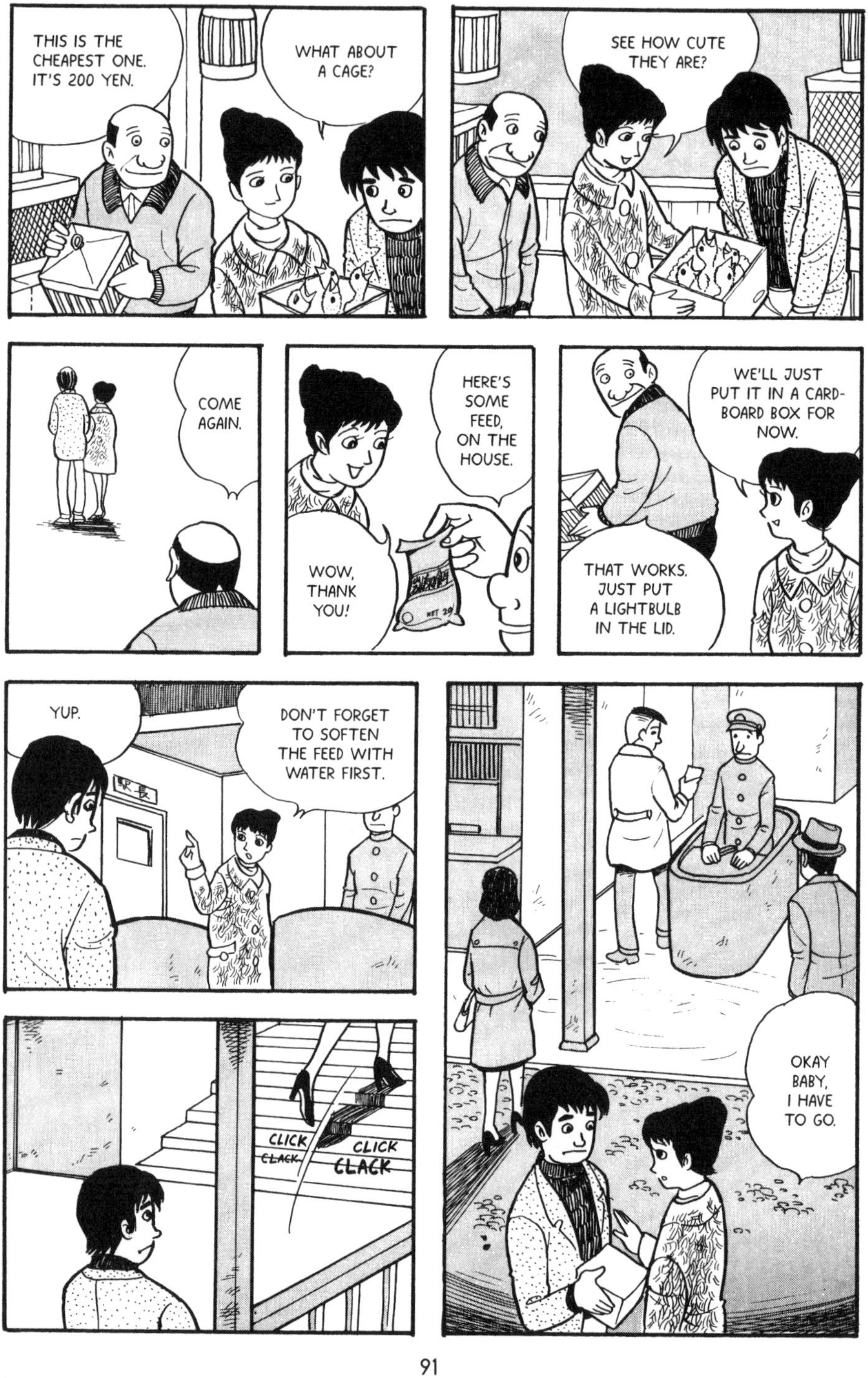
SEE HOW CUTE THEY ARE?
WHAT ABOUT A CAGE?
THIS IS THE CHEAPEST ONE. IT'S 200 YEN.
WE'LL JUST PUT IT IN A CARD-BOARD BOX FOR NOW.
THAT WORKS. JUST PUT A LIGHTBULB IN THE LID.
HERE'S SOME FEED, ON THE HOUSE.
WOW, THANK YOU!
COME AGAIN.
OKAY BABY, I HAVE TO GO.
DON'T FORGET TO SOFTEN THE FEED WITH WATER FIRST.
駅長
YUP.
CLICK CLACK
CLICK CLACK

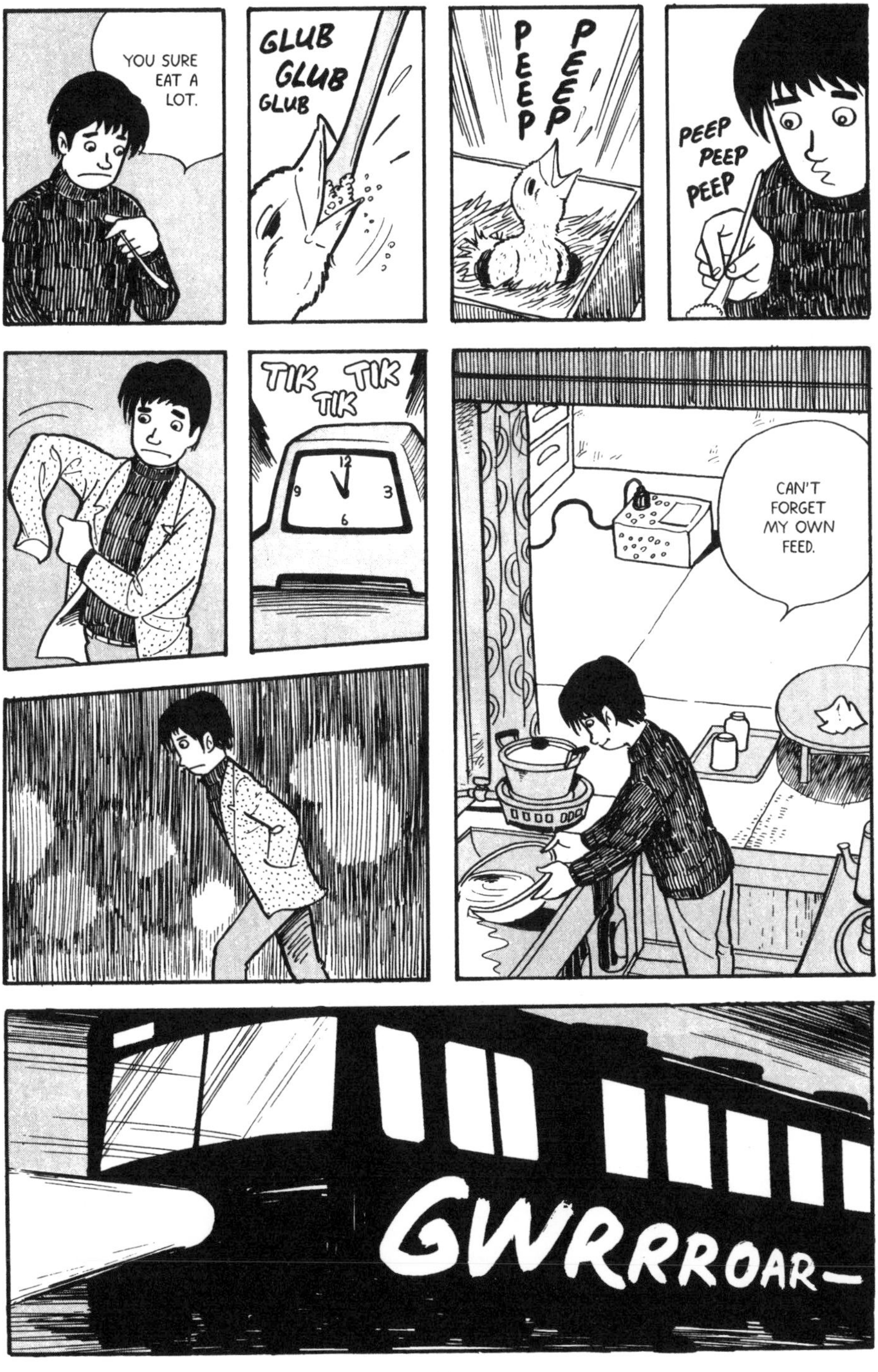
PEEP
PEEP
PEEP
PEEP
PEEP
GLUB
GLUB
GLUB
YOU SURE EAT A LOT.
CAN'T FORGET MY OWN FEED.
TIK TIK TIK
GWRRROAR–

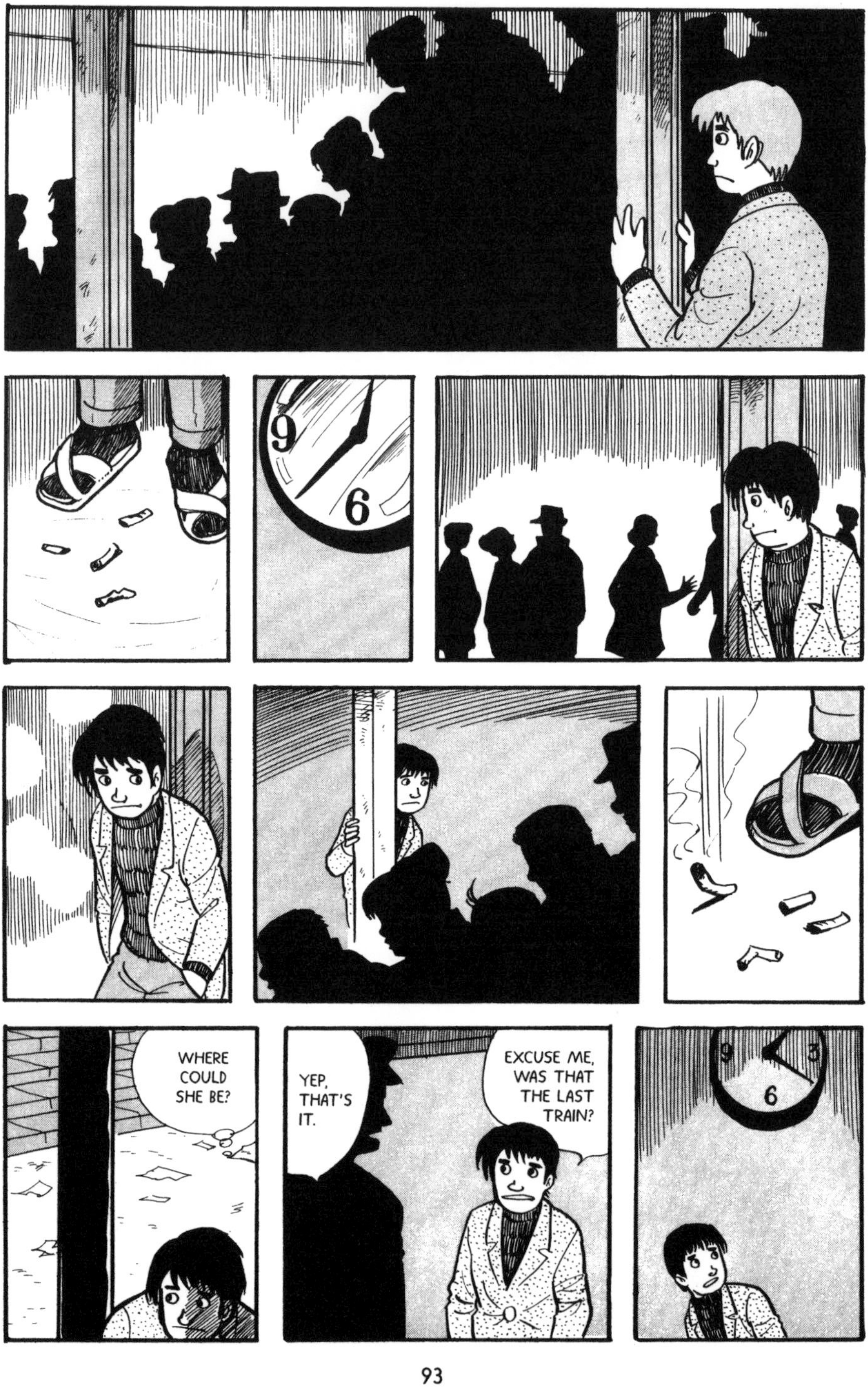
EXCUSE ME, WAS THAT THE LAST TRAIN?
YEP, THAT'S IT.
WHERE COULD SHE BE?

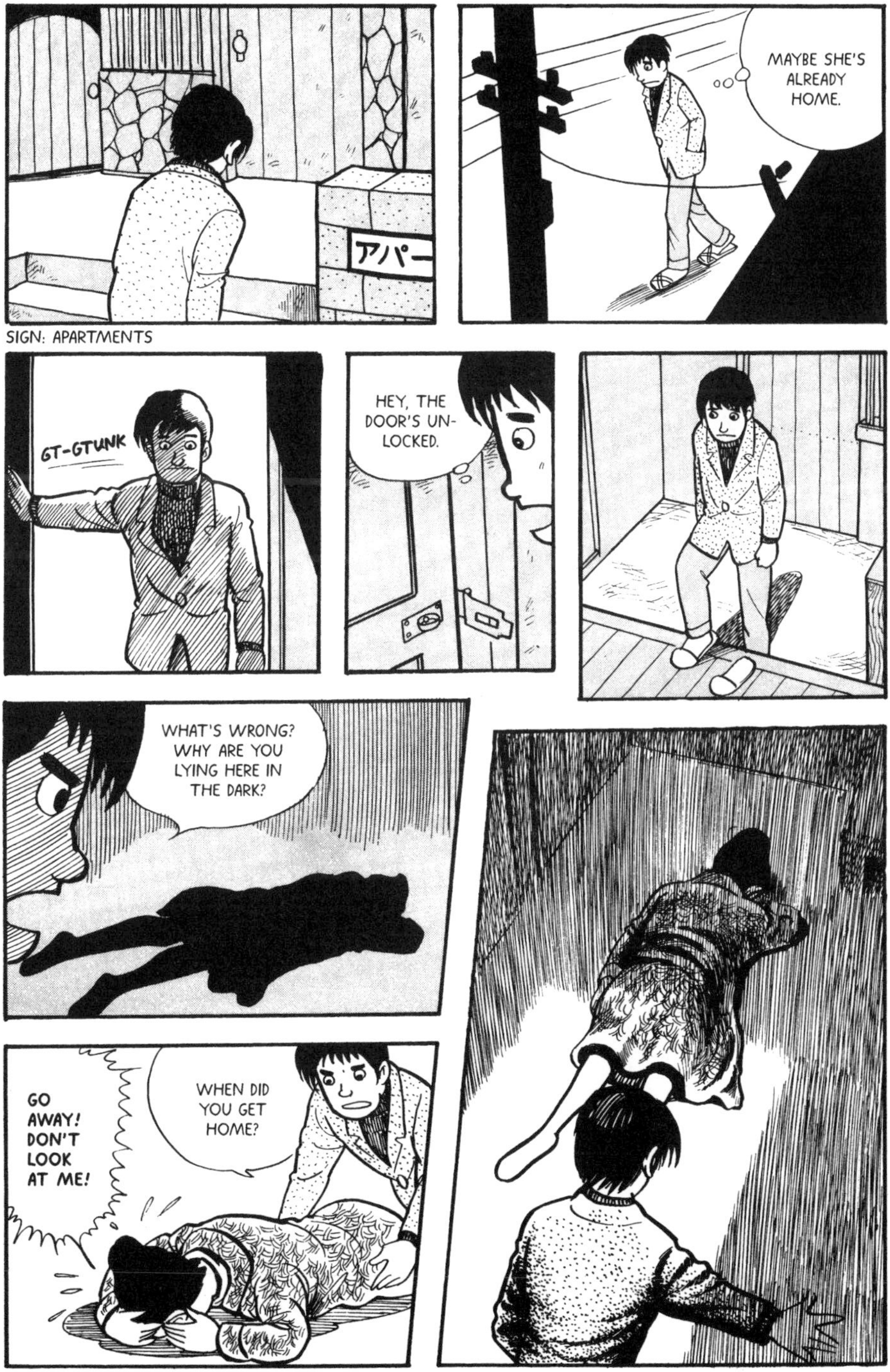
MAYBE SHE'S ALREADY HOME.
アパー
SIGN: APARTMENTS
HEY, THE DOOR'S UN-LOCKED.
GT-GTUNK
WHAT'S WRONG? WHY ARE YOU LYING HERE IN THE DARK?
WHEN DID YOU GET HOME?
GO AWAY! DON'T LOOK AT ME!

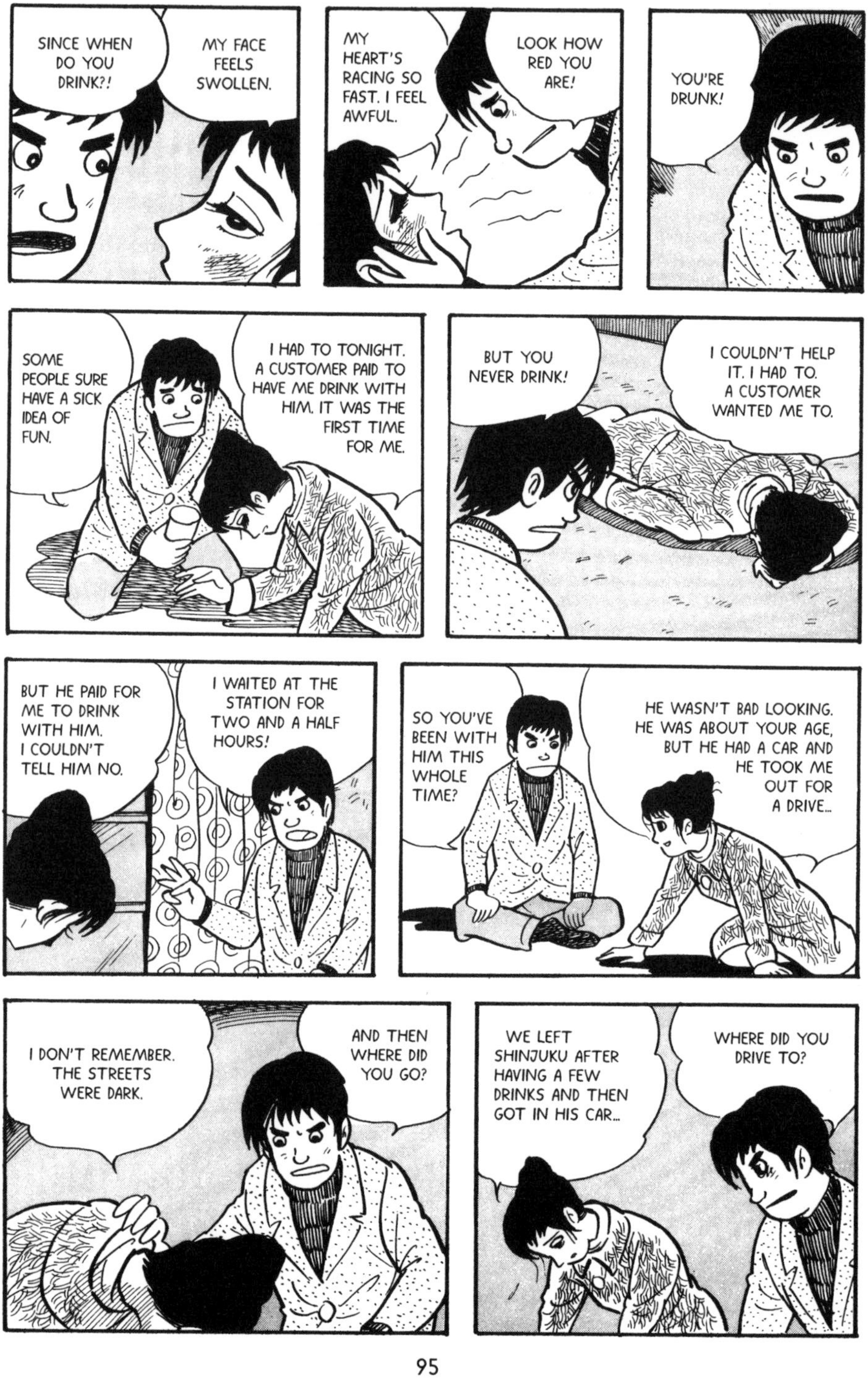
YOU'RE DRUNK!
LOOK HOW RED YOU ARE!
MY HEART'S RACING SO FAST. I FEEL AWFUL.
MY FACE FEELS SWOLLEN.
SINCE WHEN DO YOU DRINK?!
I COULDN'T HELP IT. I HAD TO. A CUSTOMER WANTED ME TO.
BUT YOU NEVER DRINK!
I HAD TO TONIGHT. A CUSTOMER PAID TO HAVE ME DRINK WITH HIM. IT WAS THE FIRST TIME FOR ME.
SOME PEOPLE SURE HAVE A SICK IDEA OF FUN.
HE WASN'T BAD LOOKING. HE WAS ABOUT YOUR AGE, BUT HE HAD A CAR AND HE TOOK ME OUT FOR A DRIVE...
SO YOU'VE BEEN WITH HIM THIS WHOLE TIME?
I WAITED AT THE STATION FOR TWO AND A HALF HOURS!
BUT HE PAID FOR ME TO DRINK WITH HIM. I COULDN'T TELL HIM NO.
WHERE DID YOU DRIVE TO?
WE LEFT SHINJUKU AFTER HAVING A FEW DRINKS AND THEN GOT IN HIS CAR...
AND THEN WHERE DID YOU GO?
I DON'T REMEMBER. THE STREETS WERE DARK.

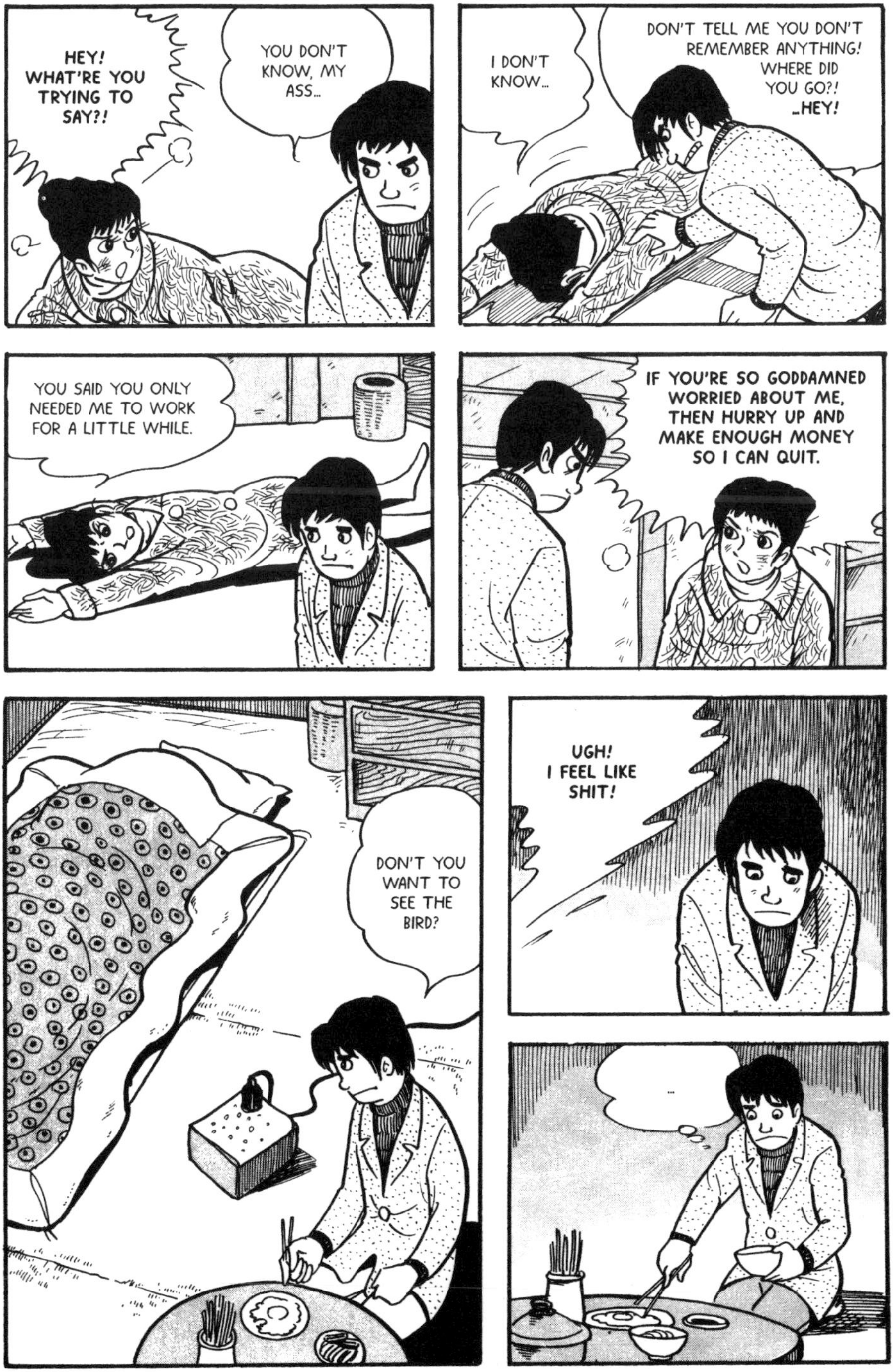
DON'T TELL ME YOU DON'T REMEMBER ANYTHING! WHERE DID YOU GO?! ..HEY!
I DON'T KNOW...
YOU DON'T KNOW, MY ASS...
HEY! WHAT'RE YOU TRYING TO SAY?!
IF YOU'RE SO GODDAMNED WORRIED ABOUT ME, THEN HURRY UP AND MAKE ENOUGH MONEY SO I CAN QUIT.
YOU SAID YOU ONLY NEEDED ME TO WORK FOR A LITTLE WHILE.
UGH! I FEEL LIKE SHIT!
...
DON'T YOU WANT TO SEE THE BIRD?

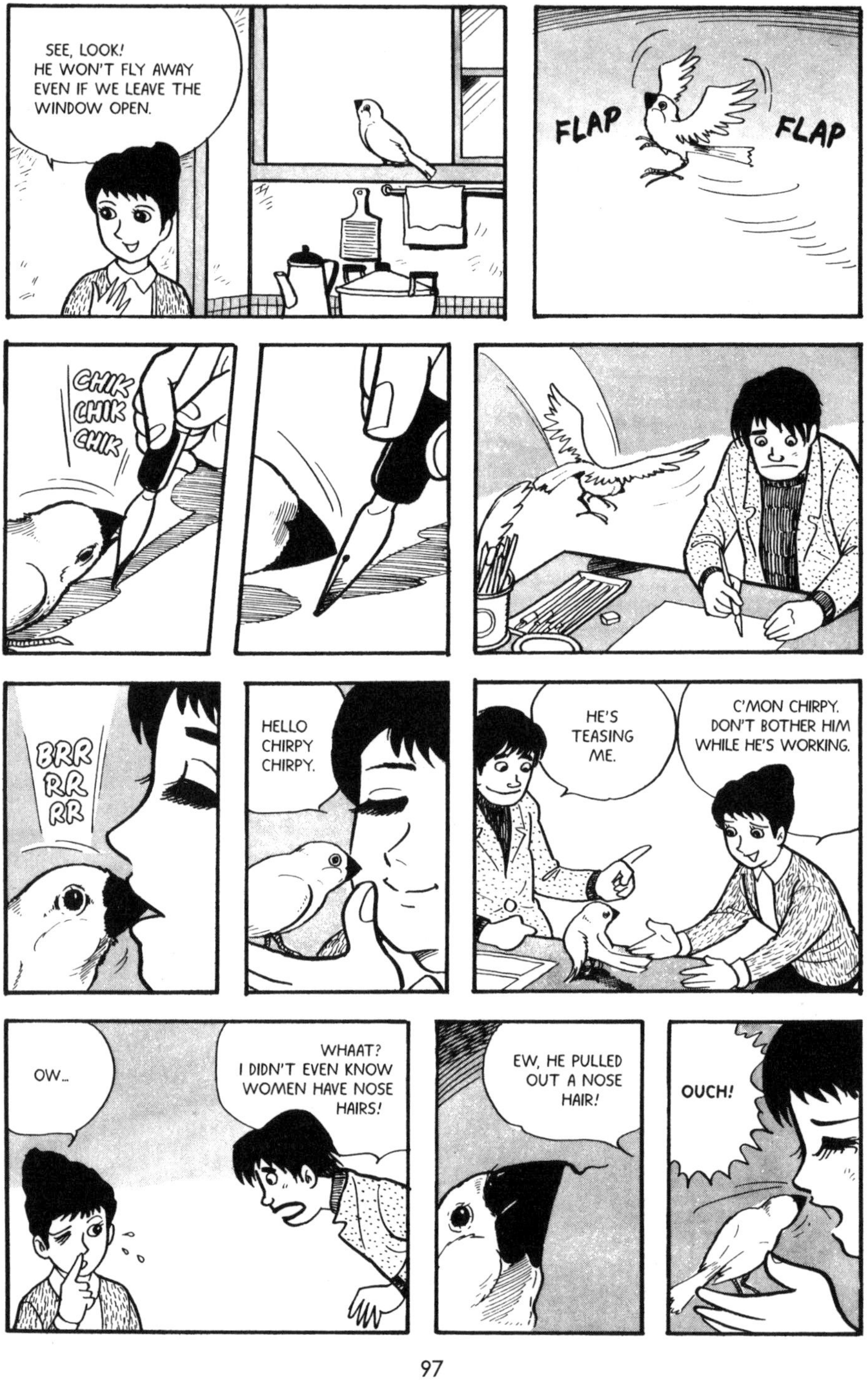
FLAP
FLAP
SEE, LOOK! HE WON'T FLY AWAY EVEN IF WE LEAVE THE WINDOW OPEN.
CHIK CHIK CHIK
C'MON CHIRPY. DON'T BOTHER HIM WHILE HE'S WORKING.
HE'S TEASING ME.
HELLO CHIRPY CHIRPY.
BRR RR RR
OUCH!
EW, HE PULLED OUT A NOSE HAIR!
WHAAT? I DIDN'T EVEN KNOW WOMEN HAVE NOSE HAIRS!
OW...

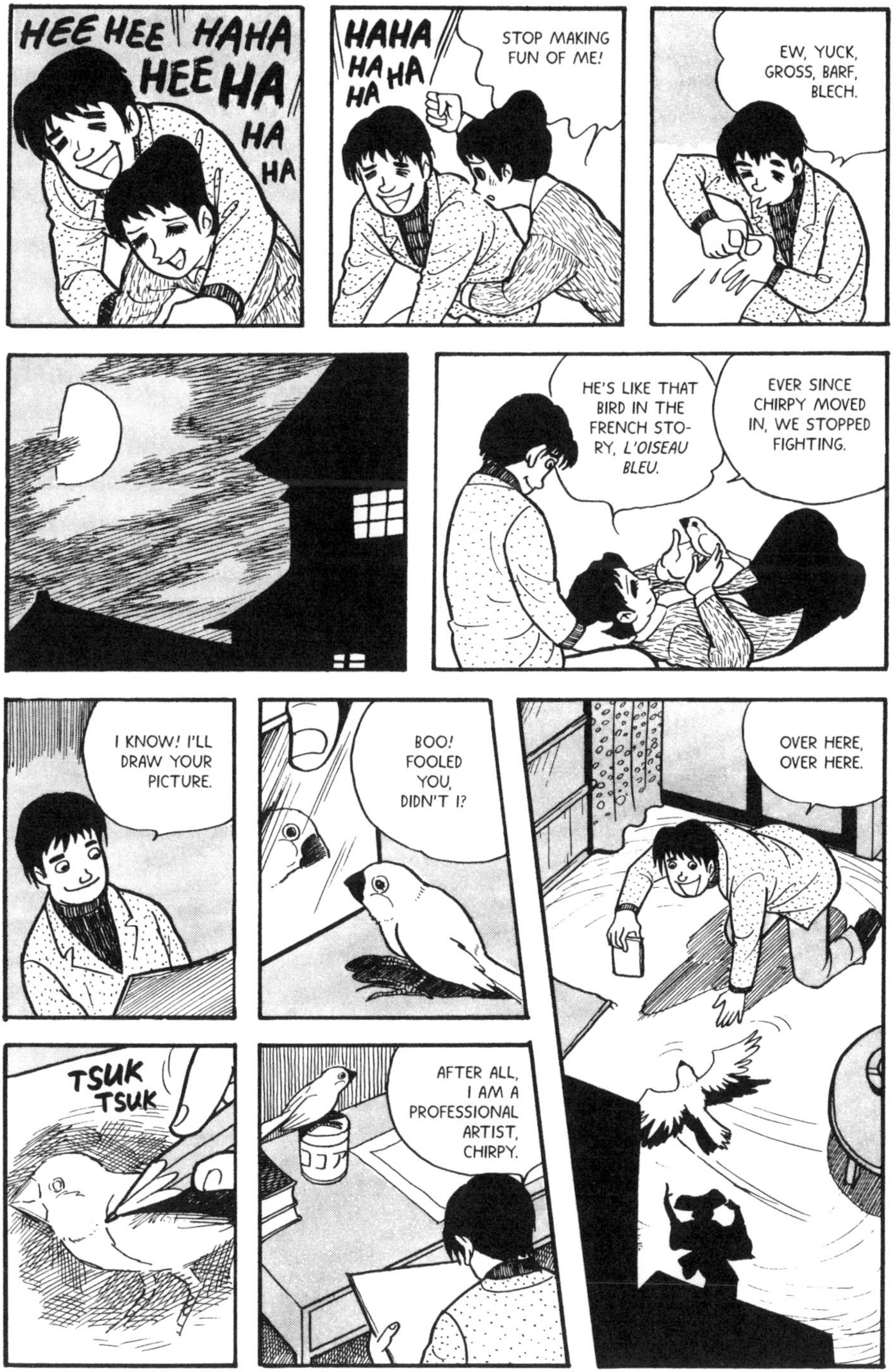
EW, YUCK, GROSS, BARF, BLECH.
HAHA HA HA HA
STOP MAKING FUN OF ME!
HEE HEE HAHA HEE HA HA HA
EVER SINCE CHIRPY MOVED IN, WE STOPPED FIGHTING.
HE'S LIKE THAT BIRD IN THE FRENCH STORY, *L'OISEAU BLEU*.
OVER HERE, OVER HERE.
BOO! FOOLED YOU, DIDN'T I?
I KNOW! I'LL DRAW YOUR PICTURE.
AFTER ALL, I AM A PROFESSIONAL ARTIST, CHIRPY.
TSUK TSUK

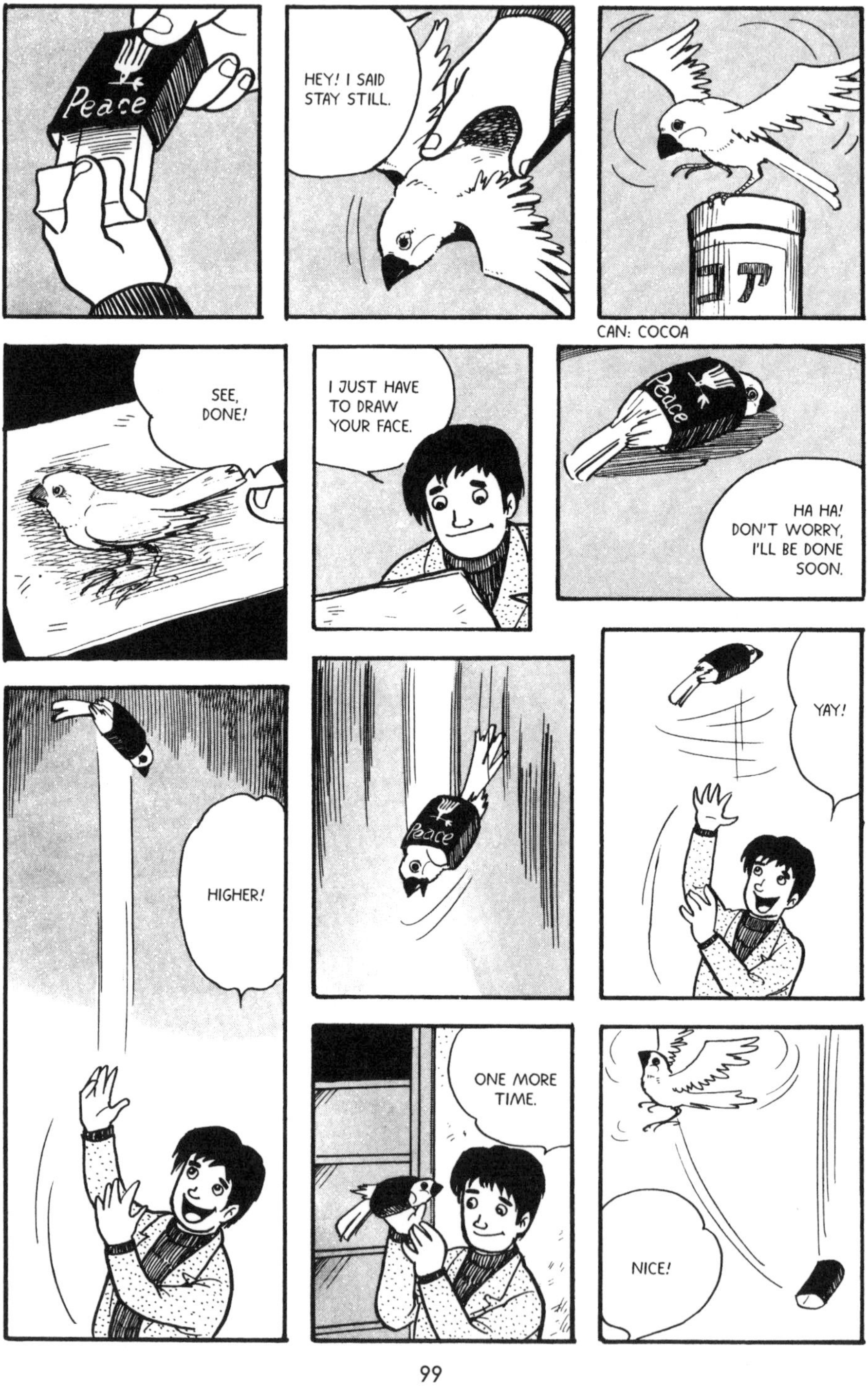
CAN: COCOA
HEY! I SAID STAY STILL.
HA HA! DON'T WORRY, I'LL BE DONE SOON.
I JUST HAVE TO DRAW YOUR FACE.
SEE, DONE!
YAY!
NICE!
ONE MORE TIME.
HIGHER!

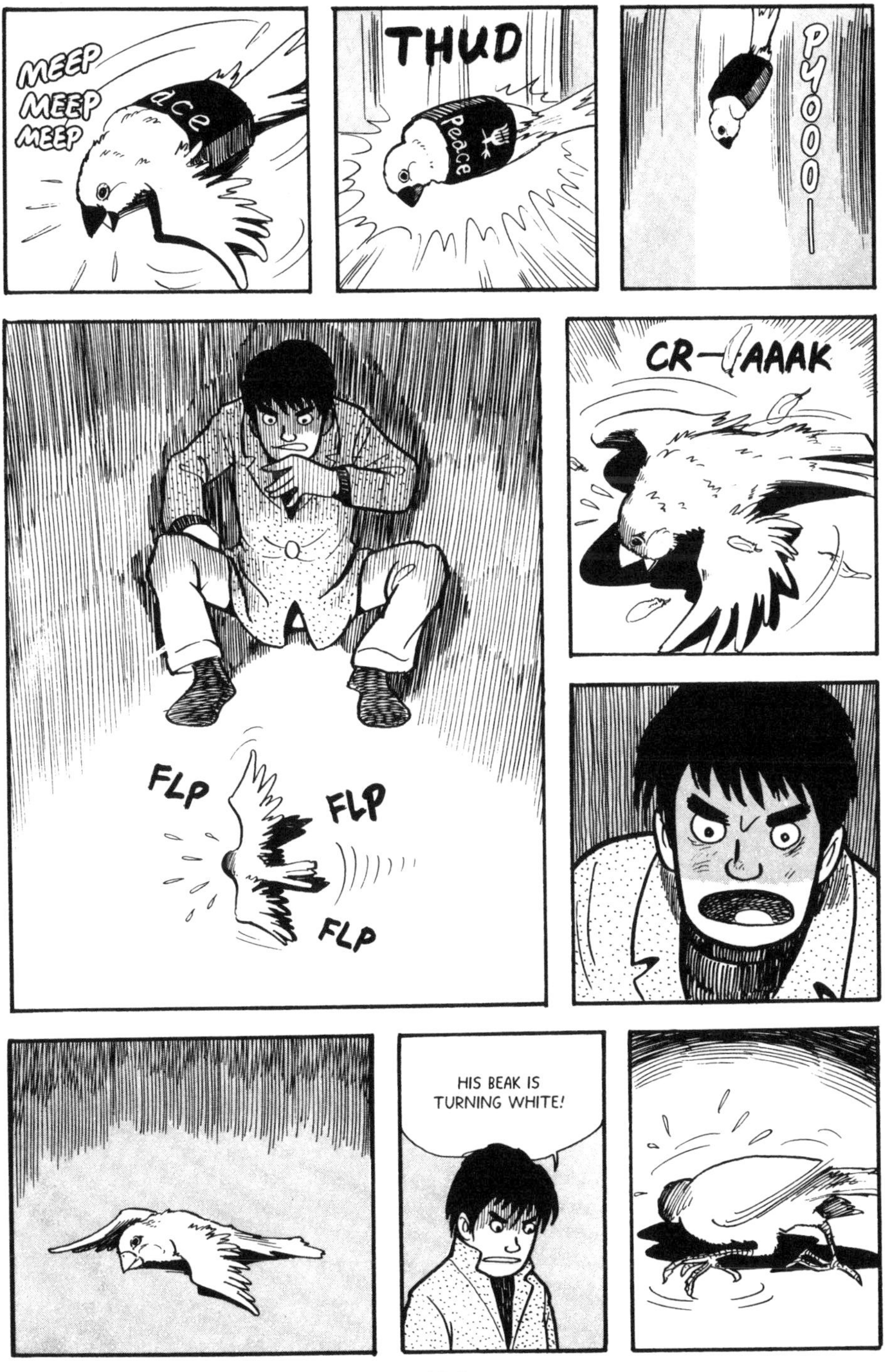
PYOOOO—
THUD
Peace
MEEP
MEEP
MEEP
ace
CR—AAAK
FLP
FLP
FLP
HIS BEAK IS TURNING WHITE!

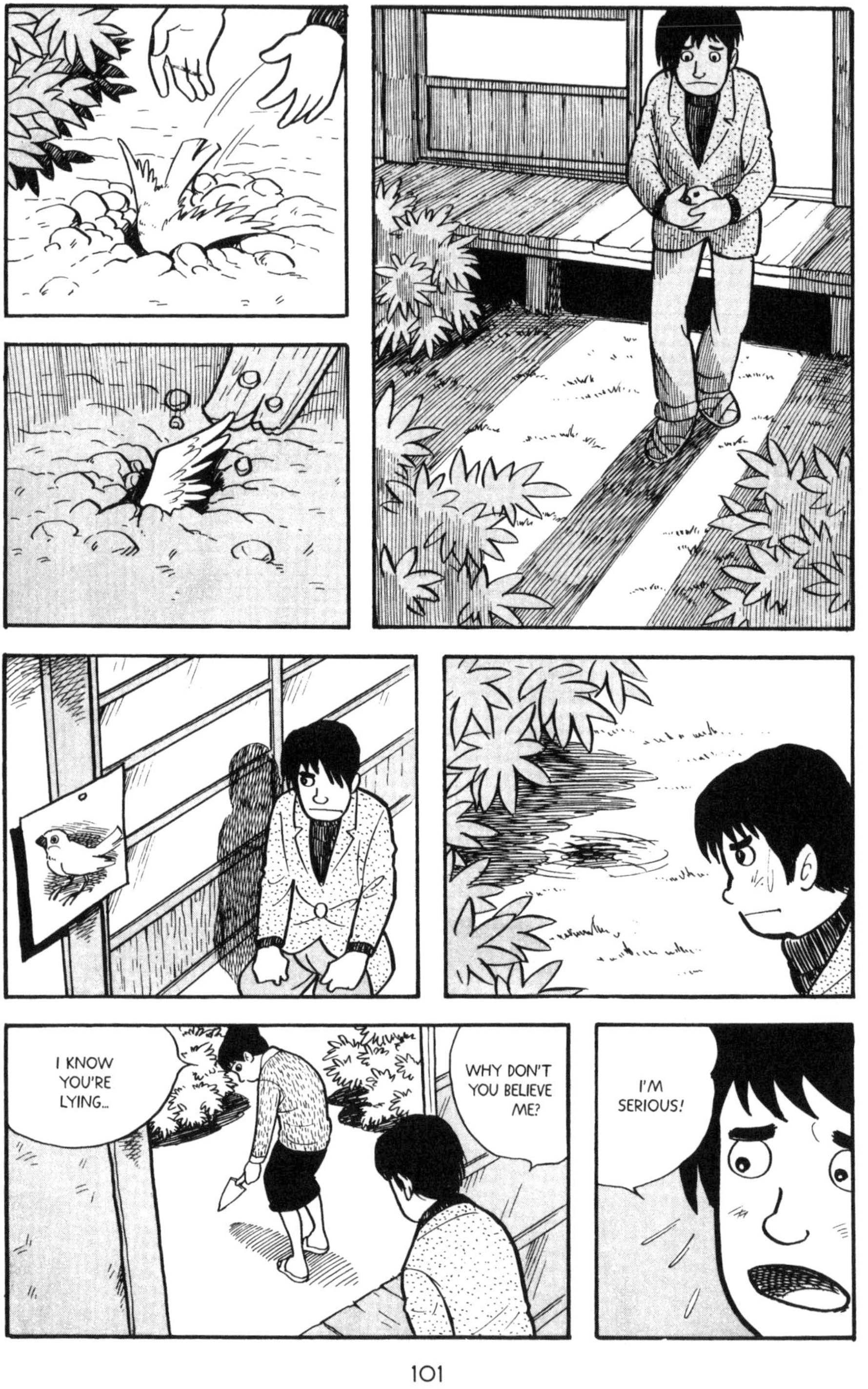
I'M SERIOUS!
WHY DON'T YOU BELIEVE ME?
I KNOW YOU'RE LYING...

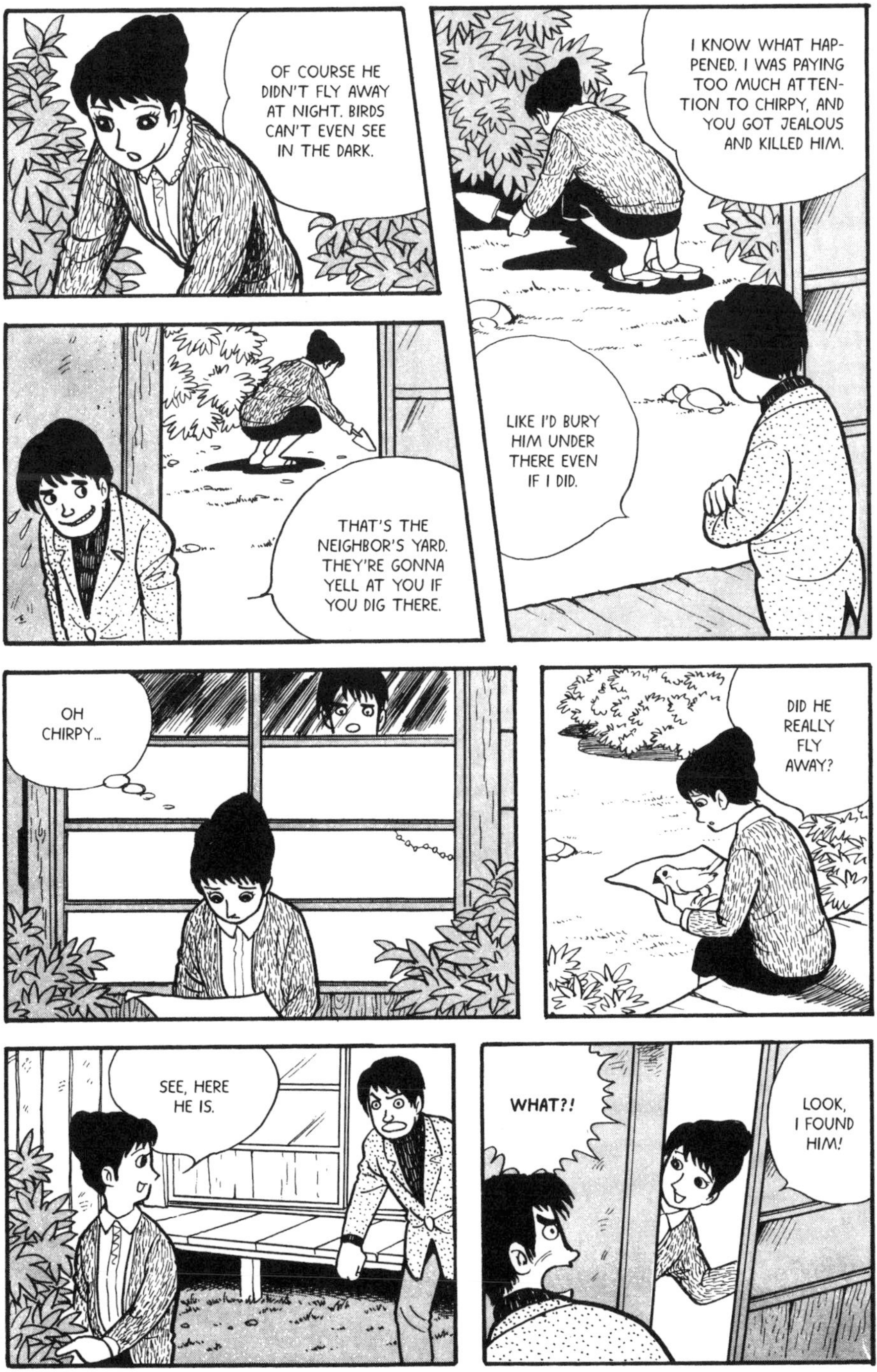
I KNOW WHAT HAP-PENED. I WAS PAYING TOO MUCH ATTENTION TO CHIRPY, AND YOU GOT JEALOUS AND KILLED HIM.
LIKE I'D BURY HIM UNDER THERE EVEN IF I DID.
OF COURSE HE DIDN'T FLY AWAY AT NIGHT. BIRDS CAN'T EVEN SEE IN THE DARK.
THAT'S THE NEIGHBOR'S YARD. THEY'RE GONNA YELL AT YOU IF YOU DIG THERE.
DID HE REALLY FLY AWAY?
OH CHIRPY...
LOOK, I FOUND HIM!
WHAT?!
SEE, HERE HE IS.

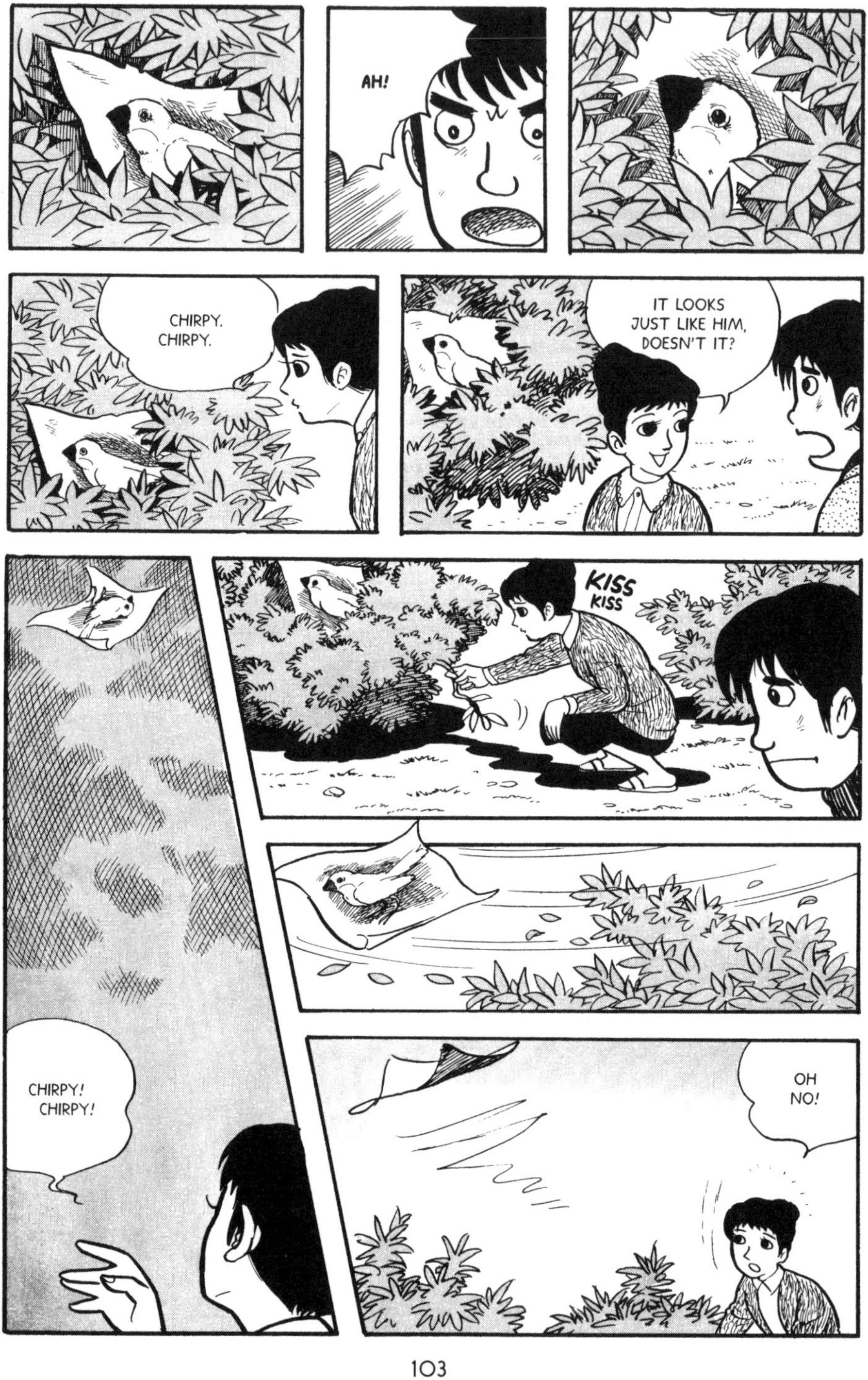
AH!
IT LOOKS JUST LIKE HIM, DOESN'T IT?
CHIRPY. CHIRPY.
KISS KISS
OH NO!
CHIRPY! CHIRPY!

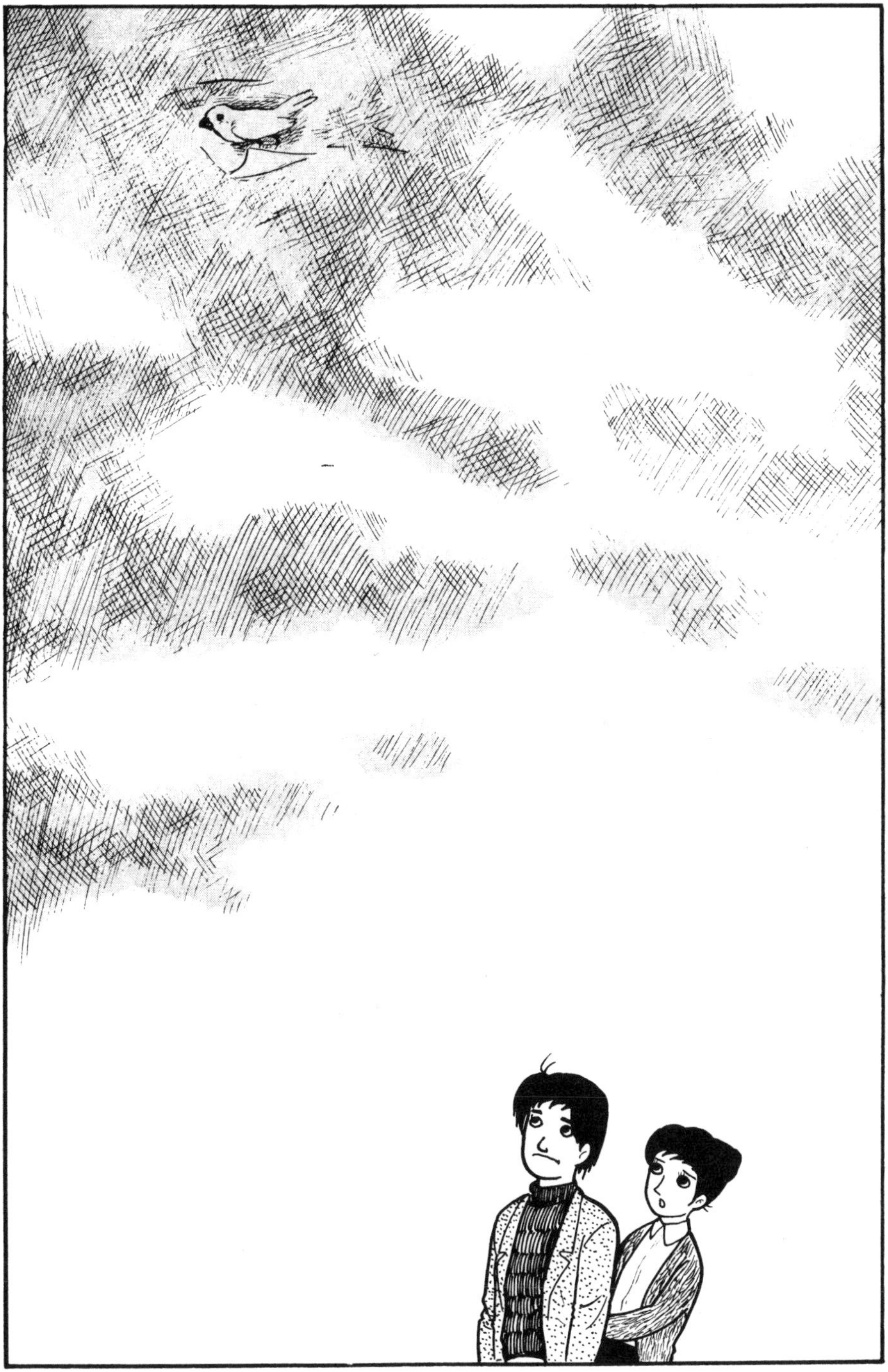

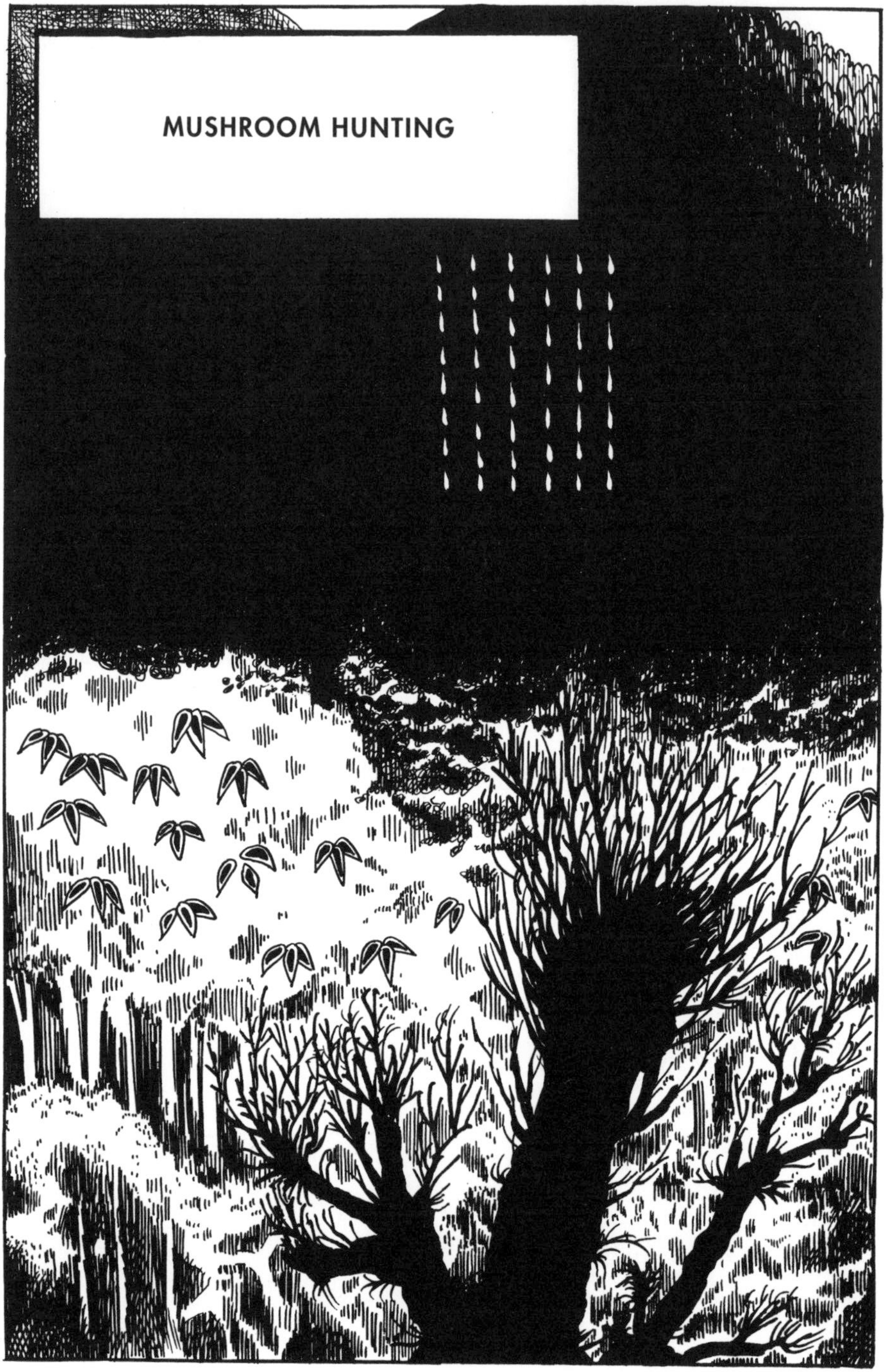
MUSHROOM HUNTING

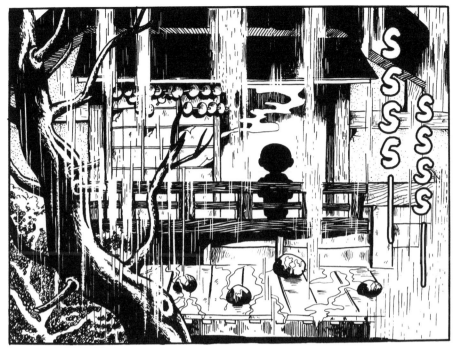

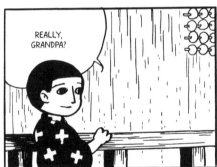

SSSS—
SSSS—
SHOTA, LET'S GO MUSHROOM HUNTING TOMORROW.
REALLY, GRANDPA?
BENEATH THOSE RED PINES SHOULD BE A GOOD PLACE.

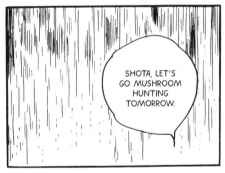

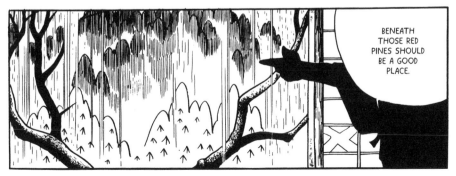

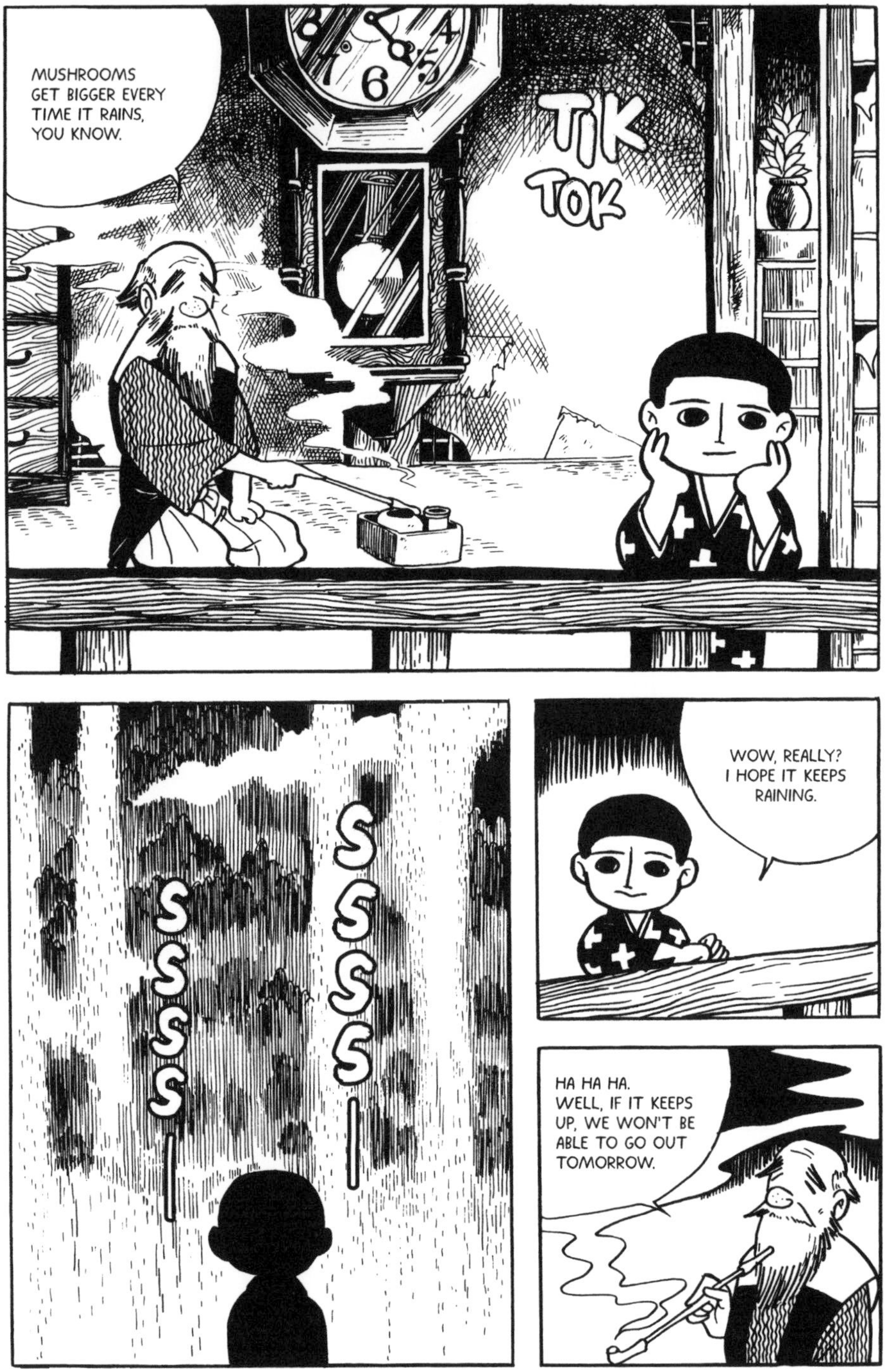
MUSHROOMS GET BIGGER EVERY TIME IT RAINS, YOU KNOW.
TIK TOK
WOW, REALLY? I HOPE IT KEEPS RAINING.
HA HA HA. WELL, IF IT KEEPS UP, WE WON'T BE ABLE TO GO OUT TOMORROW.
SSSS—
SSSS—

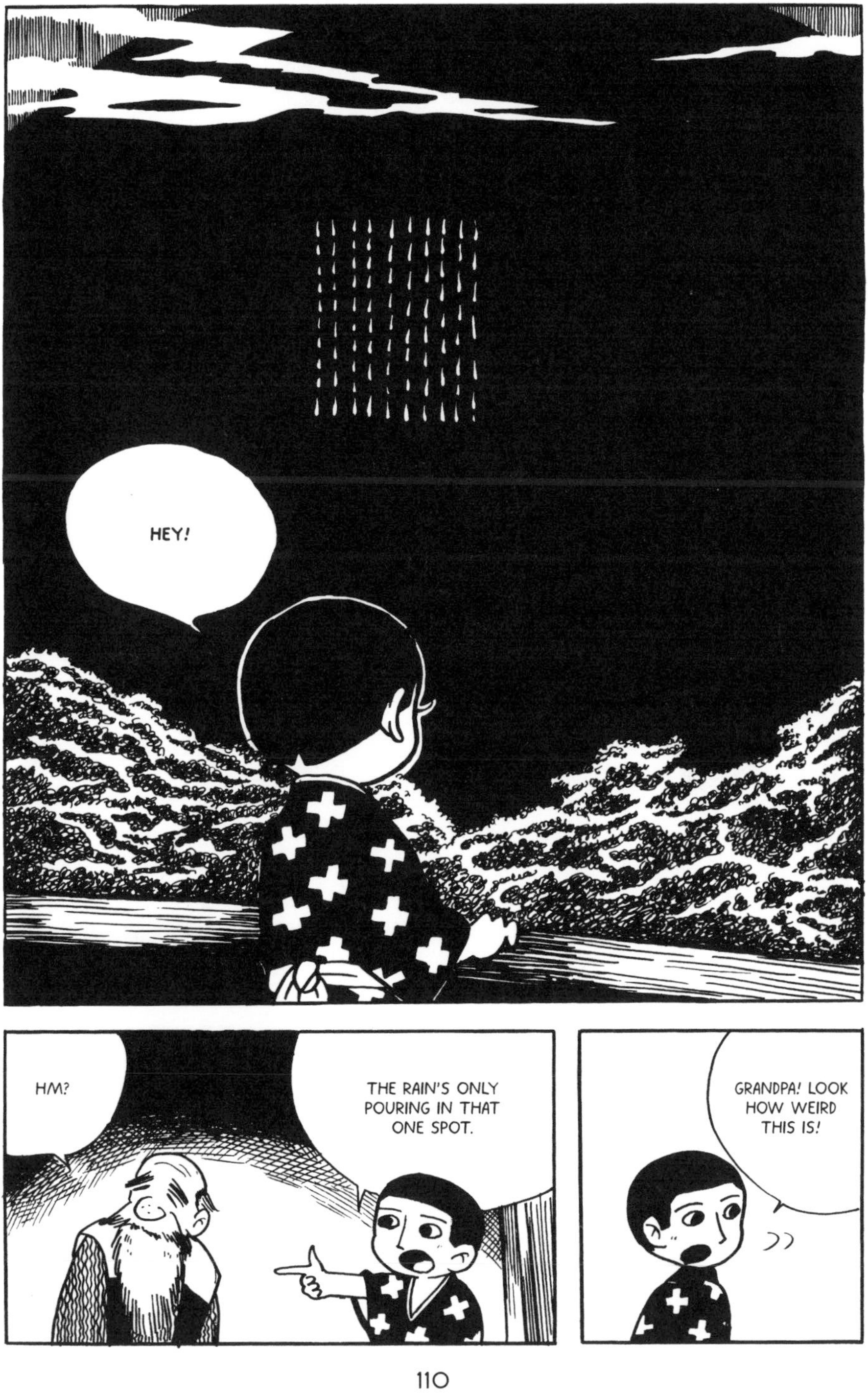
HEY!
GRANDPA! LOOK HOW WEIRD THIS IS!
THE RAIN'S ONLY POURING IN THAT ONE SPOT.
HM?

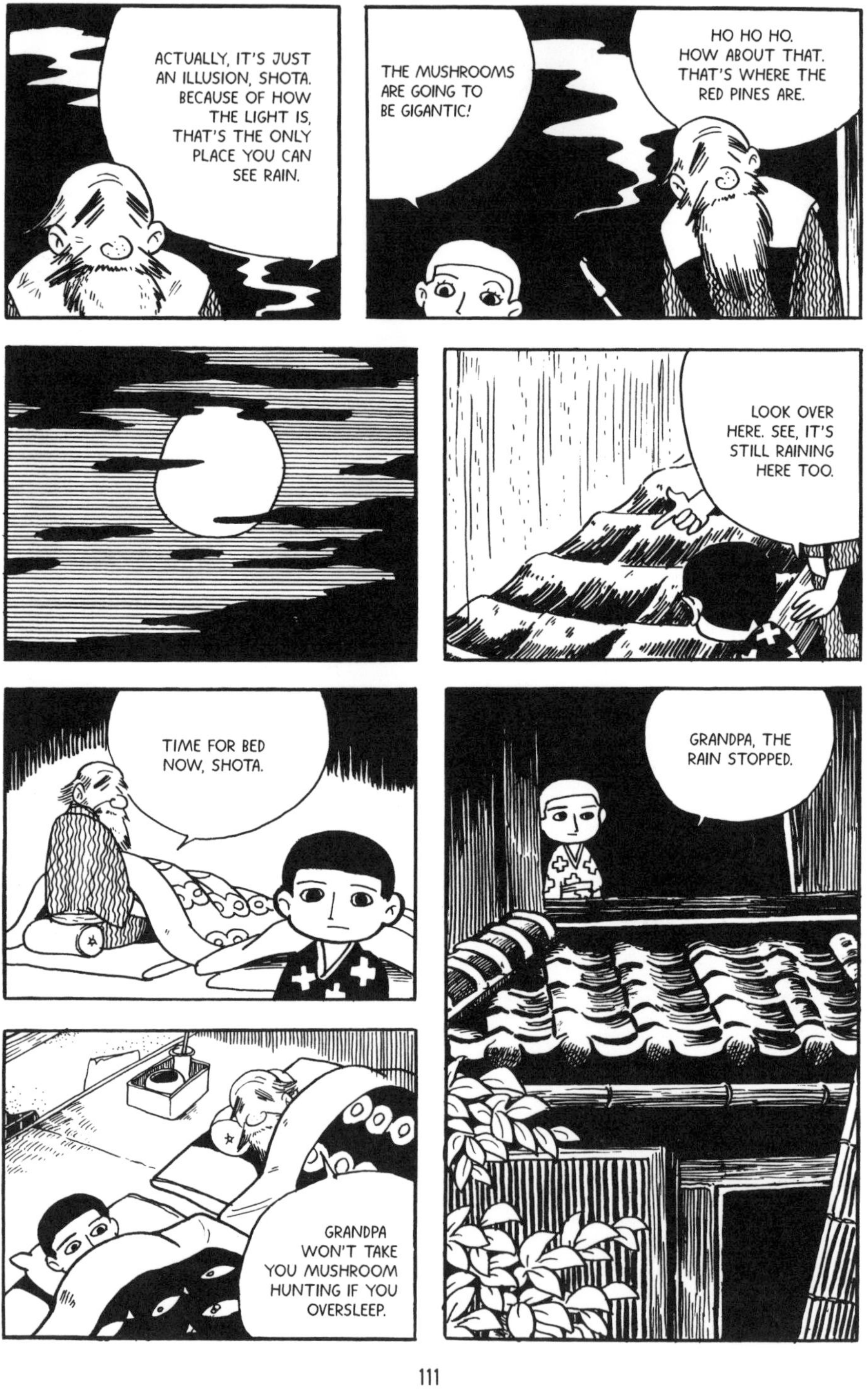
HO HO HO. HOW ABOUT THAT. THAT'S WHERE THE RED PINES ARE.
THE MUSHROOMS ARE GOING TO BE GIGANTIC!
ACTUALLY, IT'S JUST AN ILLUSION, SHOTA. BECAUSE OF HOW THE LIGHT IS, THAT'S THE ONLY PLACE YOU CAN SEE RAIN.
LOOK OVER HERE. SEE, IT'S STILL RAINING HERE TOO.
GRANDPA, THE RAIN STOPPED.
TIME FOR BED NOW, SHOTA.
GRANDPA WON'T TAKE YOU MUSHROOM HUNTING IF YOU OVERSLEEP.

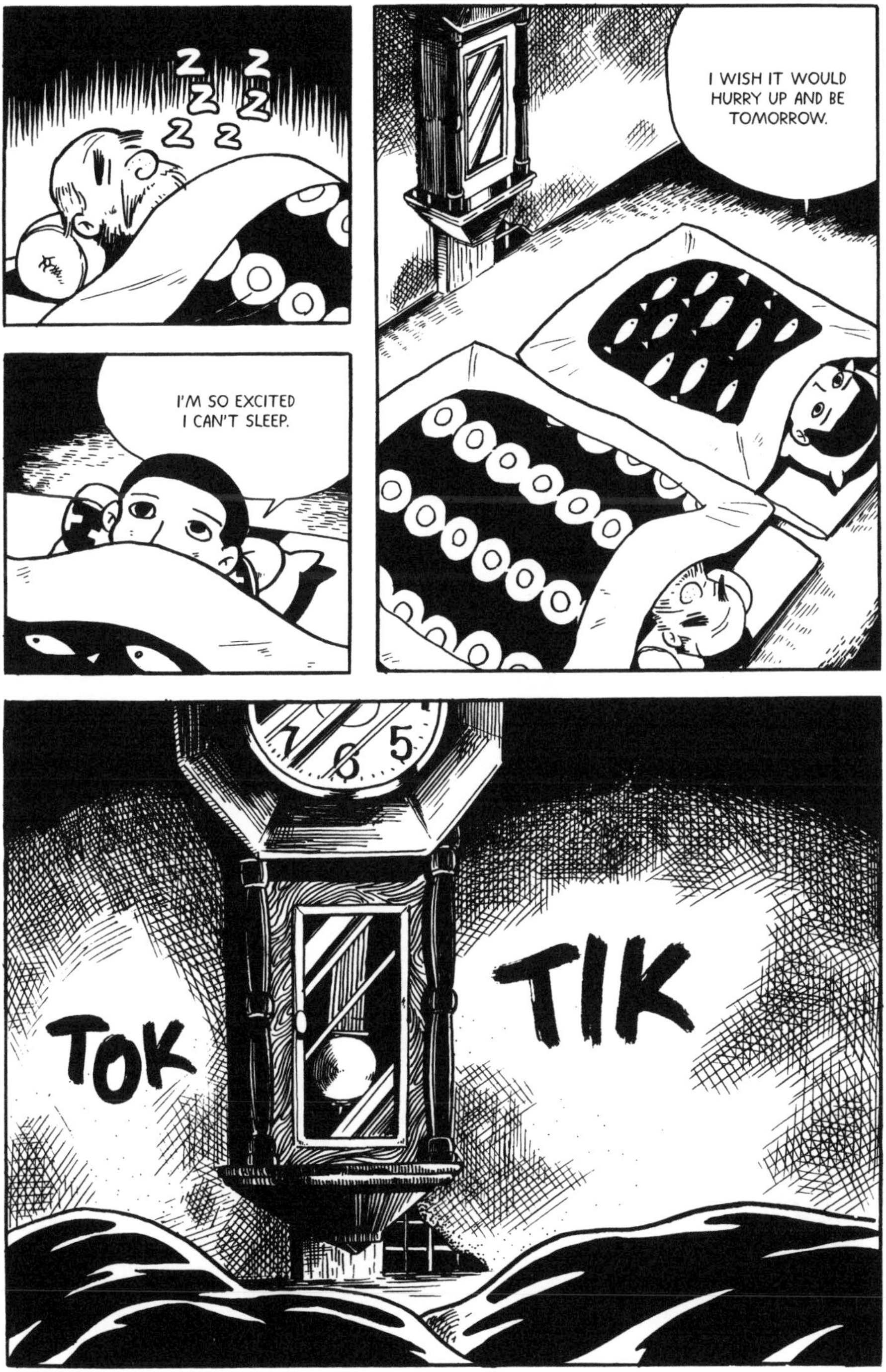
I WISH IT WOULD HURRY UP AND BE TOMORROW.
Z Z Z Z Z Z
I'M SO EXCITED I CAN'T SLEEP.
TIK
TOK

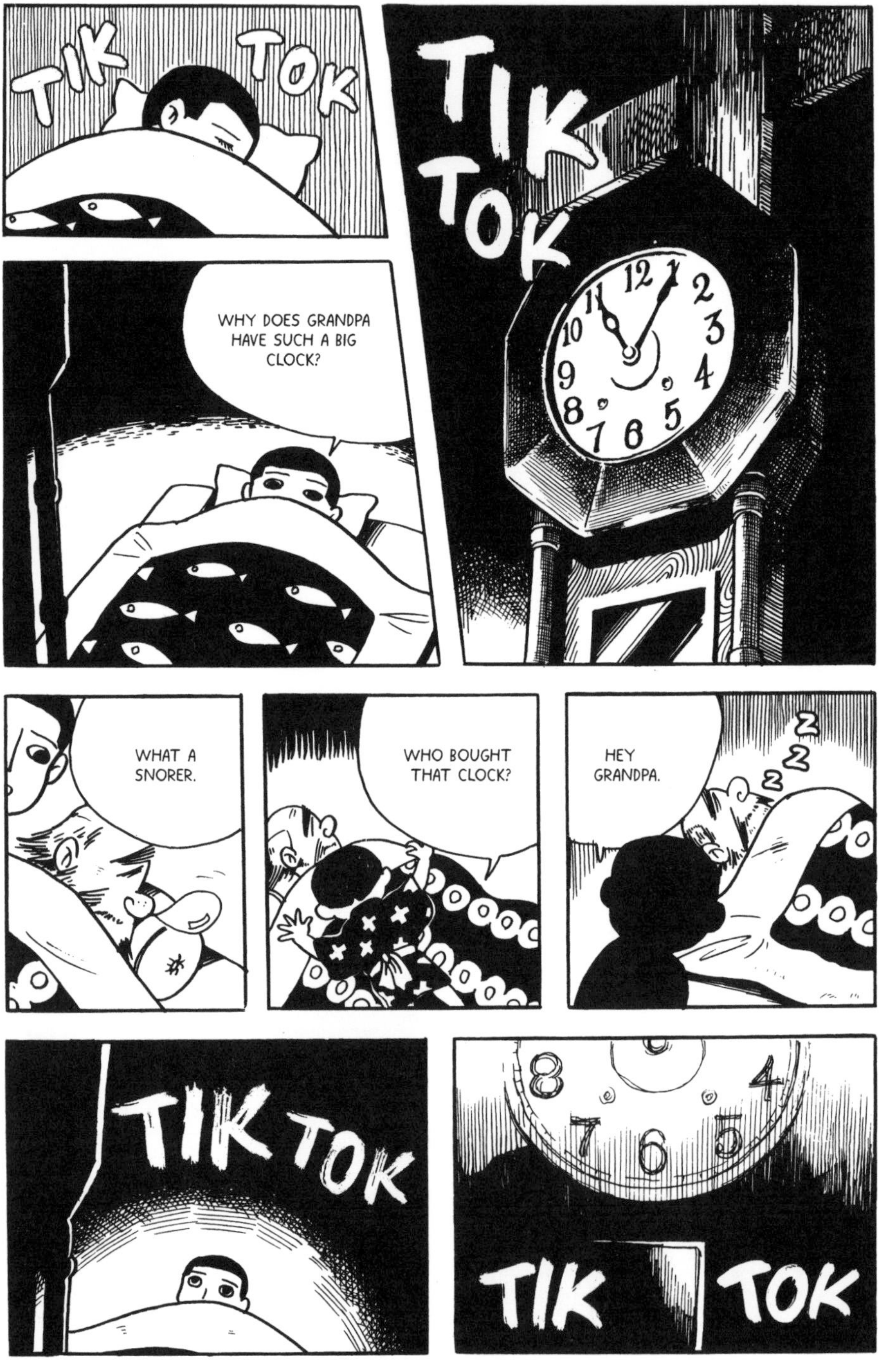
TIK
TOK
TIK TOK
WHY DOES GRANDPA HAVE SUCH A BIG CLOCK?
Z Z Z
HEY GRANDPA.
WHO BOUGHT THAT CLOCK?
WHAT A SNORER.
TIK TOK
TIK TOK

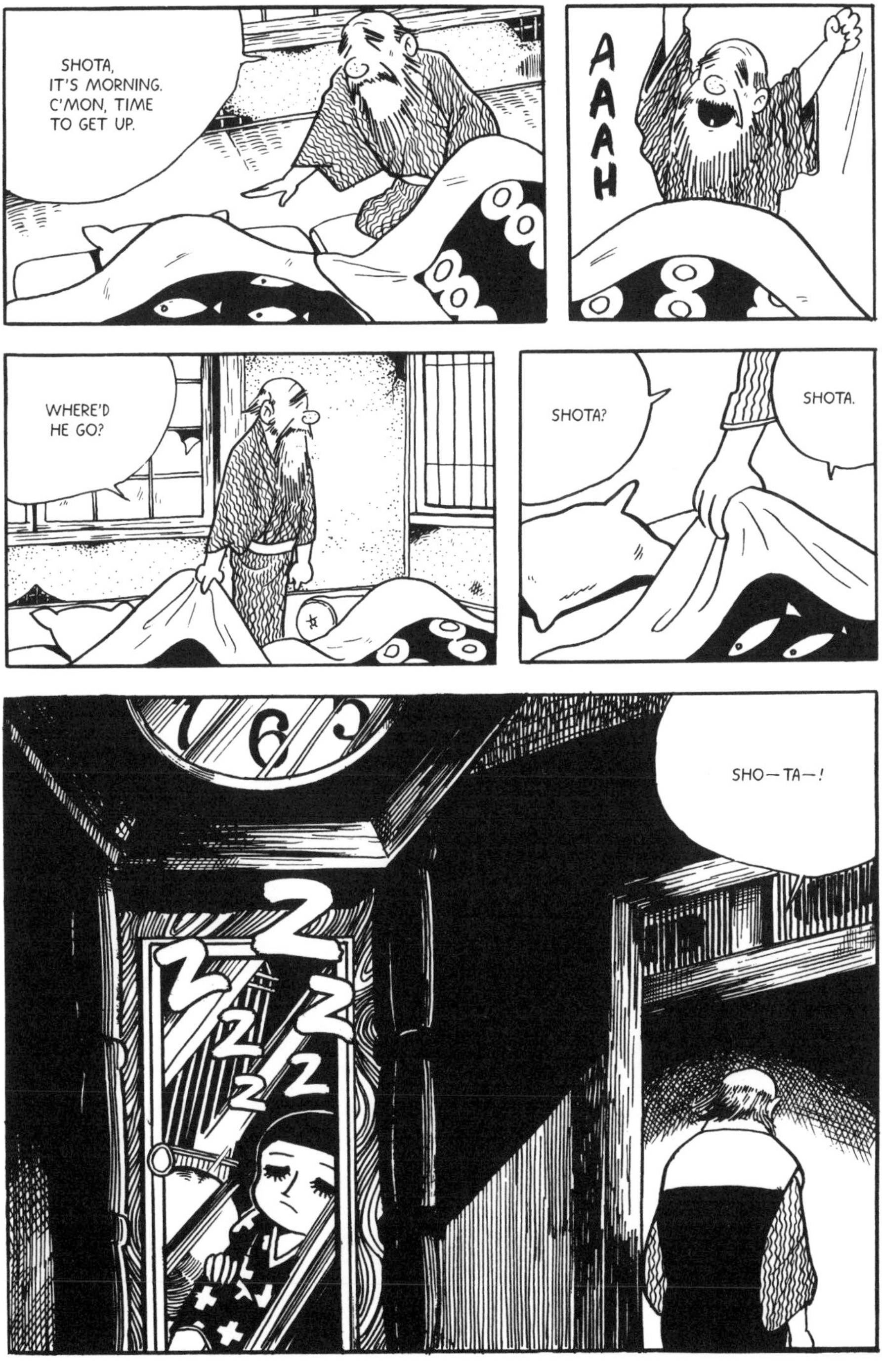
AAAH
SHOTA, IT'S MORNING. C'MON, TIME TO GET UP.
SHOTA.
SHOTA?
WHERE'D HE GO?
SHO—TA—!
ZZZZZZ

THE SECONDHAND BOOK

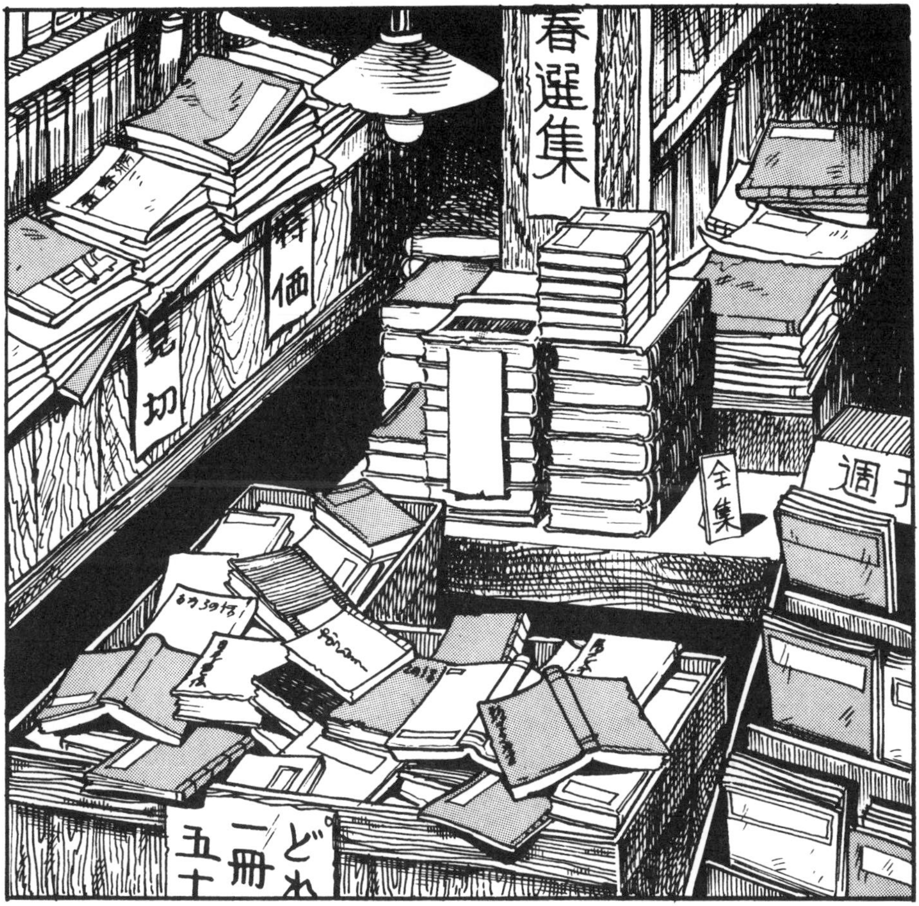
春選集
特価
見切
全集

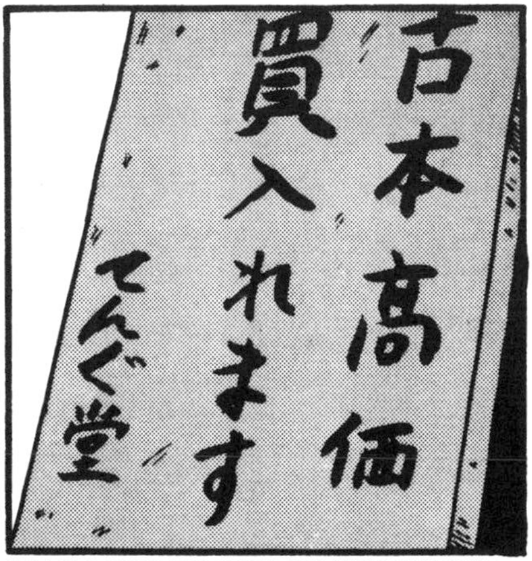
古本高価買入れます
てんぐ堂
SIGN: WE OFFER TOP PRICES FOR VINTAGE BOOKS

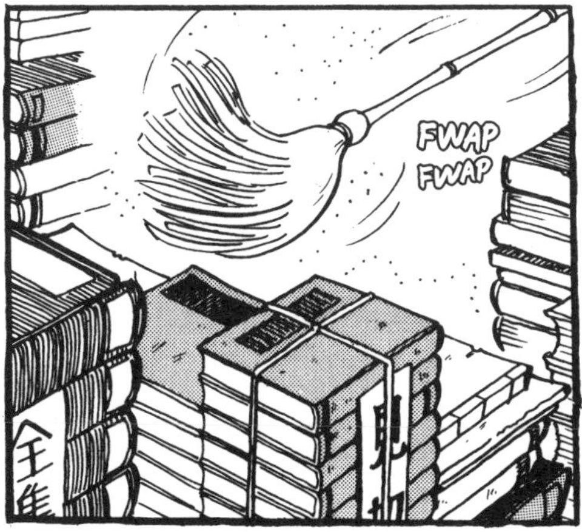
FWAP
FWAP

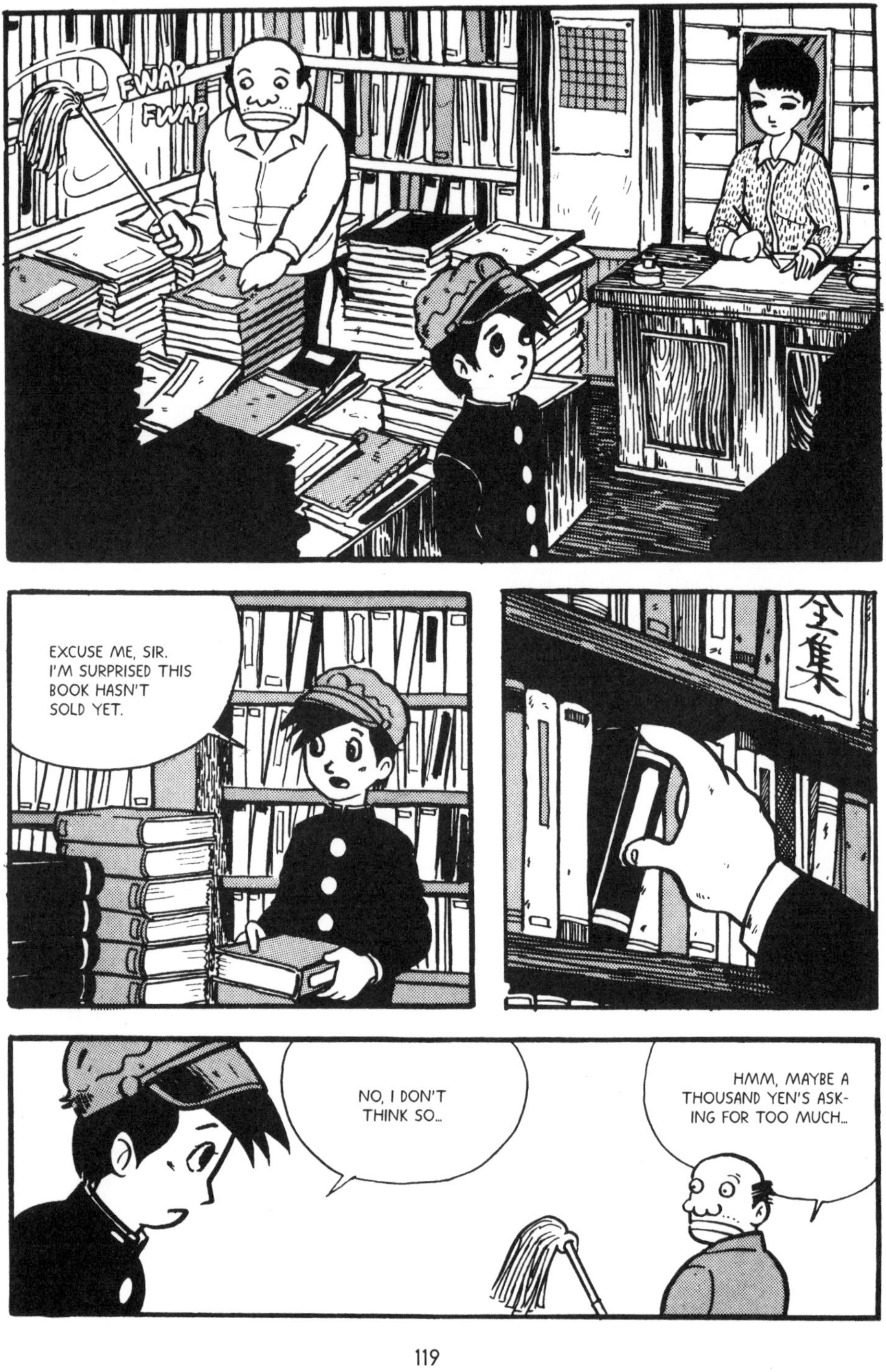
FWAP
FWAP
全集
EXCUSE ME, SIR. I'M SURPRISED THIS BOOK HASN'T SOLD YET.
HMM, MAYBE A THOUSAND YEN'S ASKING FOR TOO MUCH...
NO, I DON'T THINK SO...

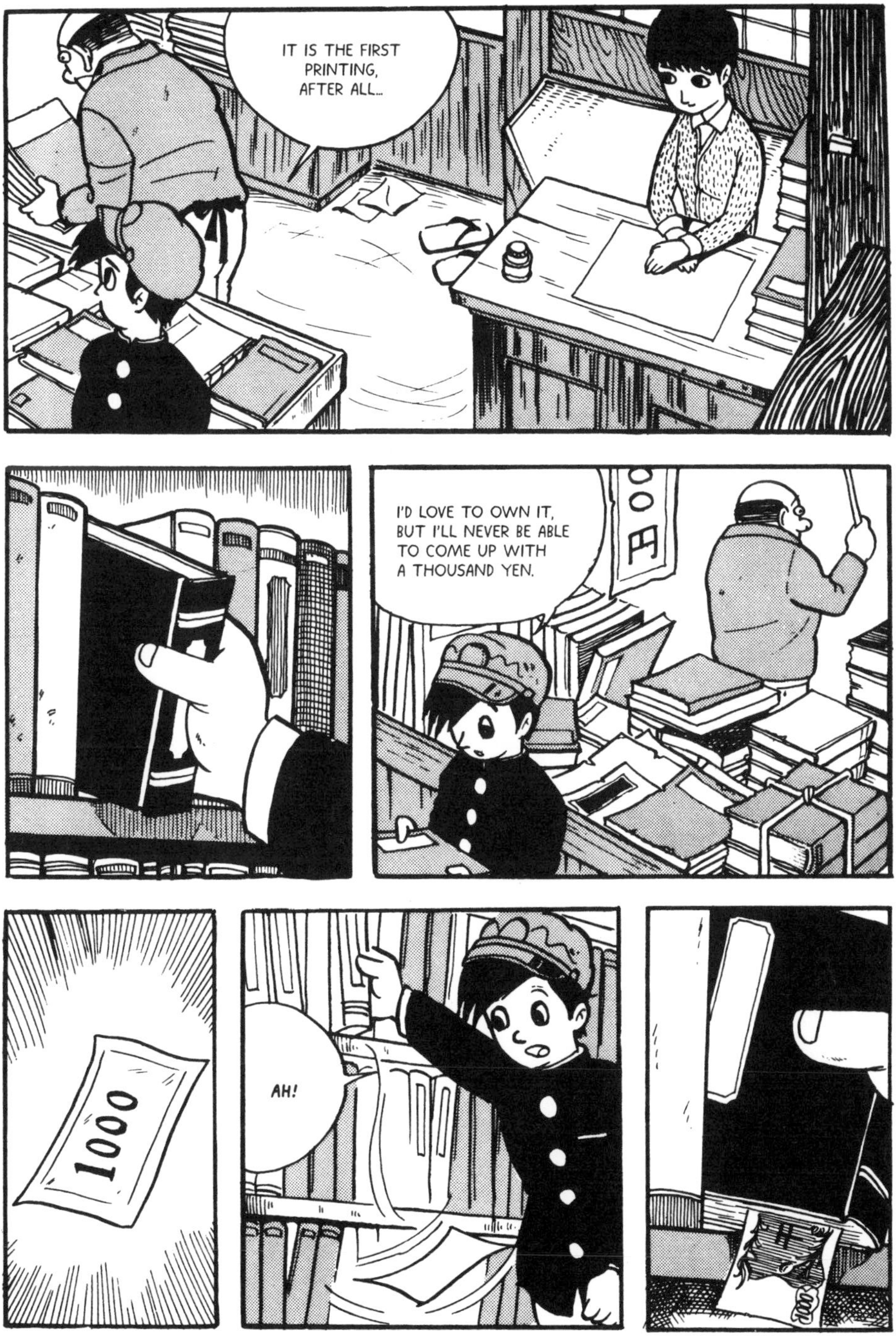
IT IS THE FIRST PRINTING, AFTER ALL...
I'D LOVE TO OWN IT, BUT I'LL NEVER BE ABLE TO COME UP WITH A THOUSAND YEN.
AH!
1000

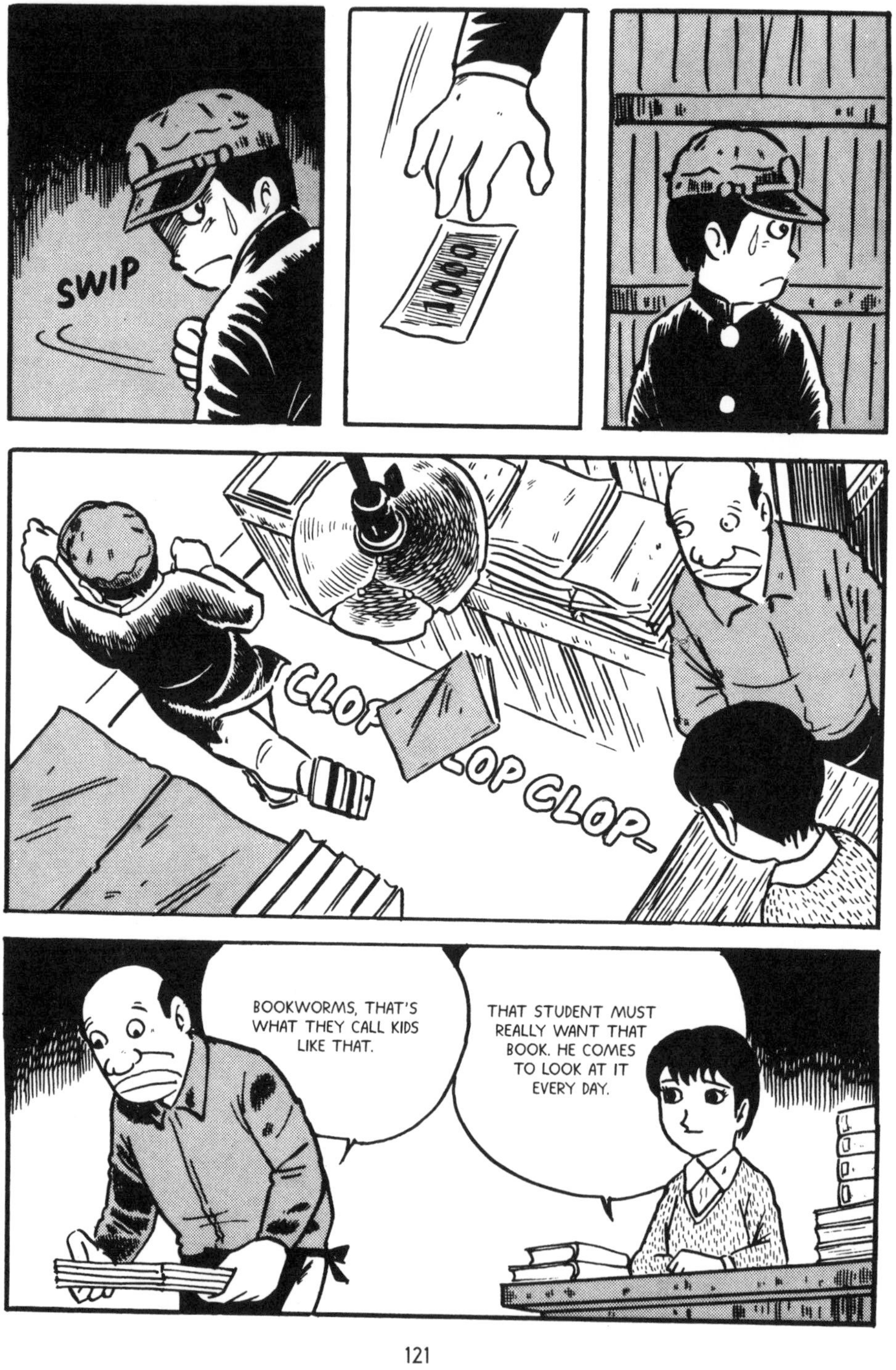
SWIP
1000
CLOP CLOP CLOP-
THAT STUDENT MUST REALLY WANT THAT BOOK. HE COMES TO LOOK AT IT EVERY DAY.
BOOKWORMS, THAT'S WHAT THEY CALL KIDS LIKE THAT.

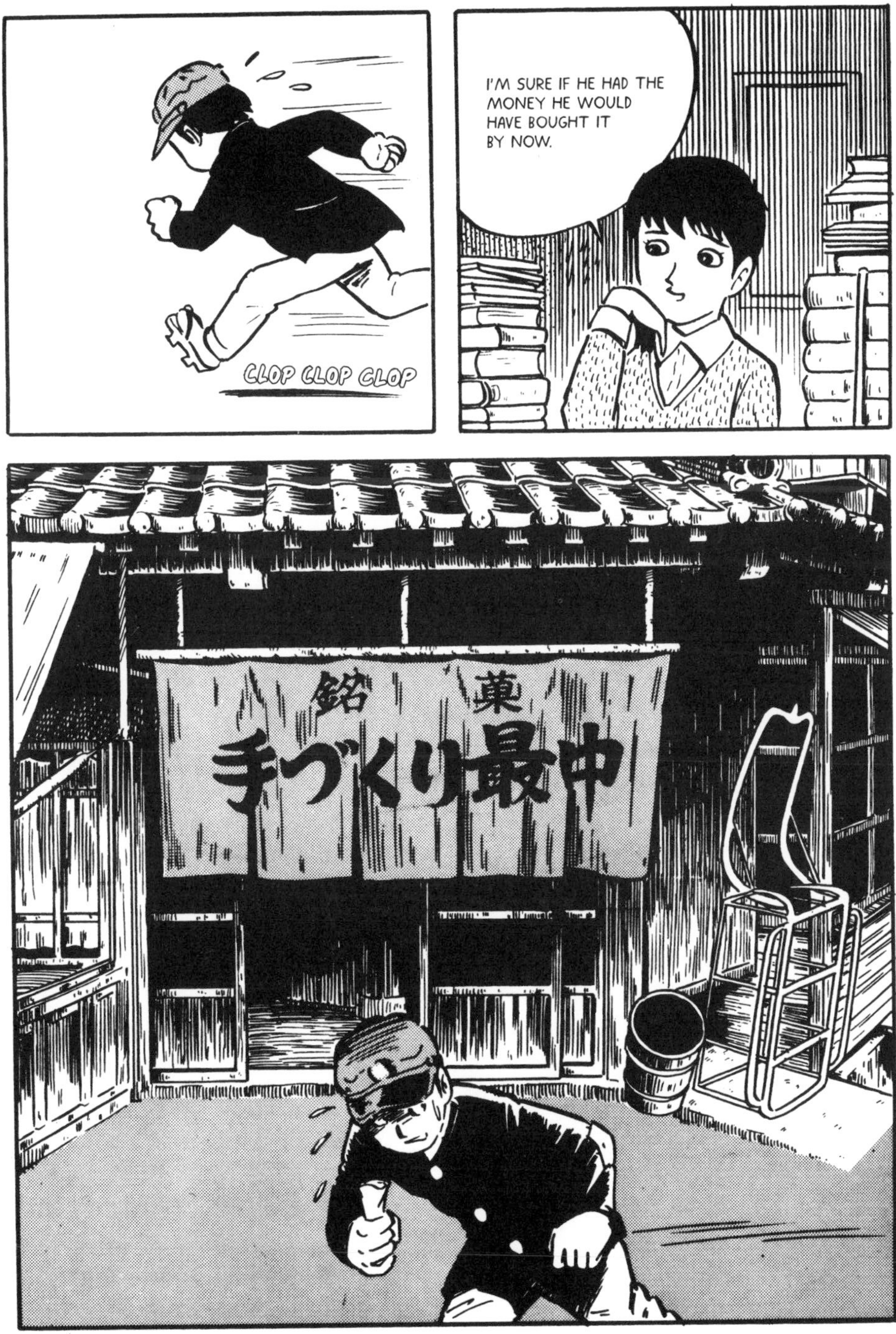
I'M SURE IF HE HAD THE MONEY HE WOULD HAVE BOUGHT IT BY NOW.
CLOP CLOP CLOP
銘菓
手づくり最中

SIGN: CONFECTIONARY,
HANDMADE BEAN-JAM WAFERS

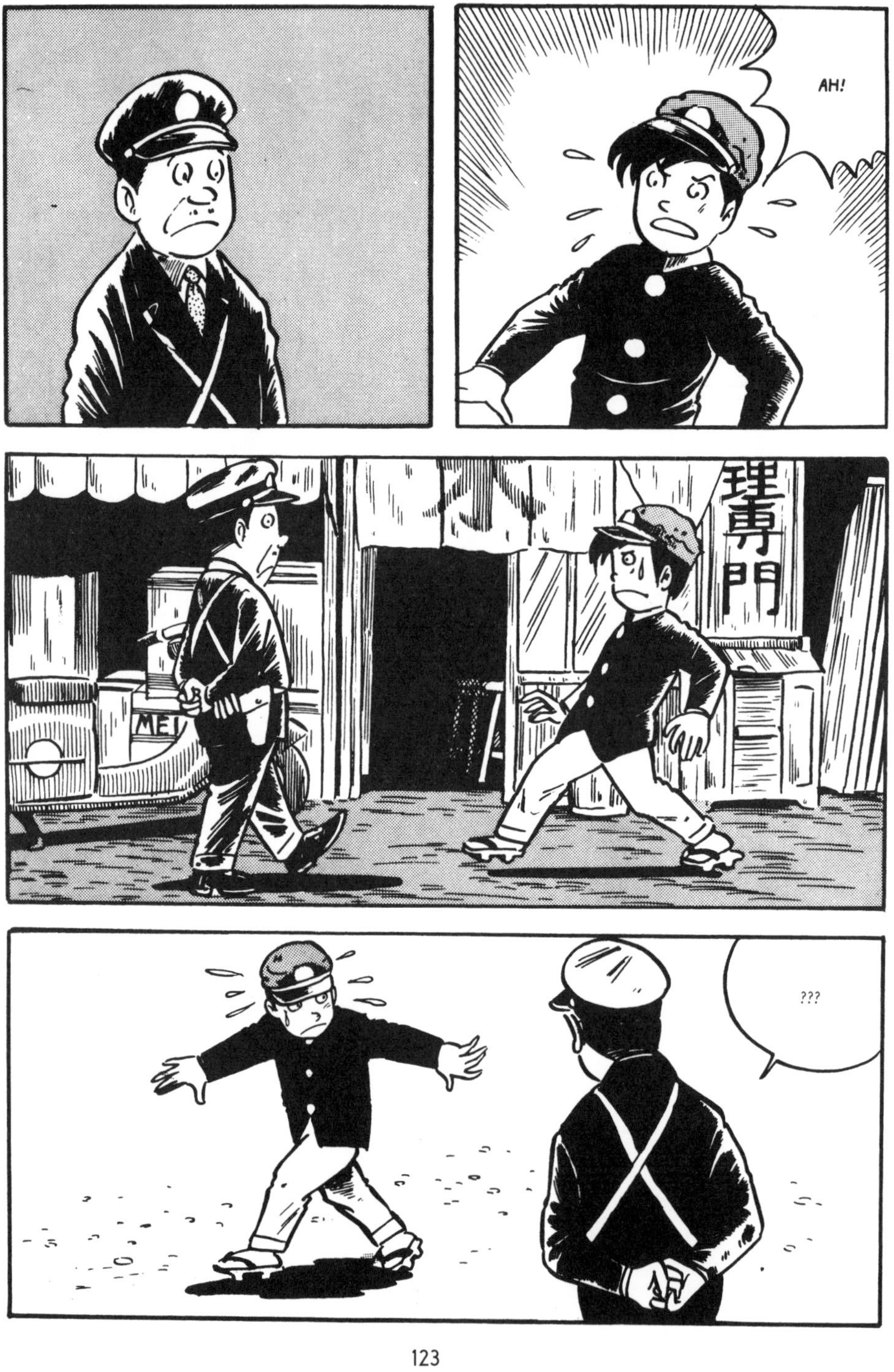
AH!
理専門
MEI
???

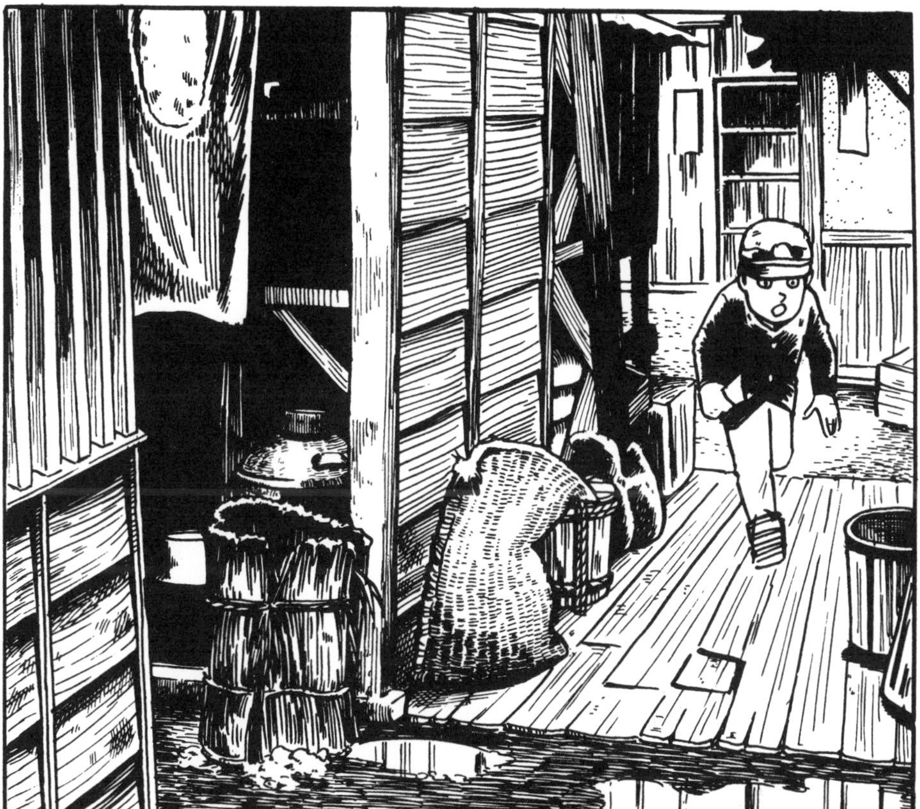

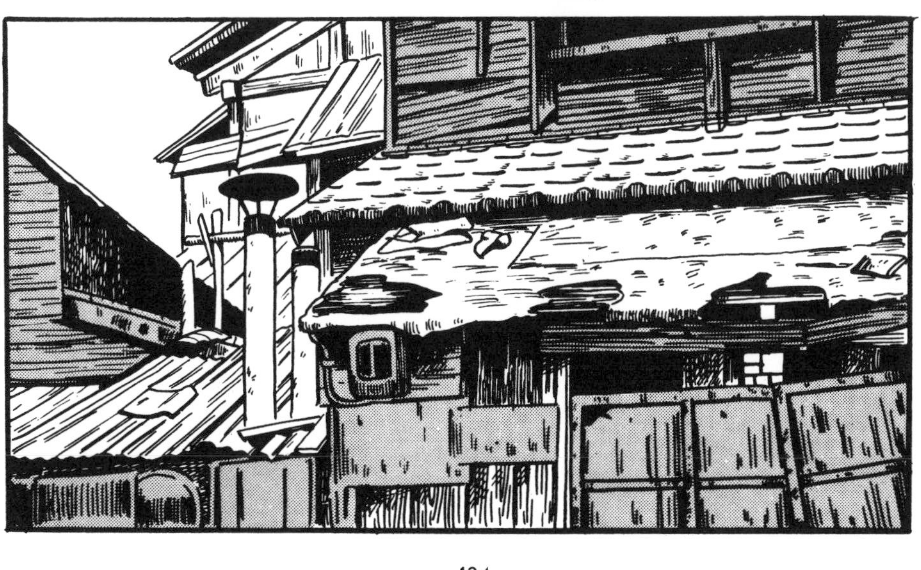

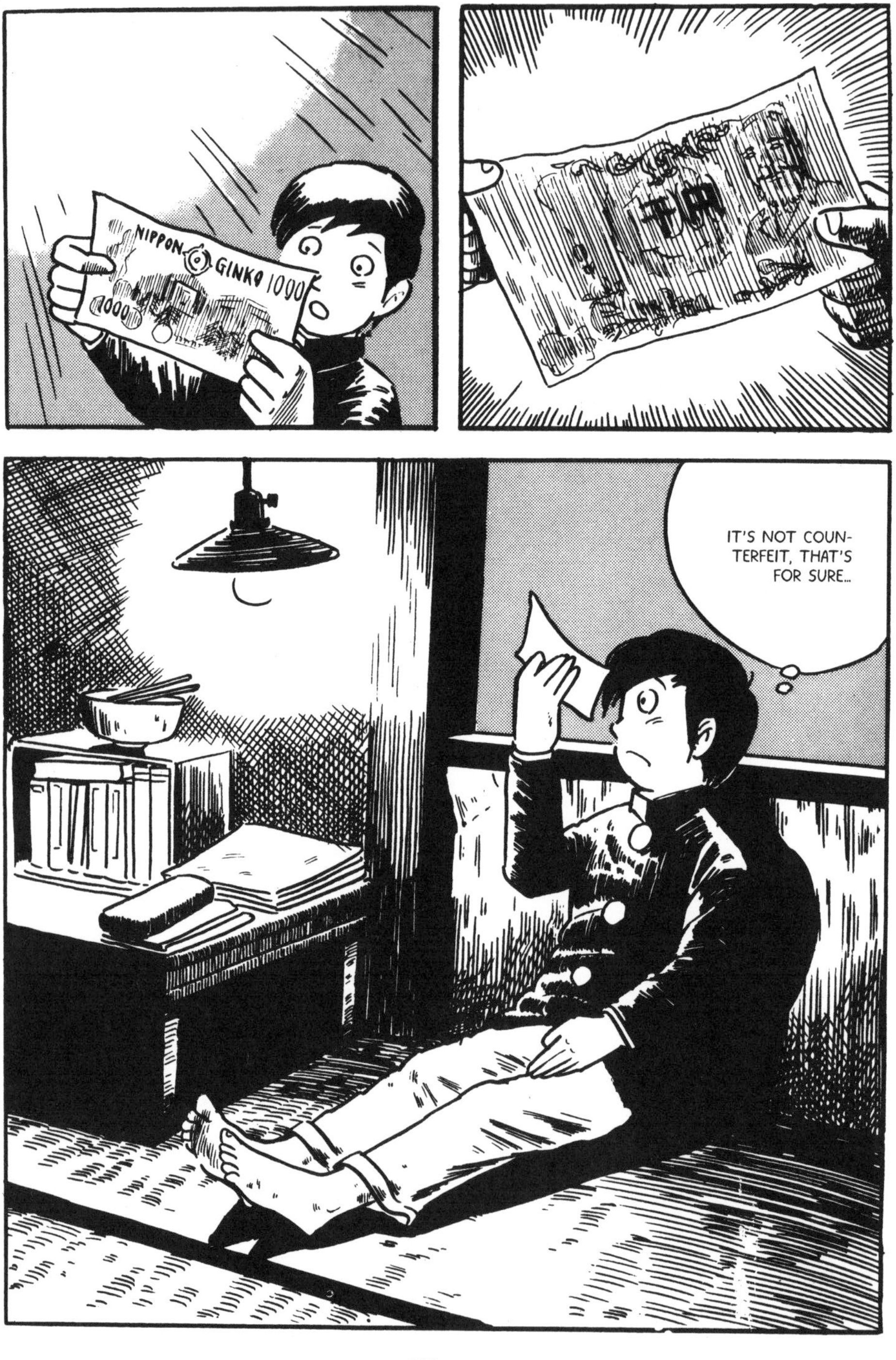
千円
NIPPON GINKO 1000
IT'S NOT COUN-
TERFEIT, THAT'S
FOR SURE...

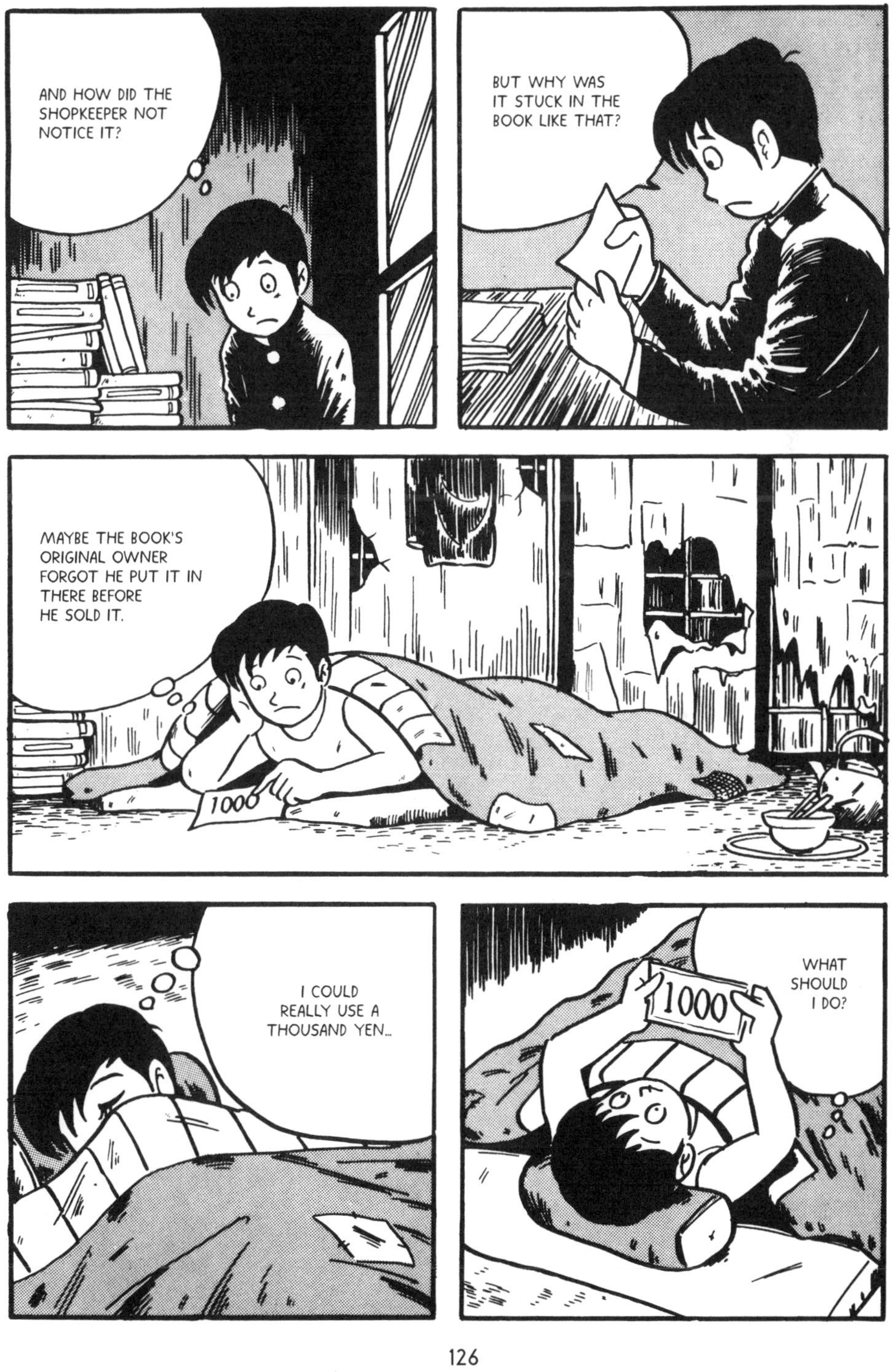
BUT WHY WAS IT STUCK IN THE BOOK LIKE THAT?
AND HOW DID THE SHOPKEEPER NOT NOTICE IT?
MAYBE THE BOOK'S ORIGINAL OWNER FORGOT HE PUT IT IN THERE BEFORE HE SOLD IT.
1000
1000
WHAT SHOULD I DO?
I COULD REALLY USE A THOUSAND YEN...

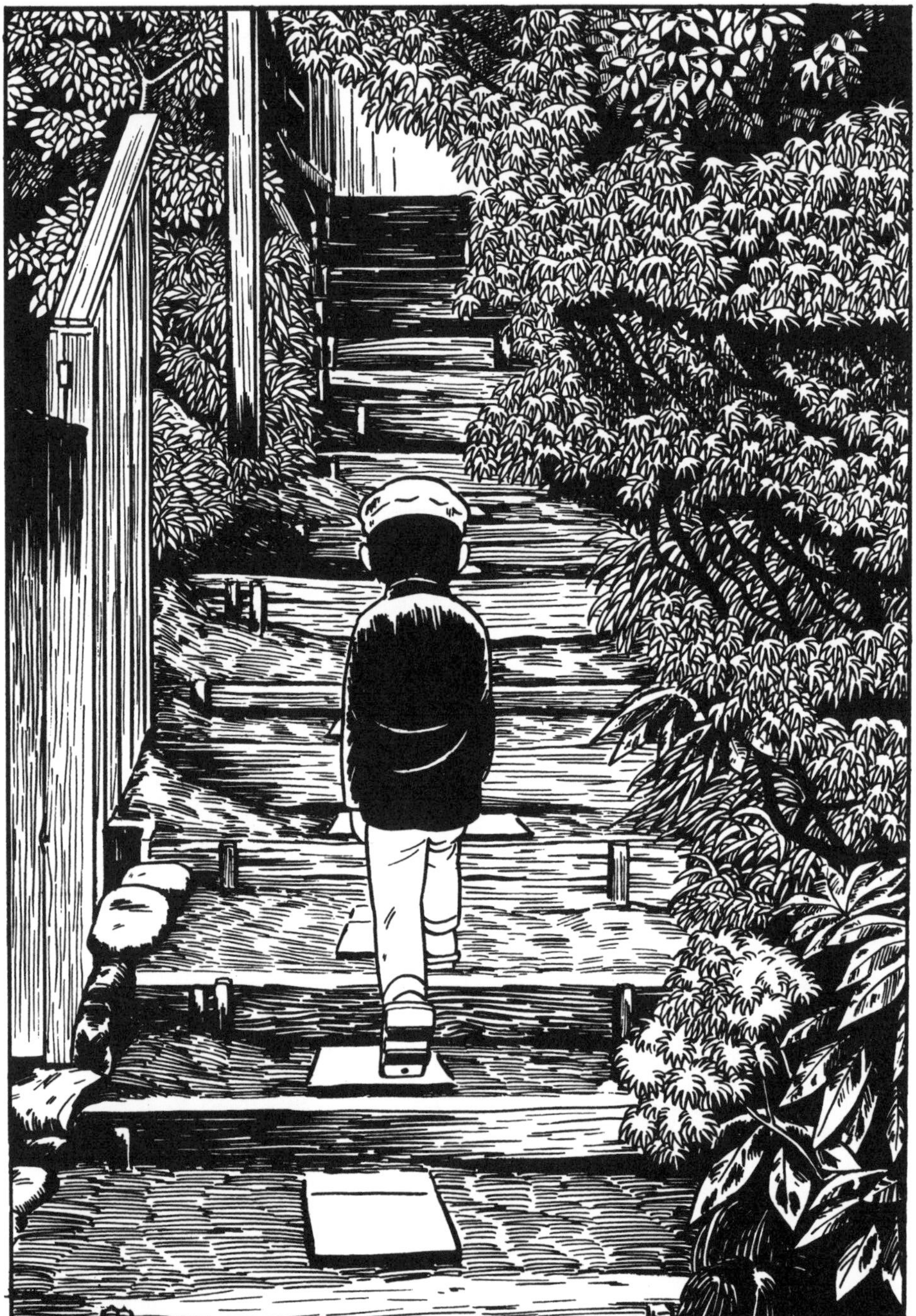

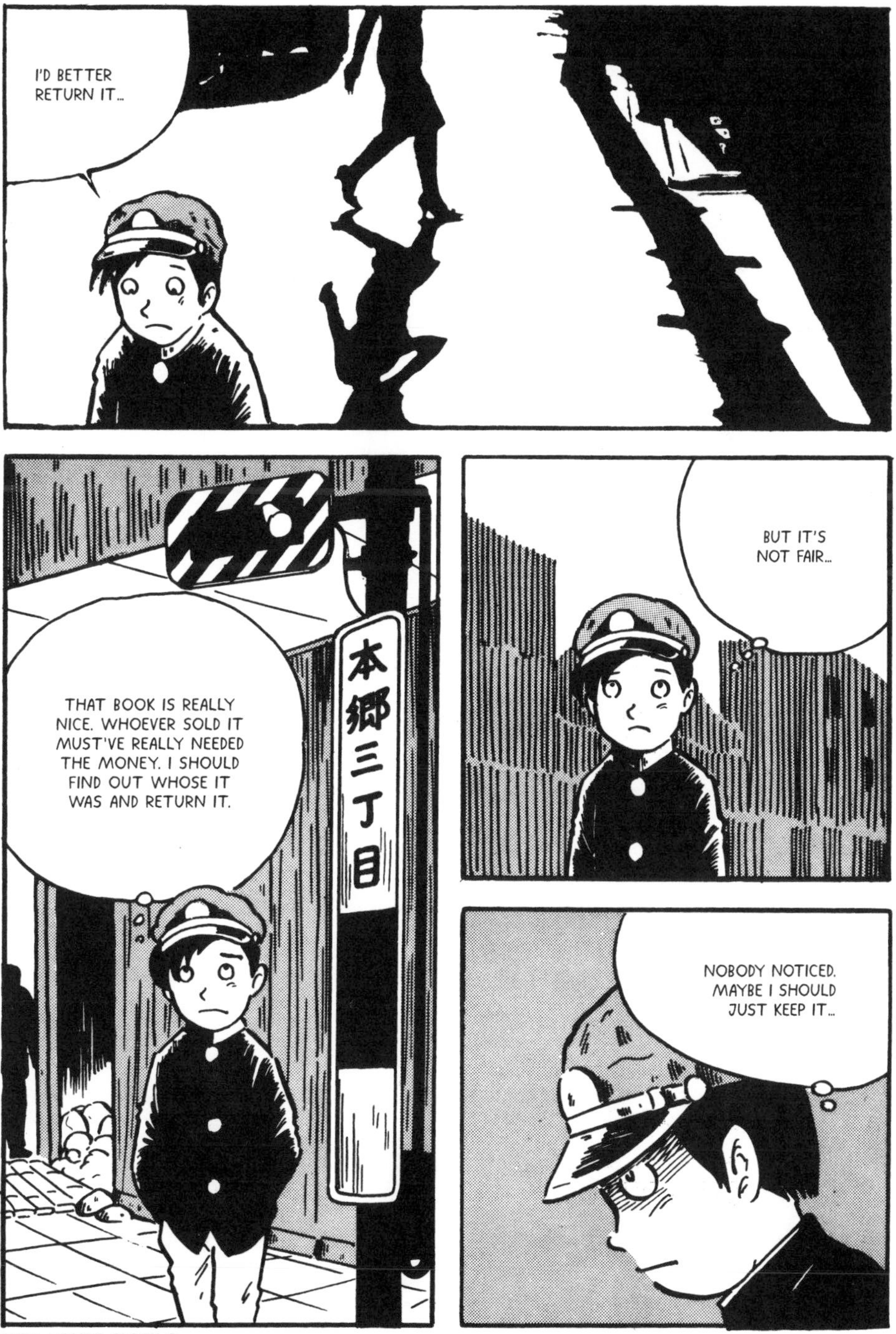
I'D BETTER RETURN IT...
BUT IT'S NOT FAIR...
NOBODY NOTICED. MAYBE I SHOULD JUST KEEP IT...
本郷三丁目
THAT BOOK IS REALLY NICE. WHOEVER SOLD IT MUST'VE REALLY NEEDED THE MONEY. I SHOULD FIND OUT WHOSE IT WAS AND RETURN IT.

SIGN: HONGO BLOCK 3

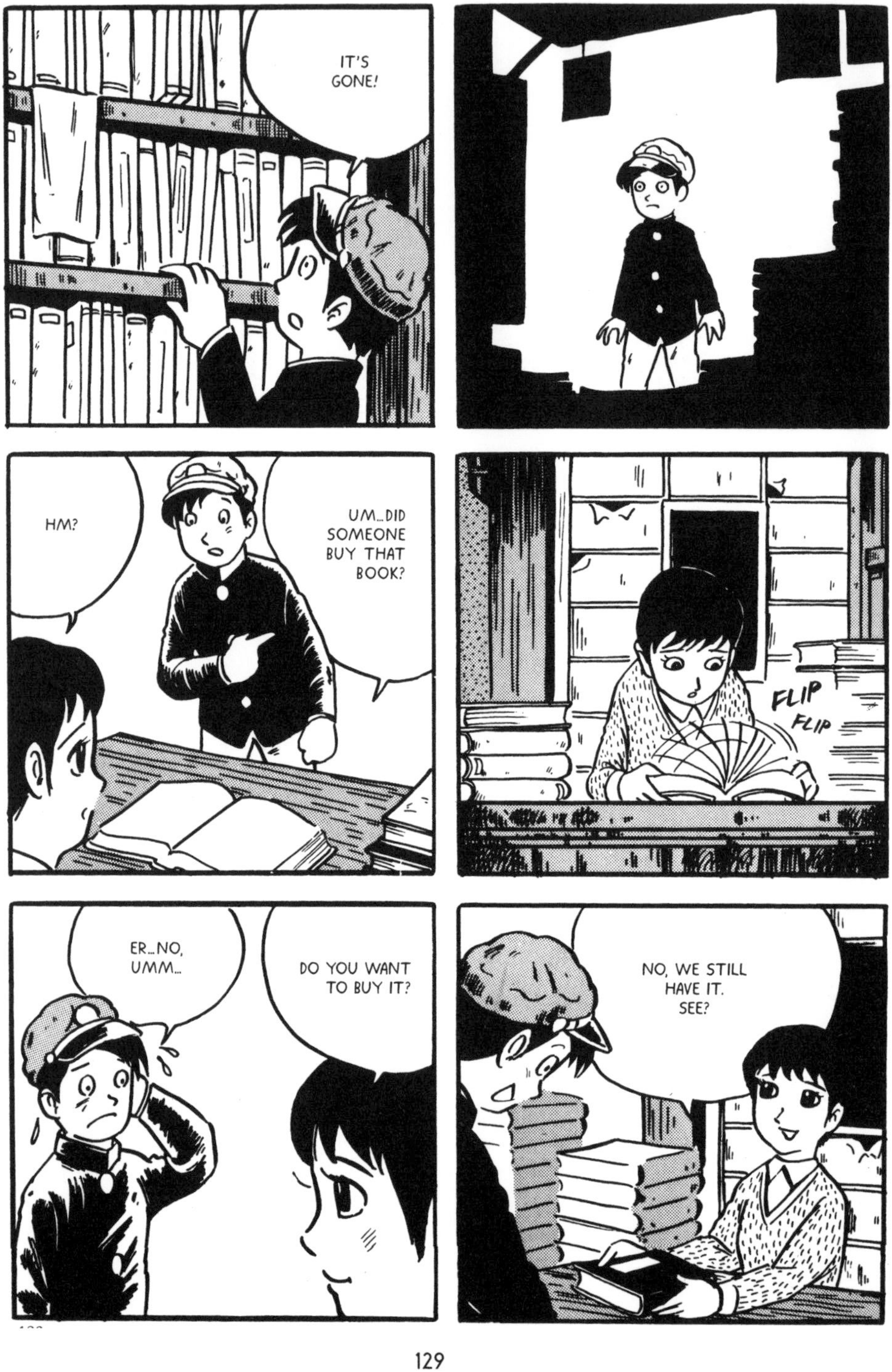
IT'S GONE!
FLIP
FLIP
UM...DID SOMEONE BUY THAT BOOK?
HM?
NO, WE STILL HAVE IT. SEE?
DO YOU WANT TO BUY IT?
ER...NO, UMM...

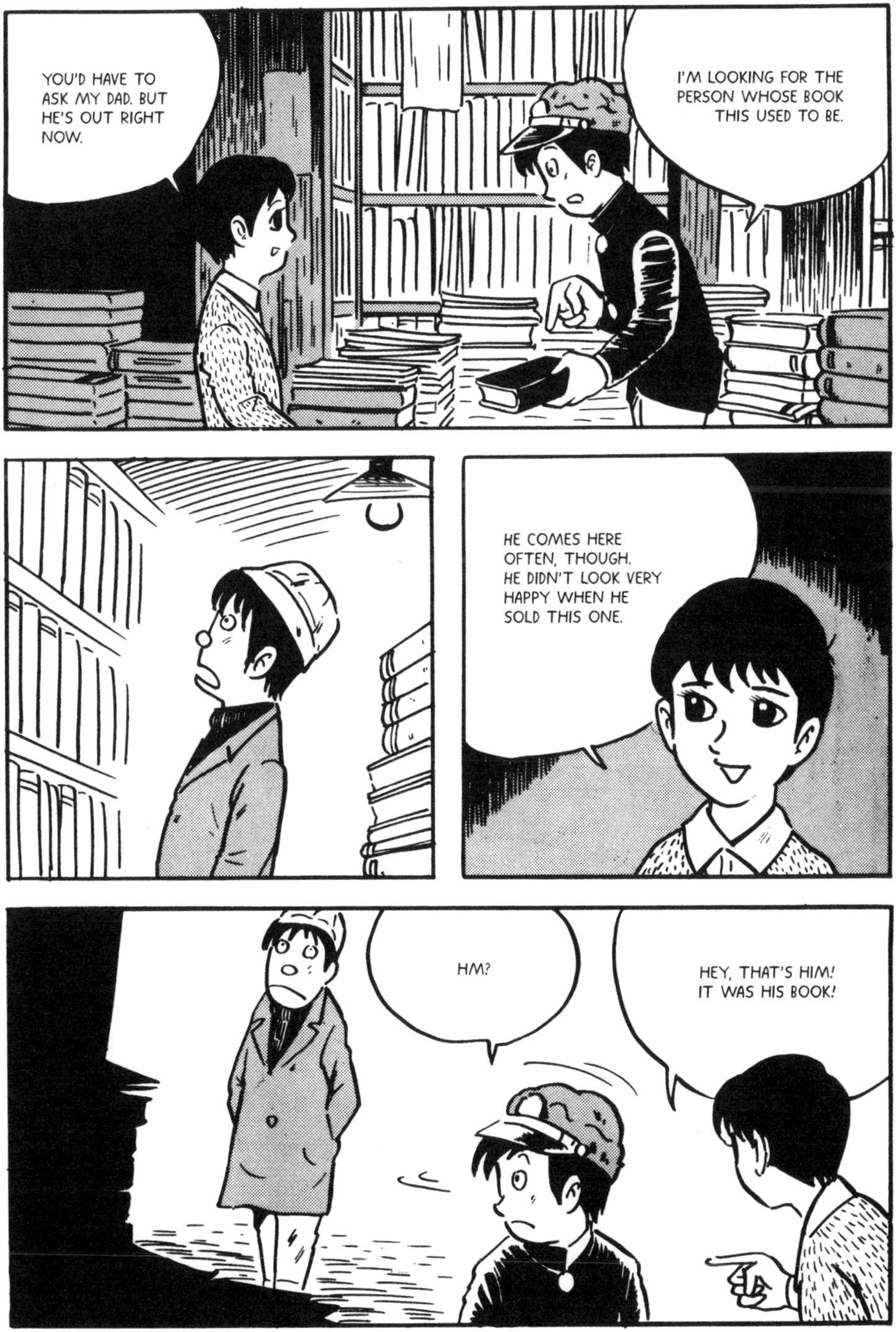
I'M LOOKING FOR THE PERSON WHOSE BOOK THIS USED TO BE.
YOU'D HAVE TO ASK MY DAD. BUT HE'S OUT RIGHT NOW.
HE COMES HERE OFTEN, THOUGH. HE DIDN'T LOOK VERY HAPPY WHEN HE SOLD THIS ONE.
HEY, THAT'S HIM! IT WAS HIS BOOK!
HM?

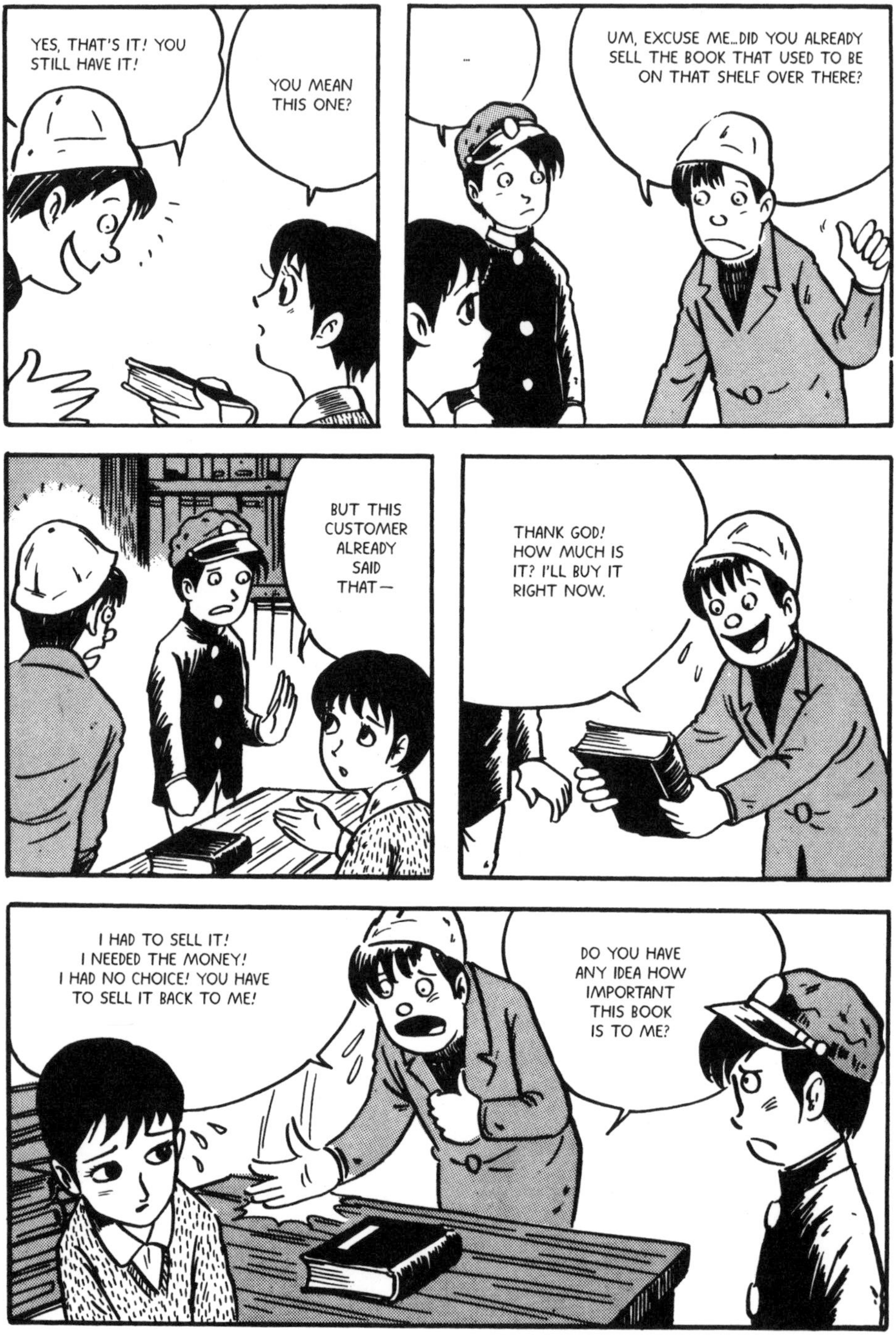
UM, EXCUSE ME...DID YOU ALREADY SELL THE BOOK THAT USED TO BE ON THAT SHELF OVER THERE?
...
YOU MEAN THIS ONE?
YES, THAT'S IT! YOU STILL HAVE IT!
THANK GOD! HOW MUCH IS IT? I'LL BUY IT RIGHT NOW.
BUT THIS CUSTOMER ALREADY SAID THAT—
DO YOU HAVE ANY IDEA HOW IMPORTANT THIS BOOK IS TO ME?
I HAD TO SELL IT! I NEEDED THE MONEY! I HAD NO CHOICE! YOU HAVE TO SELL IT BACK TO ME!

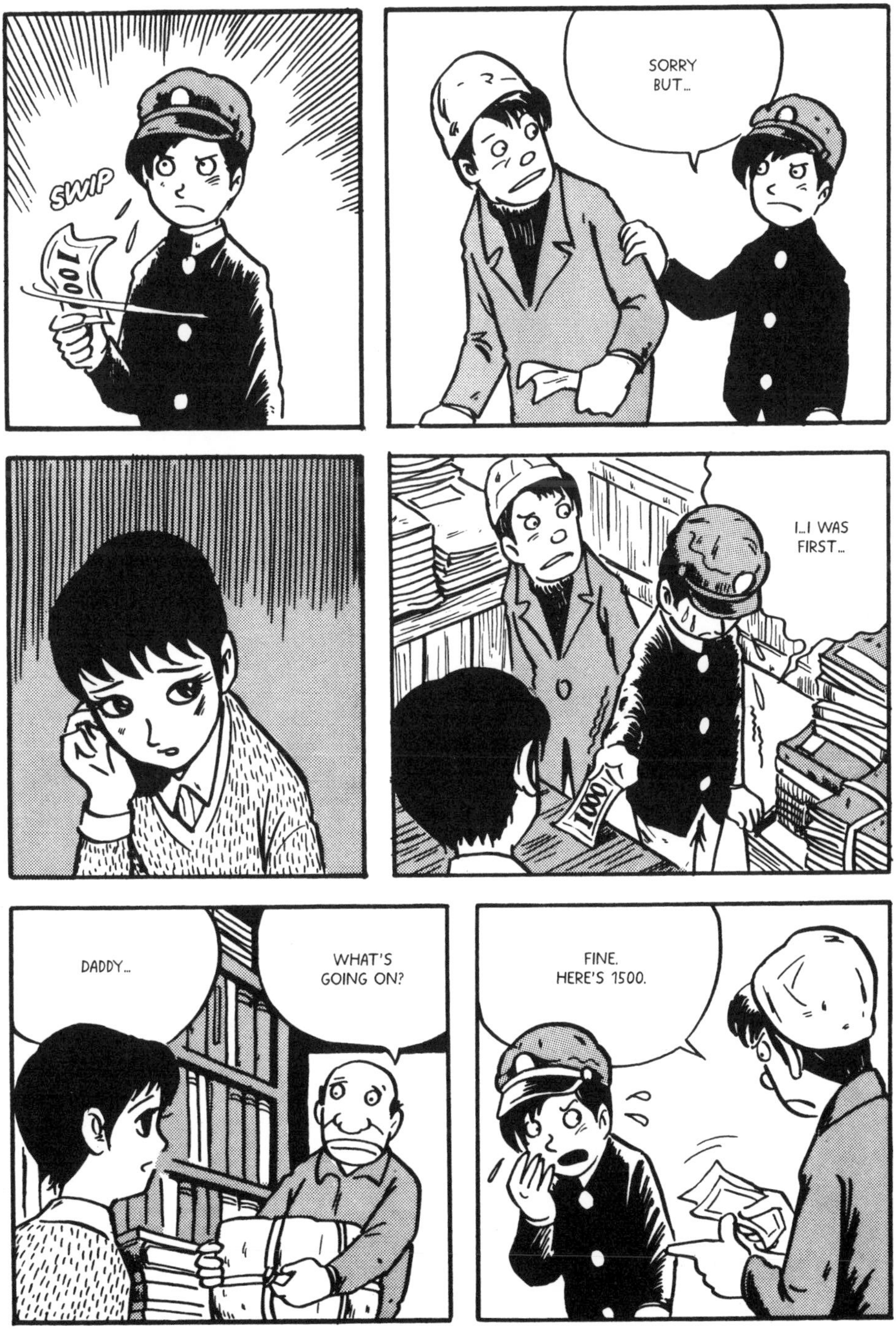
SORRY BUT...
SWIP
I...I WAS FIRST...
FINE. HERE'S 1500.
WHAT'S GOING ON?
DADDY...

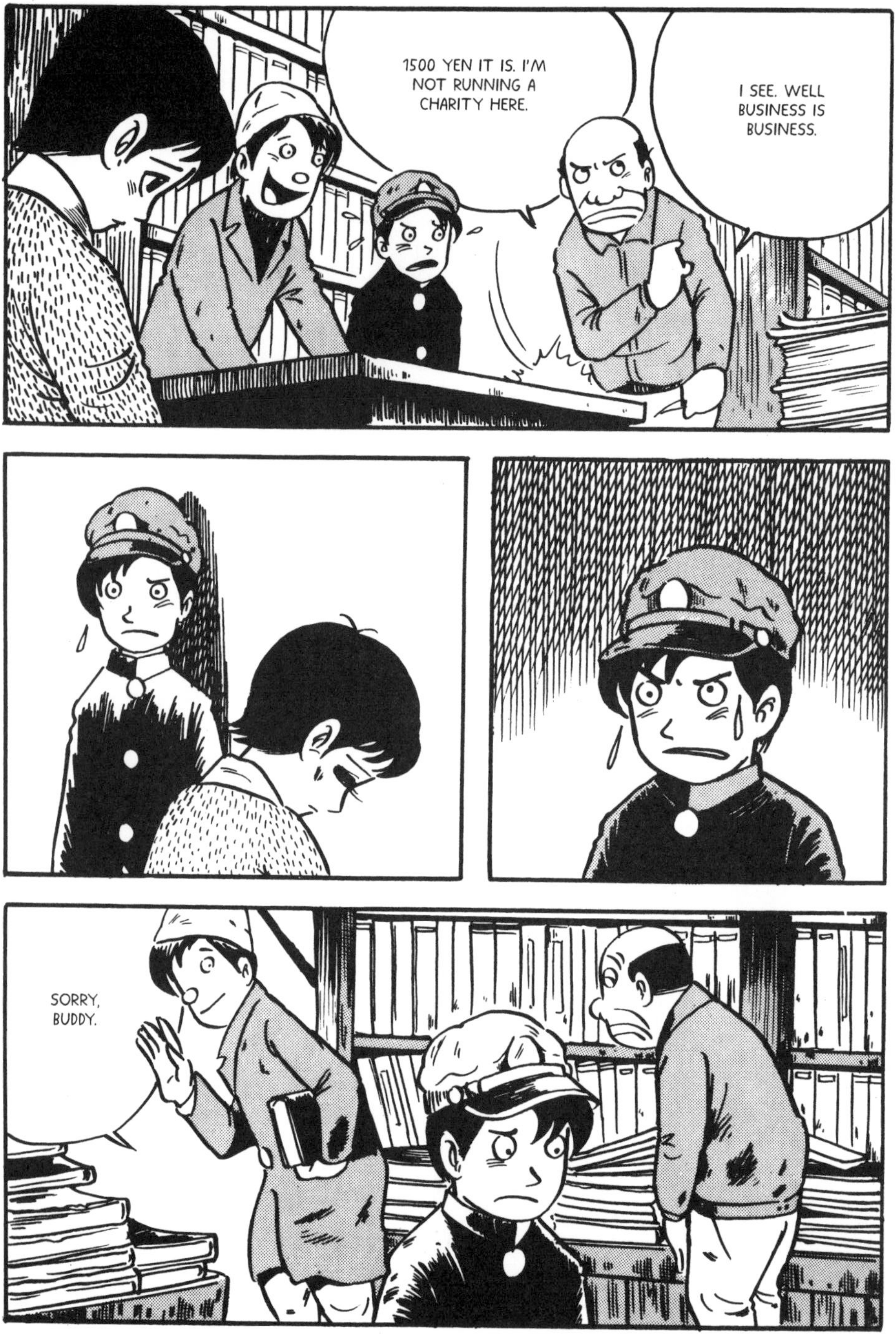
I SEE. WELL BUSINESS IS BUSINESS.
1500 YEN IT IS. I'M NOT RUNNING A CHARITY HERE.
SORRY, BUDDY.

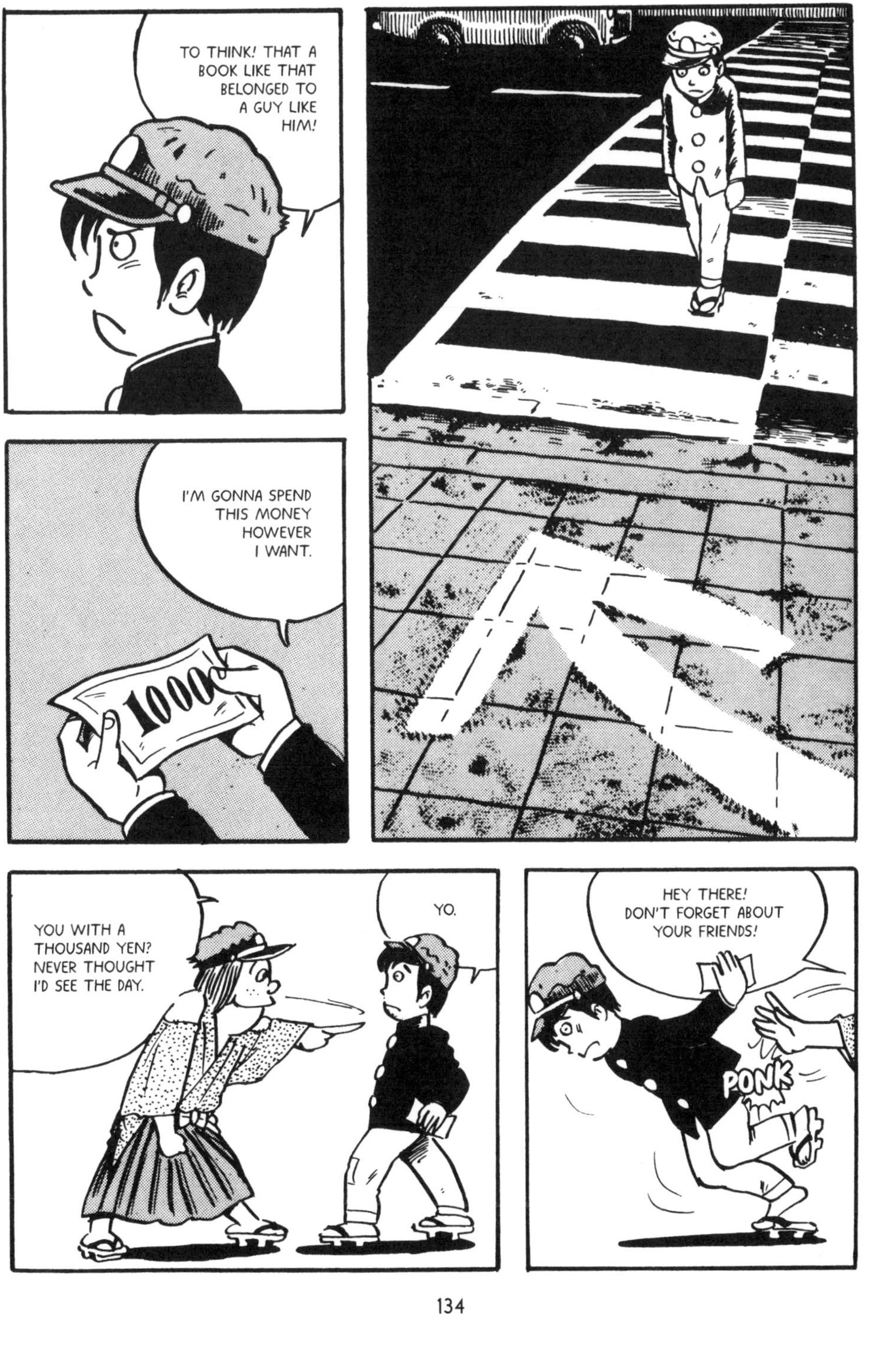
TO THINK! THAT A BOOK LIKE THAT BELONGED TO A GUY LIKE HIM!
I'M GONNA SPEND THIS MONEY HOWEVER I WANT.
1000
HEY THERE! DON'T FORGET ABOUT YOUR FRIENDS!
PONK
YO.
YOU WITH A THOUSAND YEN? NEVER THOUGHT I'D SEE THE DAY.

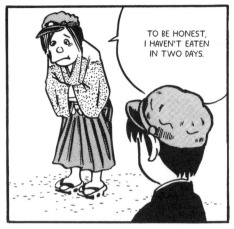

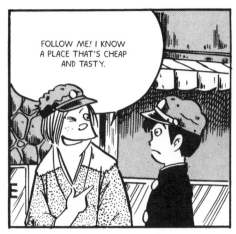

FOLLOW ME! I KNOW A PLACE THAT'S CHEAP AND TASTY.
TO BE HONEST, I HAVEN'T EATEN IN TWO DAYS.
SO C'MON! TREAT ME!
NO... I CAN'T...
WHA?!
HEY! YOU JUST GONNA LET ME STARVE TO DEATH?
FINE, YOU TIGHT-WAD! I WAS WRONG ABOUT YOU!

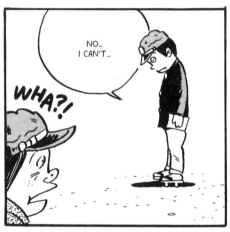

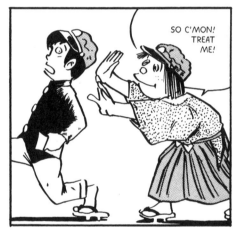

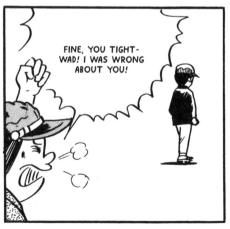

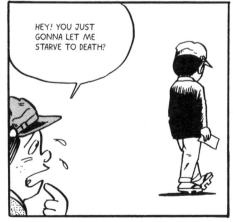

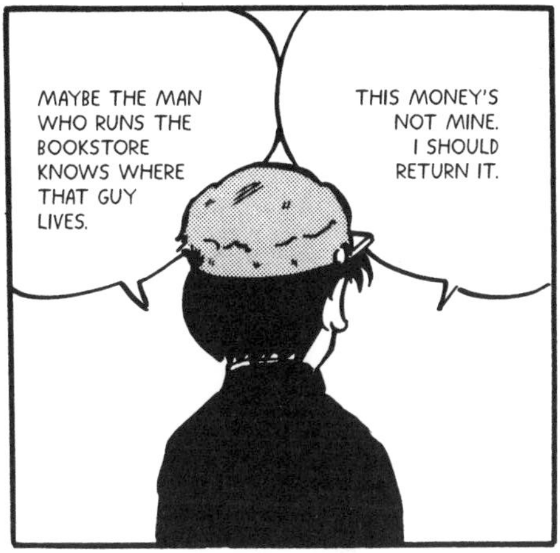
THIS MONEY'S NOT MINE. I SHOULD RETURN IT.
MAYBE THE MAN WHO RUNS THE BOOKSTORE KNOWS WHERE THAT GUY LIVES.

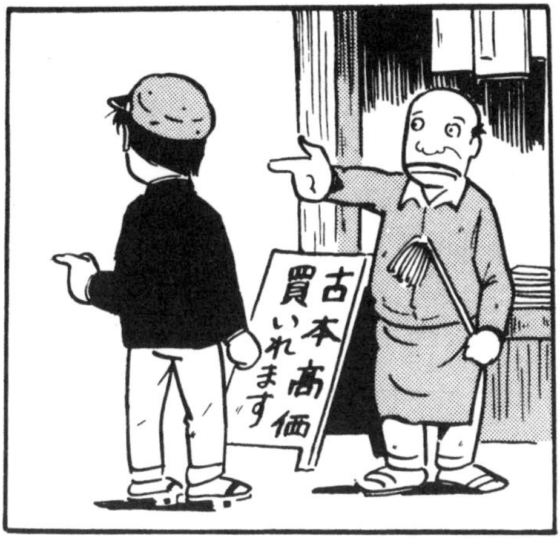
古本高価買いれます

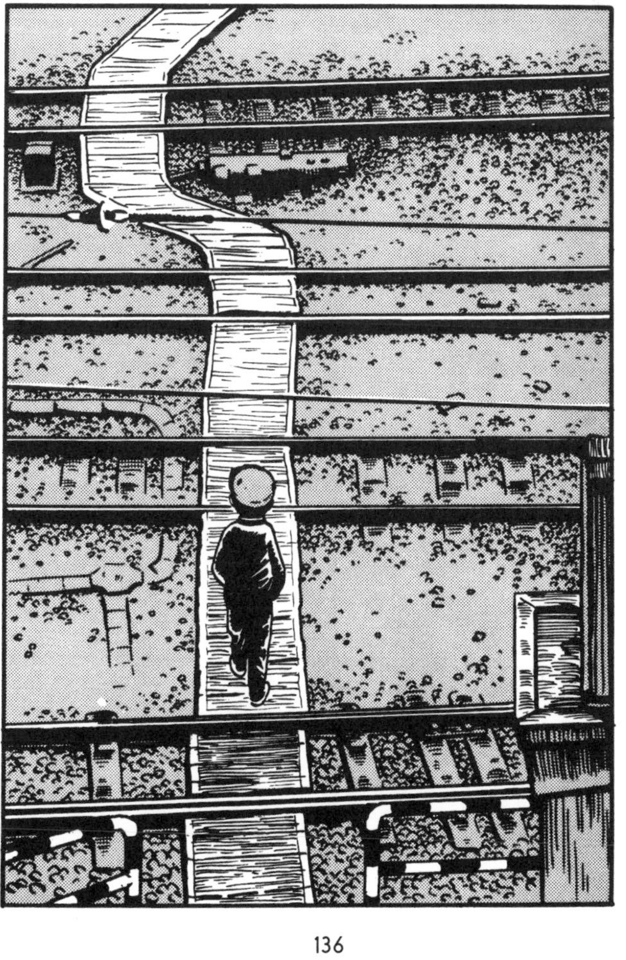

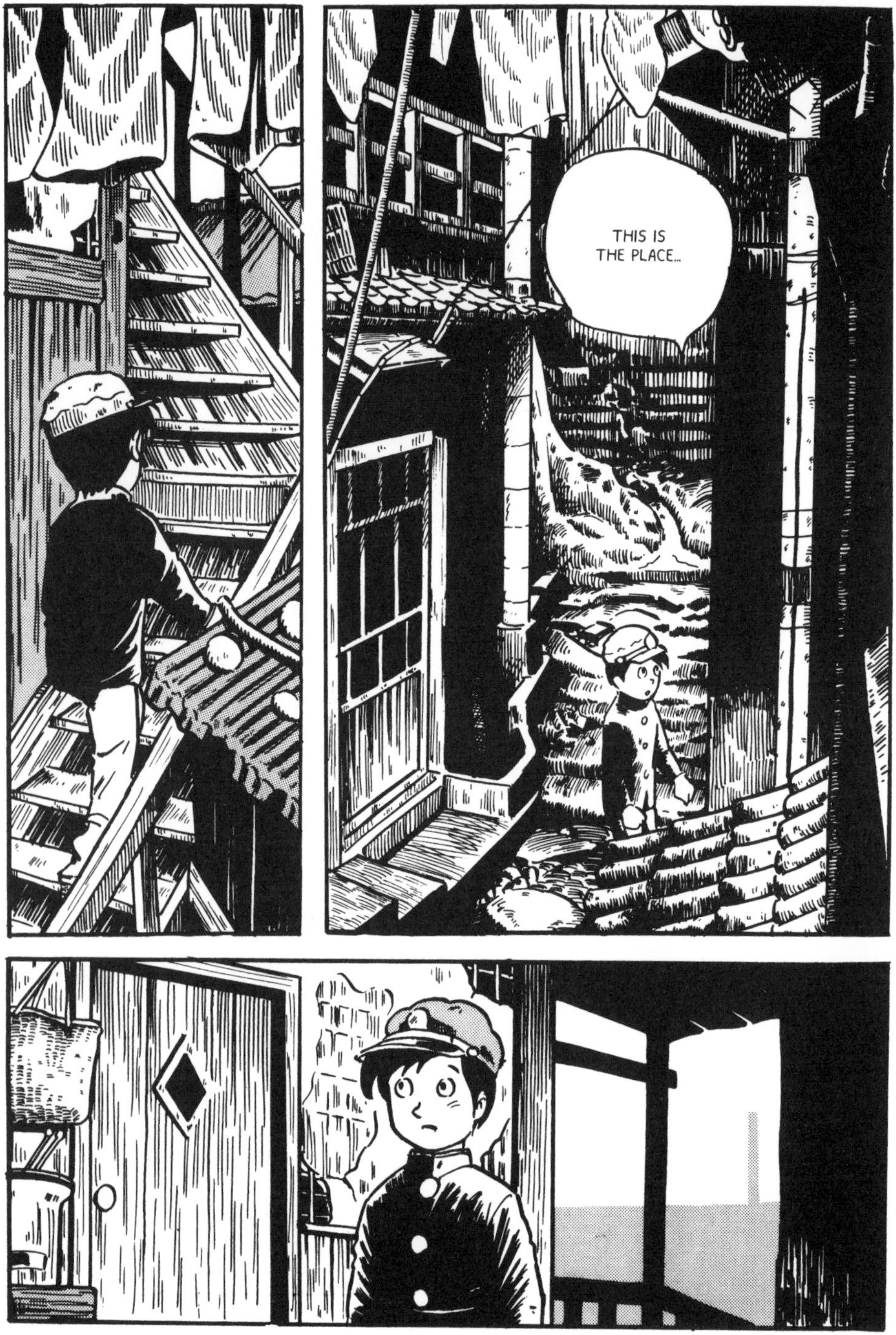
THIS IS
THE PLACE...

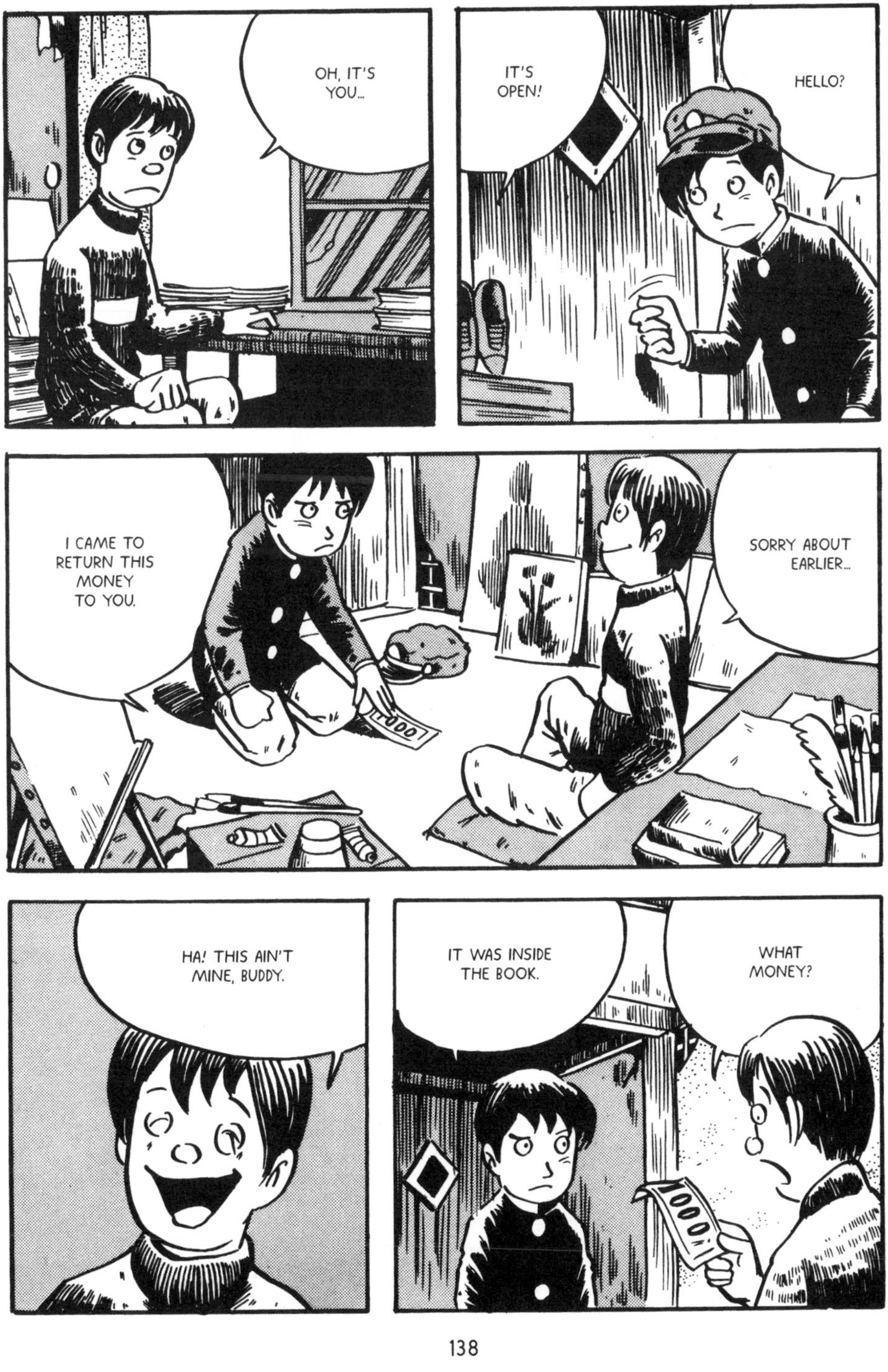
HELLO?
IT'S OPEN!
OH, IT'S YOU...
SORRY ABOUT EARLIER...
I CAME TO RETURN THIS MONEY TO YOU.
WHAT MONEY?
IT WAS INSIDE THE BOOK.
HA! THIS AIN'T MINE, BUDDY.

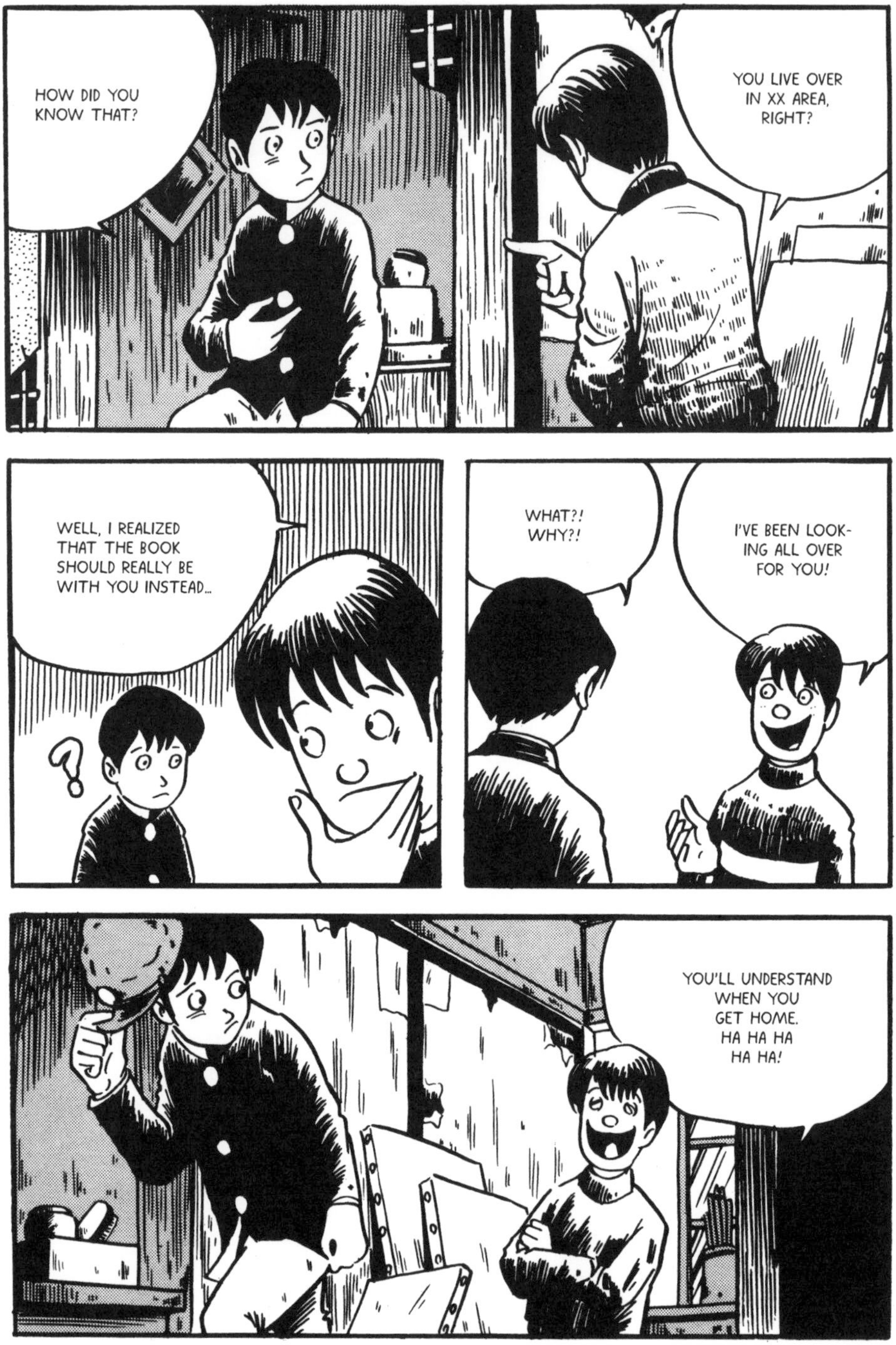
YOU LIVE OVER IN XX AREA, RIGHT?
HOW DID YOU KNOW THAT?
I'VE BEEN LOOKING ALL OVER FOR YOU!
WHAT?! WHY?!
WELL, I REALIZED THAT THE BOOK SHOULD REALLY BE WITH YOU INSTEAD...
YOU'LL UNDERSTAND WHEN YOU GET HOME. HA HA HA HA HA!

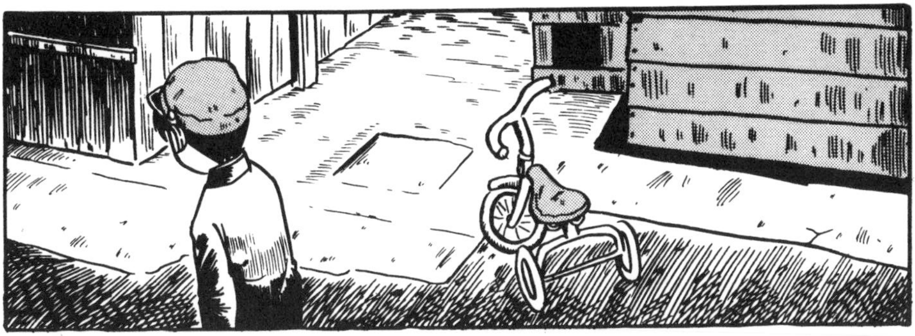

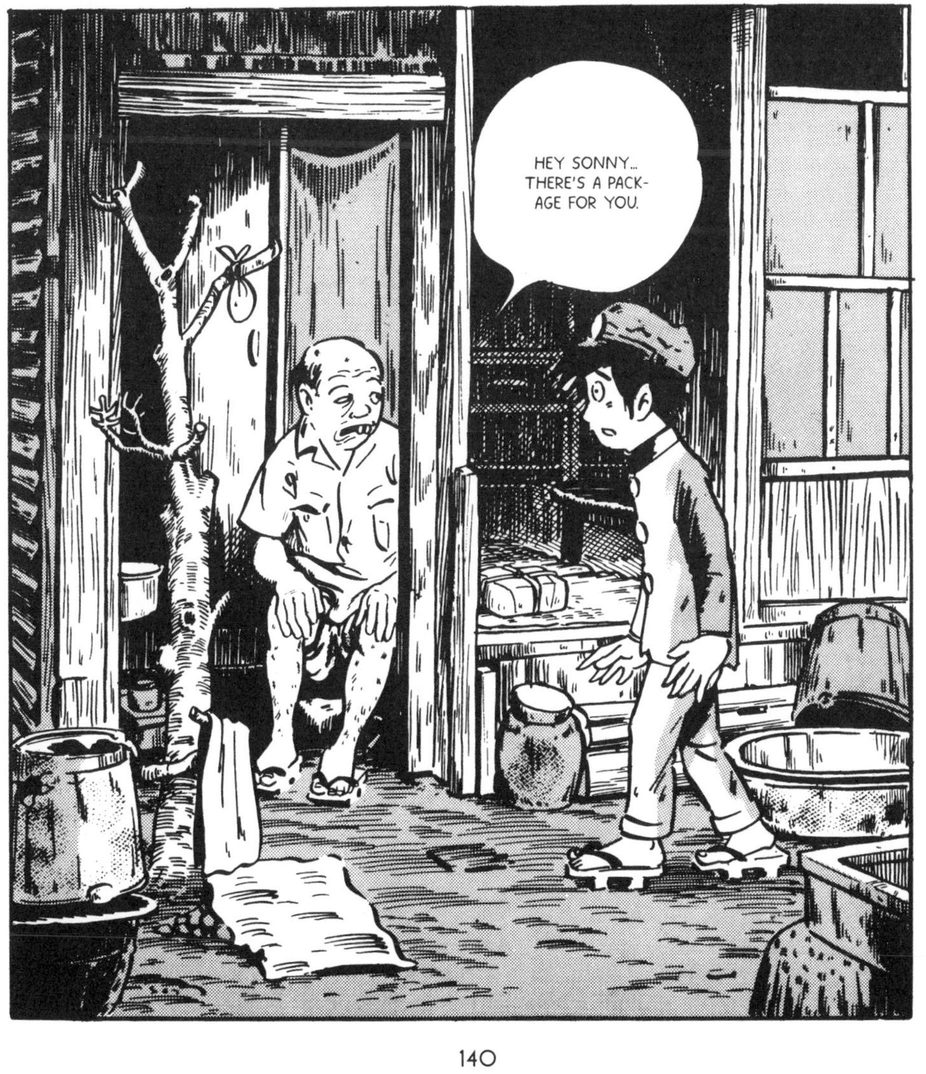
HEY SONNY... THERE'S A PACK-AGE FOR YOU.

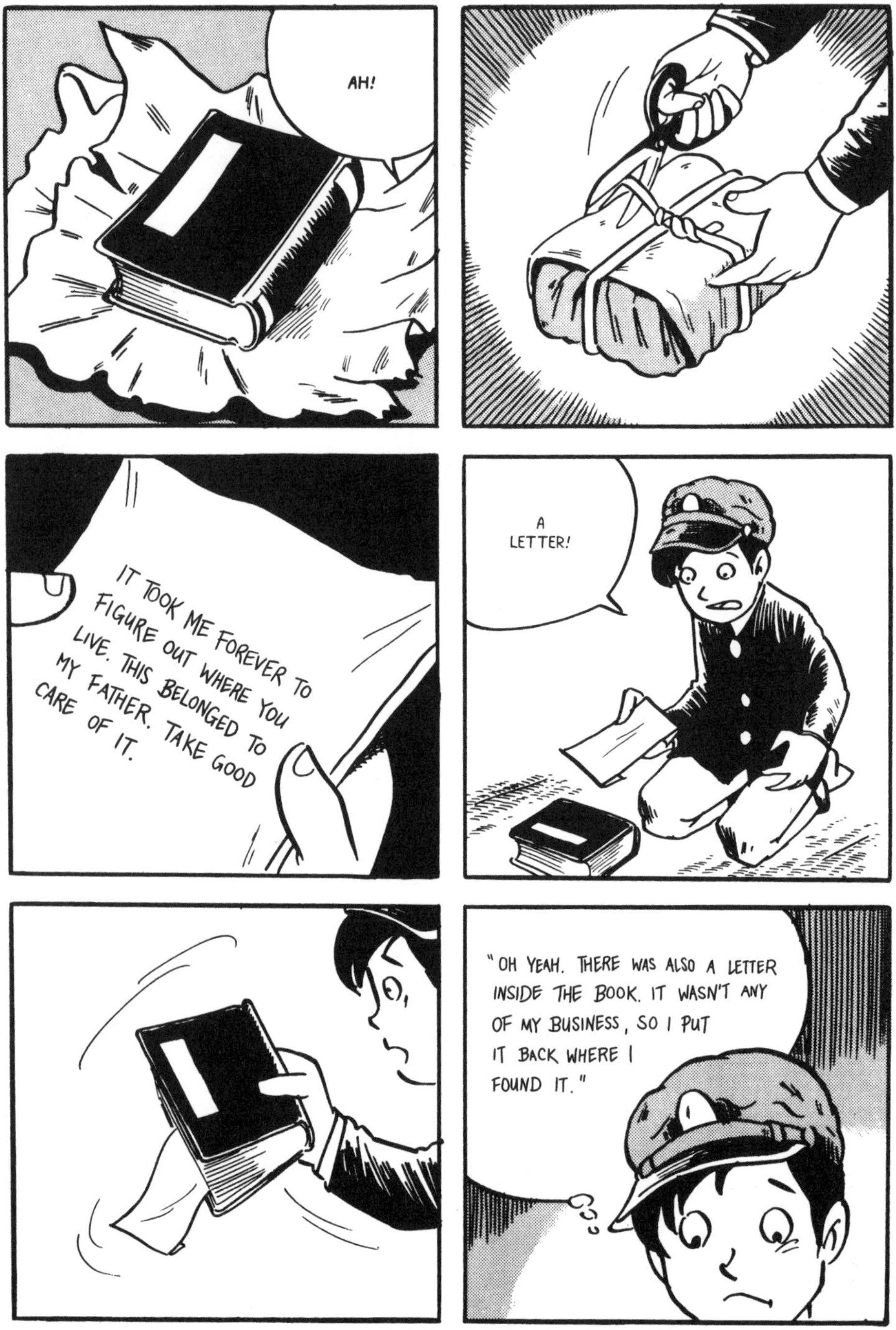
AH!
A LETTER!
IT TOOK ME FOREVER TO FIGURE OUT WHERE YOU LIVE. THIS BELONGED TO MY FATHER. TAKE GOOD CARE OF IT.
"OH YEAH. THERE WAS ALSO A LETTER INSIDE THE BOOK. IT WASN'T ANY OF MY BUSINESS, SO I PUT IT BACK WHERE I FOUND IT."

"Every day I've watched you come to the shop and look longingly at this book."
"I imagine you don't have much money, so I'm putting a thousand yen note in here for you. I worked hard to save it up."
Please use it to buy the book. And don't tell my father.

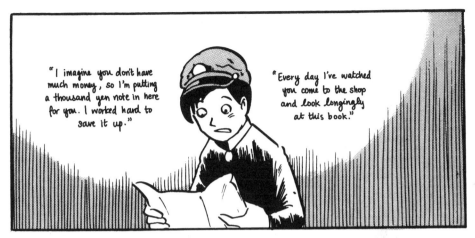

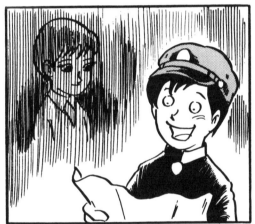

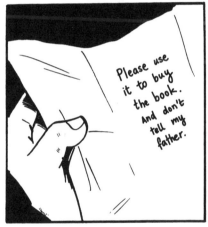

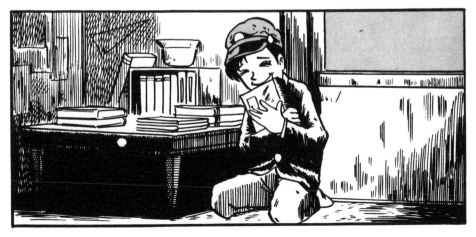

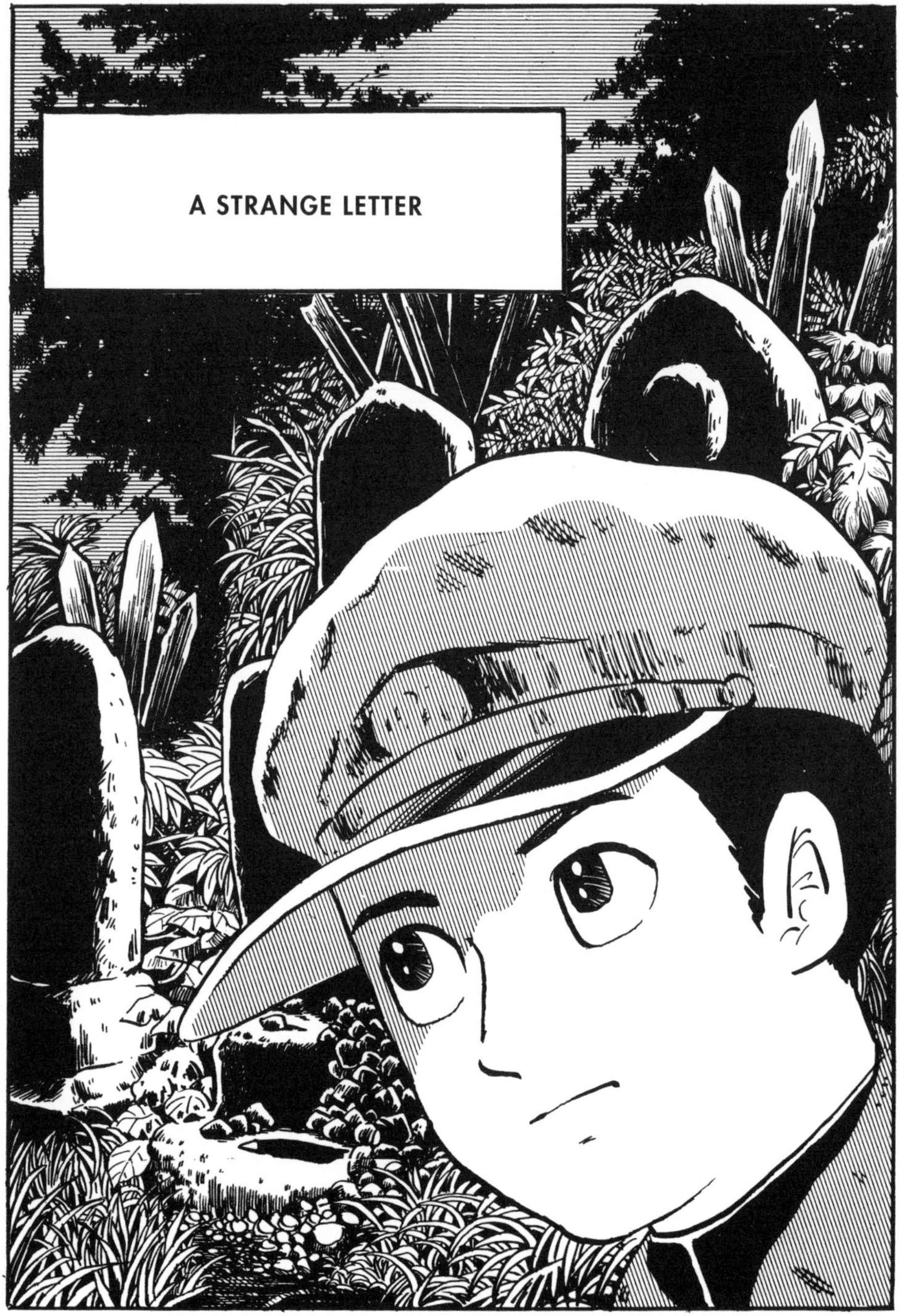
A STRANGE LETTER

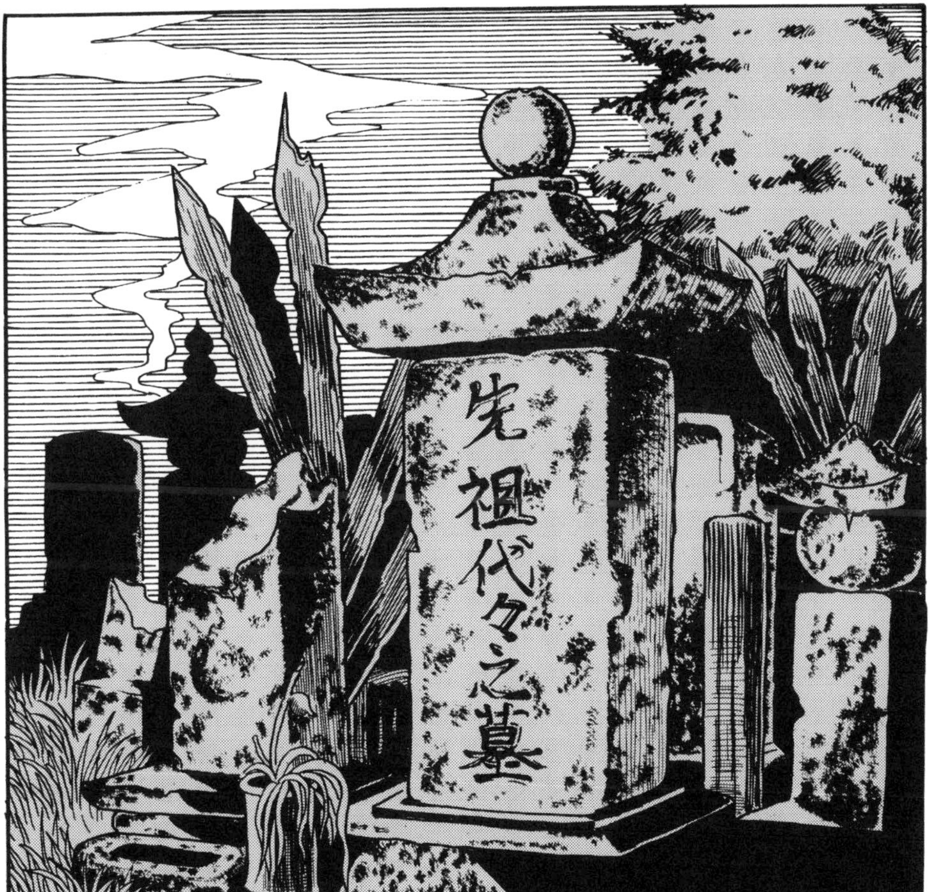
先祖代々之墓
INSCRIPTION: FAMILY GRAVE

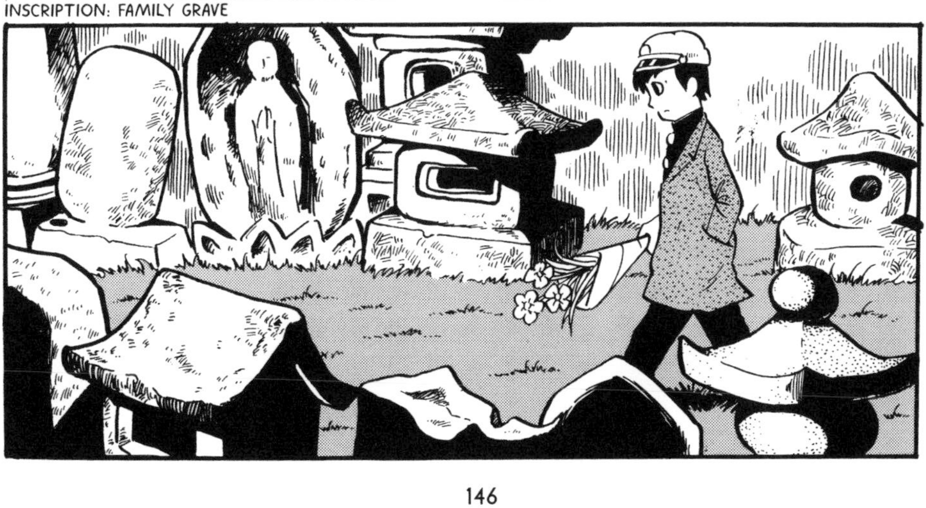

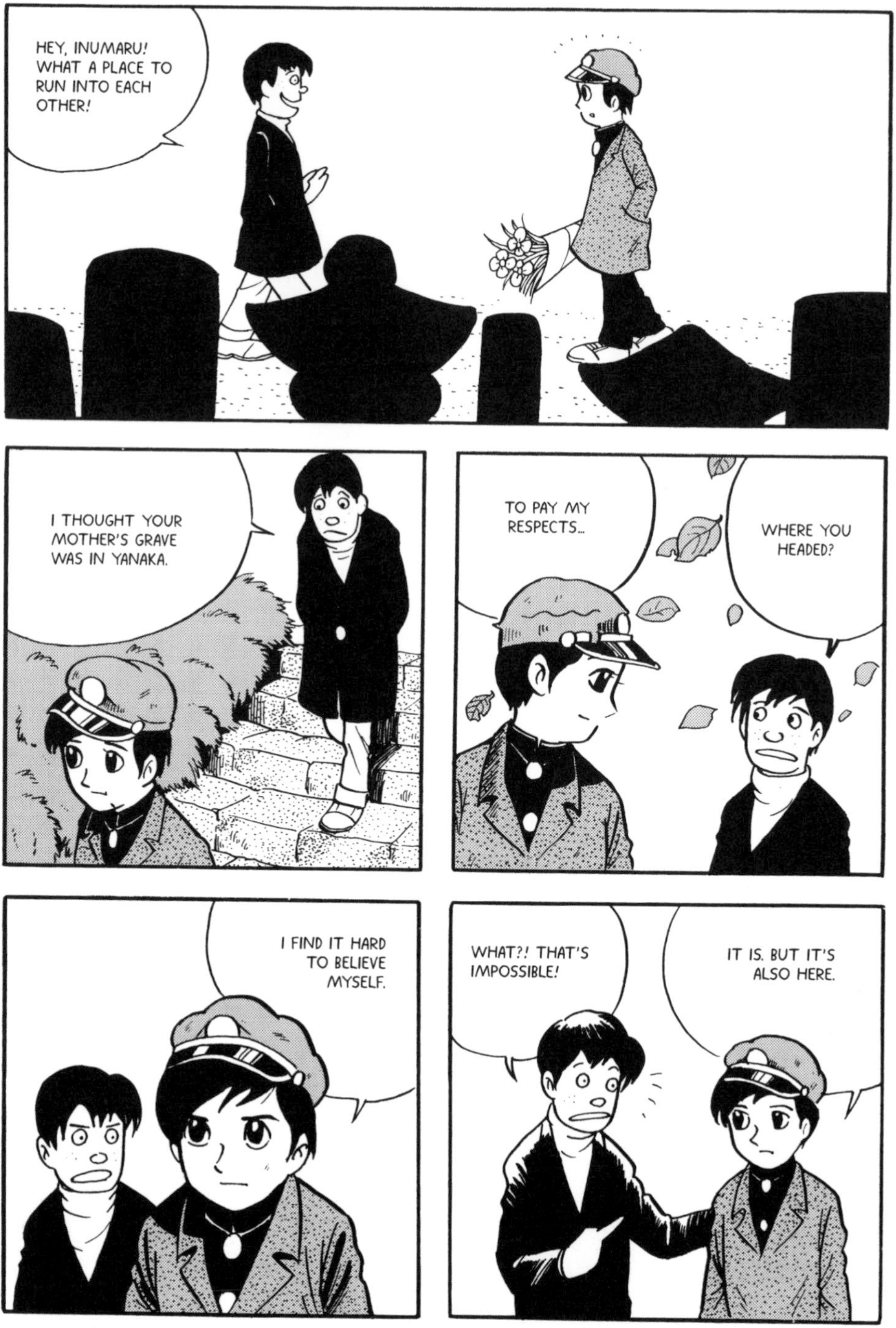
HEY, INUMARU! WHAT A PLACE TO RUN INTO EACH OTHER!
WHERE YOU HEADED?
TO PAY MY RESPECTS...
I THOUGHT YOUR MOTHER'S GRAVE WAS IN YANAKA.
IT IS. BUT IT'S ALSO HERE.
WHAT?! THAT'S IMPOSSIBLE!
I FIND IT HARD TO BELIEVE MYSELF.

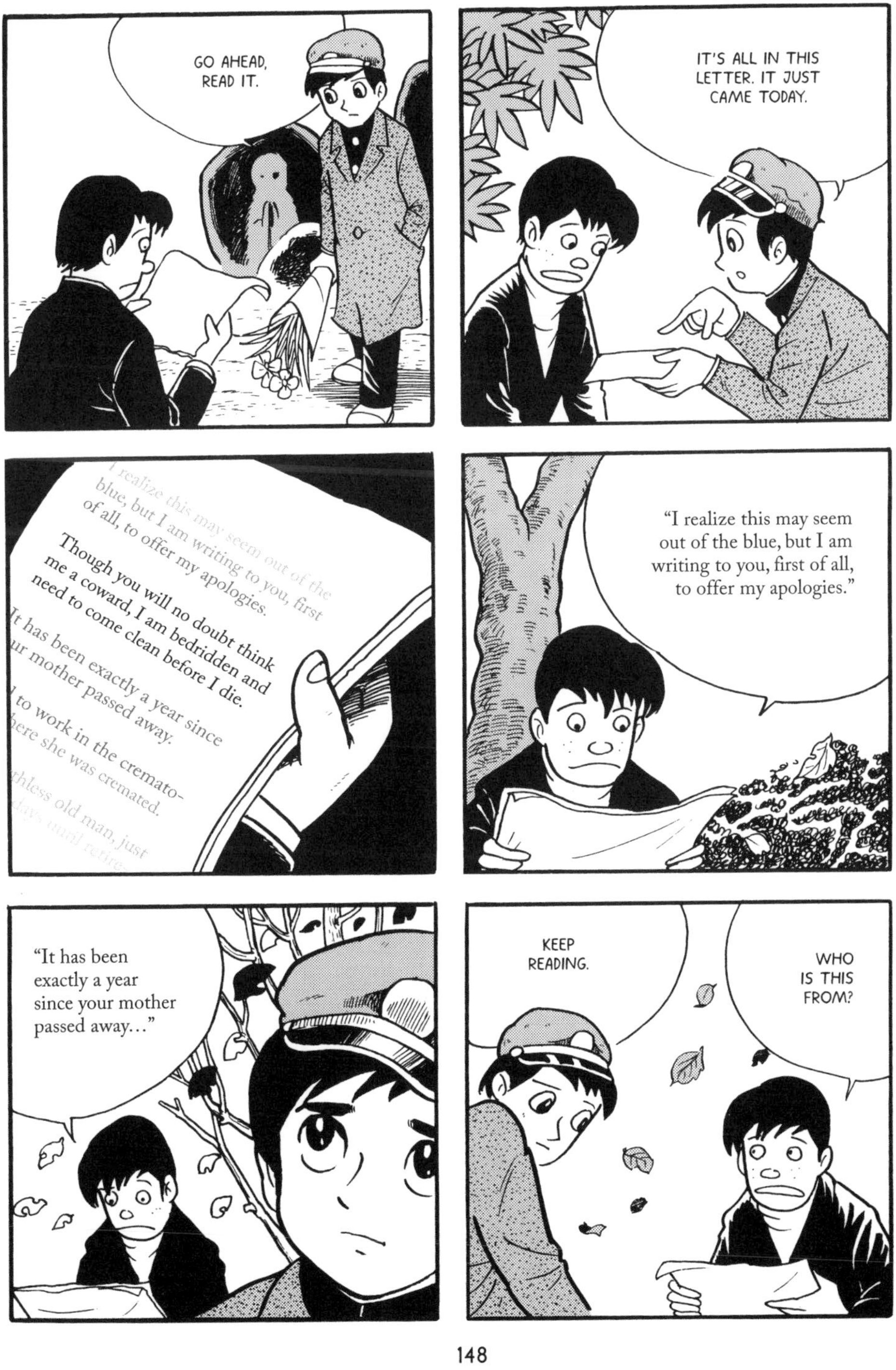
IT'S ALL IN THIS LETTER. IT JUST CAME TODAY.
GO AHEAD, READ IT.
"I realize this may seem out of the blue, but I am writing to you, first of all, to offer my apologies."
I realize this may seem out of the blue, but I am writing to you, first of all, to offer my apologies.
Though you will no doubt think me a coward, I am bedridden and need to come clean before I die.
It has been exactly a year since
mother passed away.
to work in the cremato-
here she was cremated.
old man, just
WHO IS THIS FROM?
KEEP READING.
"It has been exactly a year since your mother passed away..."

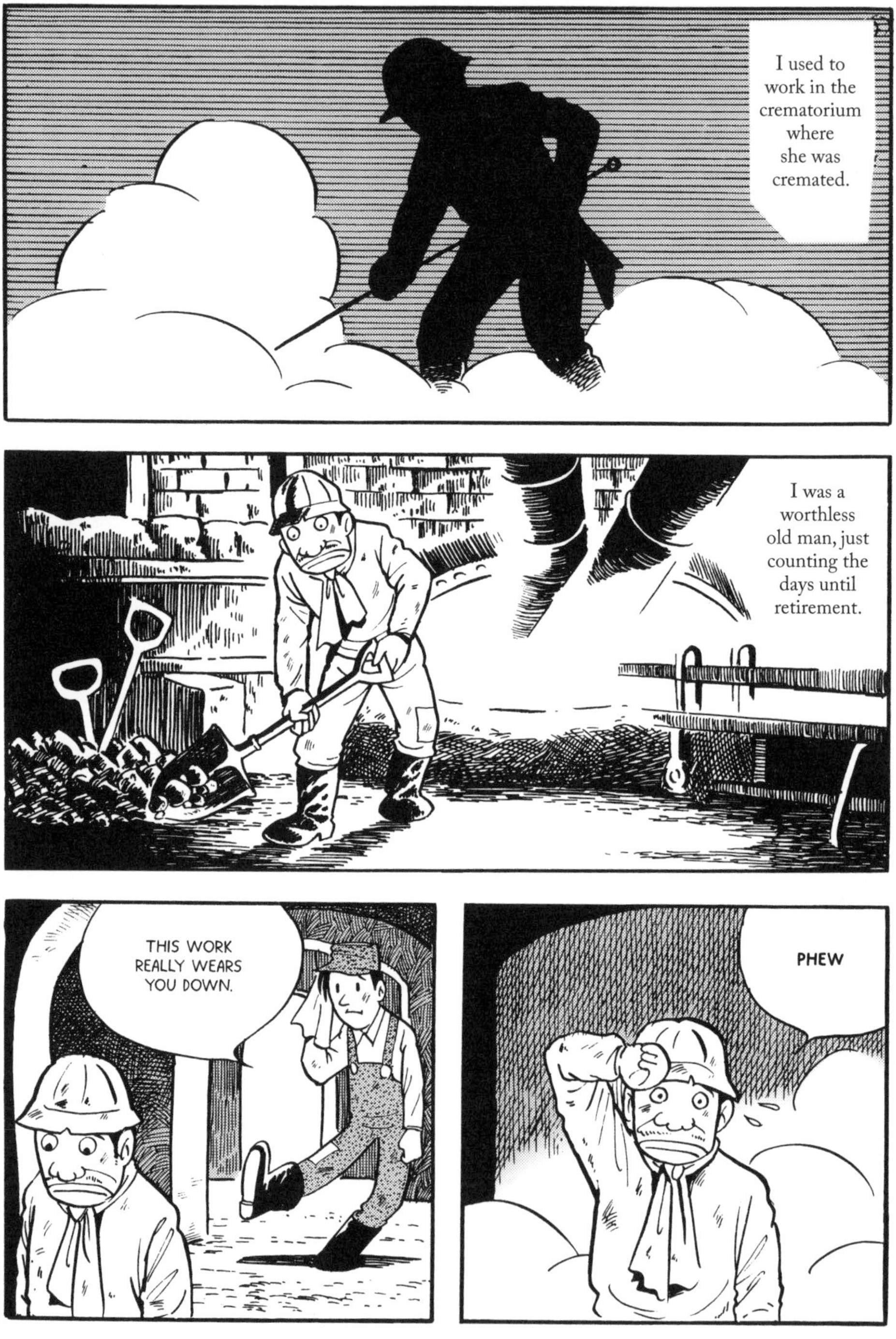
I used to work in the crematorium where she was cremated.
I was a worthless old man, just counting the days until retirement.
PHEW
THIS WORK REALLY WEARS YOU DOWN.

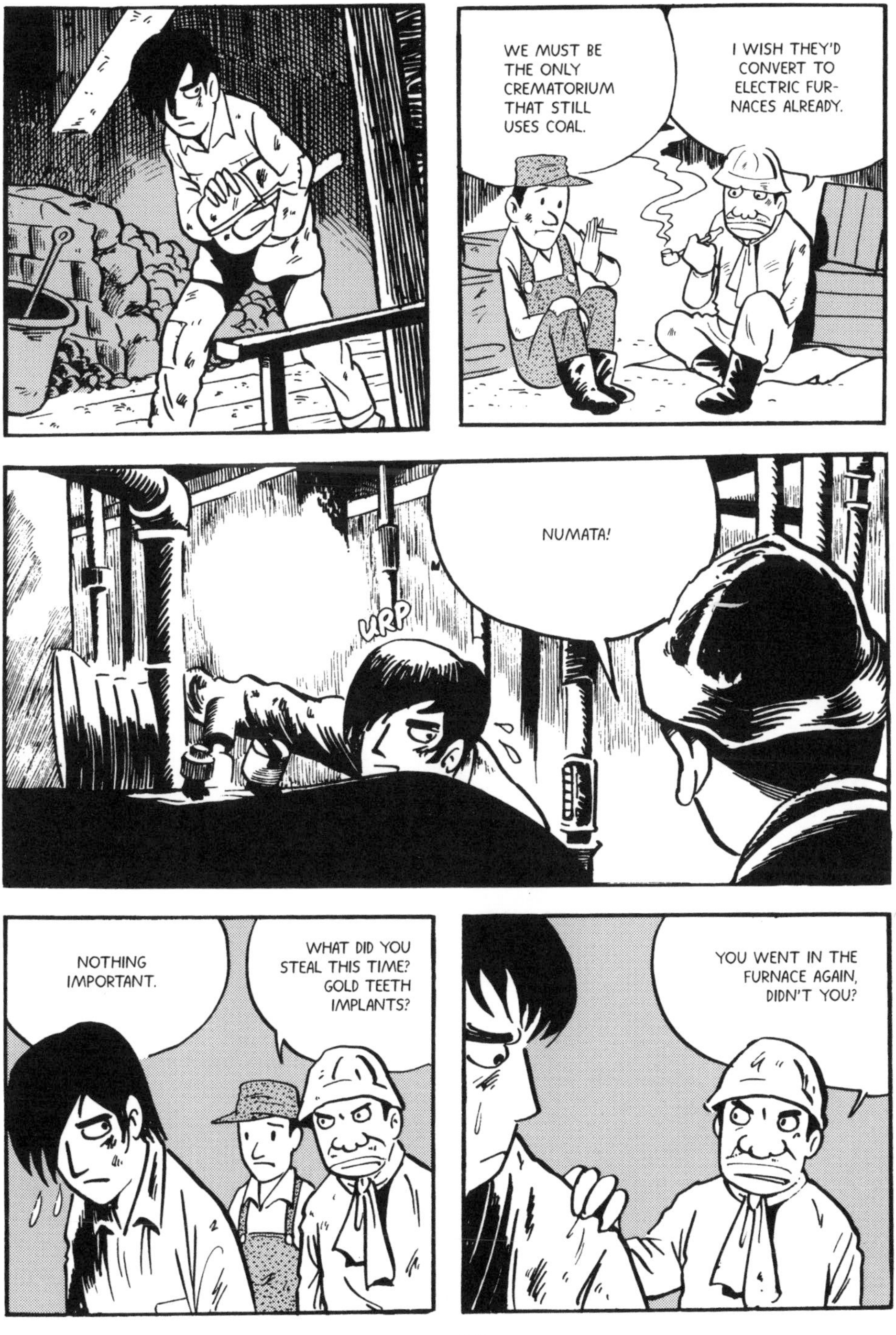

I WISH THEY'D CONVERT TO ELECTRIC FURNACES ALREADY.
WE MUST BE THE ONLY CREMATORIUM THAT STILL USES COAL.
NUMATA!
URP
YOU WENT IN THE FURNACE AGAIN, DIDN'T YOU?
WHAT DID YOU STEAL THIS TIME? GOLD TEETH IMPLANTS?
NOTHING IMPORTANT.

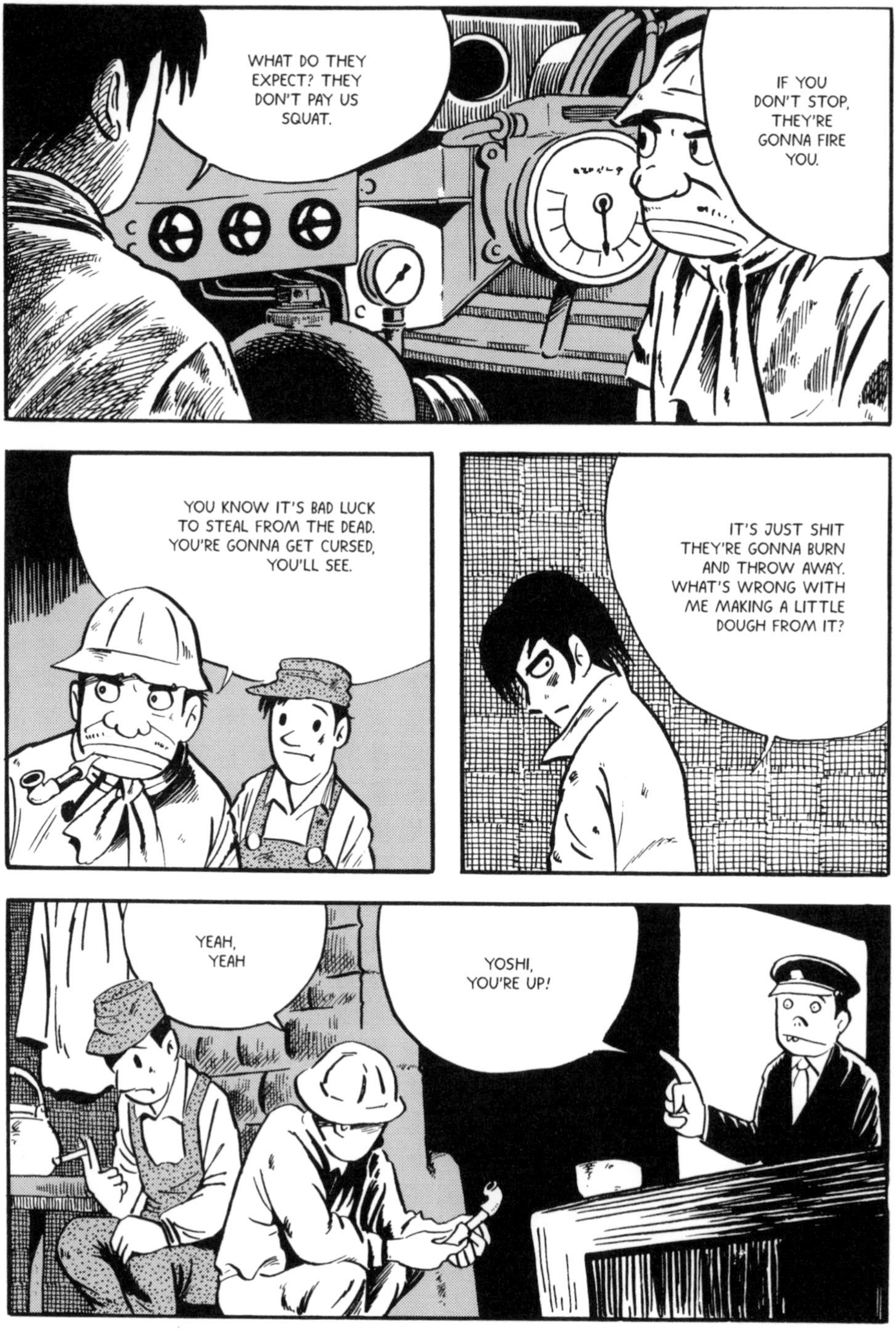
IF YOU DON'T STOP, THEY'RE GONNA FIRE YOU.
WHAT DO THEY EXPECT? THEY DON'T PAY US SQUAT.
IT'S JUST SHIT THEY'RE GONNA BURN AND THROW AWAY. WHAT'S WRONG WITH ME MAKING A LITTLE DOUGH FROM IT?
YOU KNOW IT'S BAD LUCK TO STEAL FROM THE DEAD. YOU'RE GONNA GET CURSED, YOU'LL SEE.
YOSHI, YOU'RE UP!
YEAH, YEAH

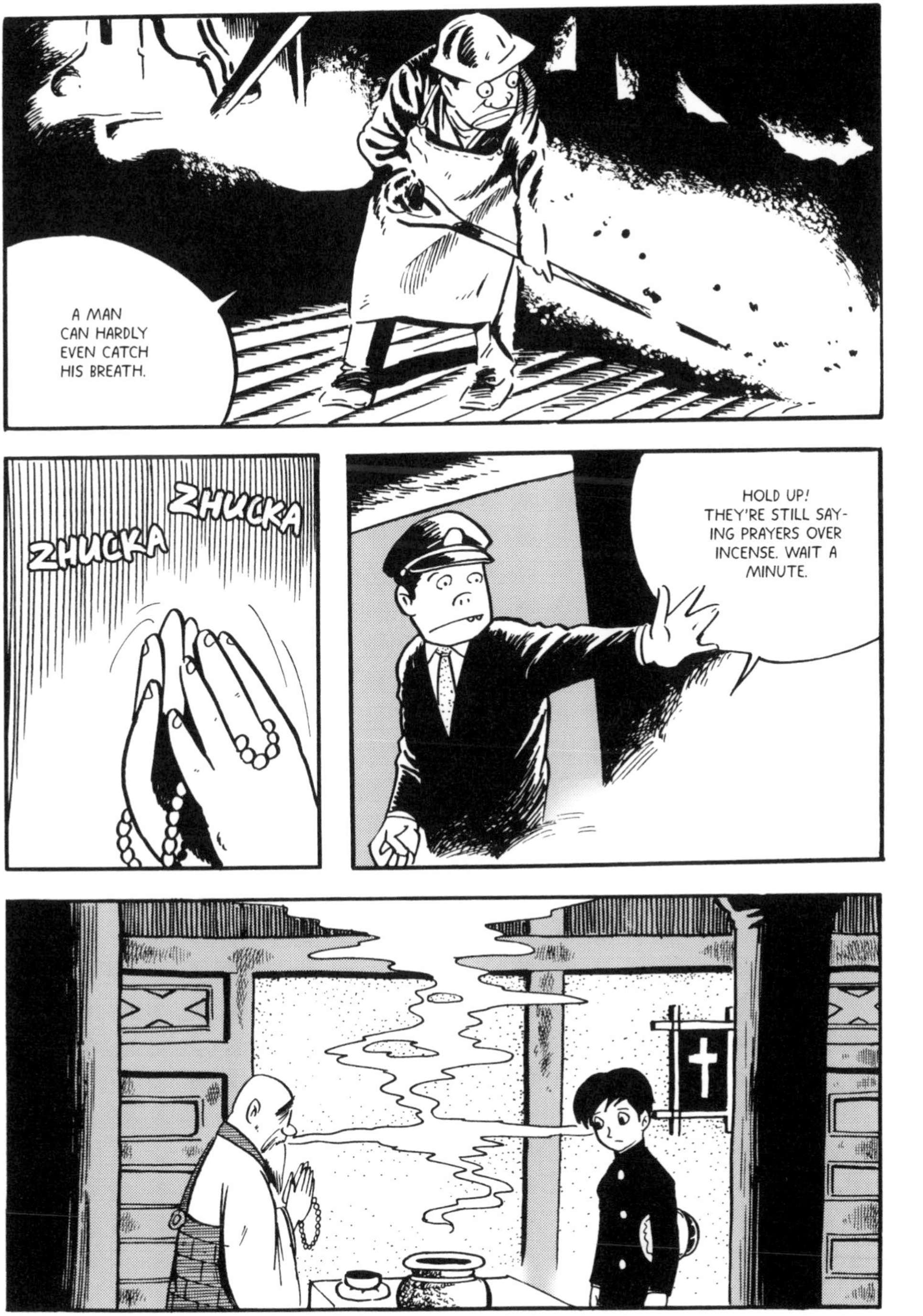
A MAN CAN HARDLY EVEN CATCH HIS BREATH.
HOLD UP! THEY'RE STILL SAY-ING PRAYERS OVER INCENSE. WAIT A MINUTE.
ZHUCKA
ZHUCKA

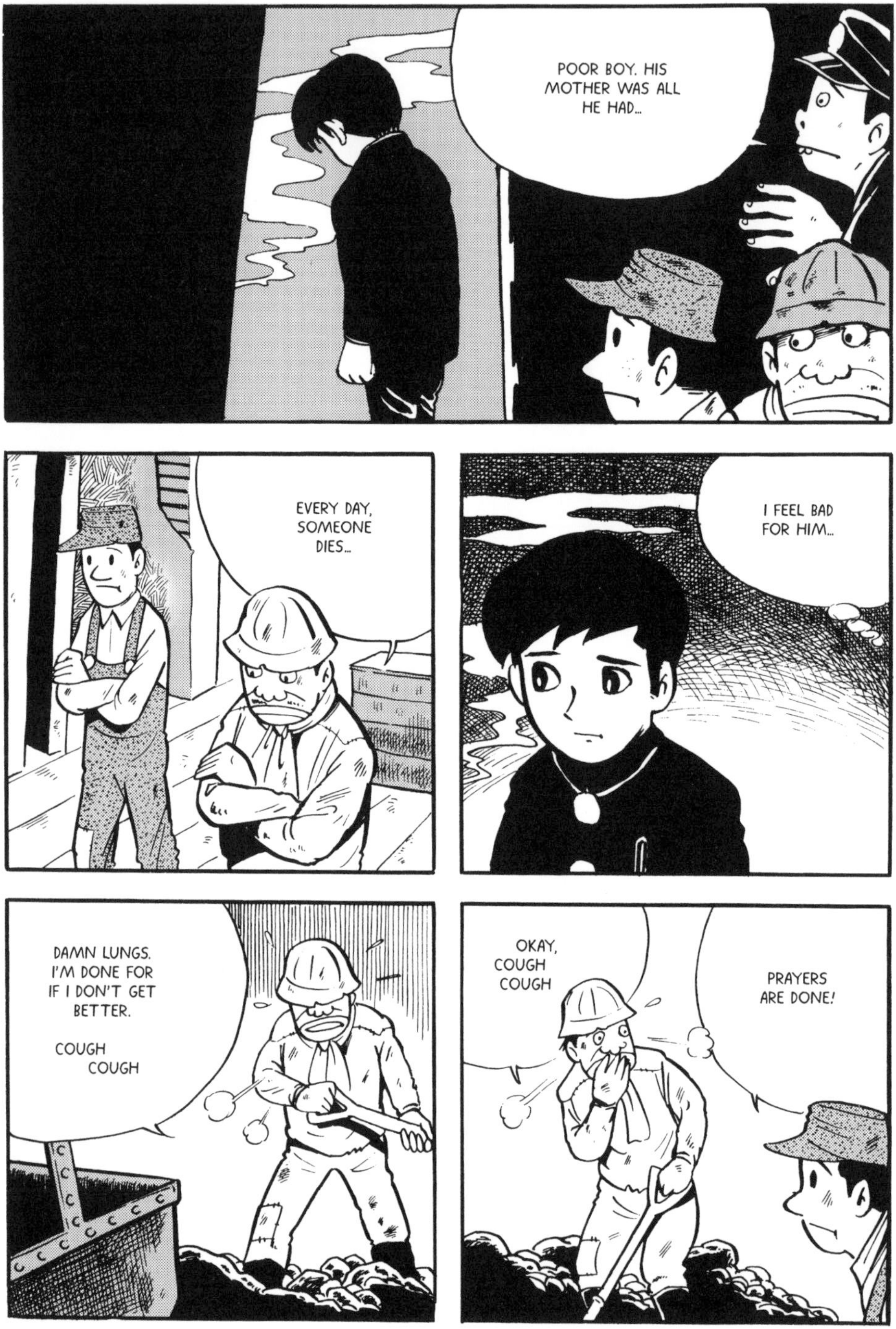
POOR BOY. HIS MOTHER WAS ALL HE HAD...
I FEEL BAD FOR HIM...
EVERY DAY, SOMEONE DIES...
PRAYERS ARE DONE!
OKAY, COUGH COUGH
DAMN LUNGS. I'M DONE FOR IF I DON'T GET BETTER.
COUGH COUGH

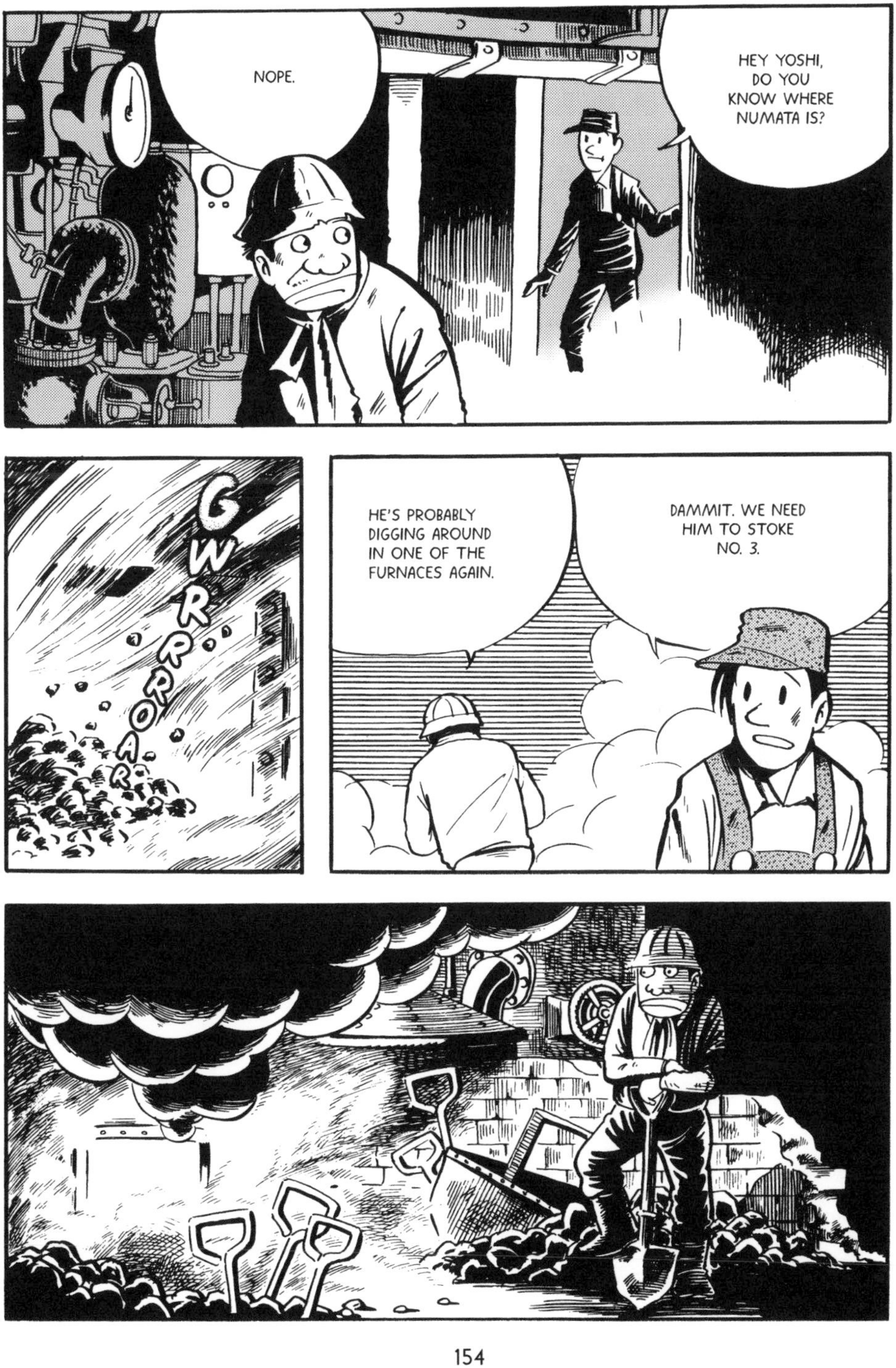
HEY YOSHI, DO YOU KNOW WHERE NUMATA IS?
NOPE.
DAMMIT. WE NEED HIM TO STOKE NO. 3.
HE'S PROBABLY DIGGING AROUND IN ONE OF THE FURNACES AGAIN.
GWRRROAR

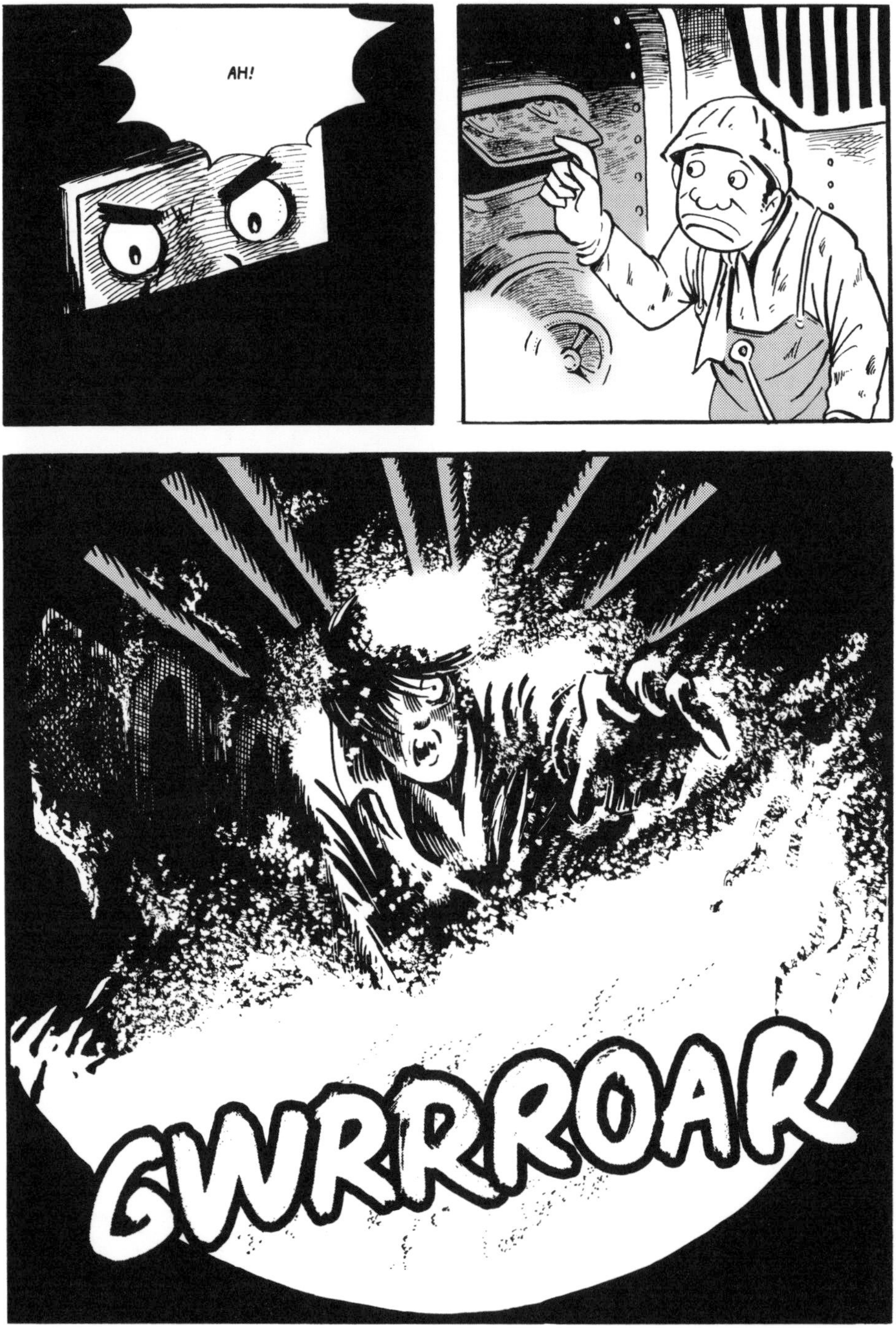
AH!
GWRRROAR

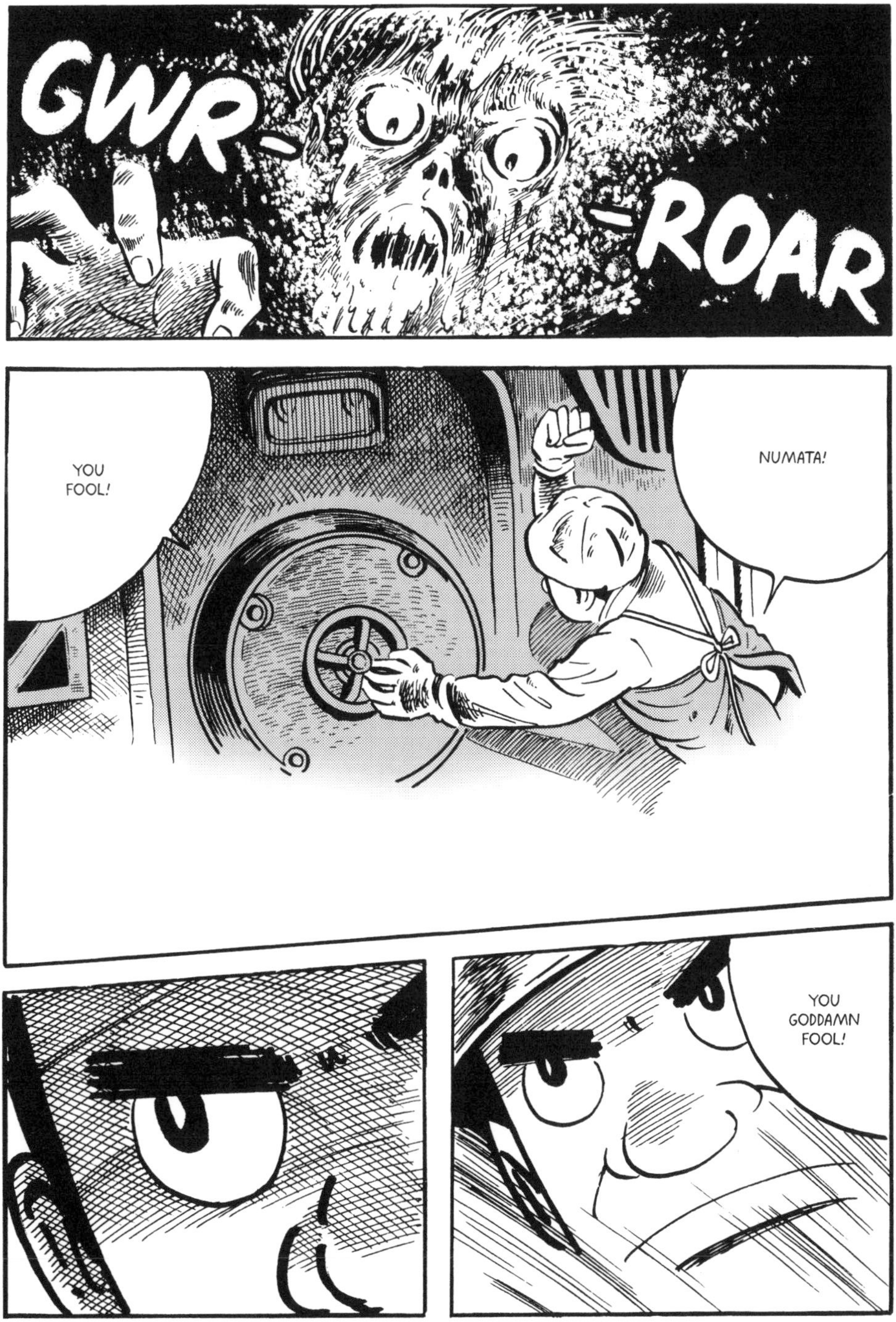
GWR-
-ROAR
NUMATA!
YOU FOOL!
YOU GODDAMN FOOL!

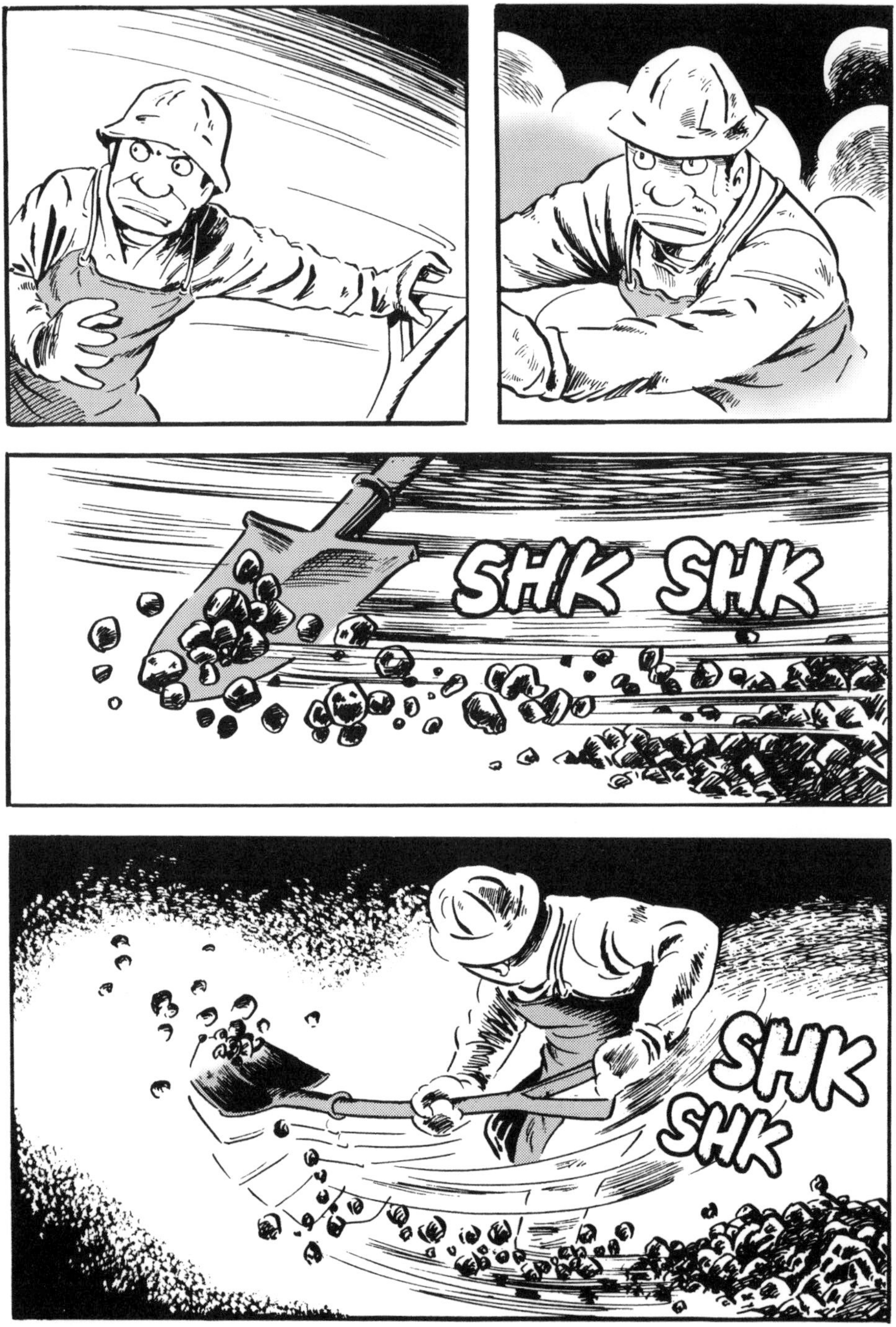
SHK SHK
SHK
SHK

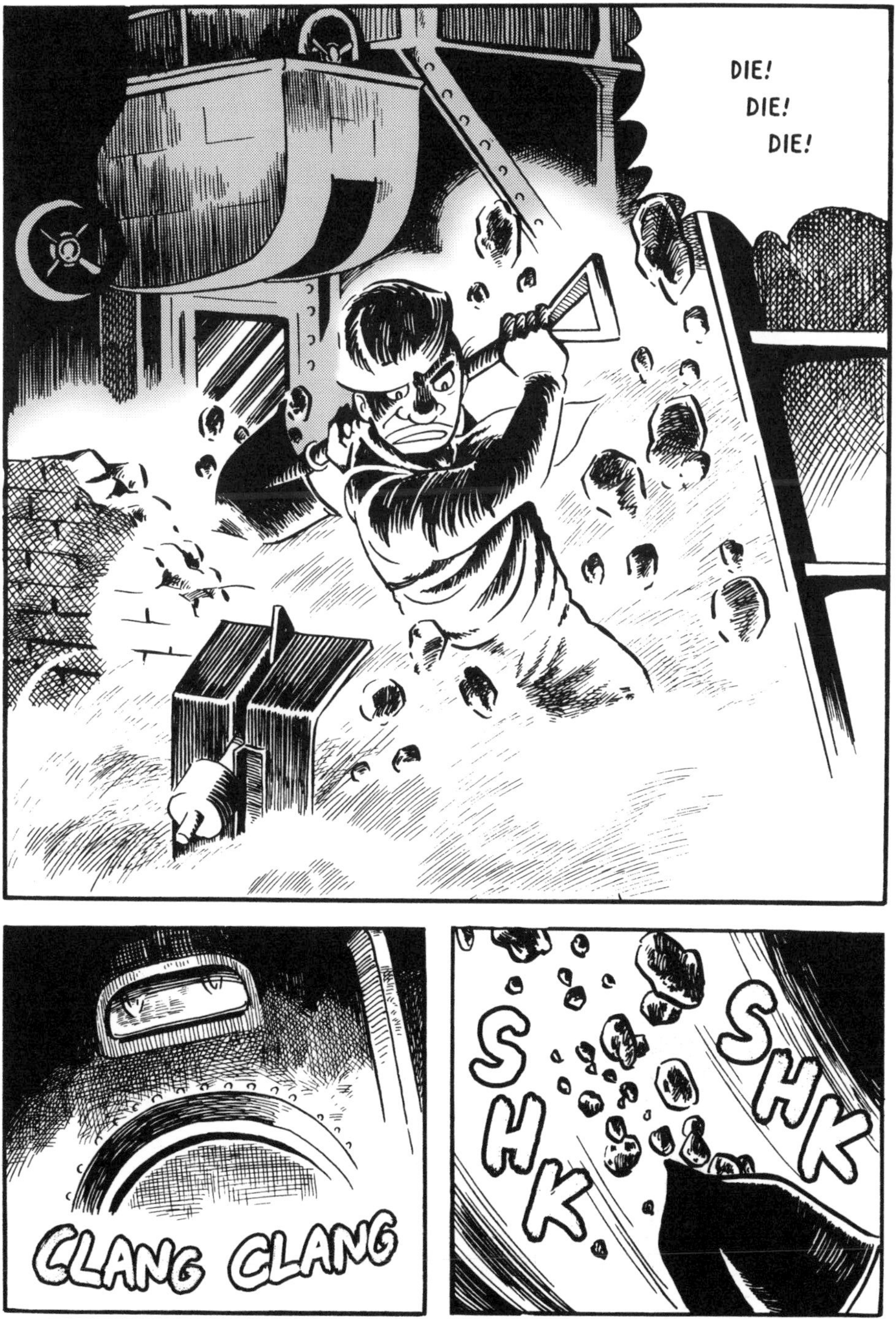
DIE!
DIE!
DIE!
SHK
SHK
CLANG CLANG

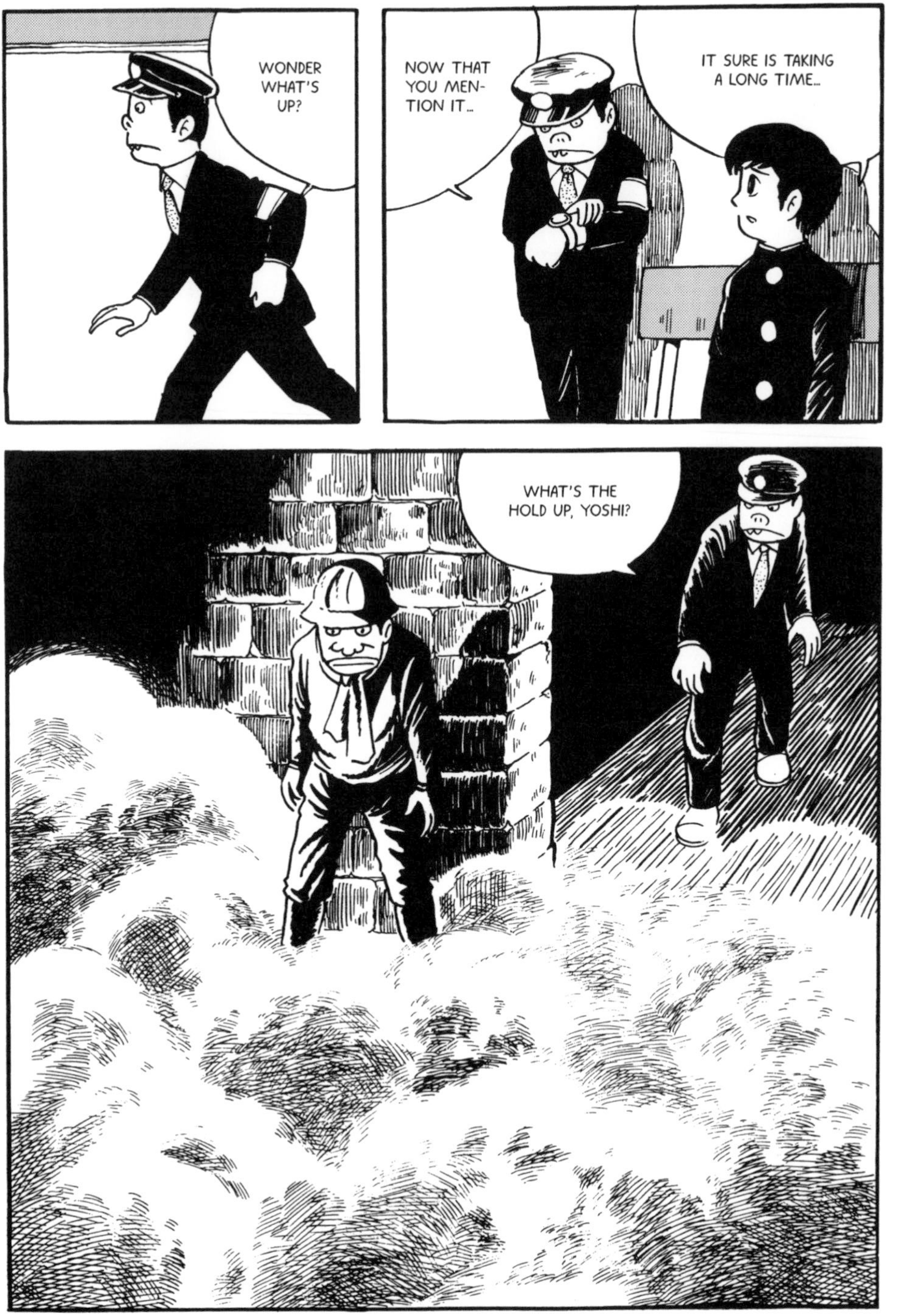
IT SURE IS TAKING A LONG TIME...
NOW THAT YOU MEN- TION IT...
WONDER WHAT'S UP?
WHAT'S THE HOLD UP, YOSHI?

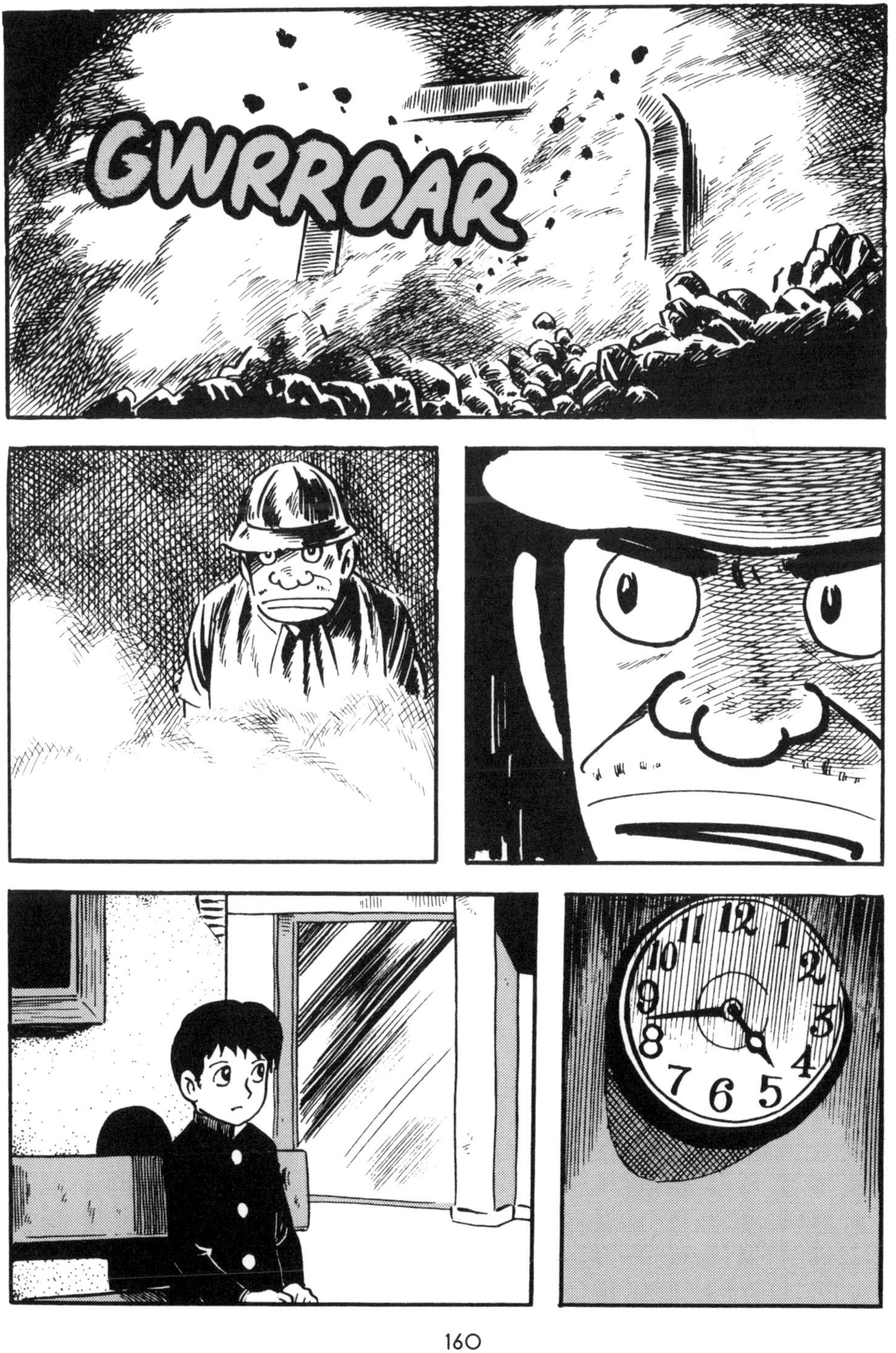
GWRROAR

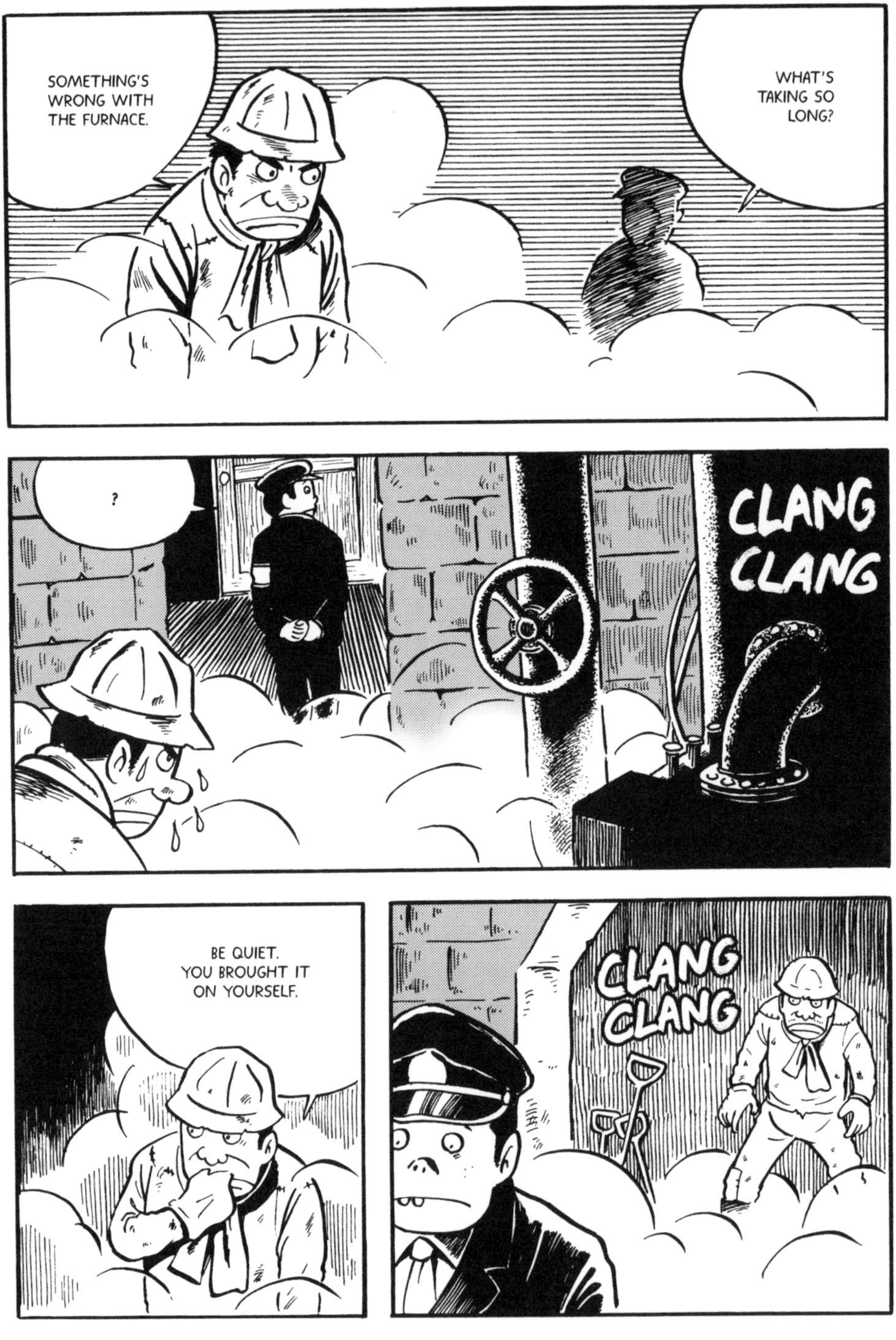
WHAT'S TAKING SO LONG?
SOMETHING'S WRONG WITH THE FURNACE.
CLANG CLANG
?
CLANG CLANG
BE QUIET. YOU BROUGHT IT ON YOURSELF.

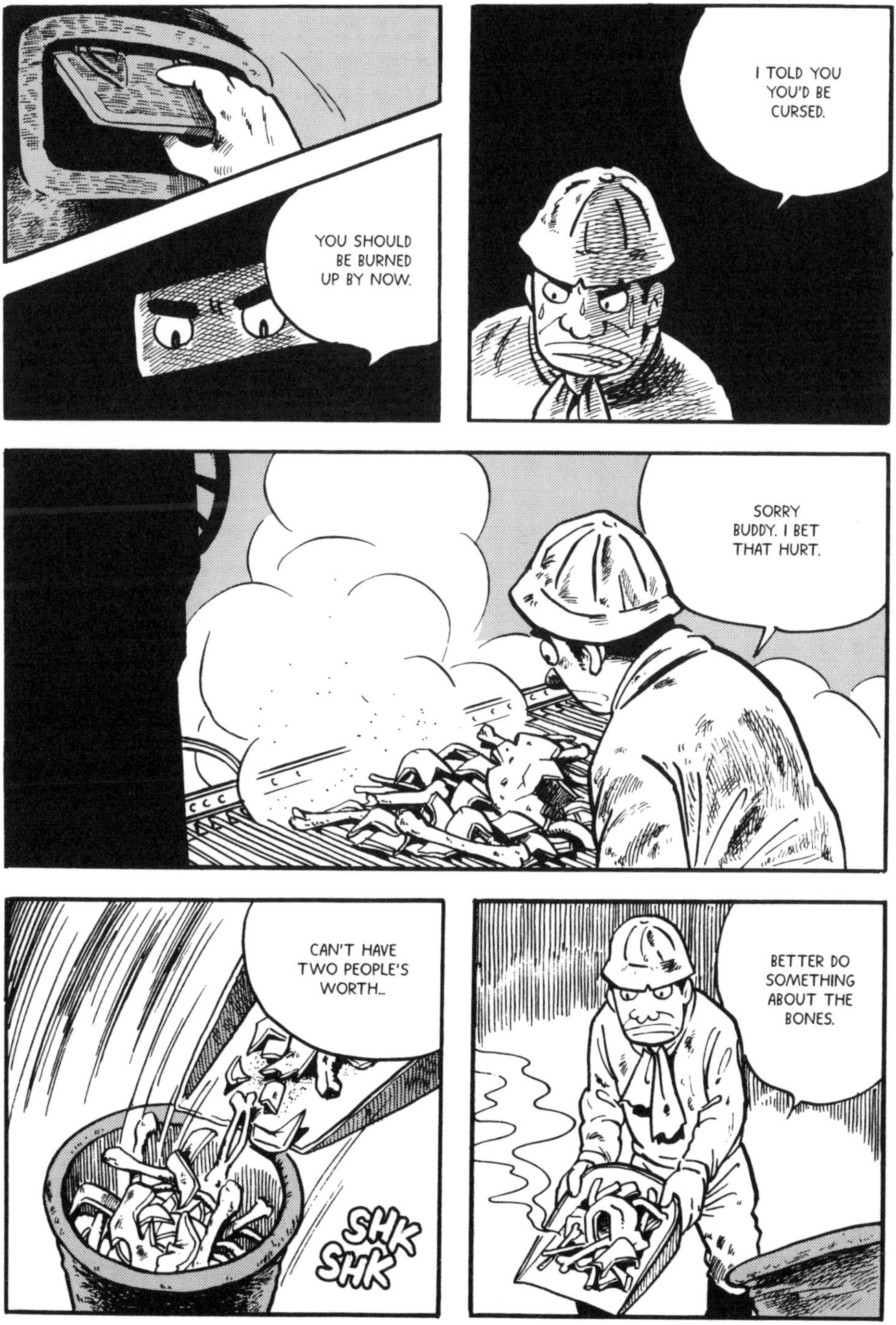
I TOLD YOU YOU'D BE CURSED.
YOU SHOULD BE BURNED UP BY NOW.
SORRY BUDDY. I BET THAT HURT.
BETTER DO SOMETHING ABOUT THE BONES.
CAN'T HAVE TWO PEOPLE'S WORTH...
SHK SHK

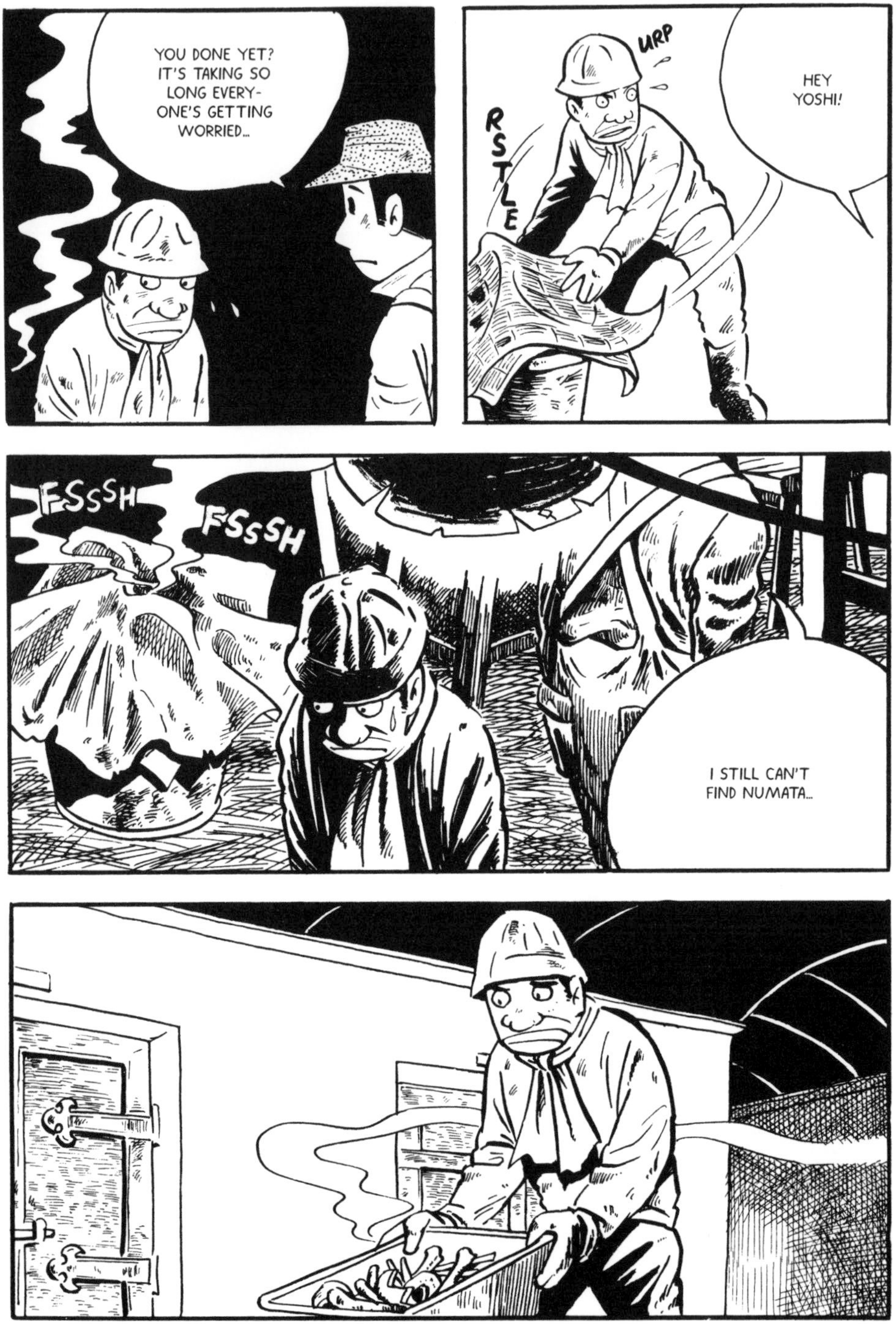
URP
RSTLE
HEY YOSHI!
YOU DONE YET? IT'S TAKING SO LONG EVERY-ONE'S GETTING WORRIED...
FSSSH
FSSSH
I STILL CAN'T FIND NUMATA...

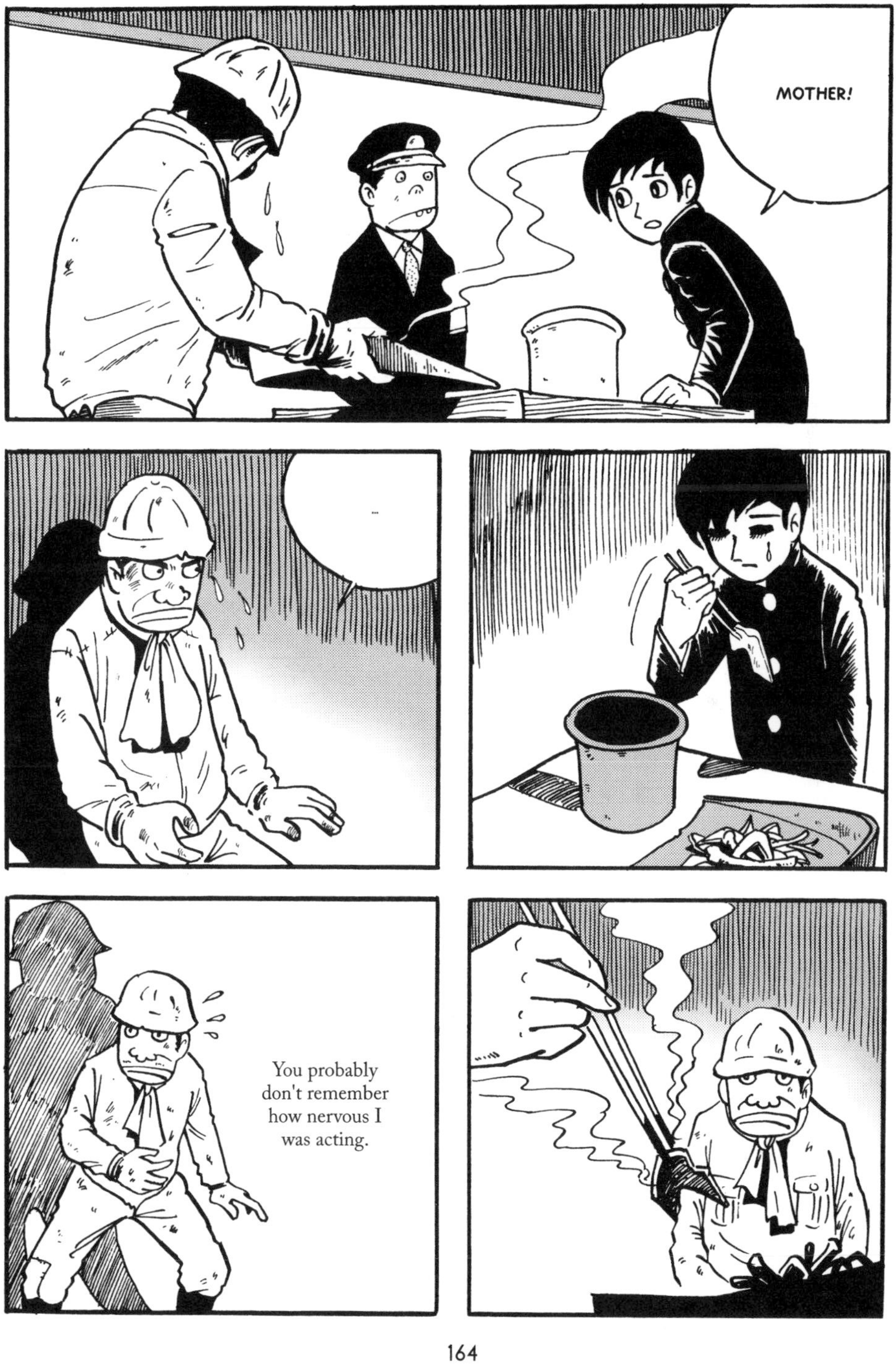
MOTHER!
...
You probably don't remember how nervous I was acting.

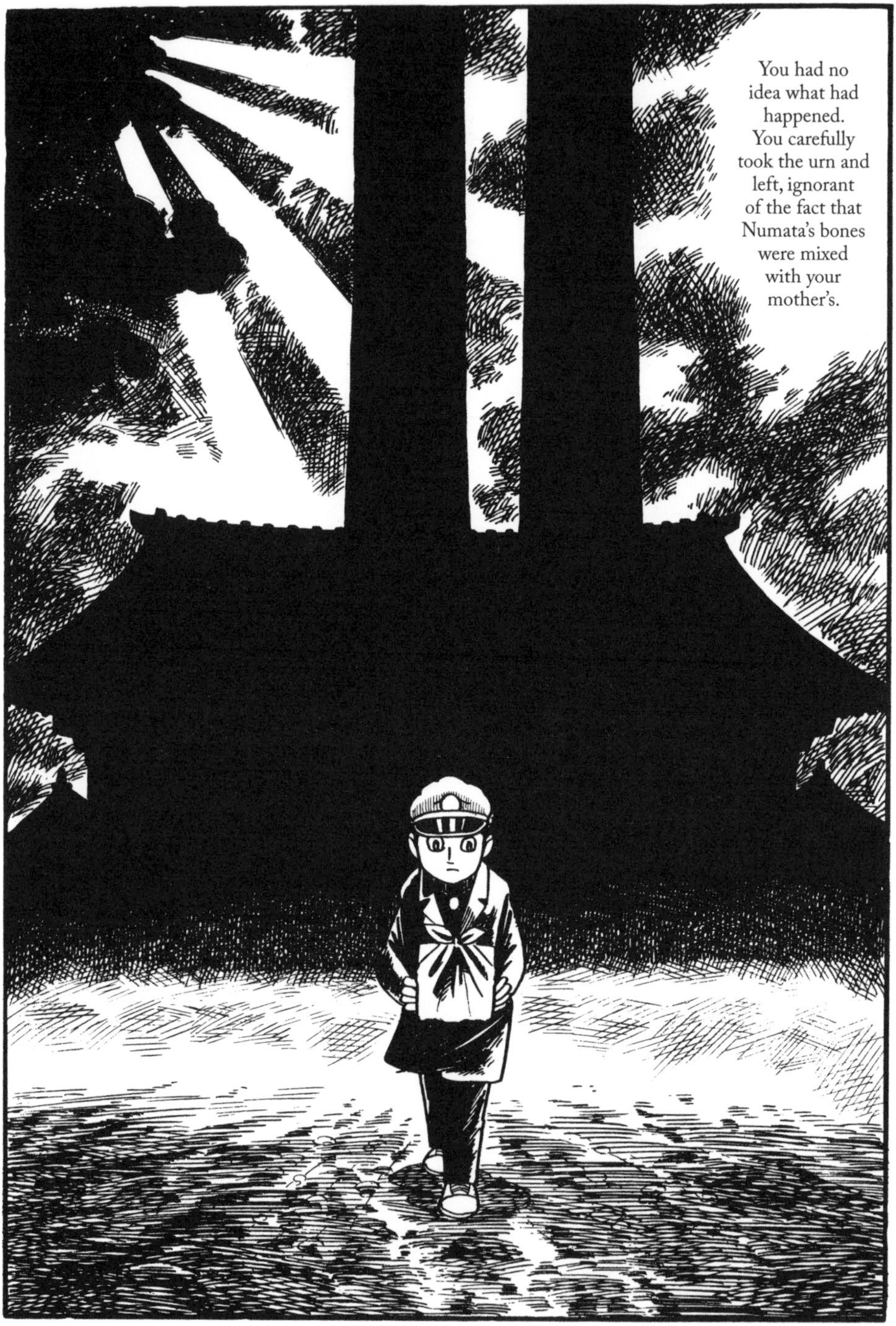
You had no idea what had happened. You carefully took the urn and left, ignorant of the fact that Numata's bones were mixed with your mother's.

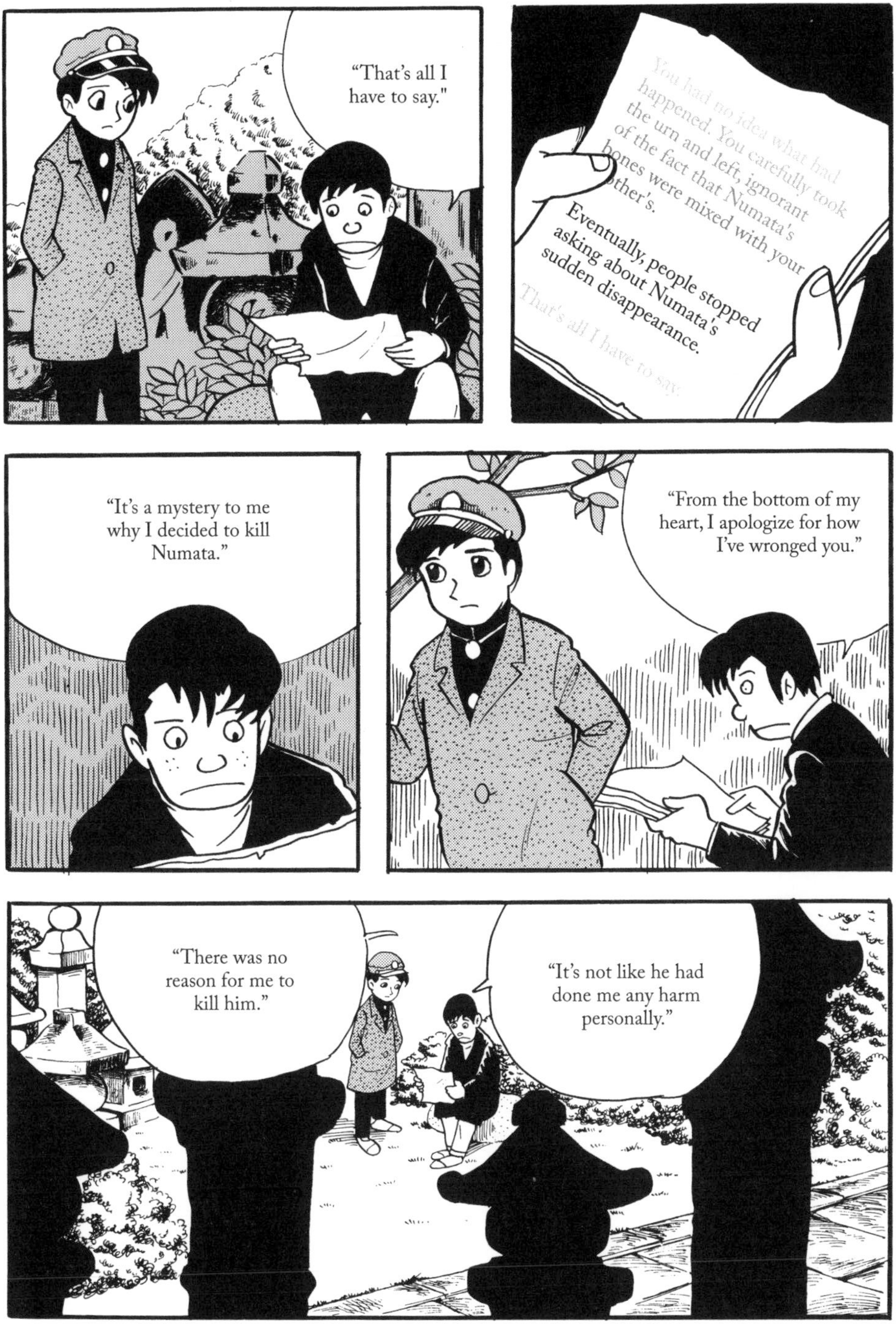
You had no idea what had happened. You carefully took the urn and left, ignorant of the fact that Numata's bones were mixed with your other's.
Eventually, people stopped asking about Numata's sudden disappearance.
That's all I have to say.
"That's all I have to say."
"From the bottom of my heart, I apologize for how I've wronged you."
"It's a mystery to me why I decided to kill Numata."
"It's not like he had done me any harm personally."
"There was no reason for me to kill him."

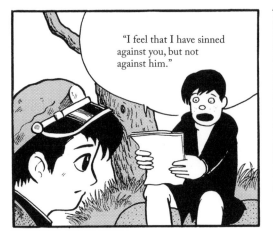

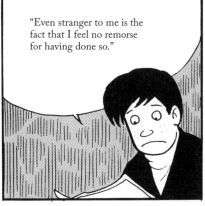

"Even stranger to me is the fact that I feel no remorse for having done so."
"I feel that I have sinned against you, but not against him."
but not against him."
I don't know how you will feel about this contradiction… at any rate, please know that the rest of the cremains are interred at Hofukuji Temple.
My sincerest apologies,
Yoshi Azuma
WHAT A STRANGE LETTER.
DO YOU THINK HE'S CRAZY?
I DOUBT IT. ONLY A SANE PERSON COULD REFLECT SO DEEPLY ABOUT WHAT HE'S DONE.

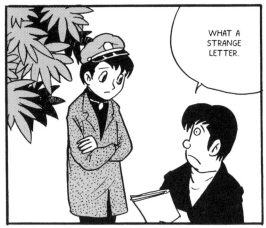

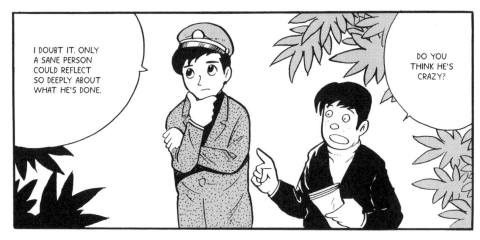

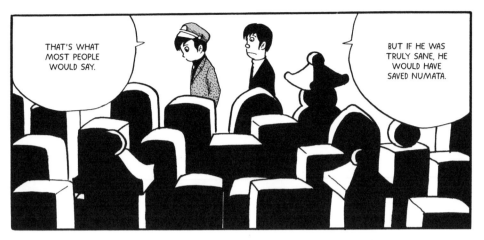

BUT IF HE WAS TRULY SANE, HE WOULD HAVE SAVED NUMATA.
THAT'S WHAT MOST PEOPLE WOULD SAY.
BUT I DON'T THINK MOST PEOPLE ARE AWARE OF THE CRUELTY THAT LIES DEEP IN THEIR HEARTS...
THIS YOSHI FELLOW TOO. I'M SURE HE THOUGHT OF HIMSELF AS A GOOD AND EARNEST MAN...
YEAH...
THEN ALL OF A SUDDEN—LITERALLY ALL OF A SUDDEN—HE FOUND HIMSELF A MURDERER.
I'M SURE HE COULDN'T BELIEVE IT HIMSELF.
IT PROBABLY DIDN'T EVEN FEEL REAL TO HIM.

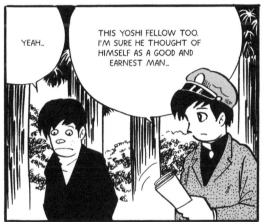

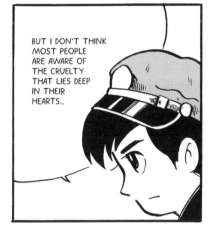

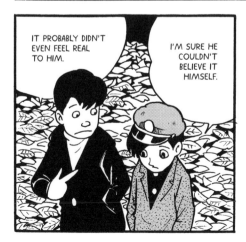

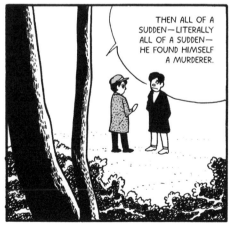

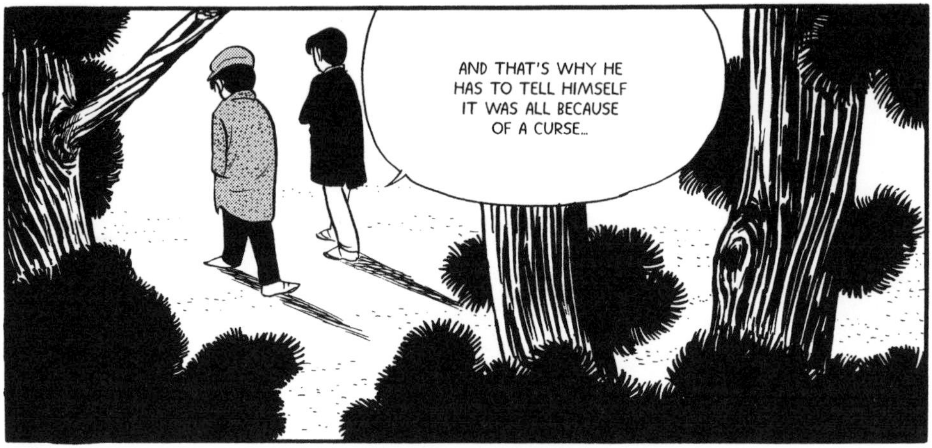
AND THAT'S WHY HE HAS TO TELL HIMSELF IT WAS ALL BECAUSE OF A CURSE...

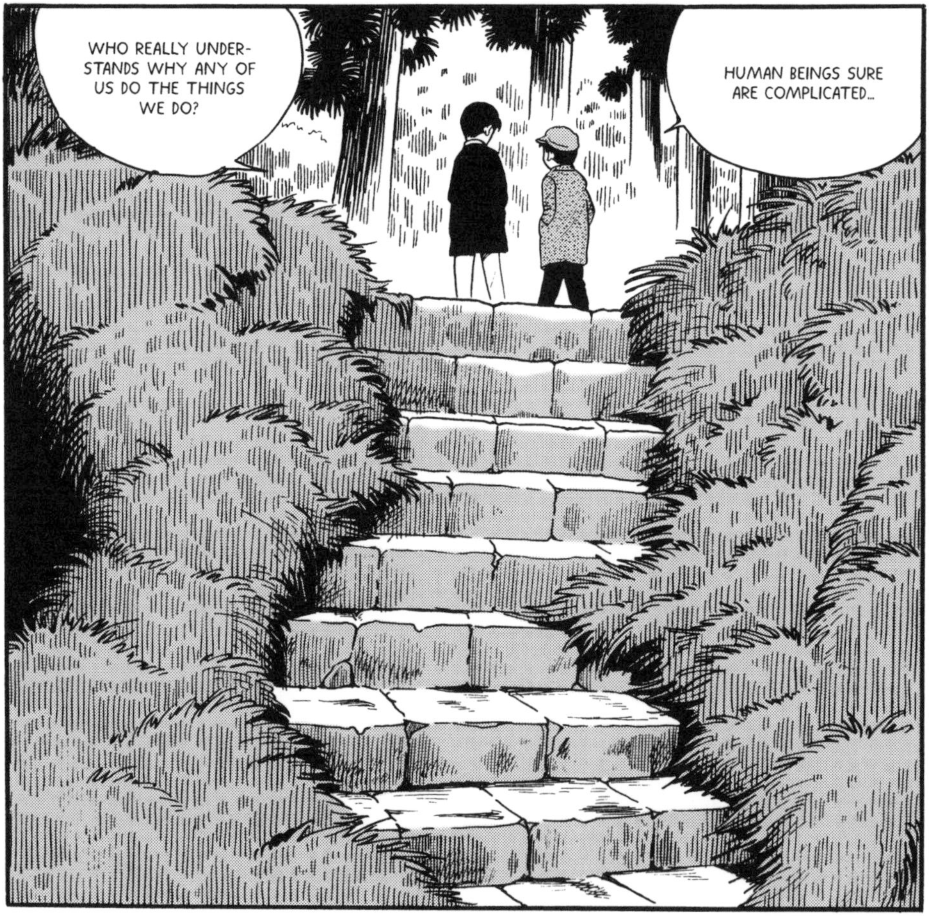
HUMAN BEINGS SURE ARE COMPLICATED...
WHO REALLY UNDER-STANDS WHY ANY OF US DO THE THINGS WE DO?

THE NINJESS

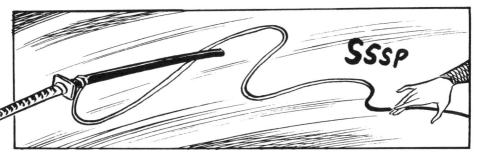

SSSP

172

THE
PALACE...

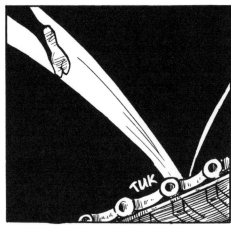

TUK

173

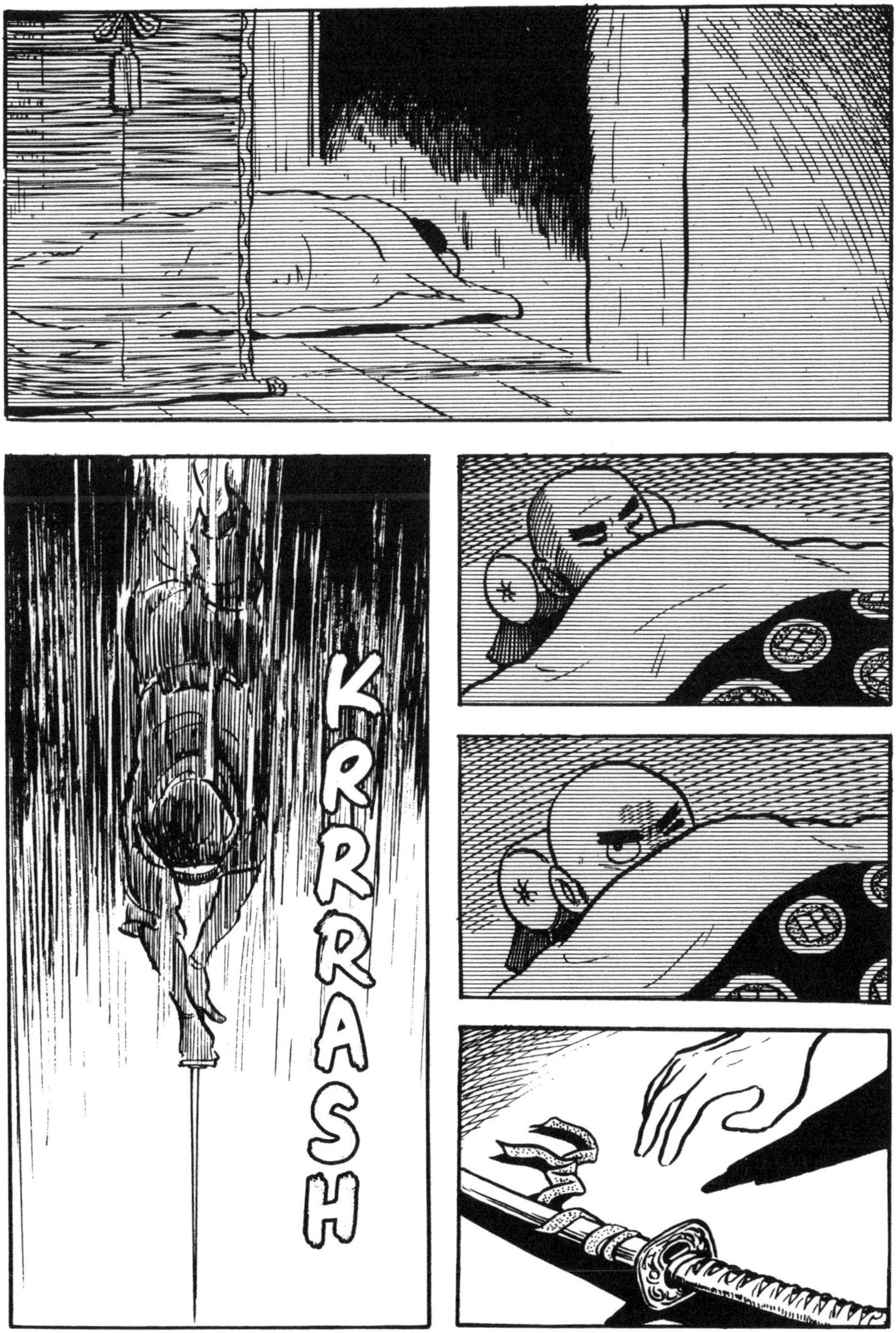
KRRASH

INTRUDER!!

INTRUDER!!
AFTER HIM!!
AFTER HIM!!

DAMN!!

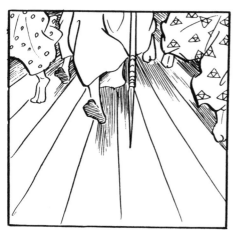

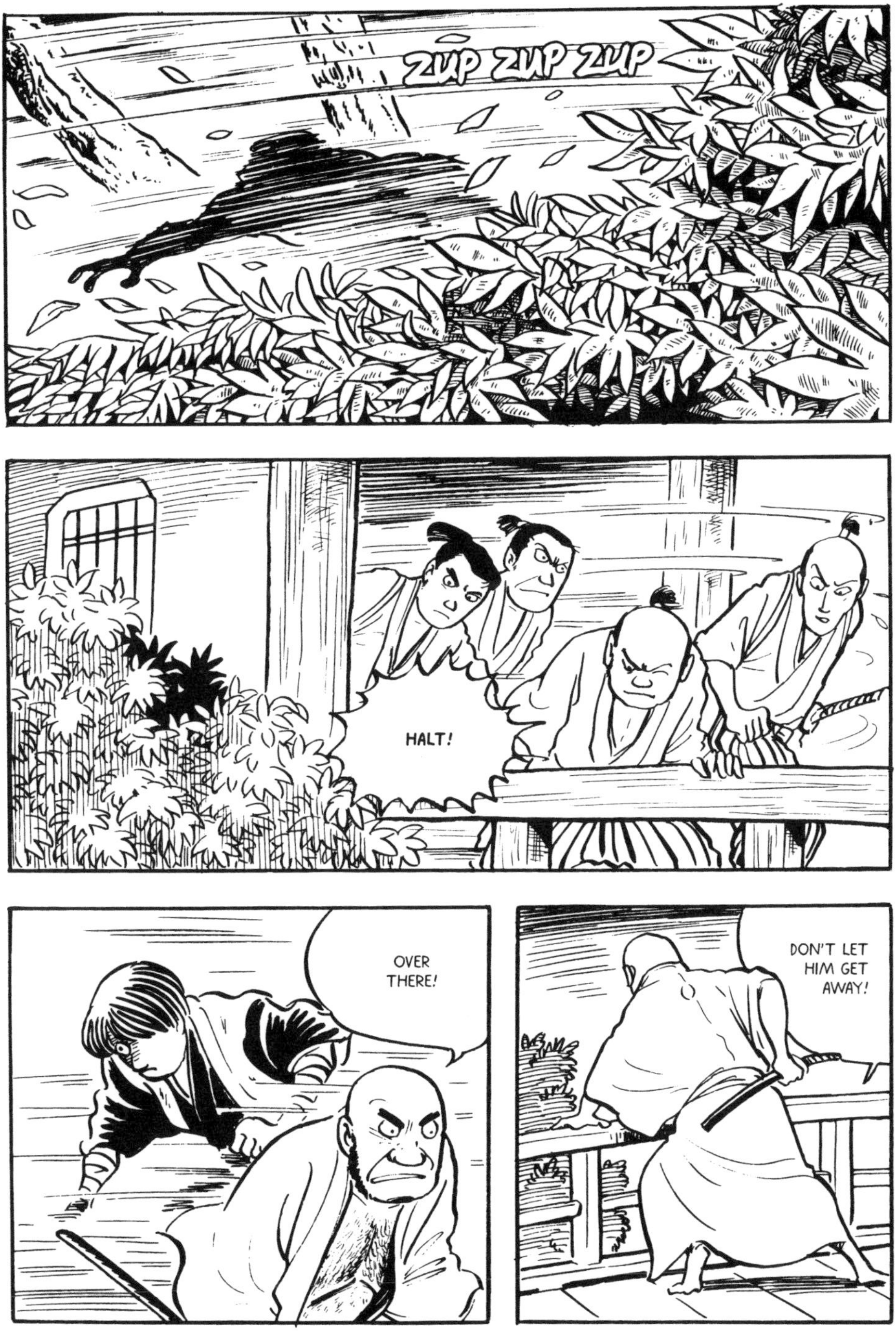
ZUP ZUP ZUP
HALT!
DON'T LET HIM GET AWAY!
OVER THERE!

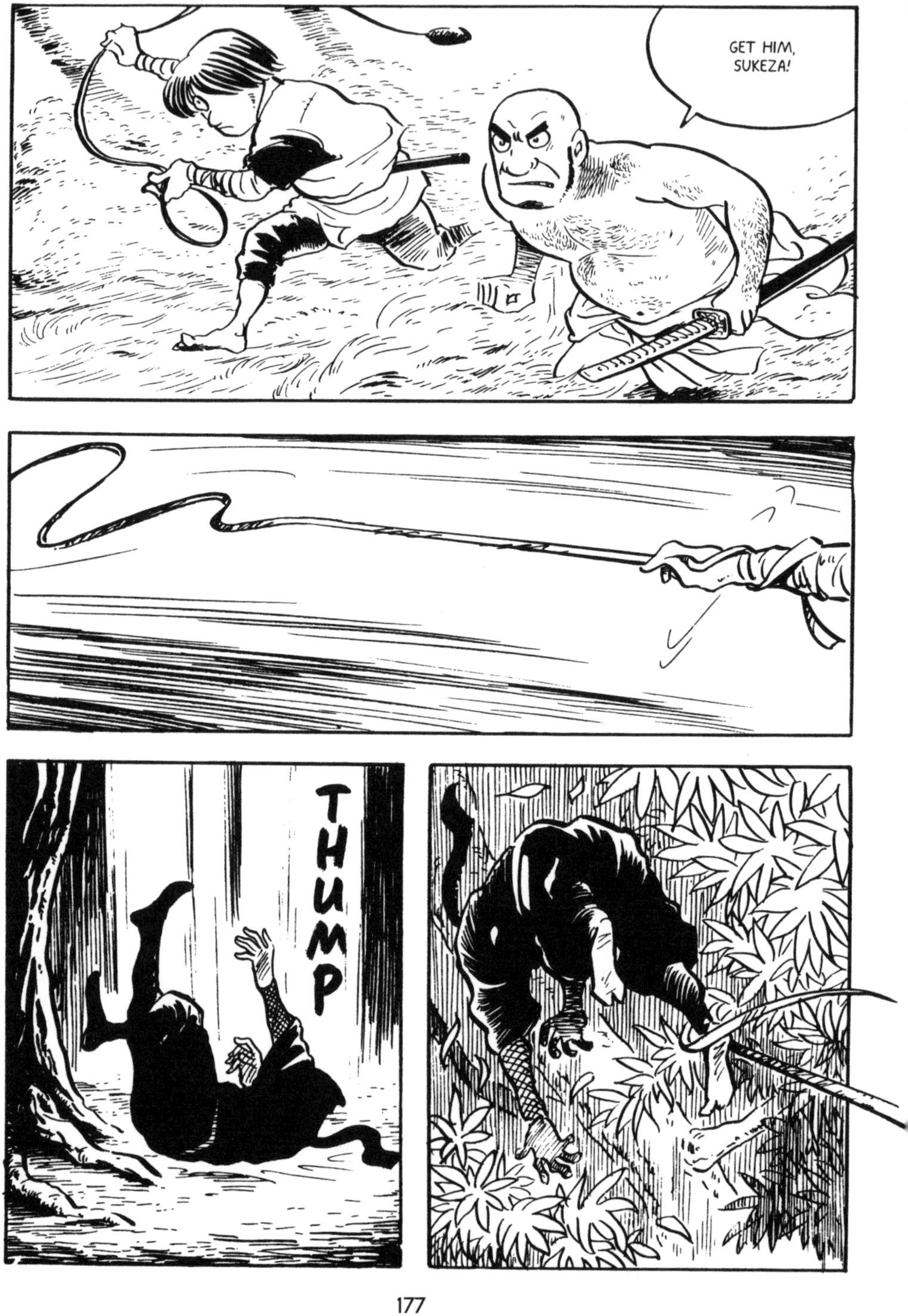
GET HIM, SUKEZA!
THUMP

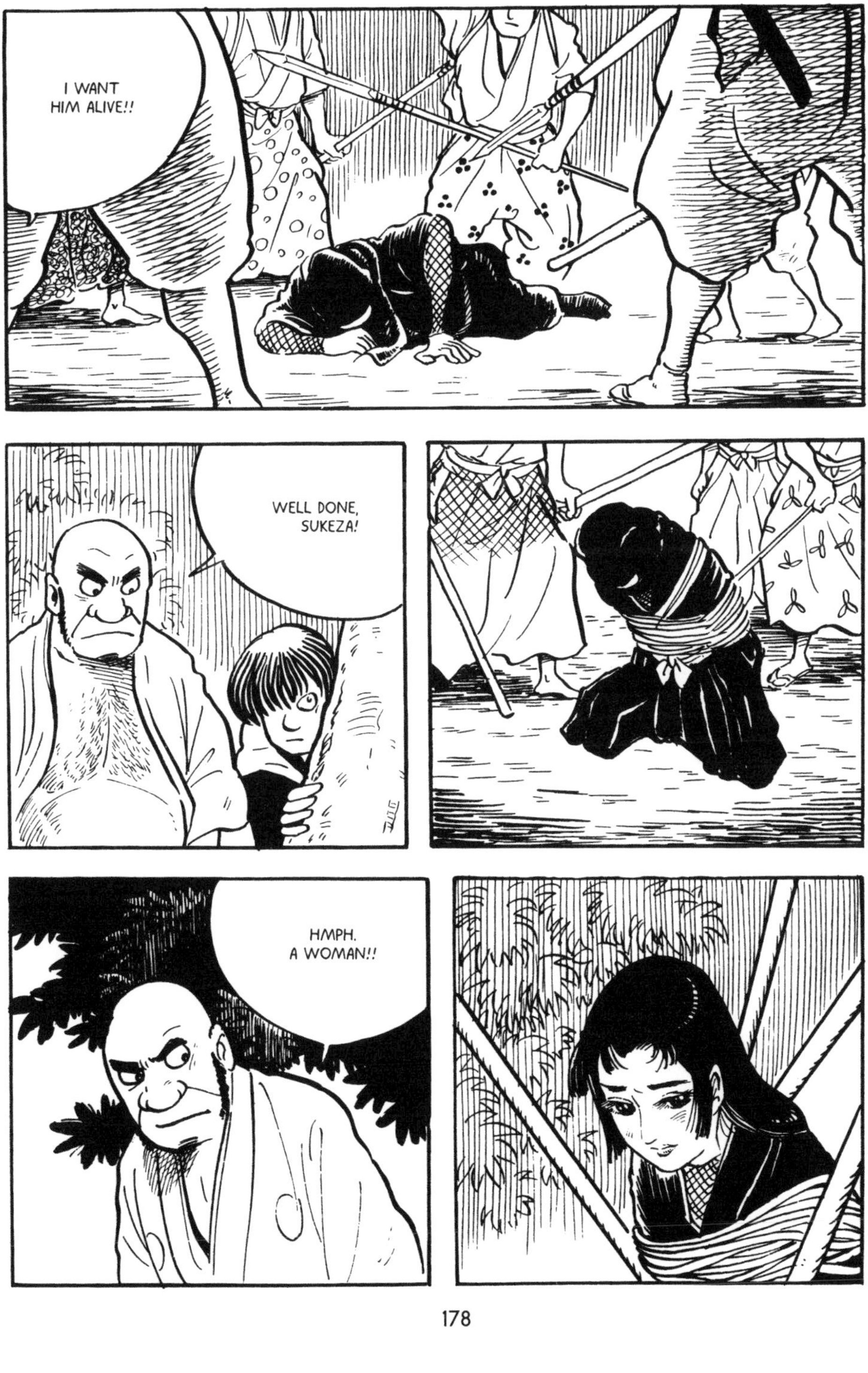
I WANT HIM ALIVE!!
WELL DONE, SUKEZA!
HMPH. A WOMAN!!

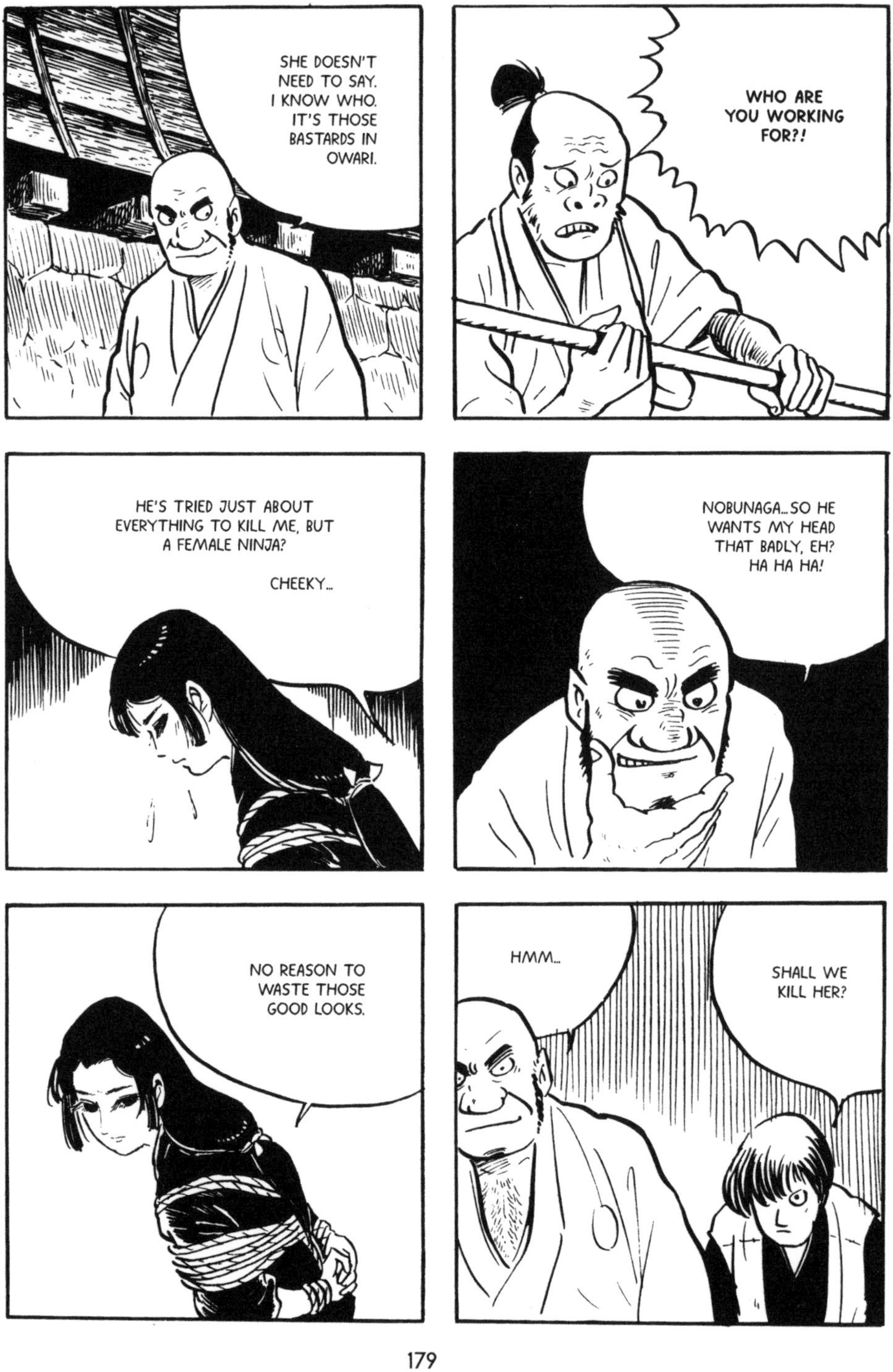
WHO ARE YOU WORKING FOR?!
SHE DOESN'T NEED TO SAY. I KNOW WHO. IT'S THOSE BASTARDS IN OWARI.
NOBUNAGA...SO HE WANTS MY HEAD THAT BADLY, EH? HA HA HA!
HE'S TRIED JUST ABOUT EVERYTHING TO KILL ME, BUT A FEMALE NINJA?
CHEEKY...
SHALL WE KILL HER?
HMM...
NO REASON TO WASTE THOSE GOOD LOOKS.

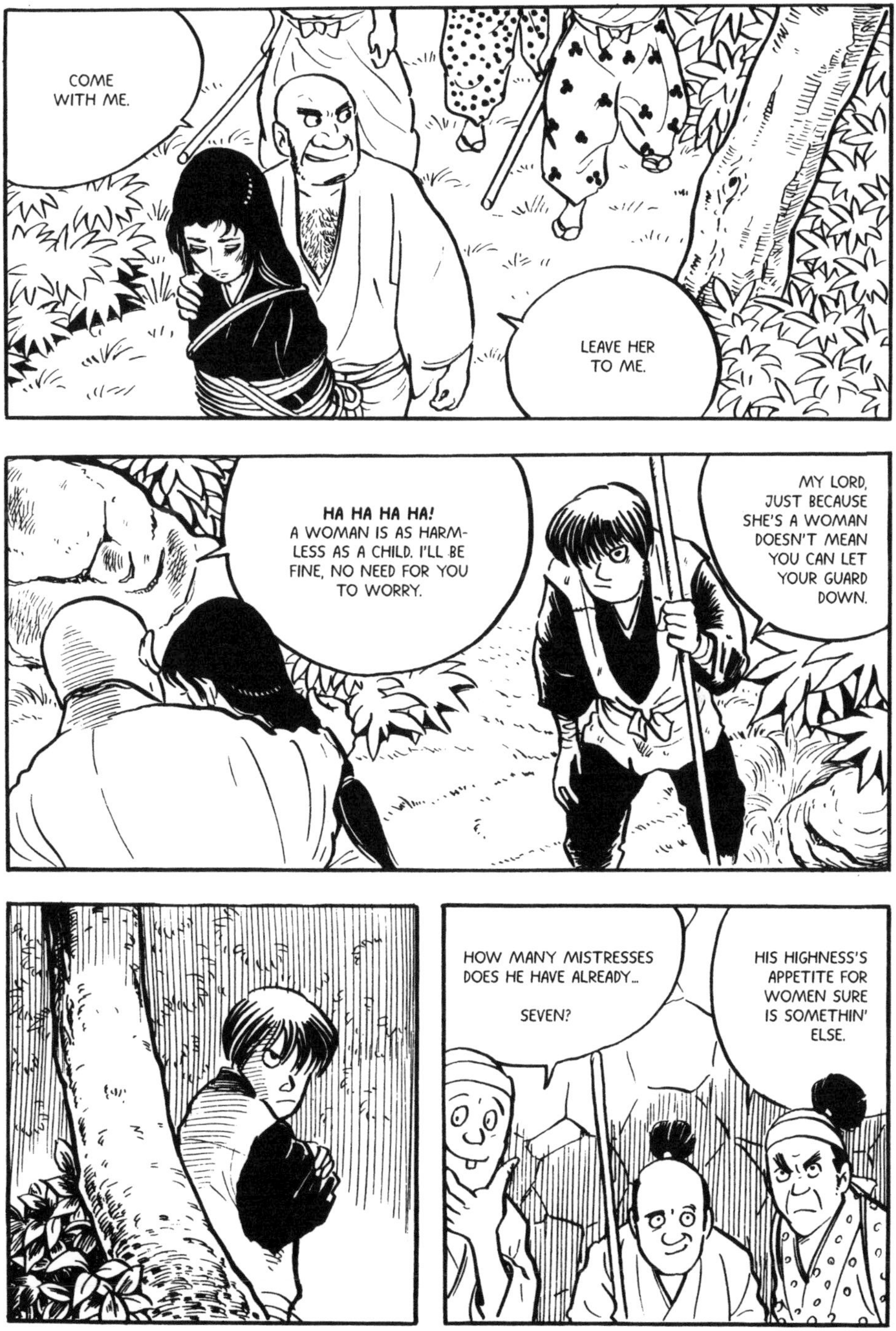
LEAVE HER TO ME.
COME WITH ME.
MY LORD, JUST BECAUSE SHE'S A WOMAN DOESN'T MEAN YOU CAN LET YOUR GUARD DOWN.
HA HA HA HA! A WOMAN IS AS HARMLESS AS A CHILD. I'LL BE FINE, NO NEED FOR YOU TO WORRY.
HIS HIGHNESS'S APPETITE FOR WOMEN SURE IS SOMETHIN' ELSE.
HOW MANY MISTRESSES DOES HE HAVE ALREADY... SEVEN?

AS THE HEAD OF A RESPECTED FAMILY OF GREAT WEALTH AND MILITARY MIGHT, SHIGEKATSU "THE PRIEST" INUMARU PRESIDED OVER A FIEFDOM LOCATED IN THE SOUTH OF MINO PROVINCE.

NOT ONLY WAS HE CAPABLE OF FELLING MULTIPLE RAGING BULLS SIMULTANEOUSLY WITH HIS BARE HANDS, BUT HE WAS ALSO A MASTER TACTICIAN ON THE BATTLEFIELD.

EVEN THE GREAT WARLORD NOBUNAGA, IN HIS VICTORIOUS RAMPAGES ACROSS THE COUNTRY, HAD BEEN UNABLE TO BRING INUMARU TO HEEL.

HEH HEH HEH. YOU'RE SHAKING. AT THE END OF THE DAY, A WOMAN IS JUST A WOMAN, EVEN IF SHE IS A NINJA.

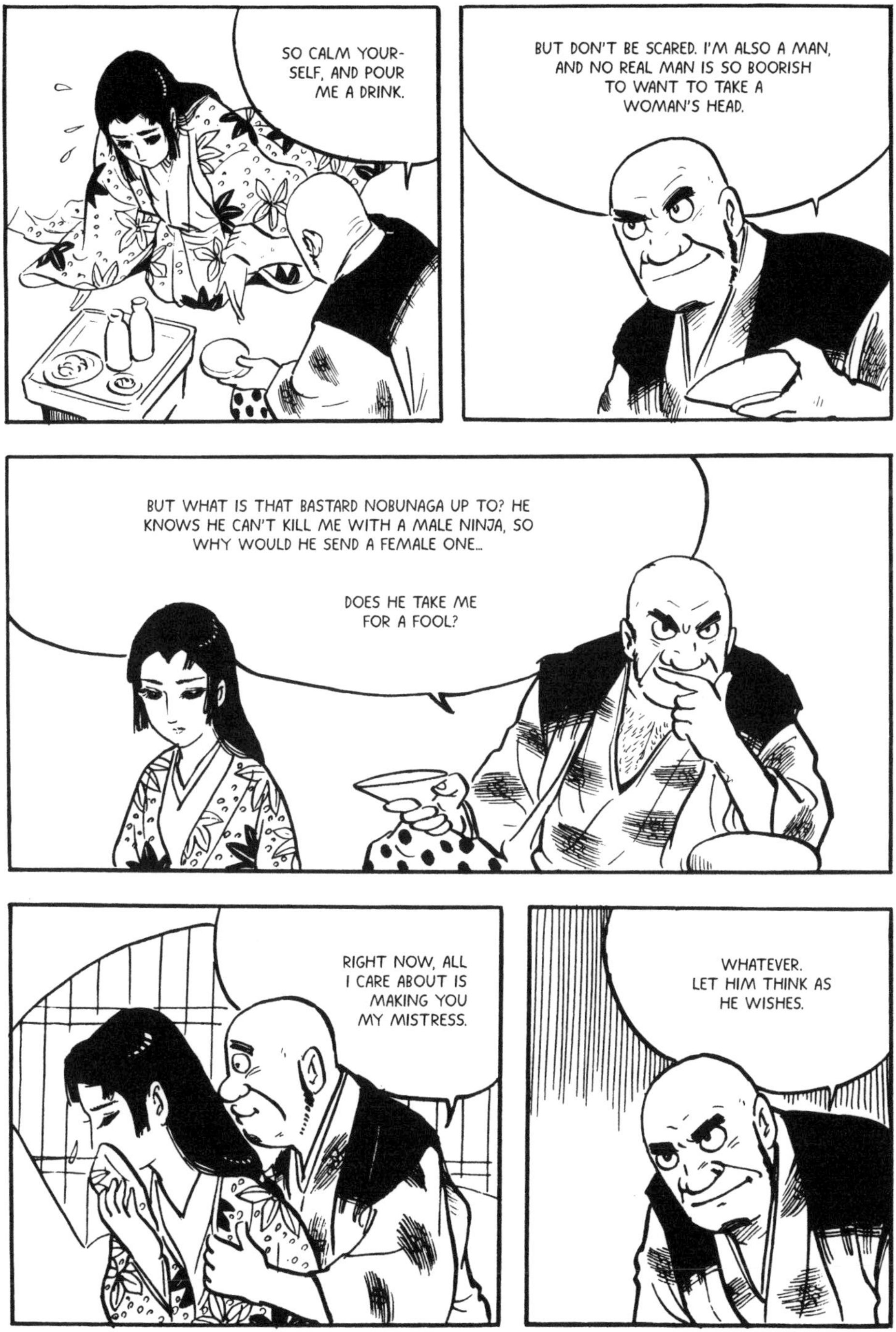
BUT DON'T BE SCARED. I'M ALSO A MAN, AND NO REAL MAN IS SO BOORISH TO WANT TO TAKE A WOMAN'S HEAD.
SO CALM YOURSELF, AND POUR ME A DRINK.
BUT WHAT IS THAT BASTARD NOBUNAGA UP TO? HE KNOWS HE CAN'T KILL ME WITH A MALE NINJA, SO WHY WOULD HE SEND A FEMALE ONE...
DOES HE TAKE ME FOR A FOOL?
WHATEVER. LET HIM THINK AS HE WISHES.
RIGHT NOW, ALL I CARE ABOUT IS MAKING YOU MY MISTRESS.

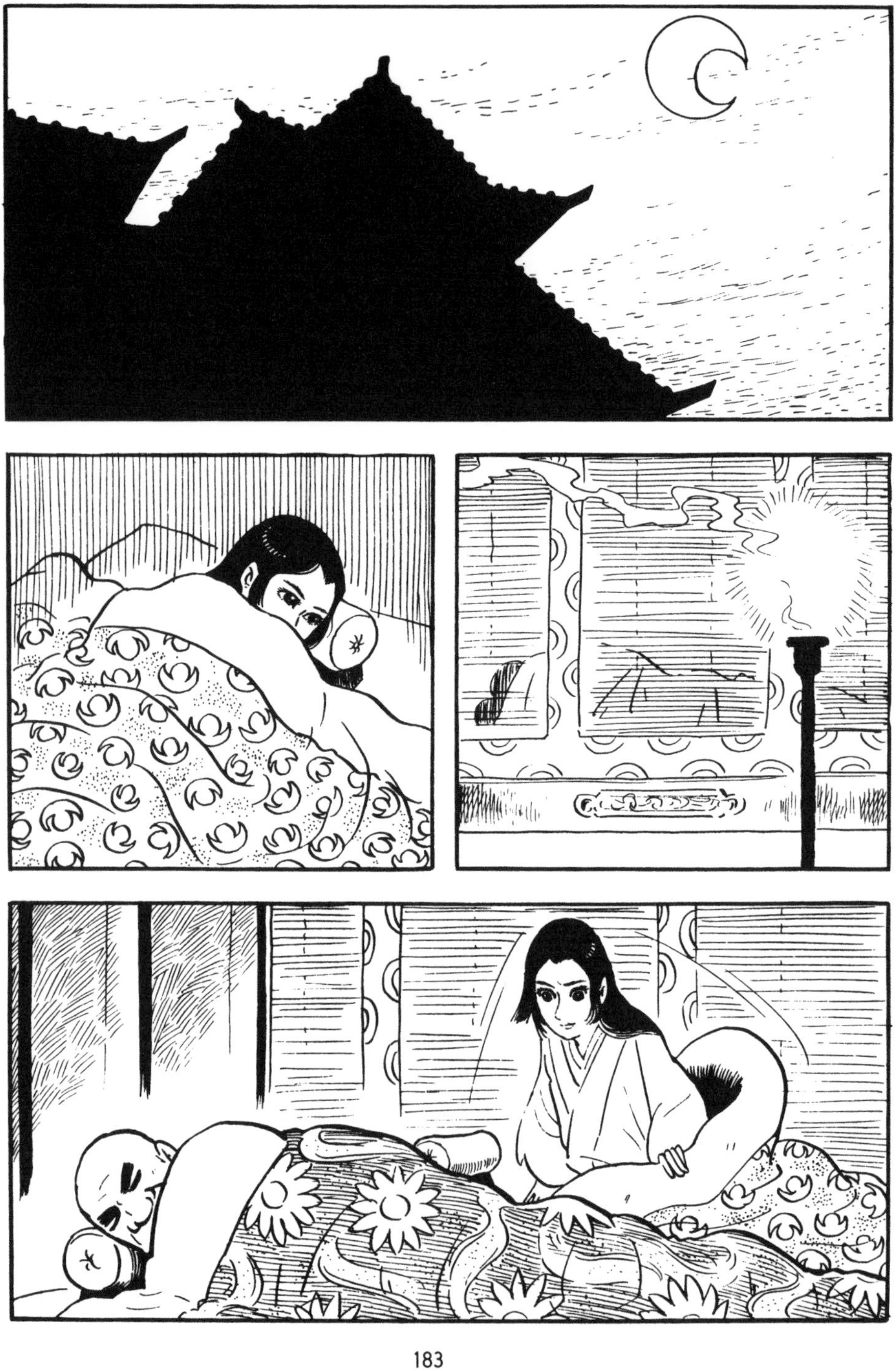

IT IS TRUE,
NO NINJA IS A
MATCH FOR HIM...

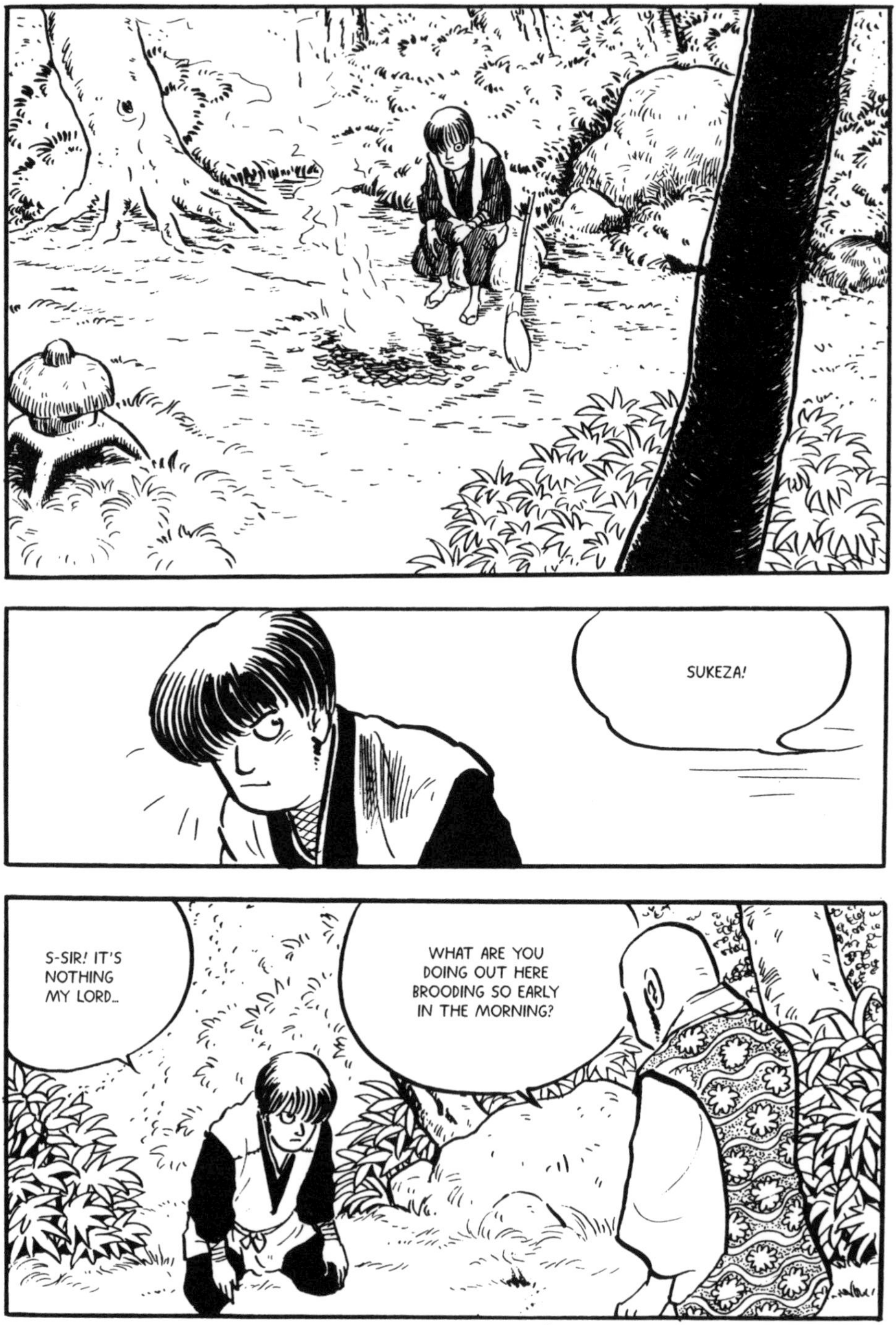
SUKEZA!
WHAT ARE YOU DOING OUT HERE BROODING SO EARLY IN THE MORNING?
S-SIR! IT'S NOTHING MY LORD...

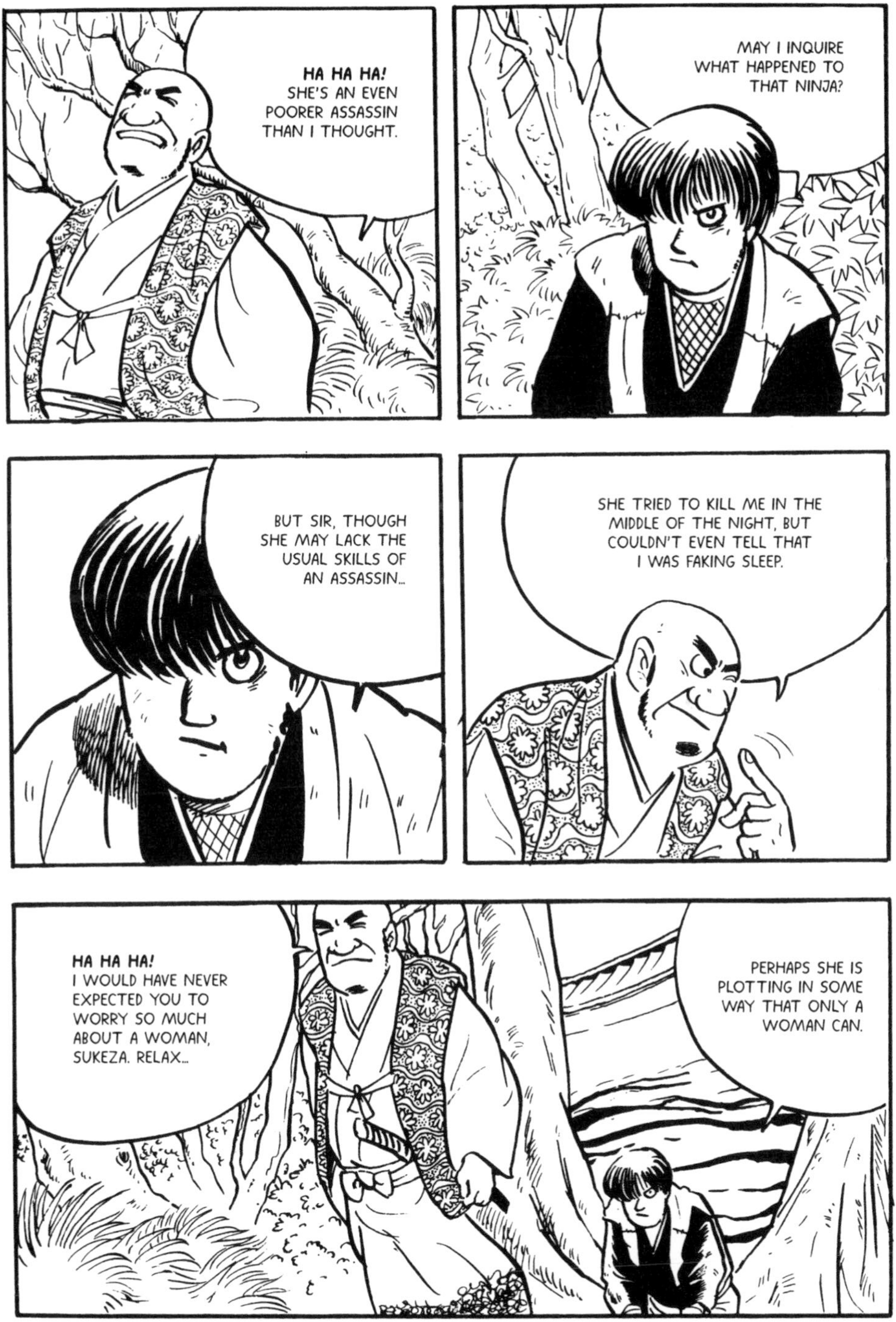
MAY I INQUIRE WHAT HAPPENED TO THAT NINJA?
HA HA HA! SHE'S AN EVEN POORER ASSASSIN THAN I THOUGHT.
SHE TRIED TO KILL ME IN THE MIDDLE OF THE NIGHT, BUT COULDN'T EVEN TELL THAT I WAS FAKING SLEEP.
BUT SIR, THOUGH SHE MAY LACK THE USUAL SKILLS OF AN ASSASSIN...
PERHAPS SHE IS PLOTTING IN SOME WAY THAT ONLY A WOMAN CAN.
HA HA HA! I WOULD HAVE NEVER EXPECTED YOU TO WORRY SO MUCH ABOUT A WOMAN, SUKEZA. RELAX...

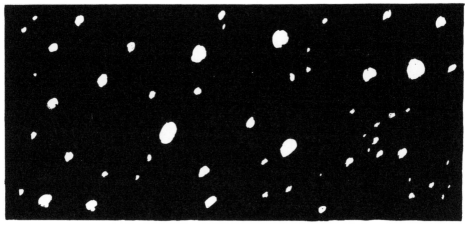

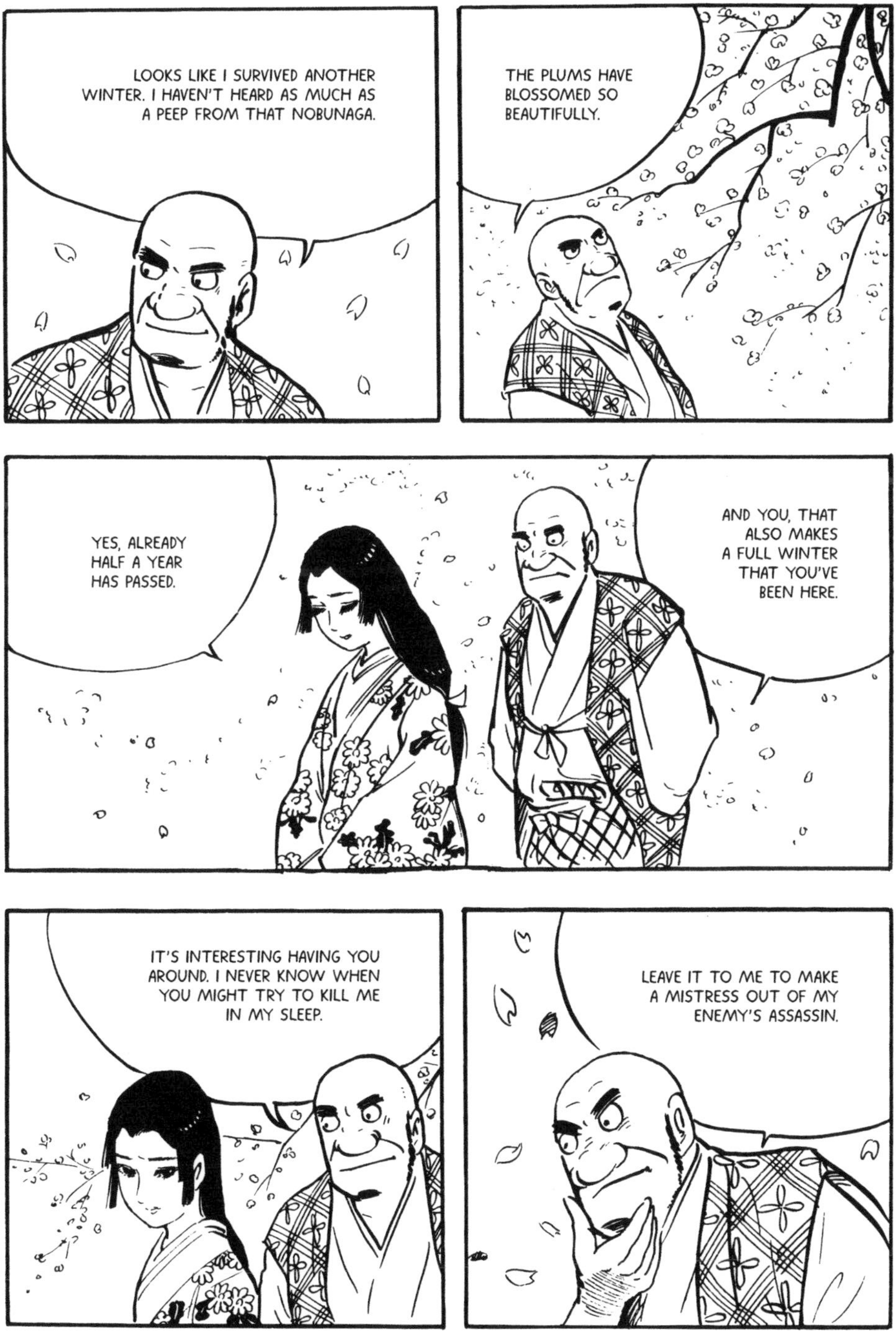
THE PLUMS HAVE BLOSSOMED SO BEAUTIFULLY.
LOOKS LIKE I SURVIVED ANOTHER WINTER. I HAVEN'T HEARD AS MUCH AS A PEEP FROM THAT NOBUNAGA.
AND YOU, THAT ALSO MAKES A FULL WINTER THAT YOU'VE BEEN HERE.
YES, ALREADY HALF A YEAR HAS PASSED.
LEAVE IT TO ME TO MAKE A MISTRESS OUT OF MY ENEMY'S ASSASSIN.
IT'S INTERESTING HAVING YOU AROUND. I NEVER KNOW WHEN YOU MIGHT TRY TO KILL ME IN MY SLEEP.

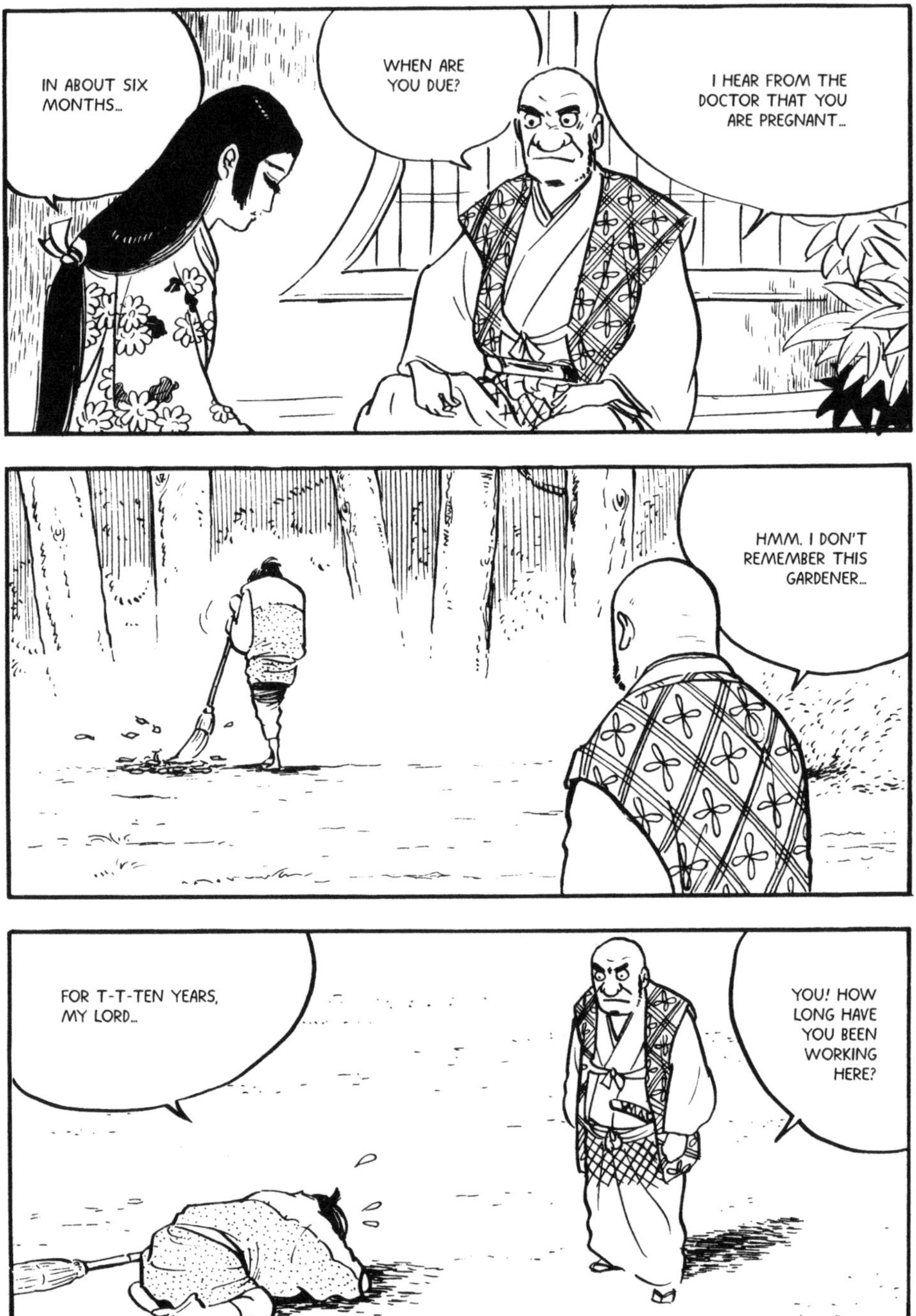
I HEAR FROM THE DOCTOR THAT YOU ARE PREGNANT...
WHEN ARE YOU DUE?
IN ABOUT SIX MONTHS...
HMM. I DON'T REMEMBER THIS GARDENER...
YOU! HOW LONG HAVE YOU BEEN WORKING HERE?
FOR T-T-TEN YEARS, MY LORD...

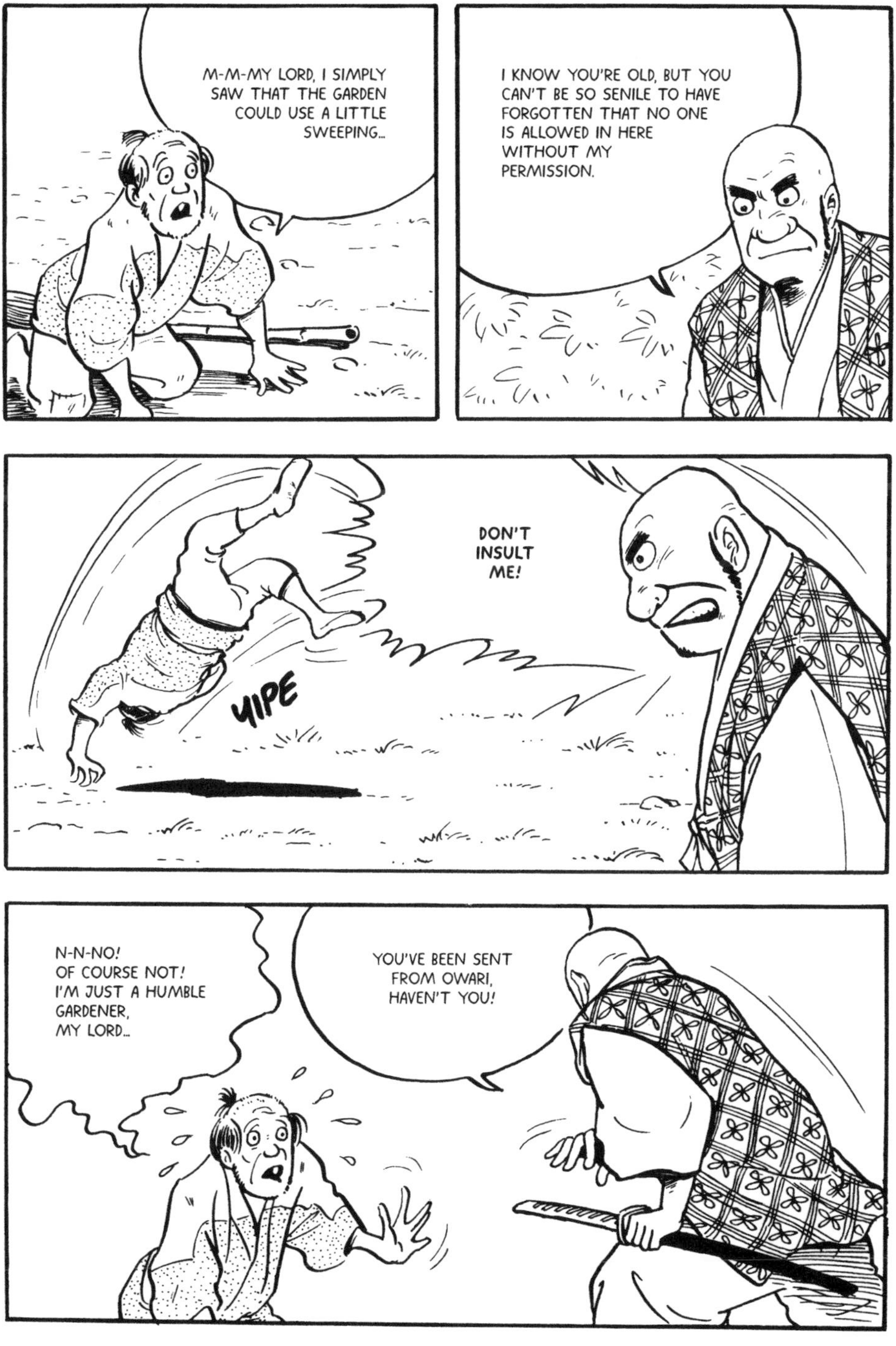
I KNOW YOU'RE OLD, BUT YOU CAN'T BE SO SENILE TO HAVE FORGOTTEN THAT NO ONE IS ALLOWED IN HERE WITHOUT MY PERMISSION.
M-M-MY LORD, I SIMPLY SAW THAT THE GARDEN COULD USE A LITTLE SWEEPING...
DON'T INSULT ME!
YIPE
YOU'VE BEEN SENT FROM OWARI, HAVEN'T YOU!
N-N-NO! OF COURSE NOT! I'M JUST A HUMBLE GARDENER, MY LORD...

OUT WITH IT! WHO IN THIS PALACE ARE YOU WORKING WITH!
TELL ME OR YOU DIE!!
MY LORD, PLEASE! I'M TELLING THE TRUTH!
SOMEBODY!!
THIS MAN'S A NINJA FROM OWARI. STRING HIM UP!
WHAT??
THIS OLD FART? A NINJA?!
BUT WE KNOW HIM...
THAT NOBUNAGA! FIRST HE SENDS A WOMAN, AND NOW AN OLD MAN...

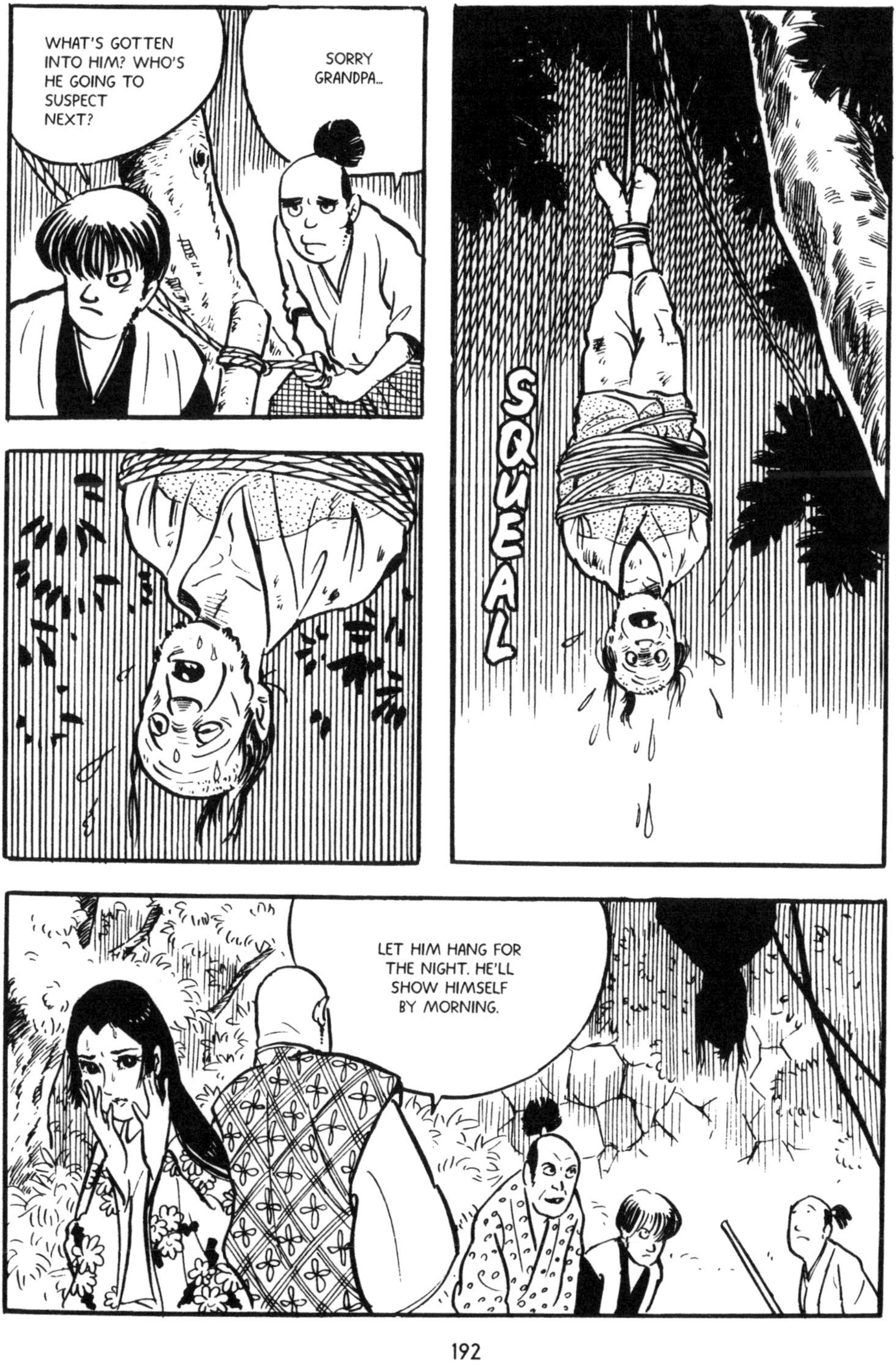
SQUEAL
SORRY GRANDPA...
WHAT'S GOTTEN INTO HIM? WHO'S HE GOING TO SUSPECT NEXT?
LET HIM HANG FOR THE NIGHT. HE'LL SHOW HIMSELF BY MORNING.

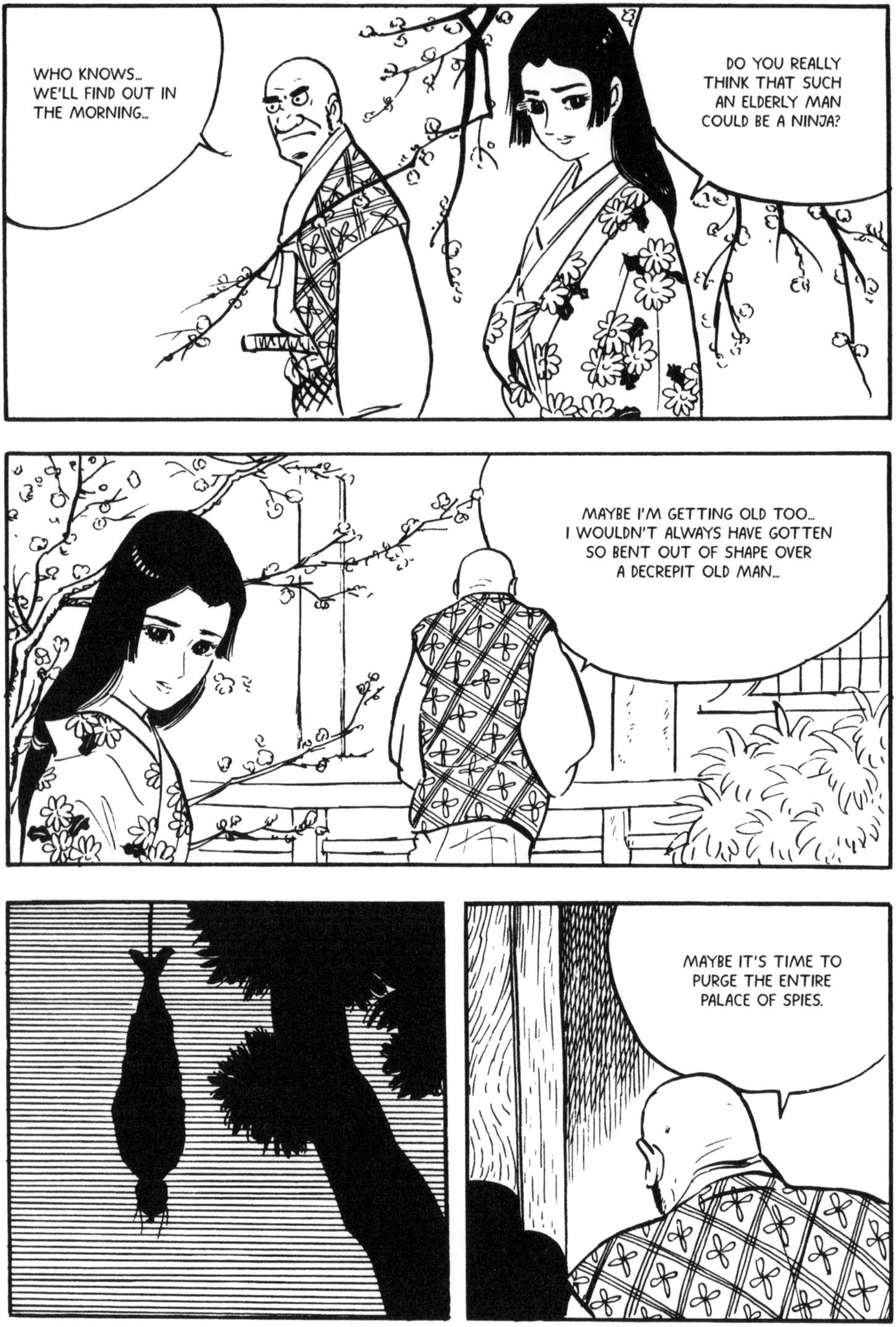
DO YOU REALLY THINK THAT SUCH AN ELDERLY MAN COULD BE A NINJA?
WHO KNOWS... WE'LL FIND OUT IN THE MORNING...
MAYBE I'M GETTING OLD TOO... I WOULDN'T ALWAYS HAVE GOTTEN SO BENT OUT OF SHAPE OVER A DECREPIT OLD MAN...
MAYBE IT'S TIME TO PURGE THE ENTIRE PALACE OF SPIES.

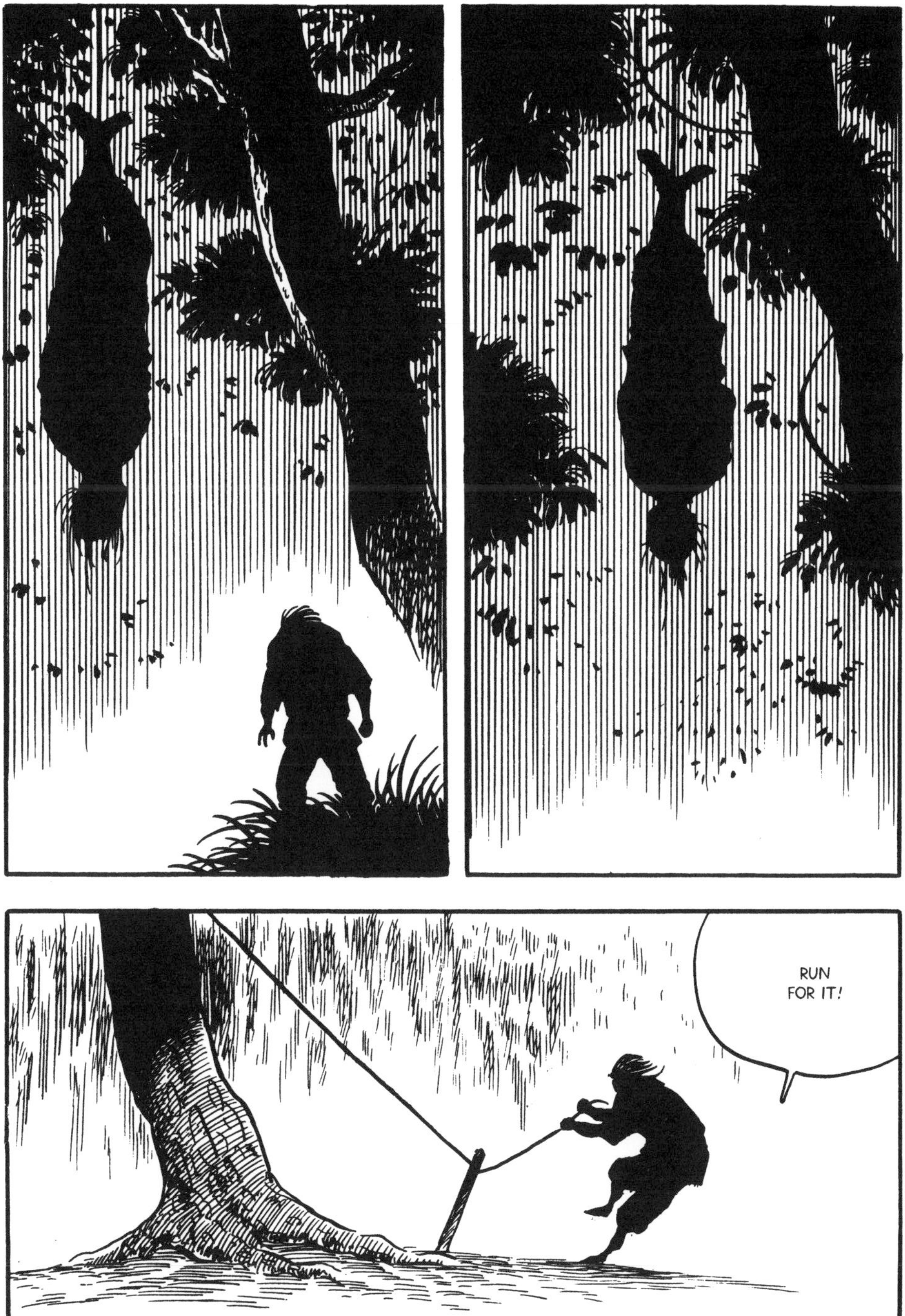
RUN FOR IT!

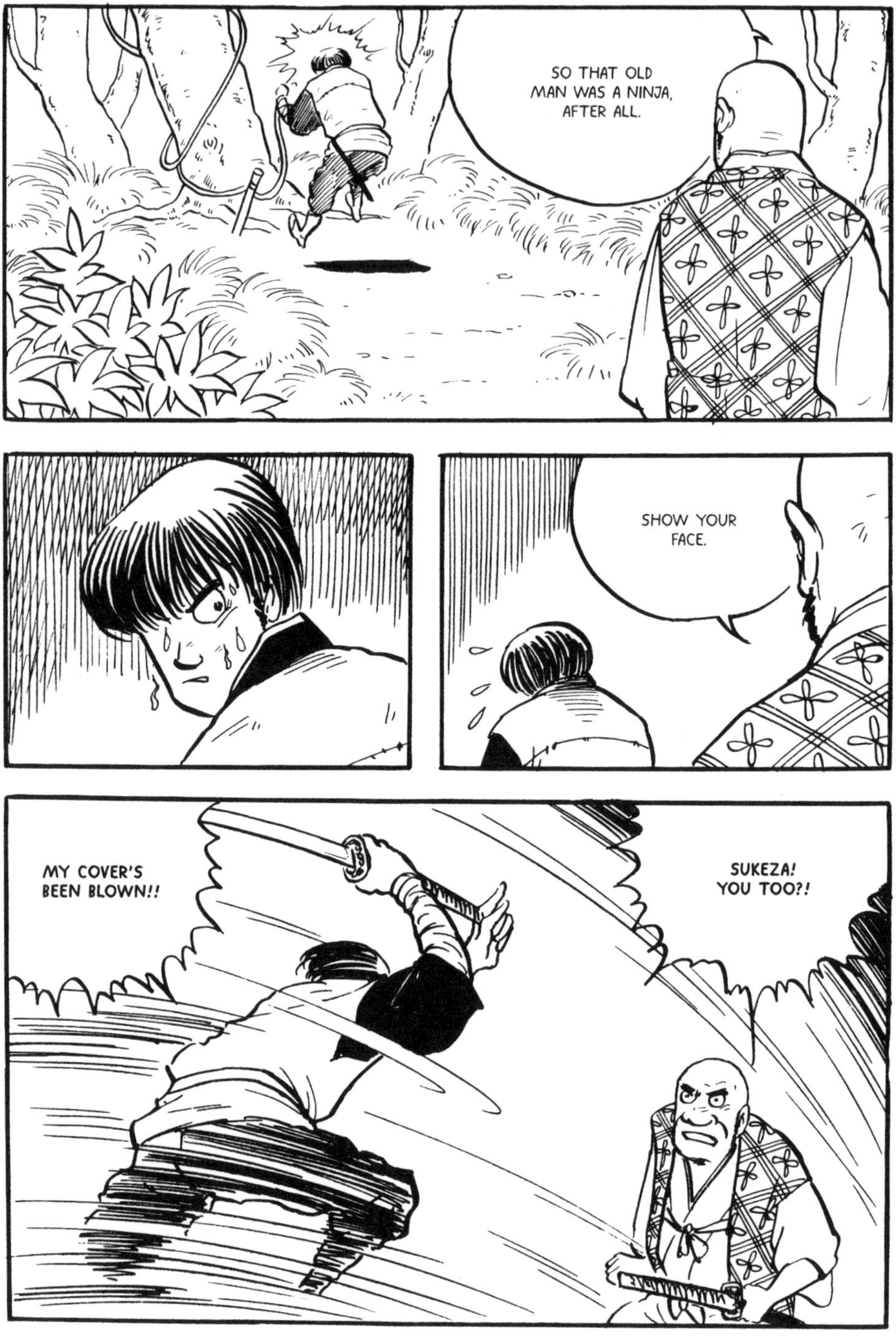
SO THAT OLD MAN WAS A NINJA, AFTER ALL.
SHOW YOUR FACE.
SUKEZA! YOU TOO?!
MY COVER'S BEEN BLOWN!!

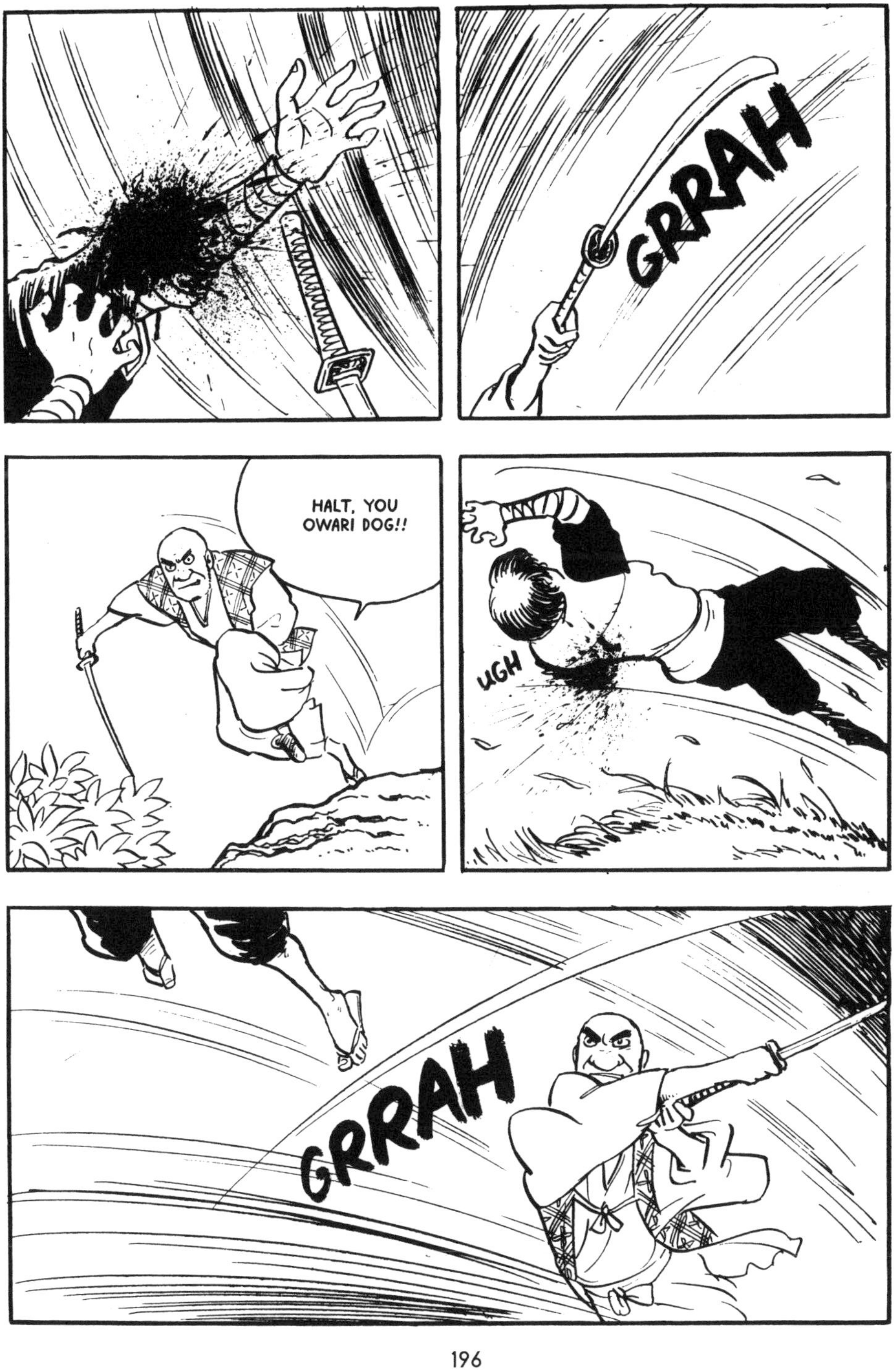
GRRAH
UGH
HALT, YOU OWARI DOG!!
GRRAH

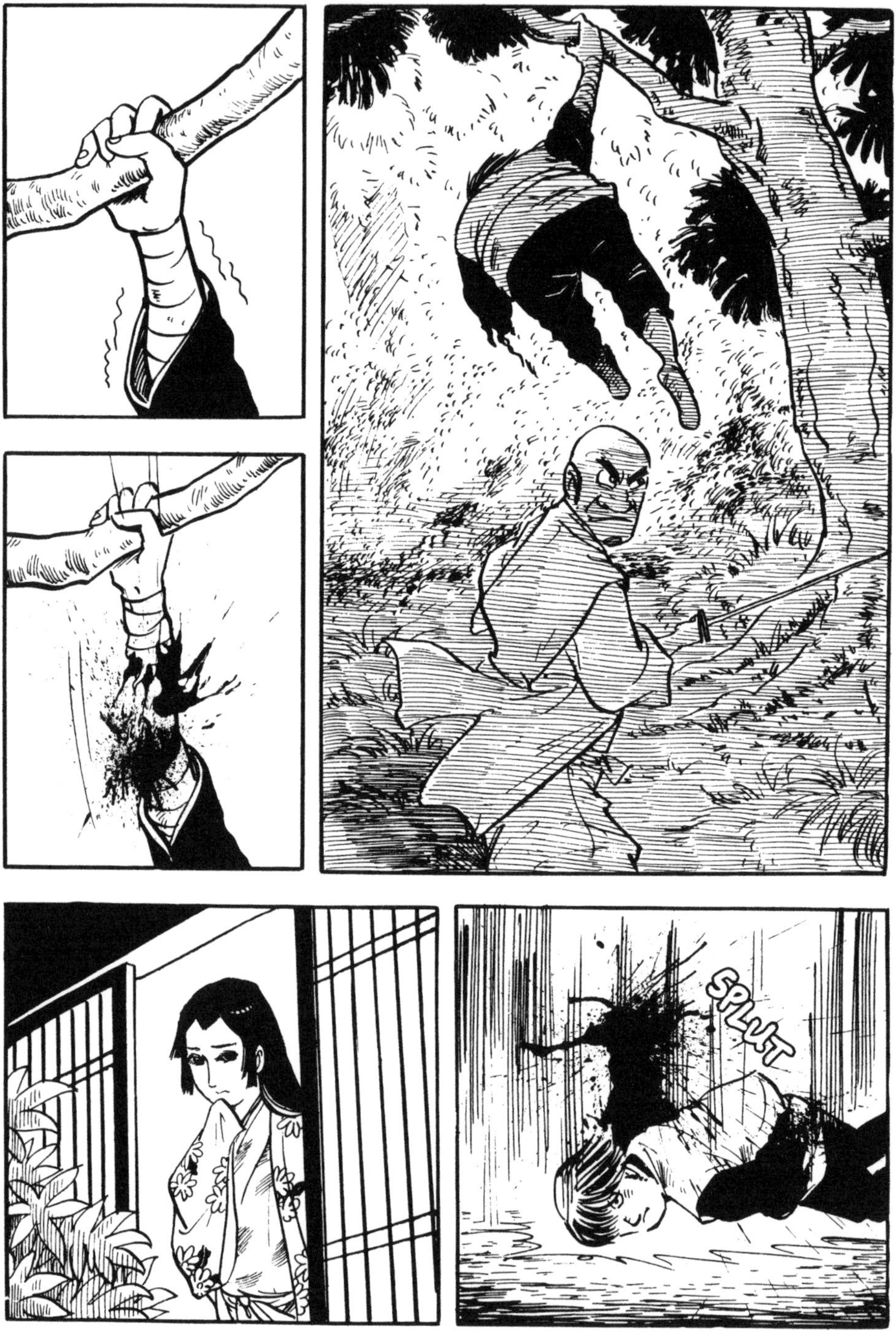
SPLUT

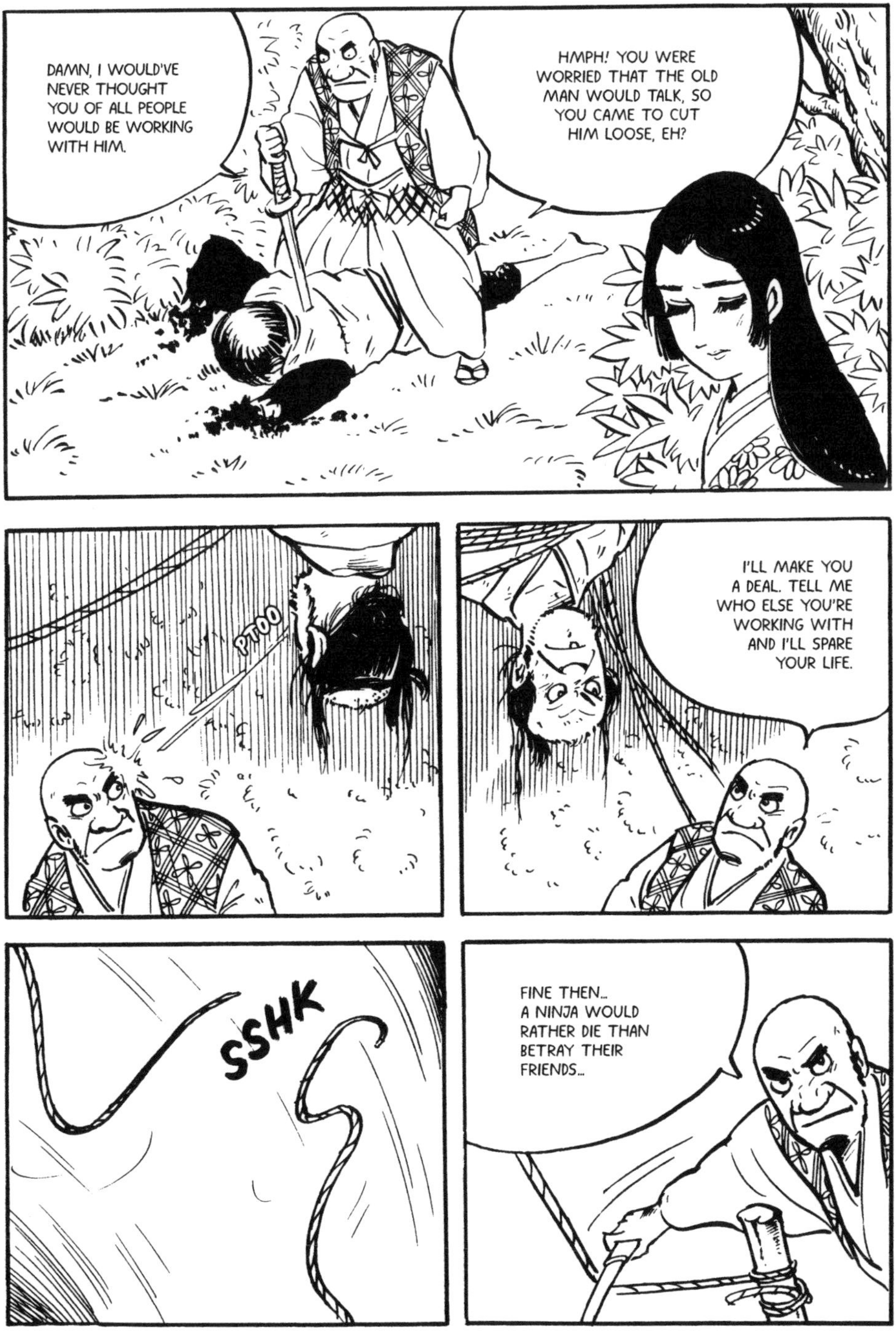
HMPH! YOU WERE WORRIED THAT THE OLD MAN WOULD TALK, SO YOU CAME TO CUT HIM LOOSE, EH?
DAMN, I WOULD'VE NEVER THOUGHT YOU OF ALL PEOPLE WOULD BE WORKING WITH HIM.
I'LL MAKE YOU A DEAL. TELL ME WHO ELSE YOU'RE WORKING WITH AND I'LL SPARE YOUR LIFE.
PTOO
FINE THEN... A NINJA WOULD RATHER DIE THAN BETRAY THEIR FRIENDS...
SSHK

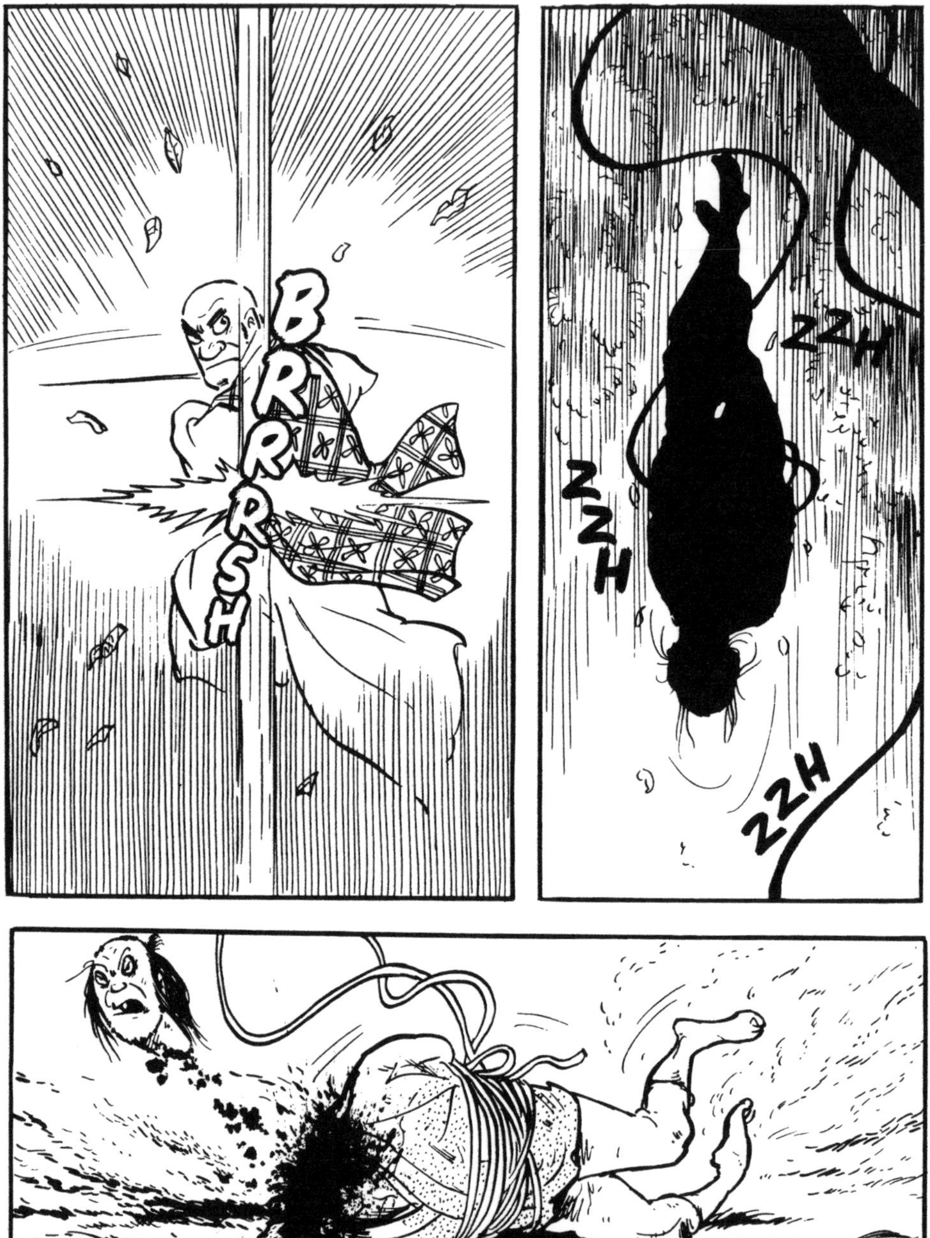
ZZH
ZZH
ZZH
BRRRSH

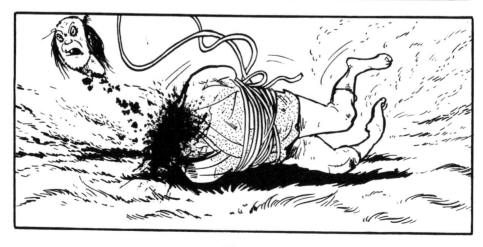

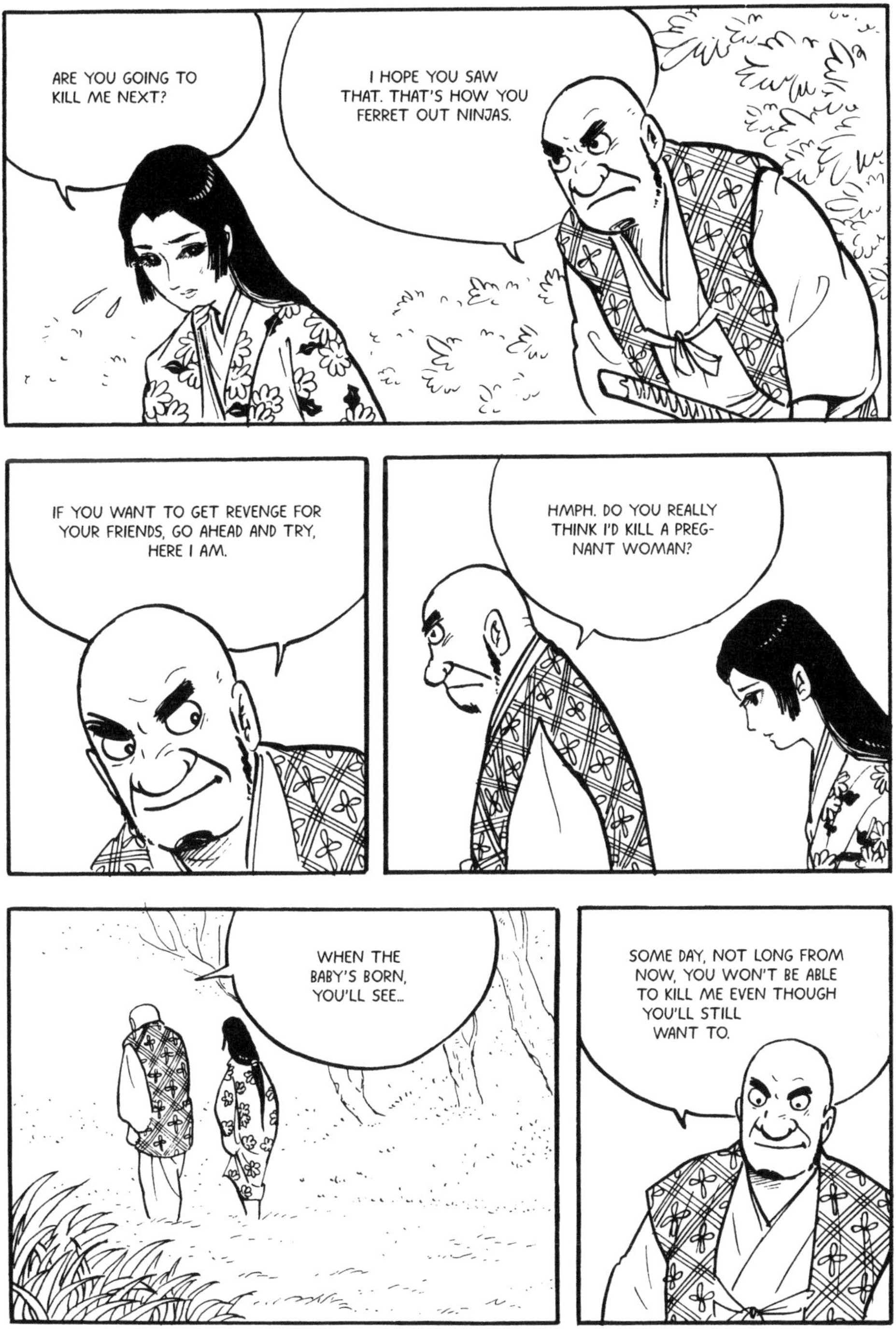
I HOPE YOU SAW THAT. THAT'S HOW YOU FERRET OUT NINJAS.
ARE YOU GOING TO KILL ME NEXT?
HMPH. DO YOU REALLY THINK I'D KILL A PREG-NANT WOMAN?
IF YOU WANT TO GET REVENGE FOR YOUR FRIENDS, GO AHEAD AND TRY, HERE I AM.
SOME DAY, NOT LONG FROM NOW, YOU WON'T BE ABLE TO KILL ME EVEN THOUGH YOU'LL STILL WANT TO.
WHEN THE BABY'S BORN, YOU'LL SEE...

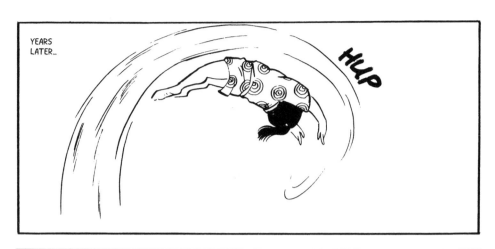

YEARS
LATER...

HUP

TUNK

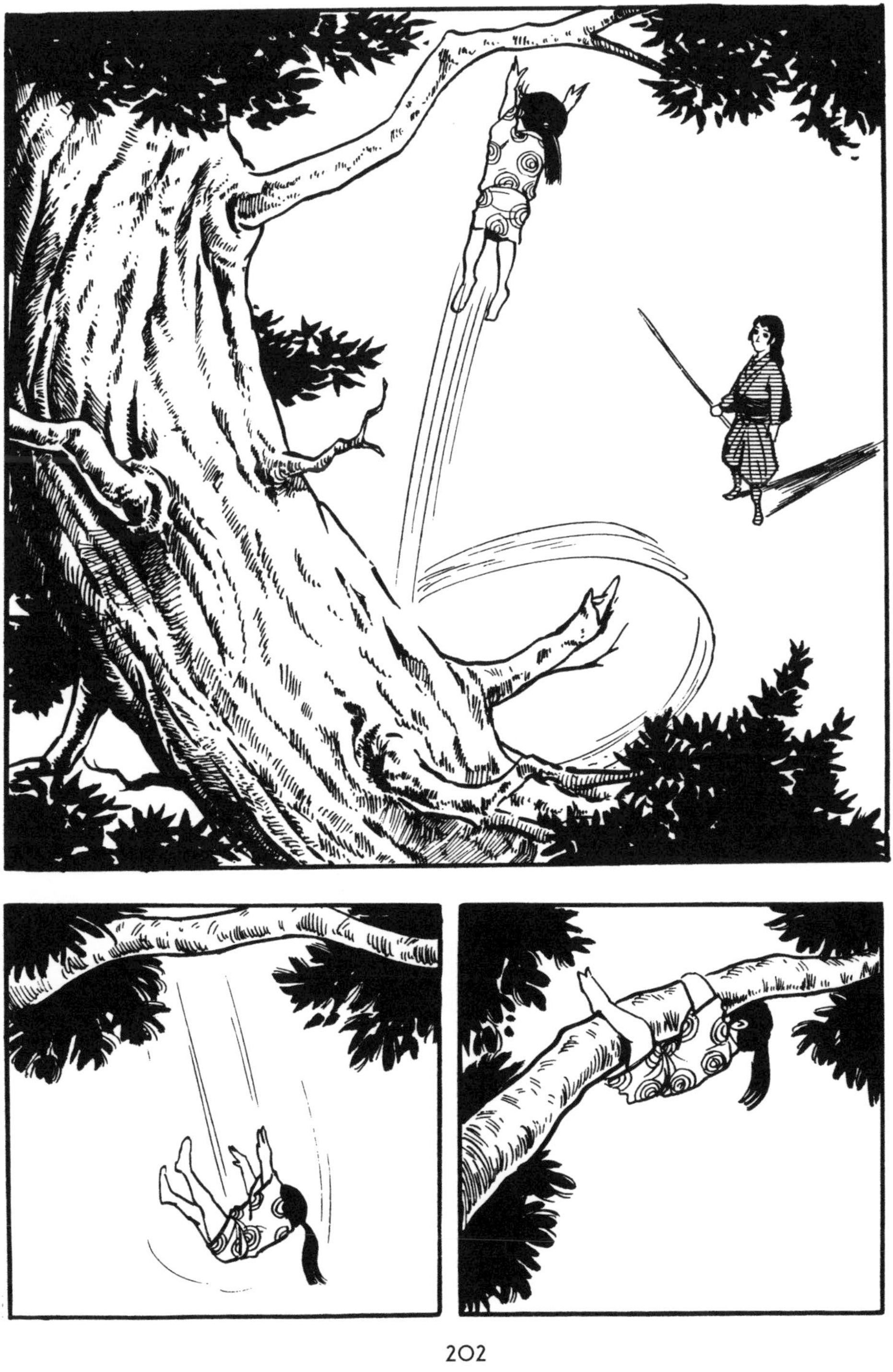

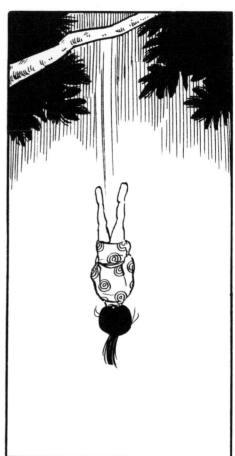

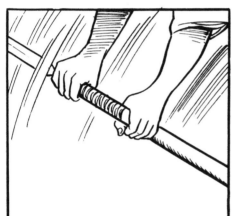

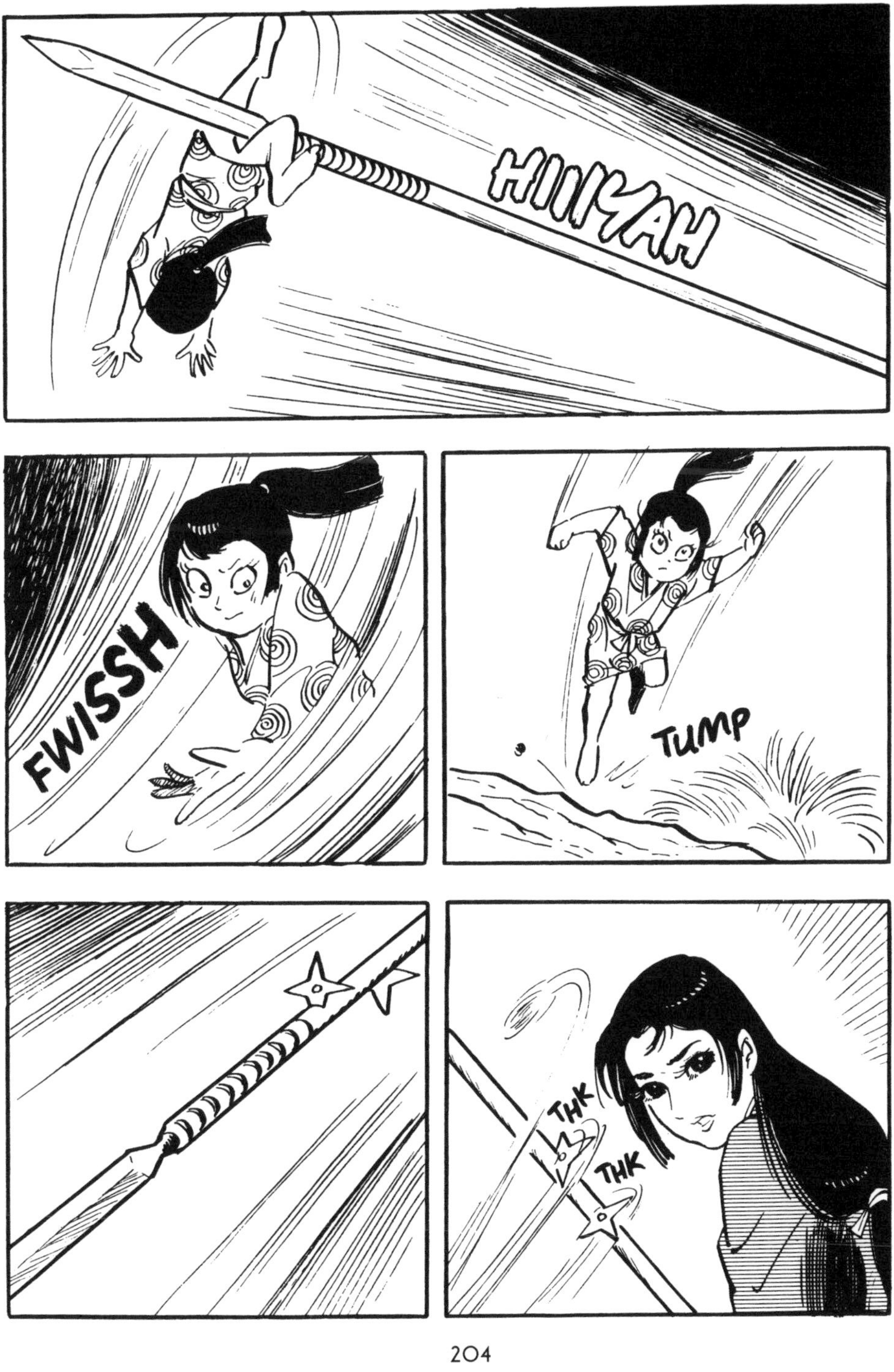
HIIYAH
TUMP
FWISSH
THK
THK

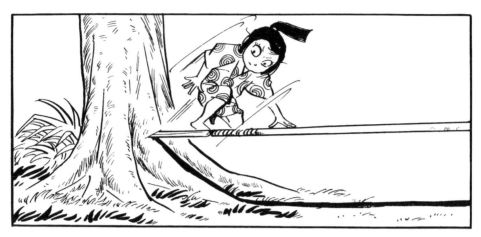

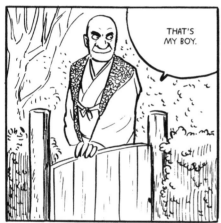

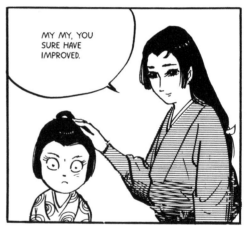

MY MY, YOU SURE HAVE IMPROVED.
THAT'S MY BOY.
HELLO, MY LORD, WHEN DID YOU RETURN?
AHH... THE WARS NEVER END. IT'S BEEN SO LONG SINCE I'VE SEEN YOU TWO.

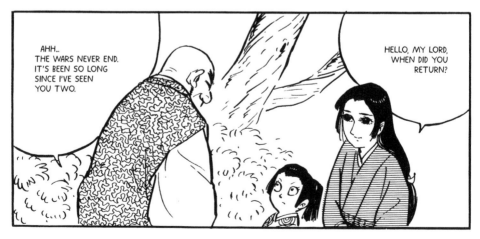

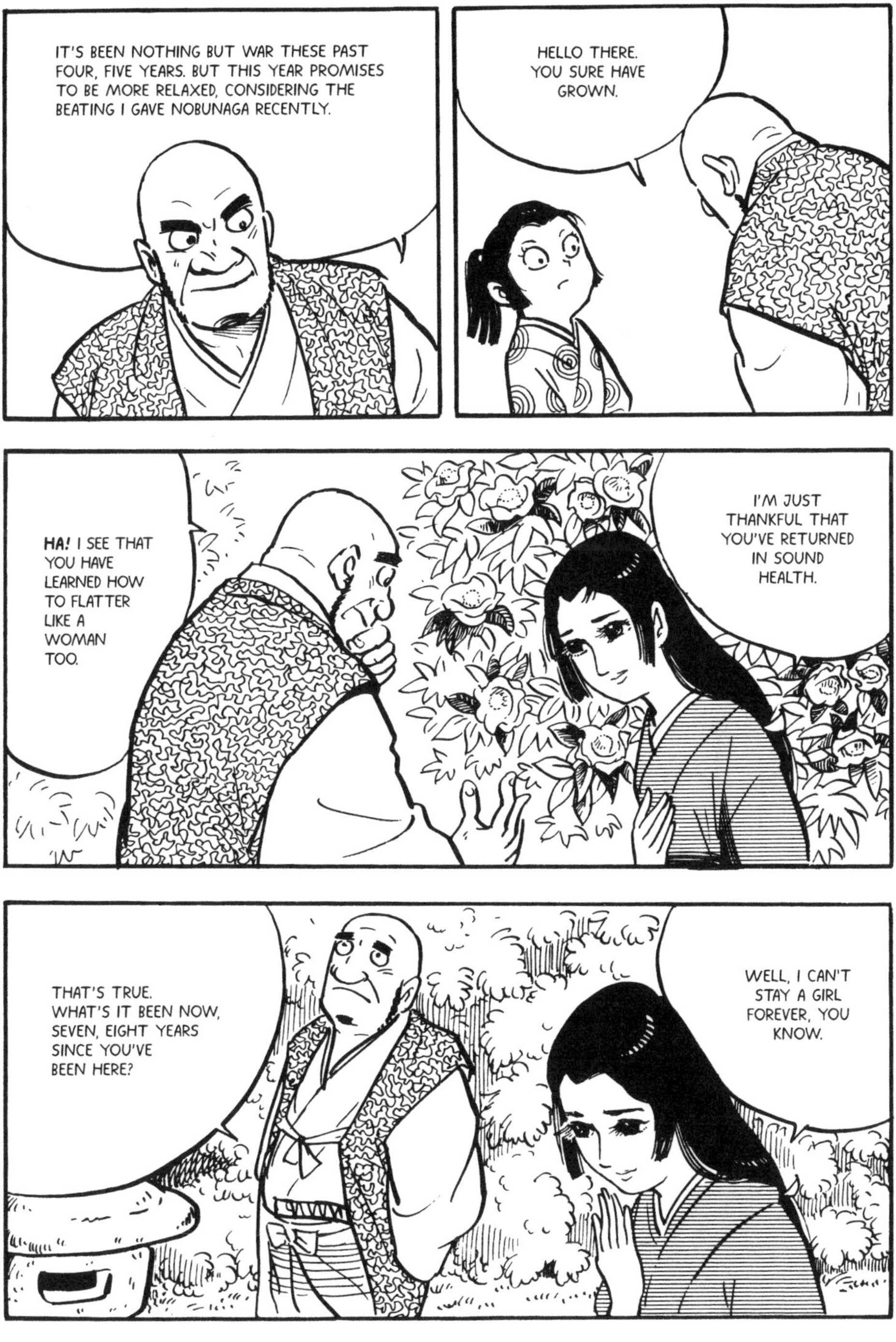
HELLO THERE. YOU SURE HAVE GROWN.
IT'S BEEN NOTHING BUT WAR THESE PAST FOUR, FIVE YEARS. BUT THIS YEAR PROMISES TO BE MORE RELAXED, CONSIDERING THE BEATING I GAVE NOBUNAGA RECENTLY.
I'M JUST THANKFUL THAT YOU'VE RETURNED IN SOUND HEALTH.
HA! I SEE THAT YOU HAVE LEARNED HOW TO FLATTER LIKE A WOMAN TOO.
WELL, I CAN'T STAY A GIRL FOREVER, YOU KNOW.
THAT'S TRUE. WHAT'S IT BEEN NOW, SEVEN, EIGHT YEARS SINCE YOU'VE BEEN HERE?

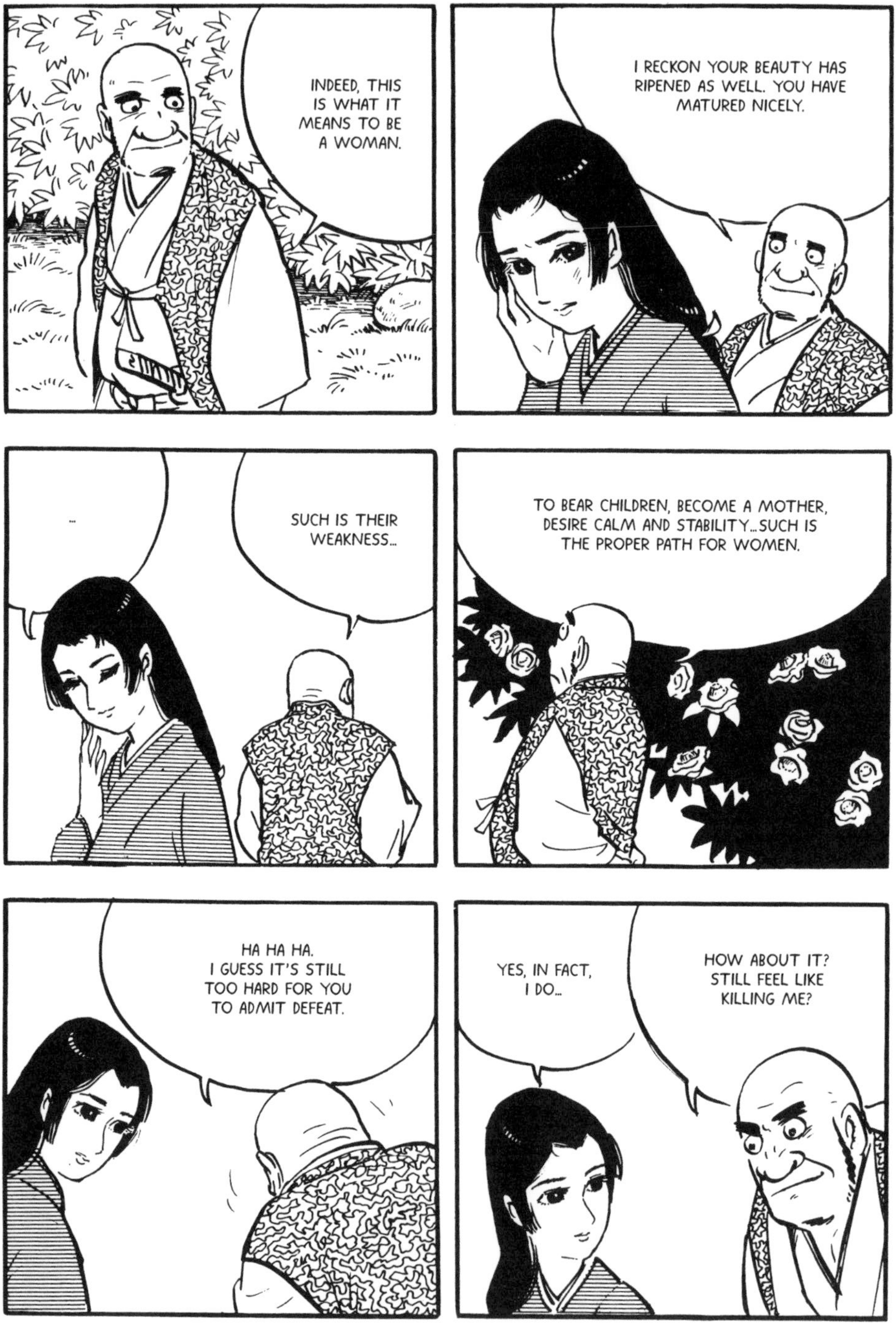

I RECKON YOUR BEAUTY HAS RIPENED AS WELL. YOU HAVE MATURED NICELY.
INDEED, THIS IS WHAT IT MEANS TO BE A WOMAN.
TO BEAR CHILDREN, BECOME A MOTHER, DESIRE CALM AND STABILITY...SUCH IS THE PROPER PATH FOR WOMEN.
SUCH IS THEIR WEAKNESS...
...
HOW ABOUT IT? STILL FEEL LIKE KILLING ME?
YES, IN FACT, I DO...
HA HA HA. I GUESS IT'S STILL TOO HARD FOR YOU TO ADMIT DEFEAT.

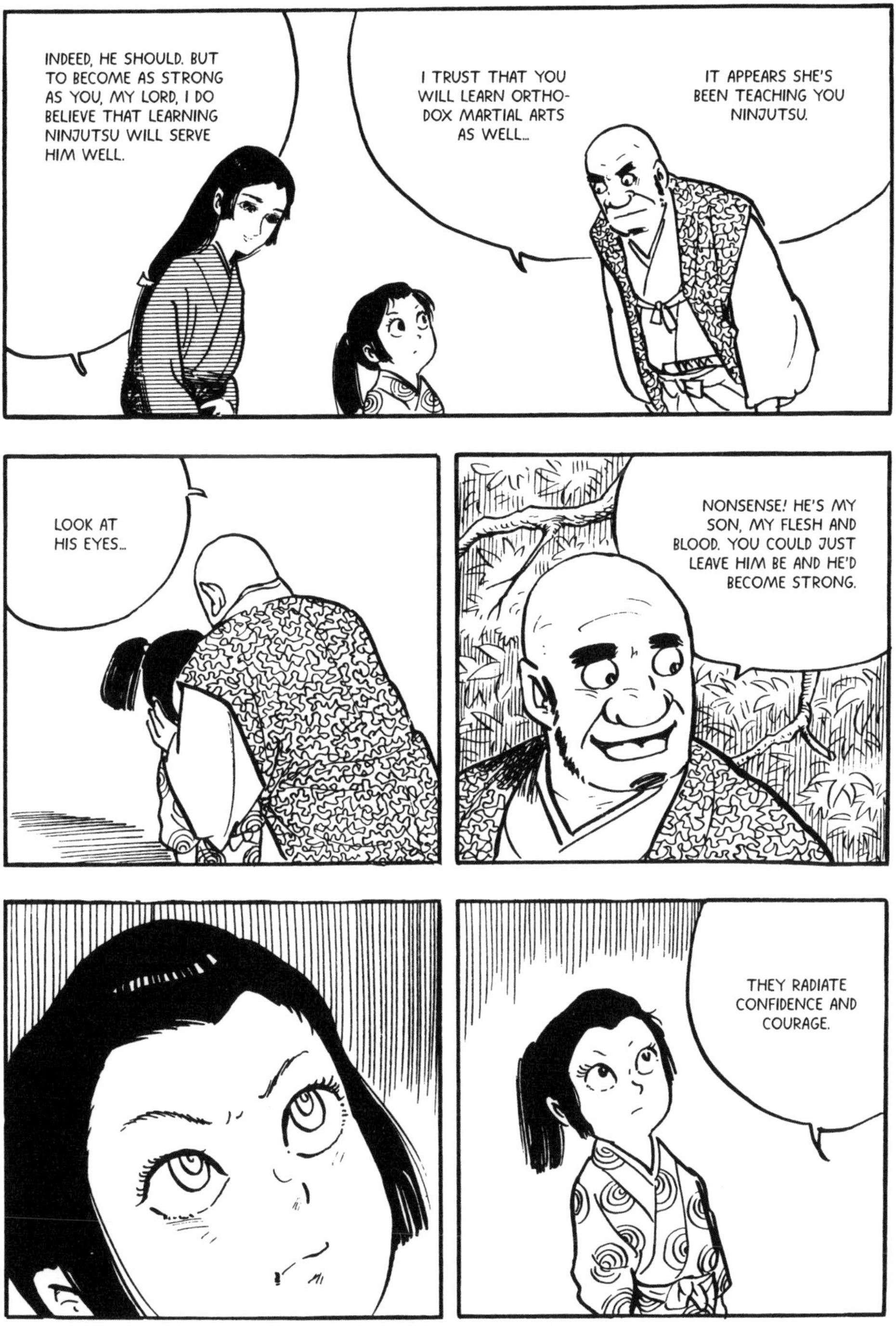
IT APPEARS SHE'S BEEN TEACHING YOU NINJUTSU.
I TRUST THAT YOU WILL LEARN ORTHODOX MARTIAL ARTS AS WELL...
INDEED, HE SHOULD. BUT TO BECOME AS STRONG AS YOU, MY LORD, I DO BELIEVE THAT LEARNING NINJUTSU WILL SERVE HIM WELL.
NONSENSE! HE'S MY SON, MY FLESH AND BLOOD. YOU COULD JUST LEAVE HIM BE AND HE'D BECOME STRONG.
LOOK AT HIS EYES...
THEY RADIATE CONFIDENCE AND COURAGE.

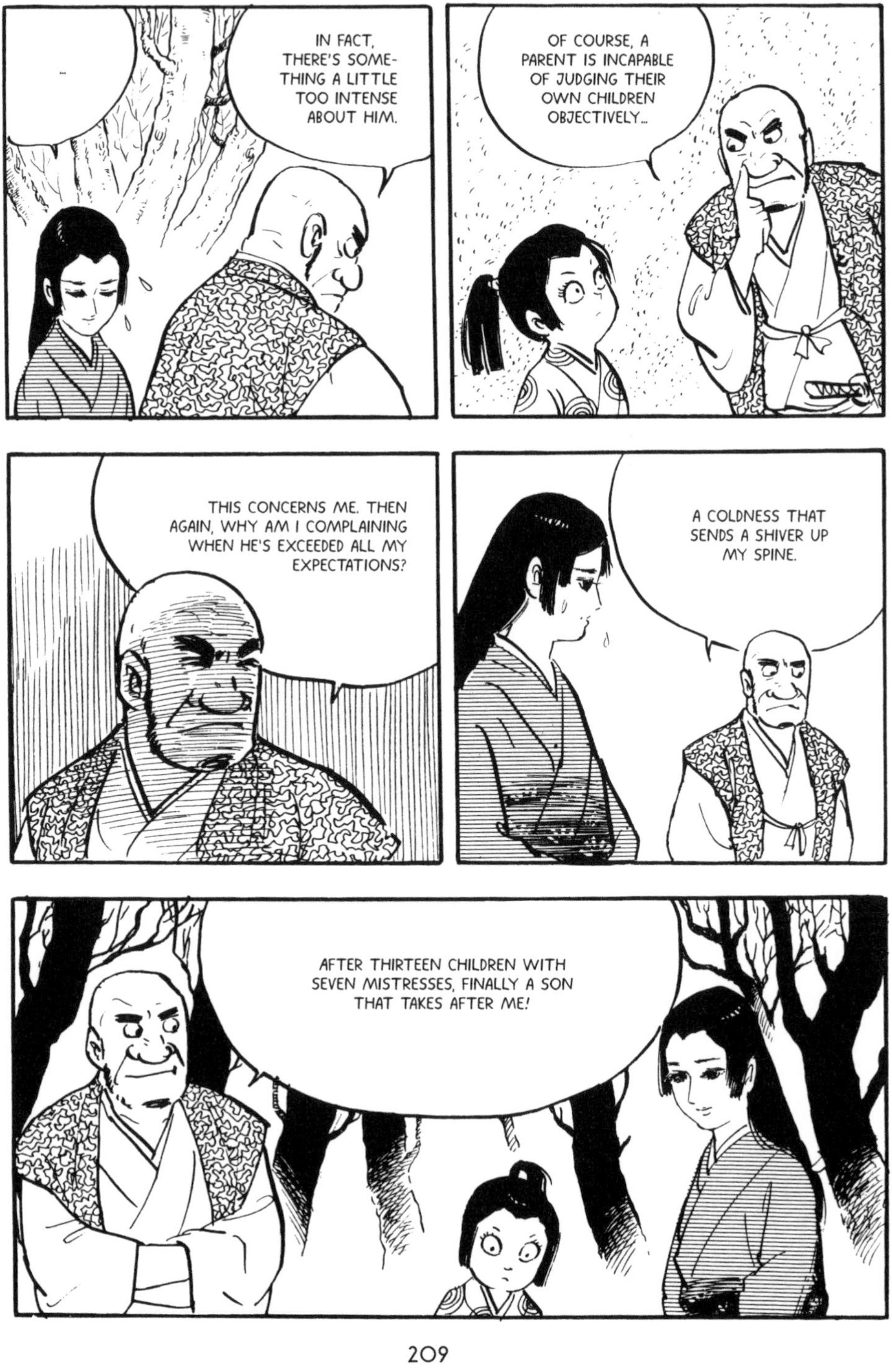
OF COURSE, A PARENT IS INCAPABLE OF JUDGING THEIR OWN CHILDREN OBJECTIVELY...
IN FACT, THERE'S SOME-THING A LITTLE TOO INTENSE ABOUT HIM.
...
A COLDNESS THAT SENDS A SHIVER UP MY SPINE.
THIS CONCERNS ME. THEN AGAIN, WHY AM I COMPLAINING WHEN HE'S EXCEEDED ALL MY EXPECTATIONS?
AFTER THIRTEEN CHILDREN WITH SEVEN MISTRESSES, FINALLY A SON THAT TAKES AFTER ME!

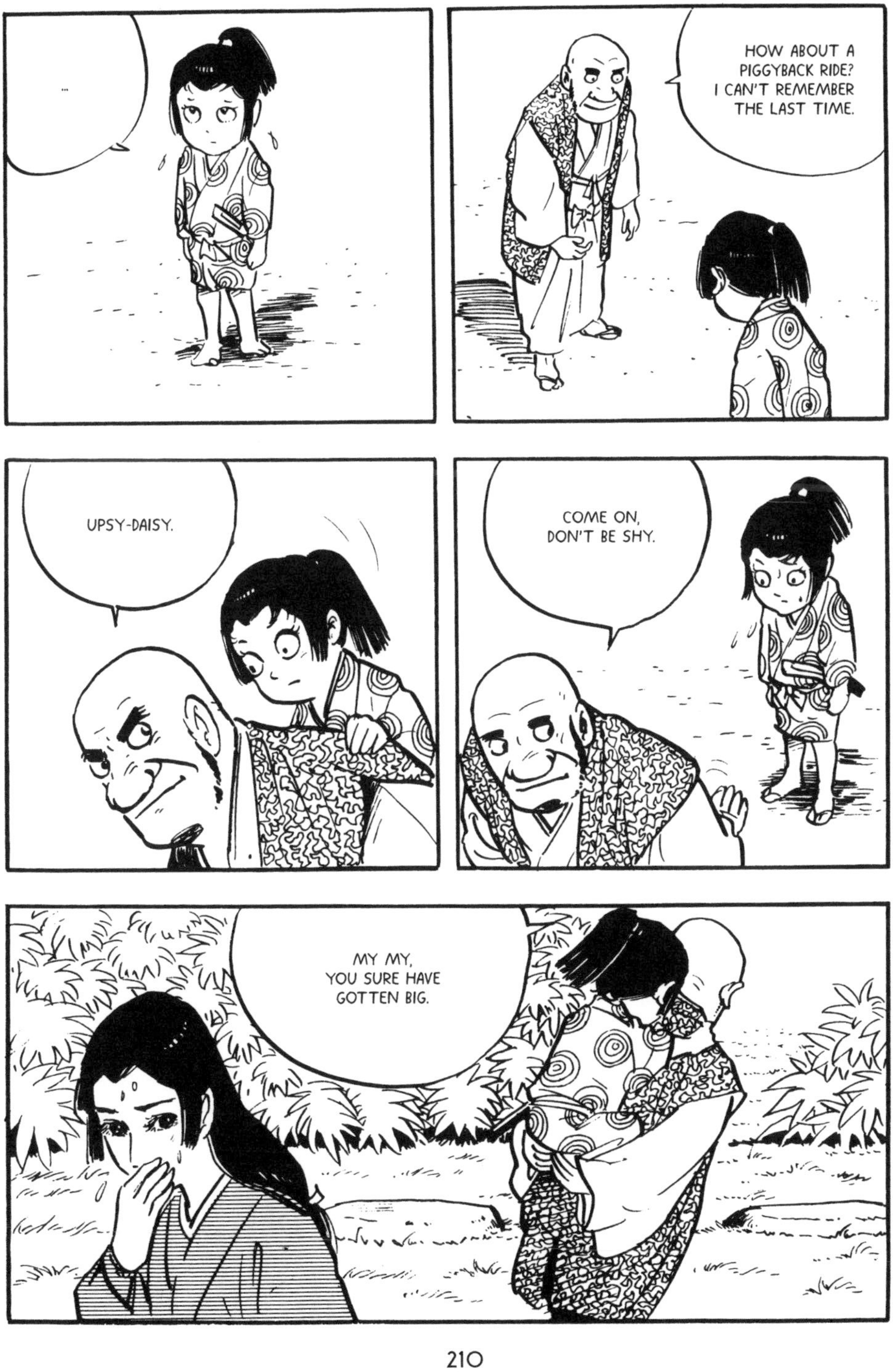
HOW ABOUT A PIGGYBACK RIDE? I CAN'T REMEMBER THE LAST TIME.
...
COME ON, DON'T BE SHY.
UPSY-DAISY.
MY MY, YOU SURE HAVE GOTTEN BIG.

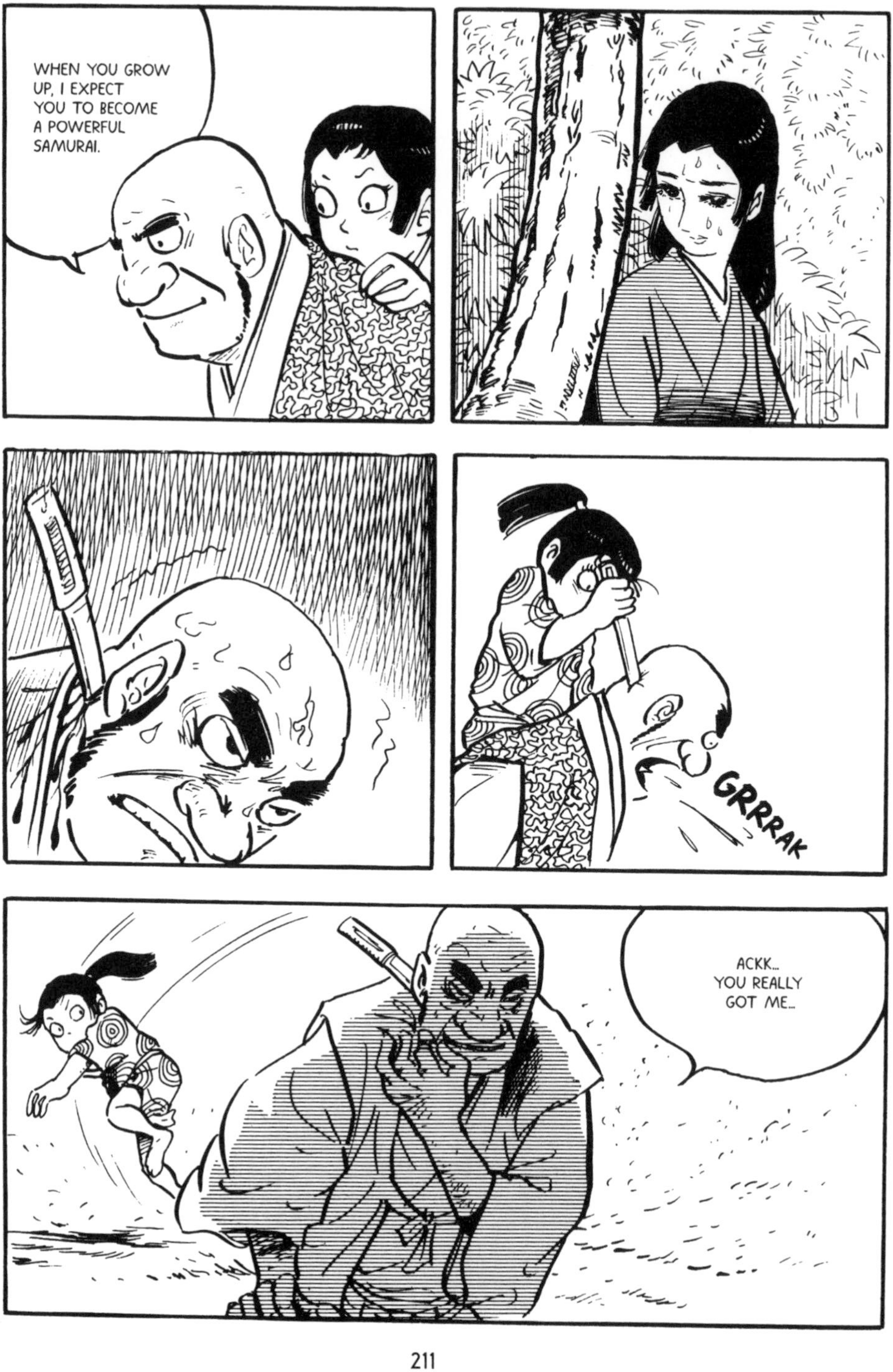
WHEN YOU GROW UP, I EXPECT YOU TO BECOME A POWERFUL SAMURAI.
GRRRAK
ACKK... YOU REALLY GOT ME...

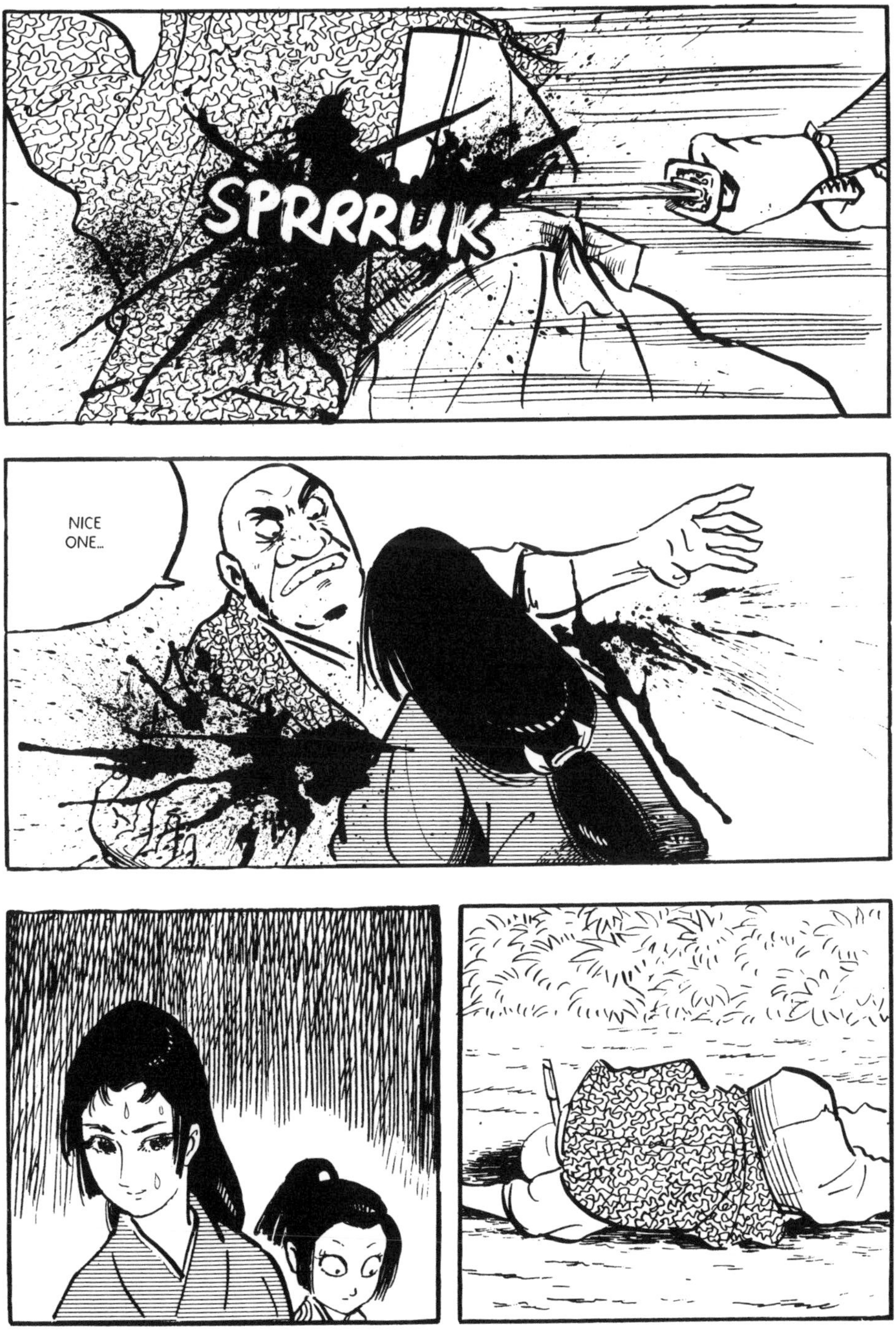
SPRRRUK
NICE ONE...

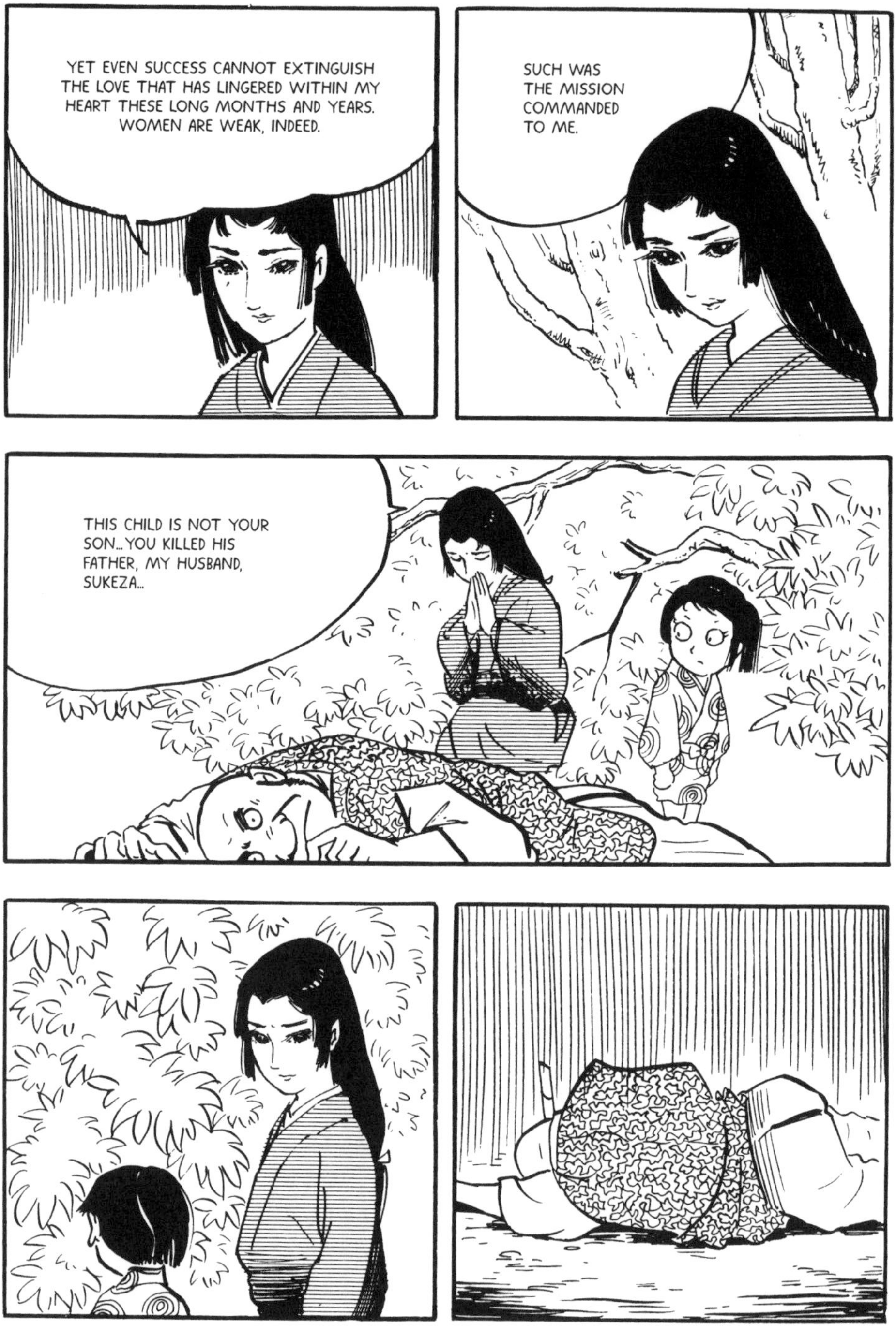
SUCH WAS THE MISSION COMMANDED TO ME.
YET EVEN SUCCESS CANNOT EXTINGUISH THE LOVE THAT HAS LINGERED WITHIN MY HEART THESE LONG MONTHS AND YEARS. WOMEN ARE WEAK, INDEED.
THIS CHILD IS NOT YOUR SON... YOU KILLED HIS FATHER, MY HUSBAND, SUKEZA...

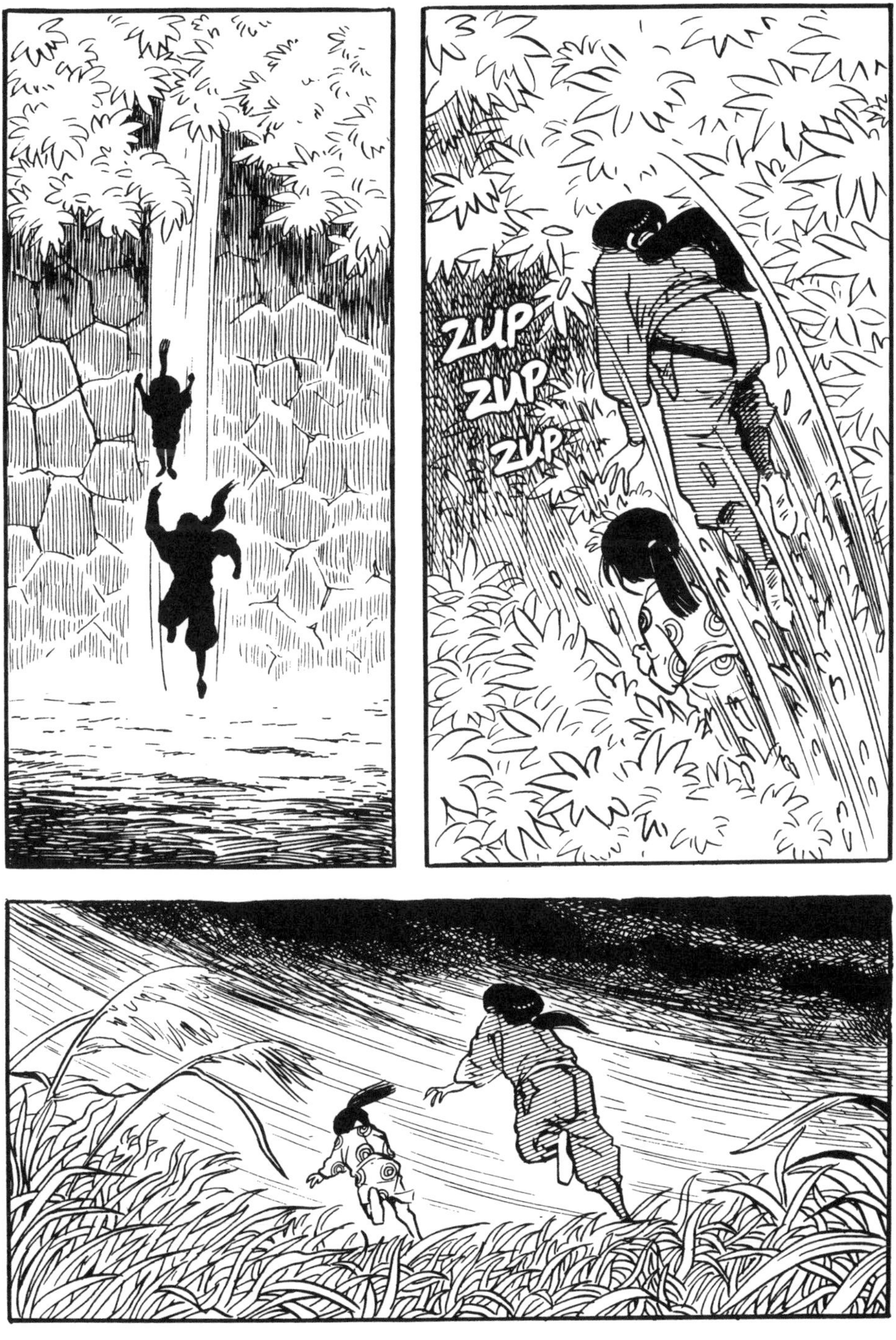
ZUP
ZUP
ZUP

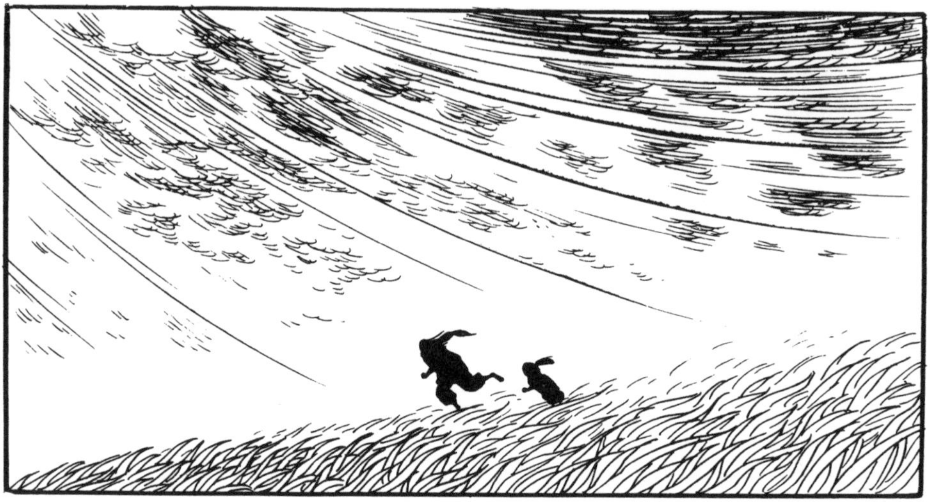

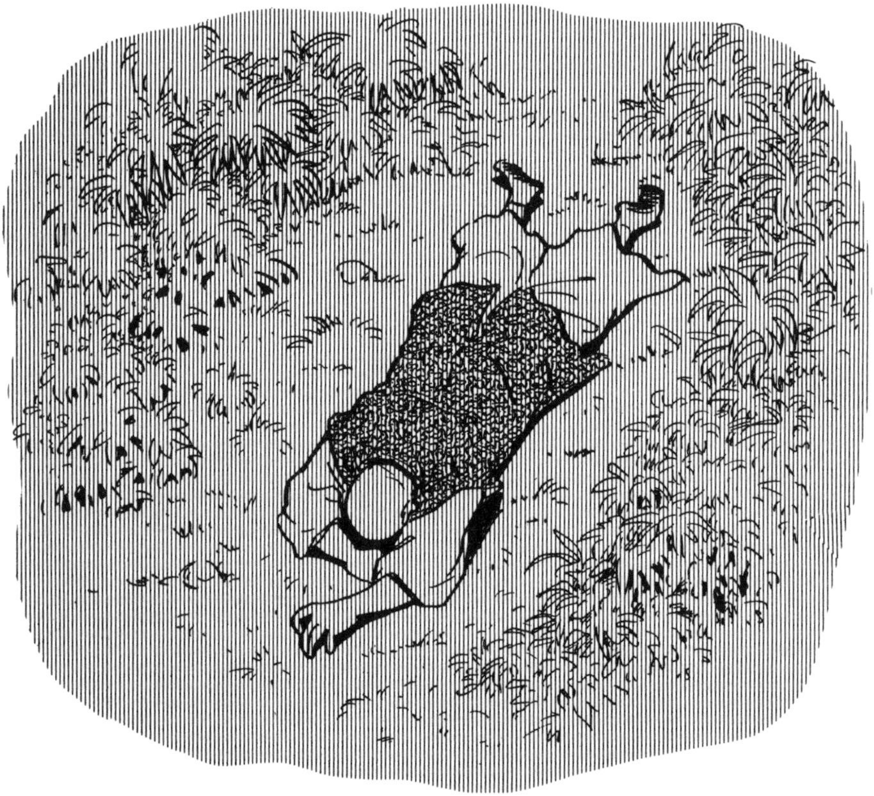

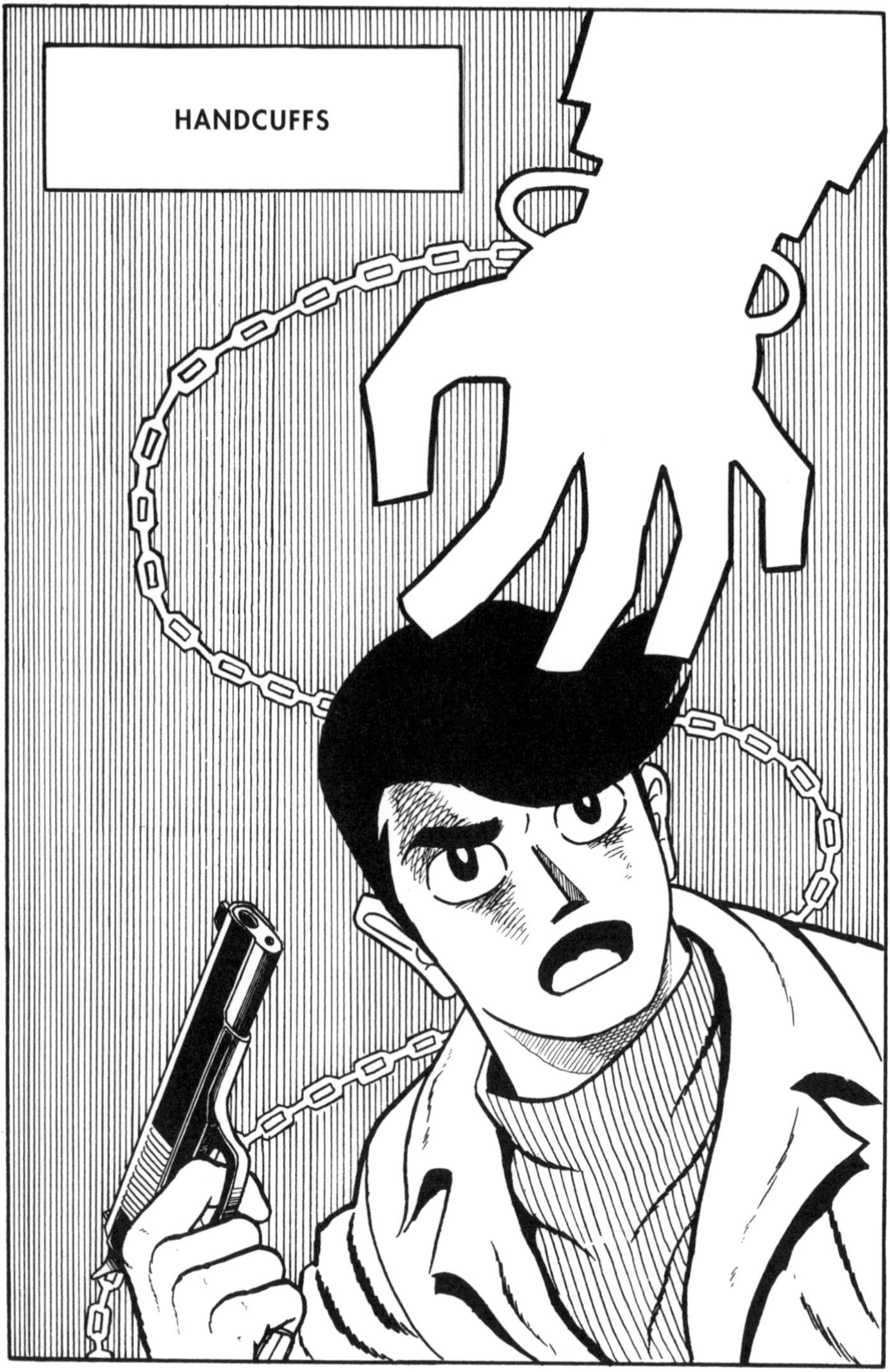
HANDCUFFS

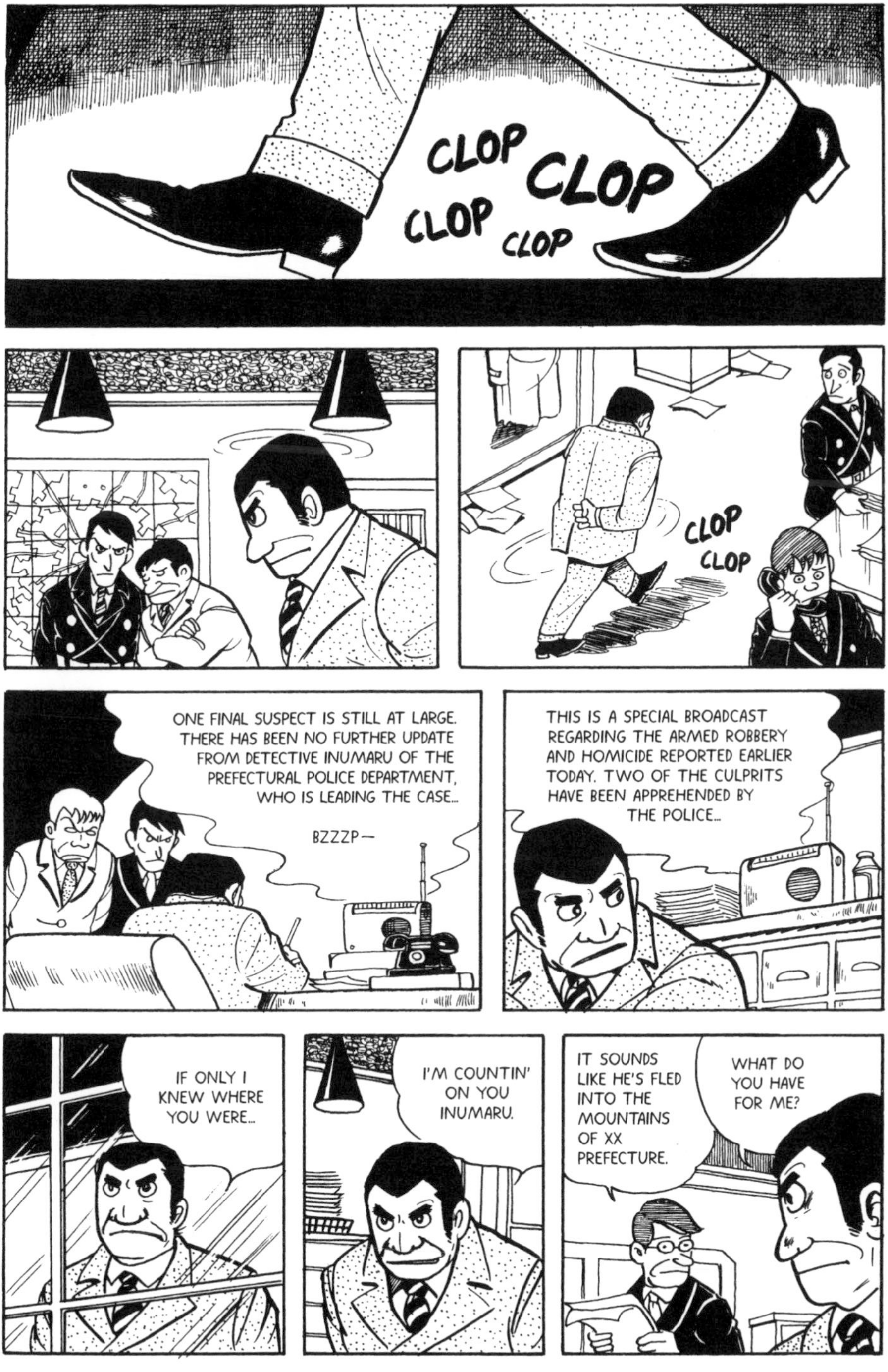
CLOP
CLOP
CLOP
CLOP
CLOP
CLOP
THIS IS A SPECIAL BROADCAST REGARDING THE ARMED ROBBERY AND HOMICIDE REPORTED EARLIER TODAY. TWO OF THE CULPRITS HAVE BEEN APPREHENDED BY THE POLICE...
ONE FINAL SUSPECT IS STILL AT LARGE. THERE HAS BEEN NO FURTHER UPDATE FROM DETECTIVE INUMARU OF THE PREFECTURAL POLICE DEPARTMENT, WHO IS LEADING THE CASE...
BZZZP—
WHAT DO YOU HAVE FOR ME?
IT SOUNDS LIKE HE'S FLED INTO THE MOUNTAINS OF XX PREFECTURE.
I'M COUNTIN' ON YOU INUMARU.
IF ONLY I KNEW WHERE YOU WERE...

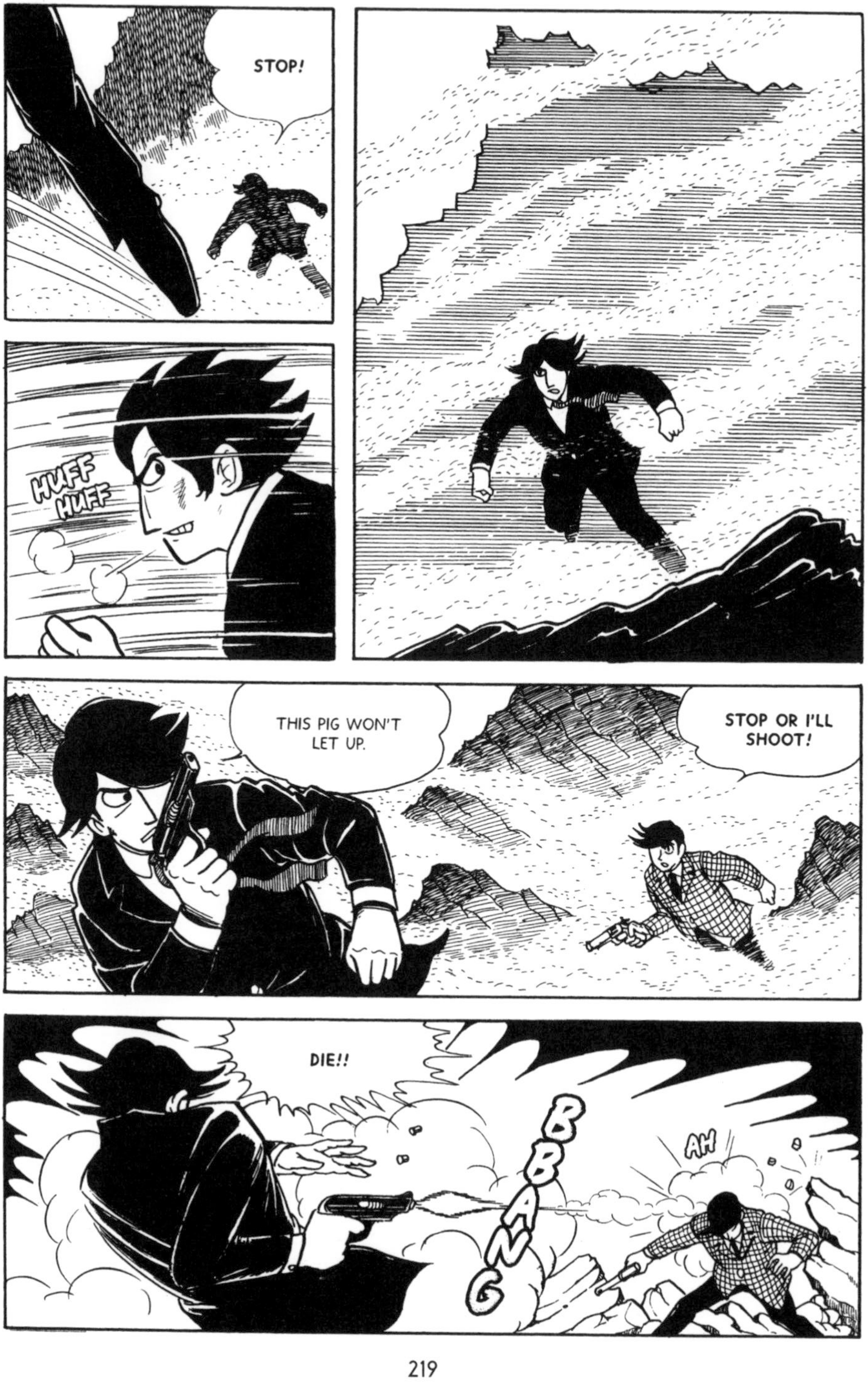
STOP!
HUFF HUFF
STOP OR I'LL SHOOT!
THIS PIG WON'T LET UP.
DIE!!
BBANG
AH

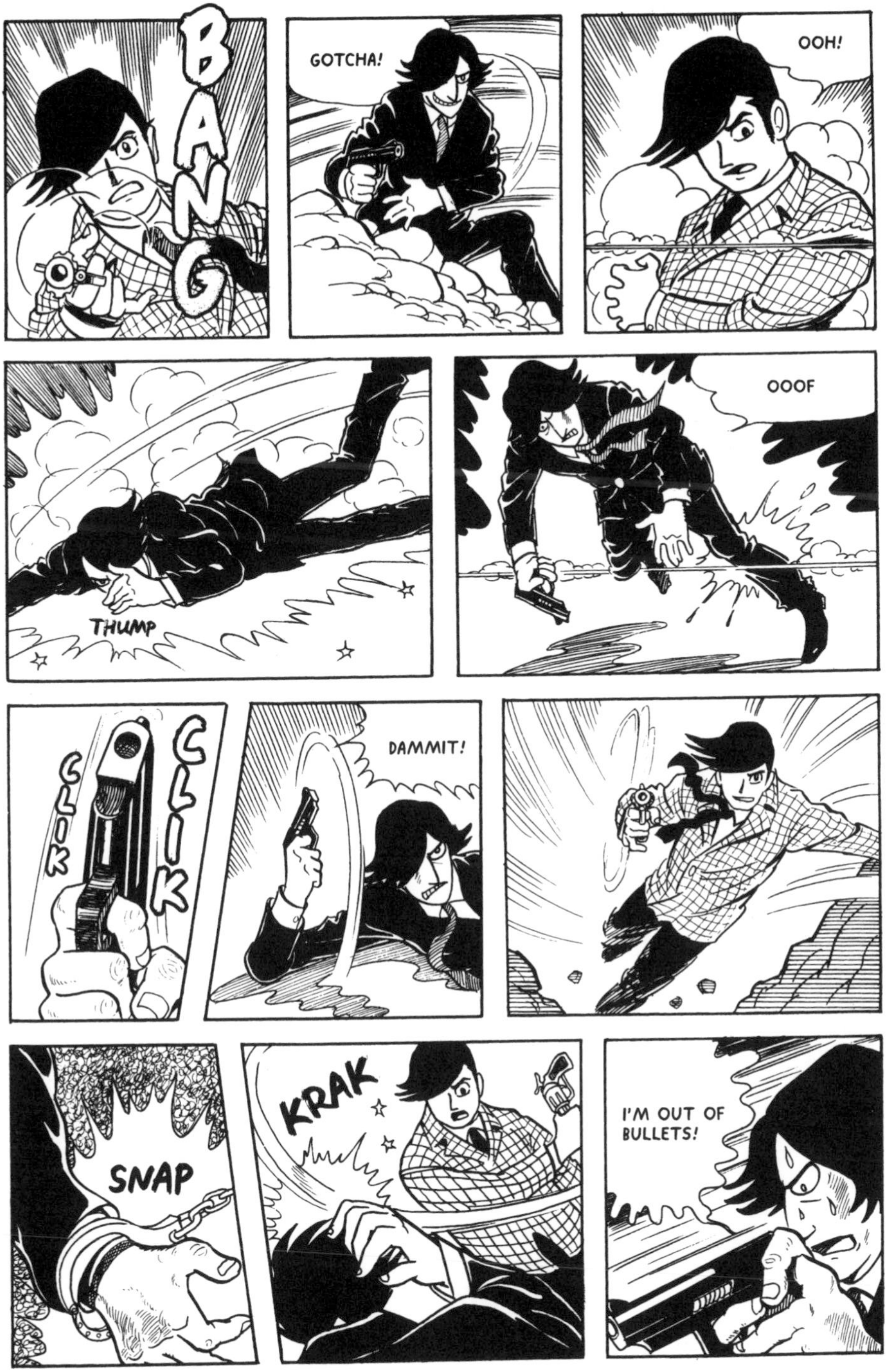
OOH!
GOTCHA!
BANG
OOOF
THUMP
DAMMIT!
CLIK
CLIK
I'M OUT OF BULLETS!
KRAK
SNAP

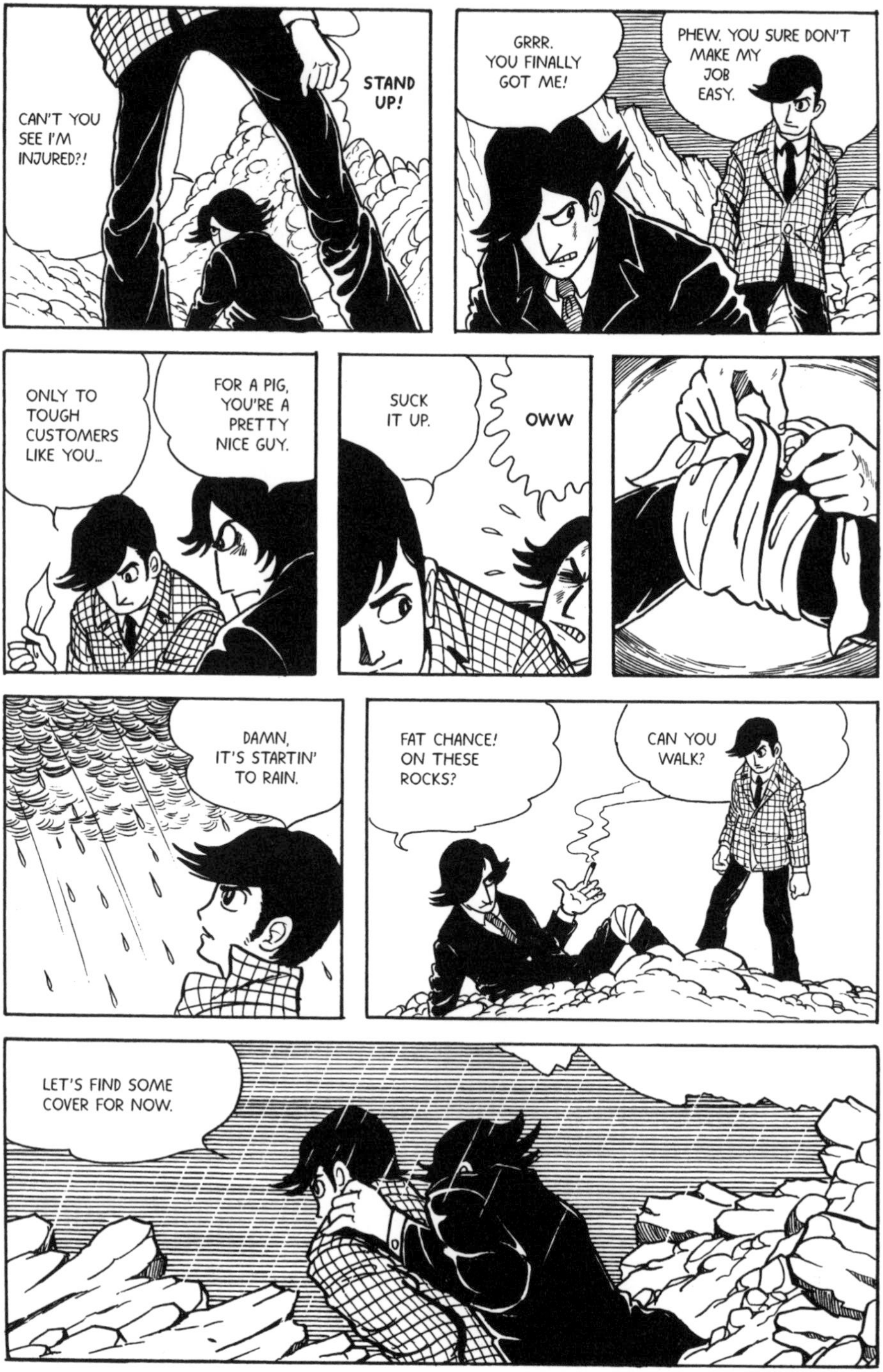
PHEW. YOU SURE DON'T MAKE MY JOB EASY.
GRRR. YOU FINALLY GOT ME!
STAND UP!
CAN'T YOU SEE I'M INJURED?!
OWW
SUCK IT UP.
FOR A PIG, YOU'RE A PRETTY NICE GUY.
ONLY TO TOUGH CUSTOMERS LIKE YOU...
CAN YOU WALK?
FAT CHANCE! ON THESE ROCKS?
DAMN, IT'S STARTIN' TO RAIN.
LET'S FIND SOME COVER FOR NOW.

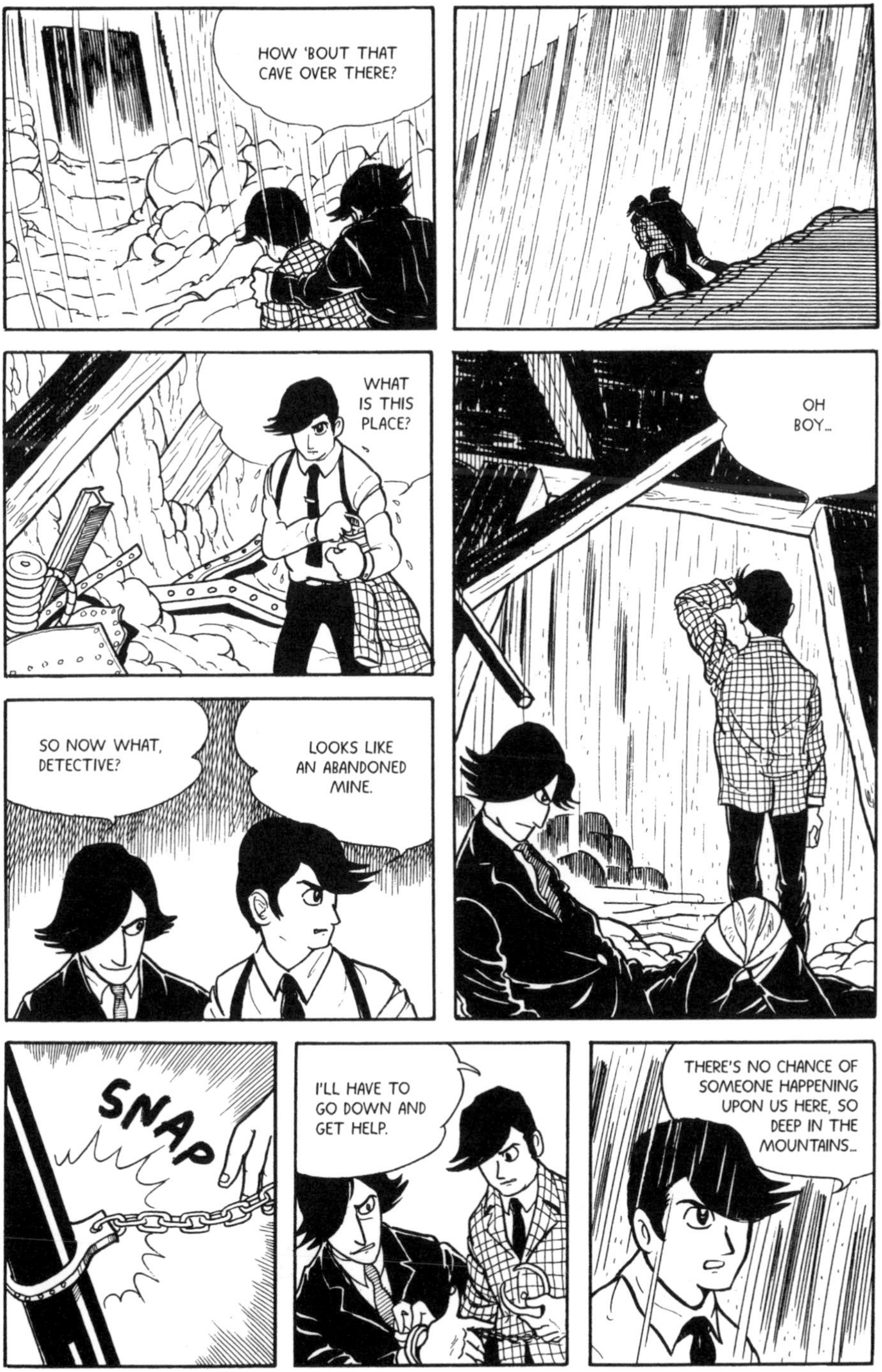
HOW 'BOUT THAT CAVE OVER THERE?
OH BOY...
WHAT IS THIS PLACE?
LOOKS LIKE AN ABANDONED MINE.
SO NOW WHAT, DETECTIVE?
THERE'S NO CHANCE OF SOMEONE HAPPENING UPON US HERE, SO DEEP IN THE MOUNTAINS...
I'LL HAVE TO GO DOWN AND GET HELP.
SNAP

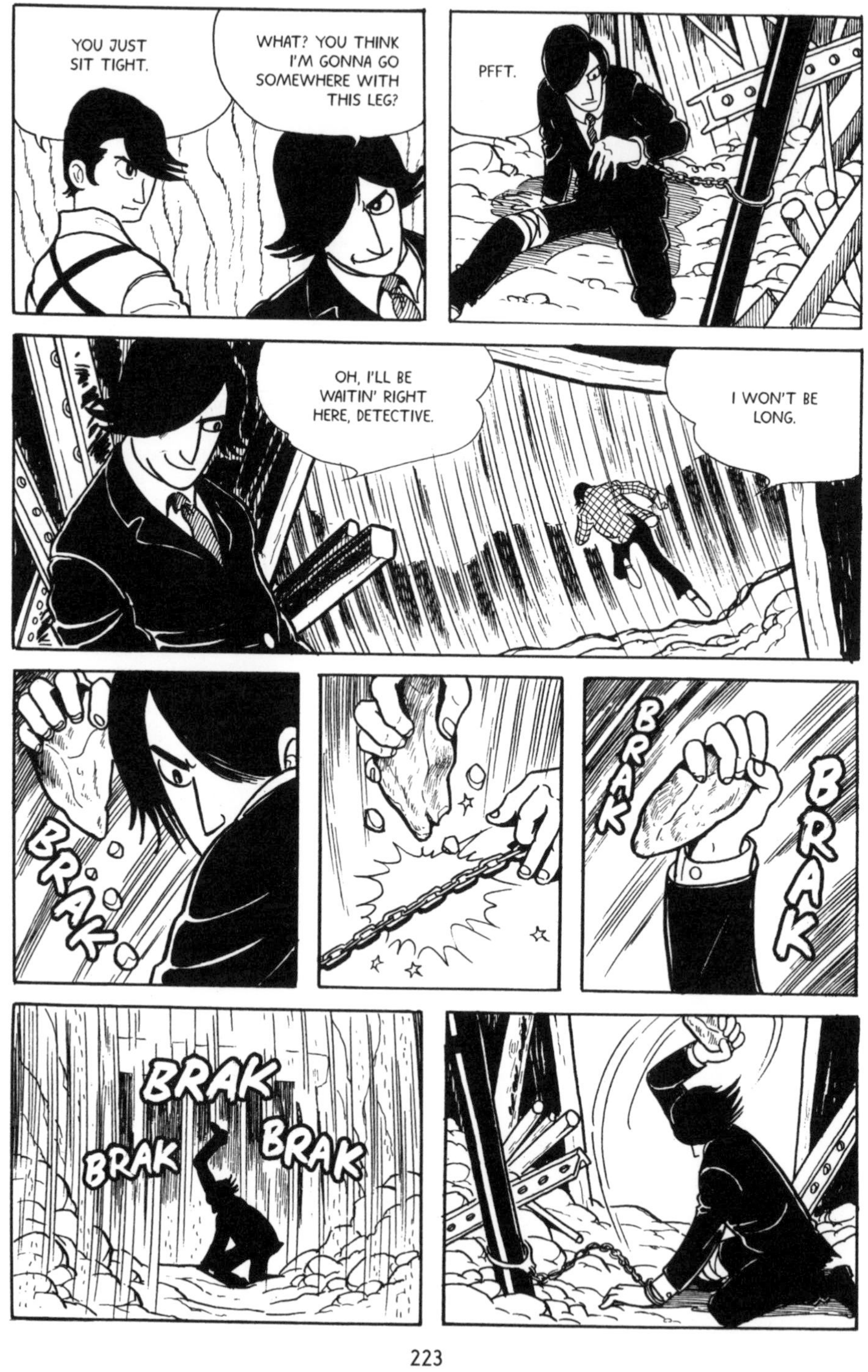
PFFT.
WHAT? YOU THINK I'M GONNA GO SOMEWHERE WITH THIS LEG?
YOU JUST SIT TIGHT.
I WON'T BE LONG.
OH, I'LL BE WAITIN' RIGHT HERE, DETECTIVE.
BRAK
BRAK
BRAK
BRAK
BRAK
BRAK

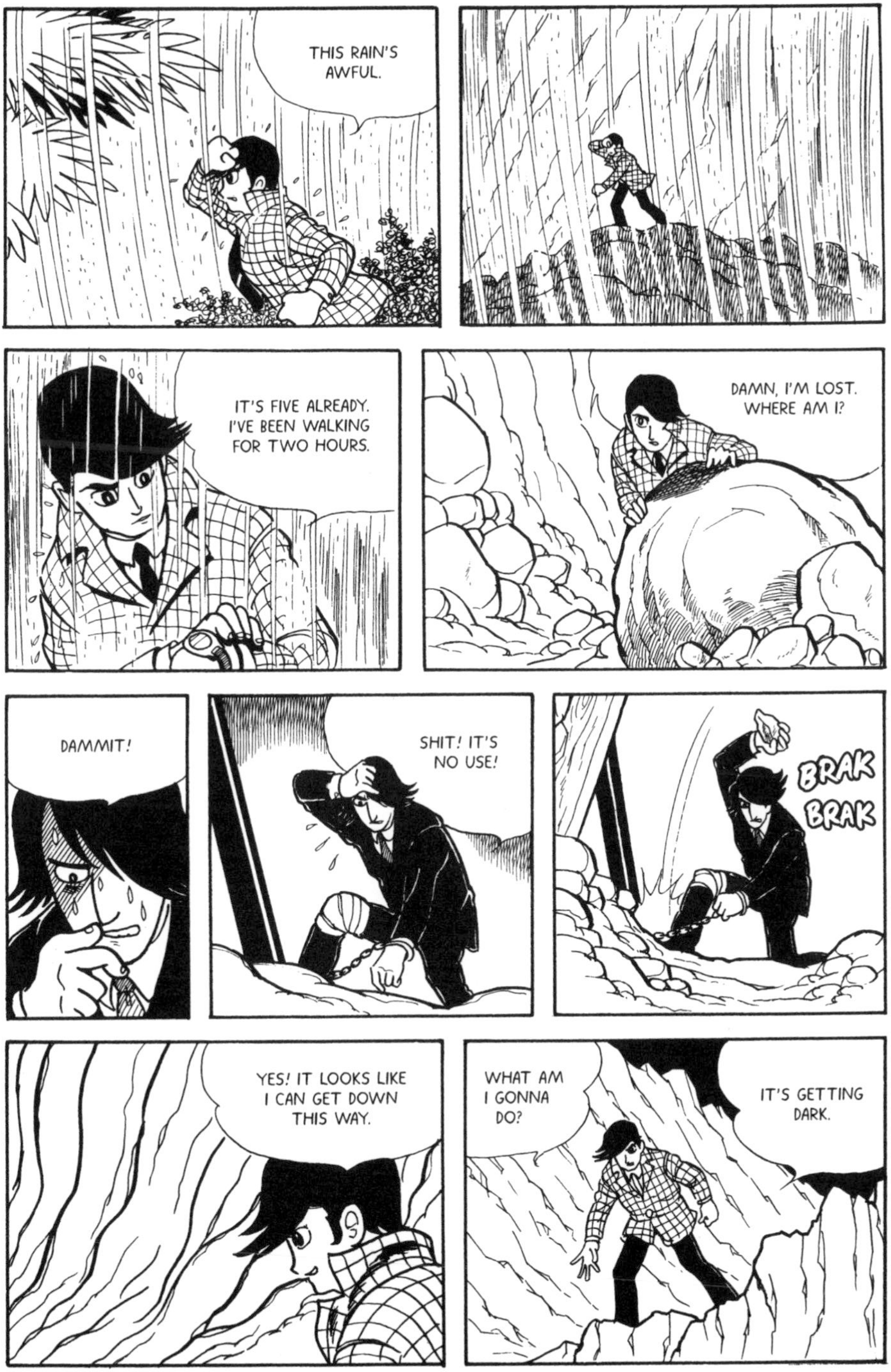
THIS RAIN'S AWFUL.
DAMN, I'M LOST. WHERE AM I?
IT'S FIVE ALREADY. I'VE BEEN WALKING FOR TWO HOURS.
BRAK BRAK
SHIT! IT'S NO USE!
DAMMIT!
IT'S GETTING DARK.
WHAT AM I GONNA DO?
YES! IT LOOKS LIKE I CAN GET DOWN THIS WAY.

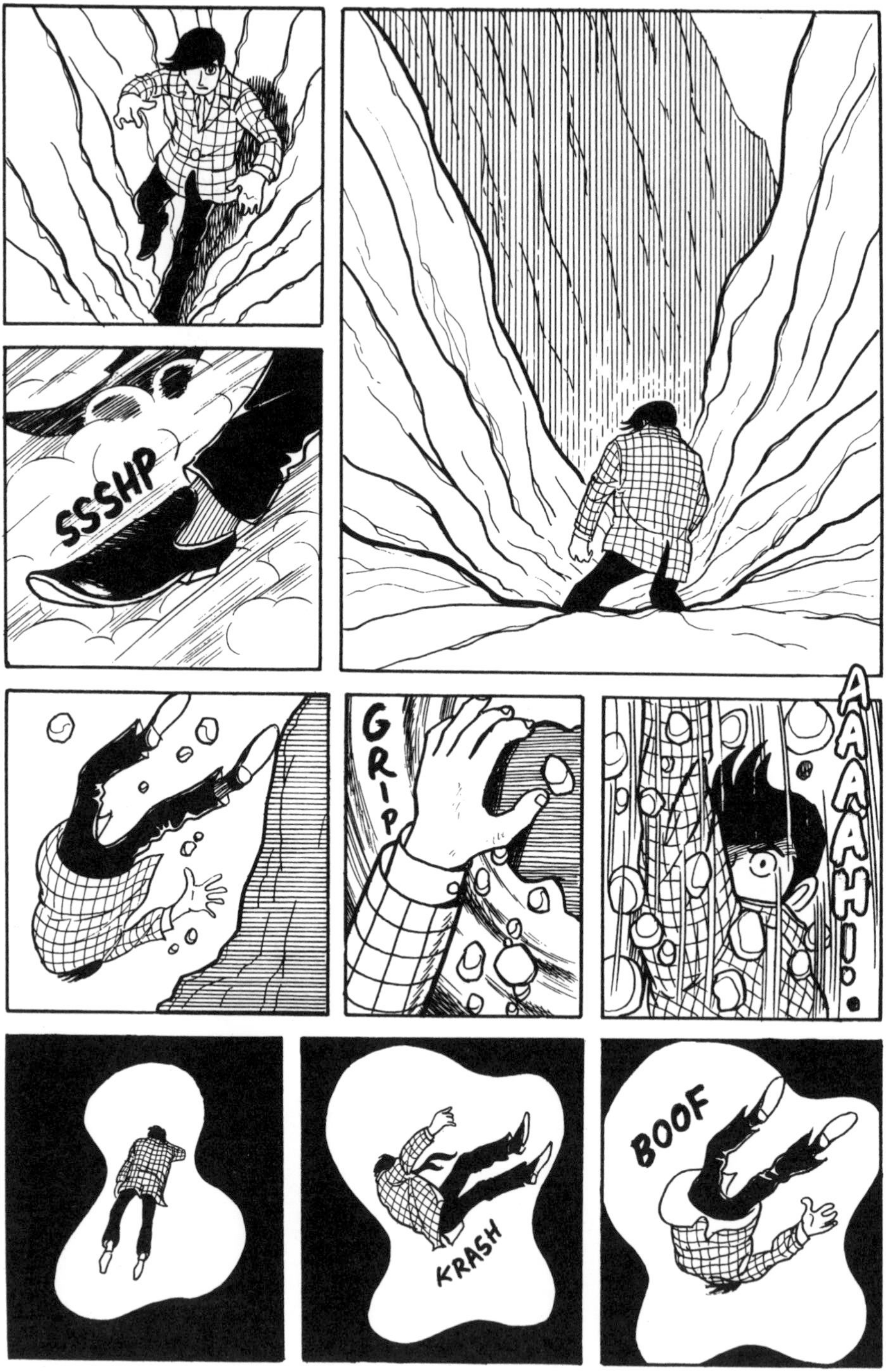
SSSHP
AAAAH!!
GRIP
BOOF
KRASH

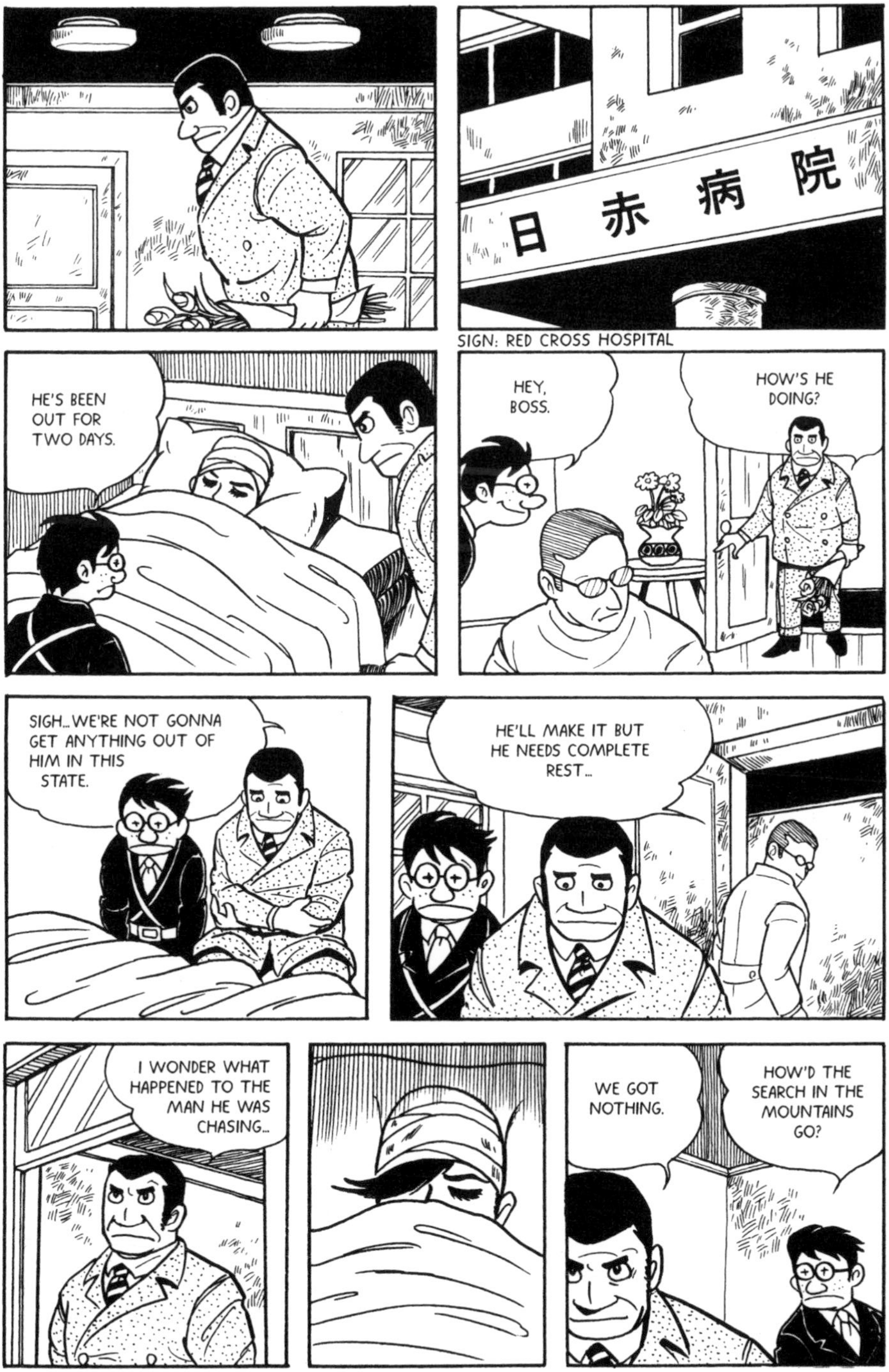
日赤病院
SIGN: RED CROSS HOSPITAL
HOW'S HE DOING?
HEY, BOSS.
HE'S BEEN OUT FOR TWO DAYS.
HE'LL MAKE IT BUT HE NEEDS COMPLETE REST...
SIGH...WE'RE NOT GONNA GET ANYTHING OUT OF HIM IN THIS STATE.
HOW'D THE SEARCH IN THE MOUNTAINS GO?
WE GOT NOTHING.
I WONDER WHAT HAPPENED TO THE MAN HE WAS CHASING...

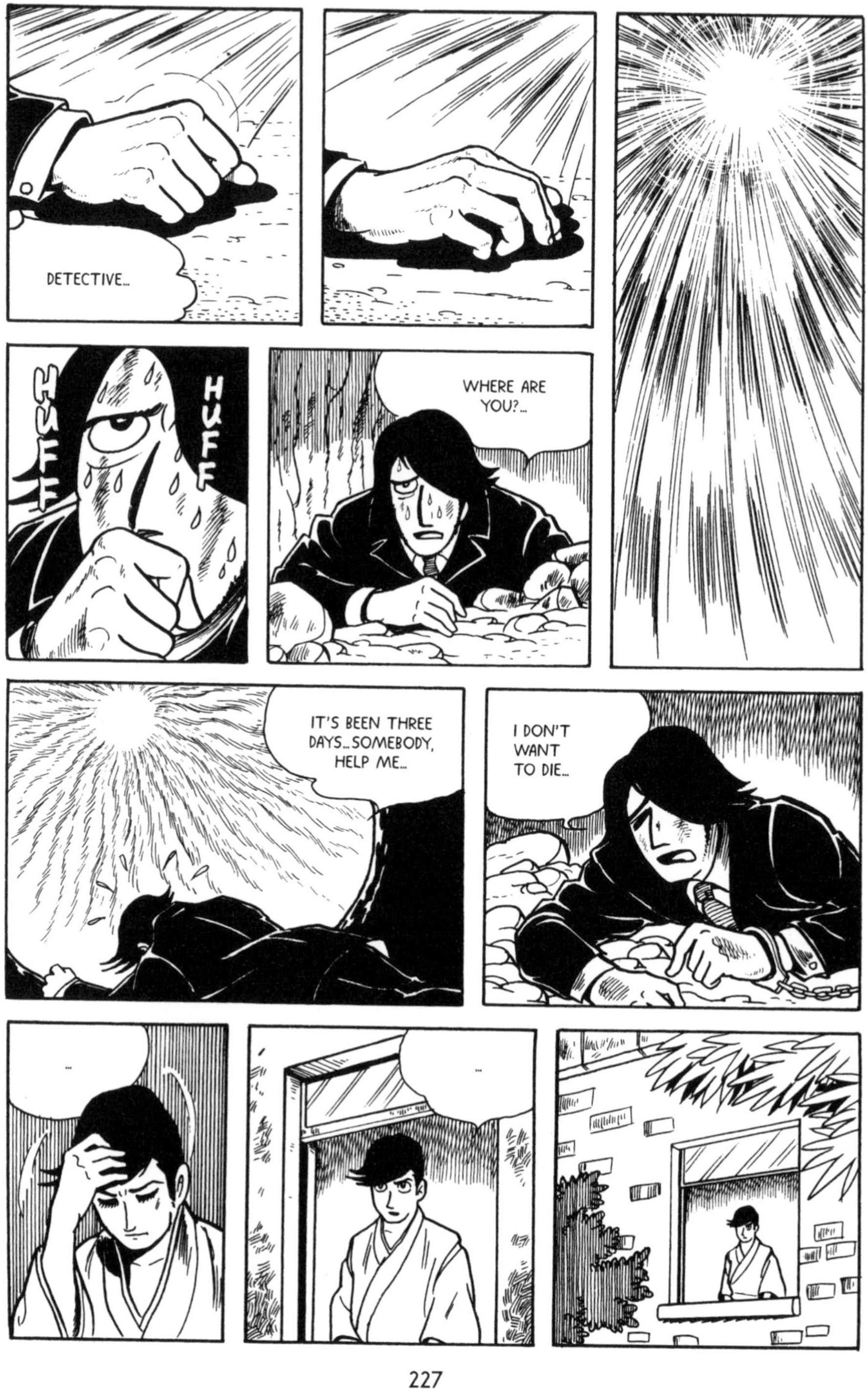
DETECTIVE...
WHERE ARE YOU?...
HUFF
HUFF
I DON'T WANT TO DIE...
IT'S BEEN THREE DAYS...SOMEBODY, HELP ME...
...
...

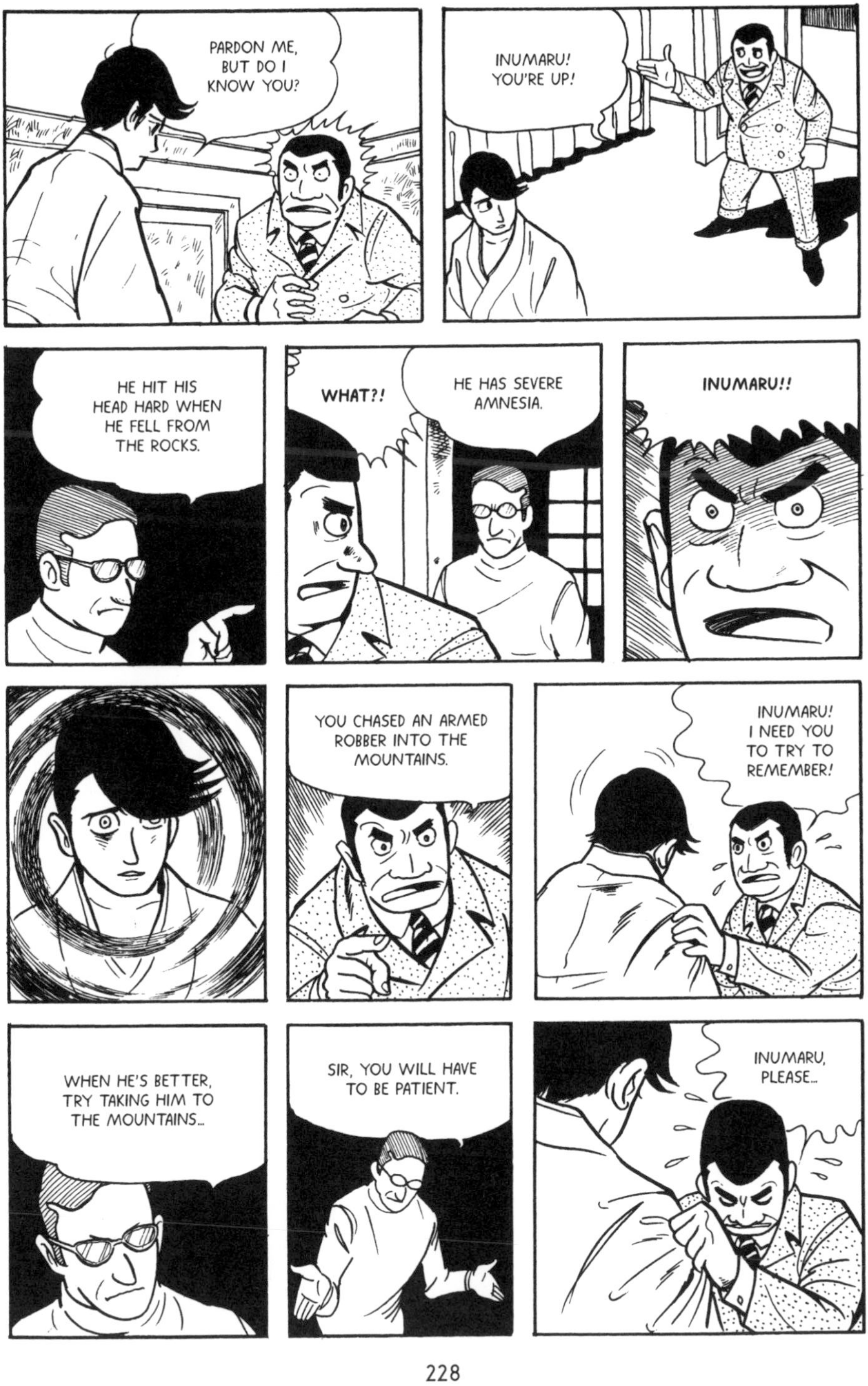
INUMARU! YOU'RE UP!
PARDON ME, BUT DO I KNOW YOU?
INUMARU!!
HE HAS SEVERE AMNESIA.
WHAT?!
HE HIT HIS HEAD HARD WHEN HE FELL FROM THE ROCKS.
INUMARU! I NEED YOU TO TRY TO REMEMBER!
YOU CHASED AN ARMED ROBBER INTO THE MOUNTAINS.
INUMARU, PLEASE...
SIR, YOU WILL HAVE TO BE PATIENT.
WHEN HE'S BETTER, TRY TAKING HIM TO THE MOUNTAINS...

...

POOR INUMARU...

I CAN'T GUARANTEE ANYTHING, BUT THAT MIGHT JOG HIS MEMORY.

IF SOMEBODY DOESN'T COME SOON, MY LEG'S GONNA ROT OFF...

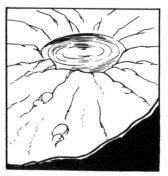

WATER... WATER...

I NEED WATER.

PLEASE HURRY...

CAN'T REACH...

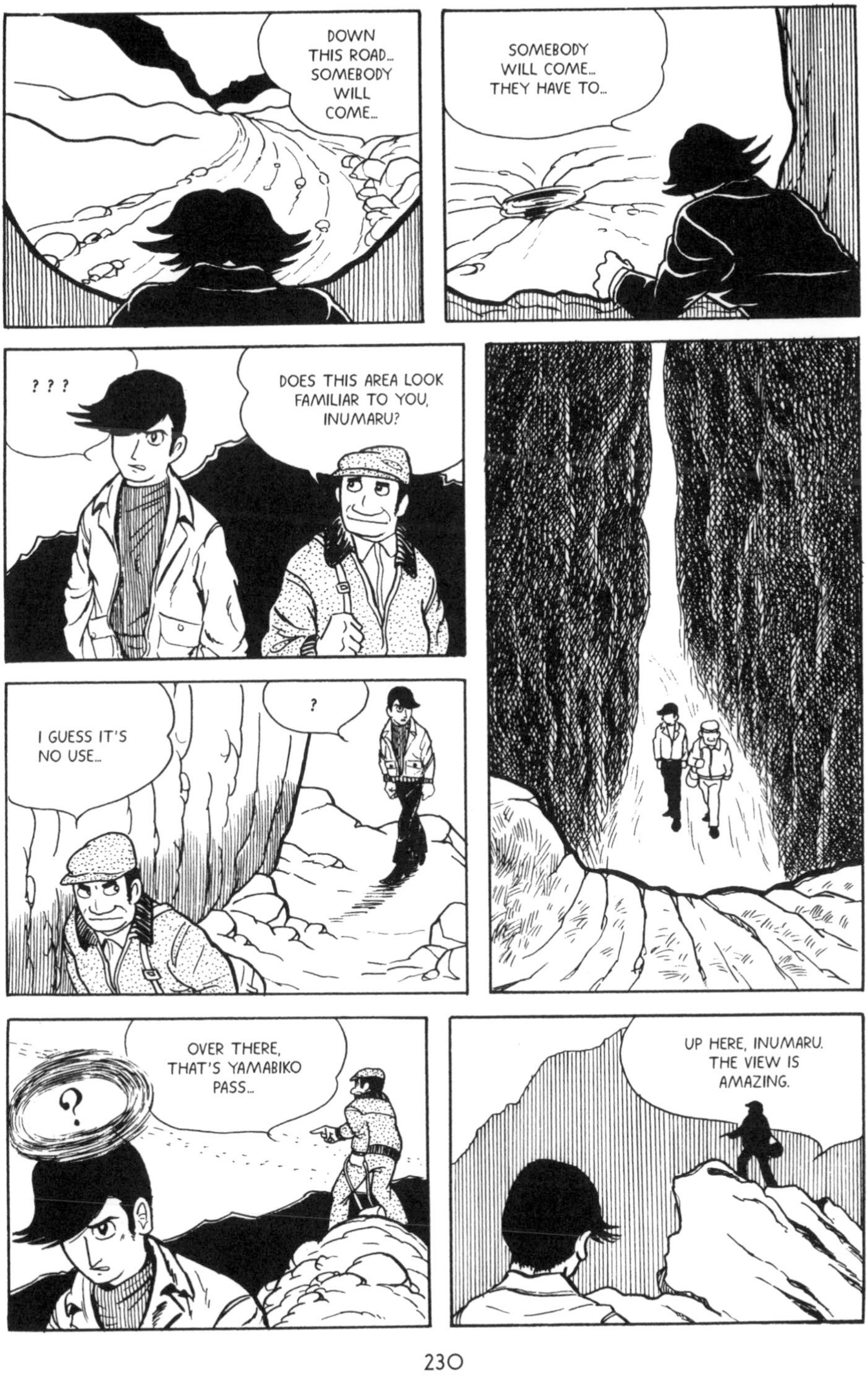
SOMEBODY WILL COME... THEY HAVE TO...
DOWN THIS ROAD... SOMEBODY WILL COME...
DOES THIS AREA LOOK FAMILIAR TO YOU, INUMARU?
? ? ?
?
I GUESS IT'S NO USE...
UP HERE, INUMARU. THE VIEW IS AMAZING.
OVER THERE, THAT'S YAMABIKO PASS...
?

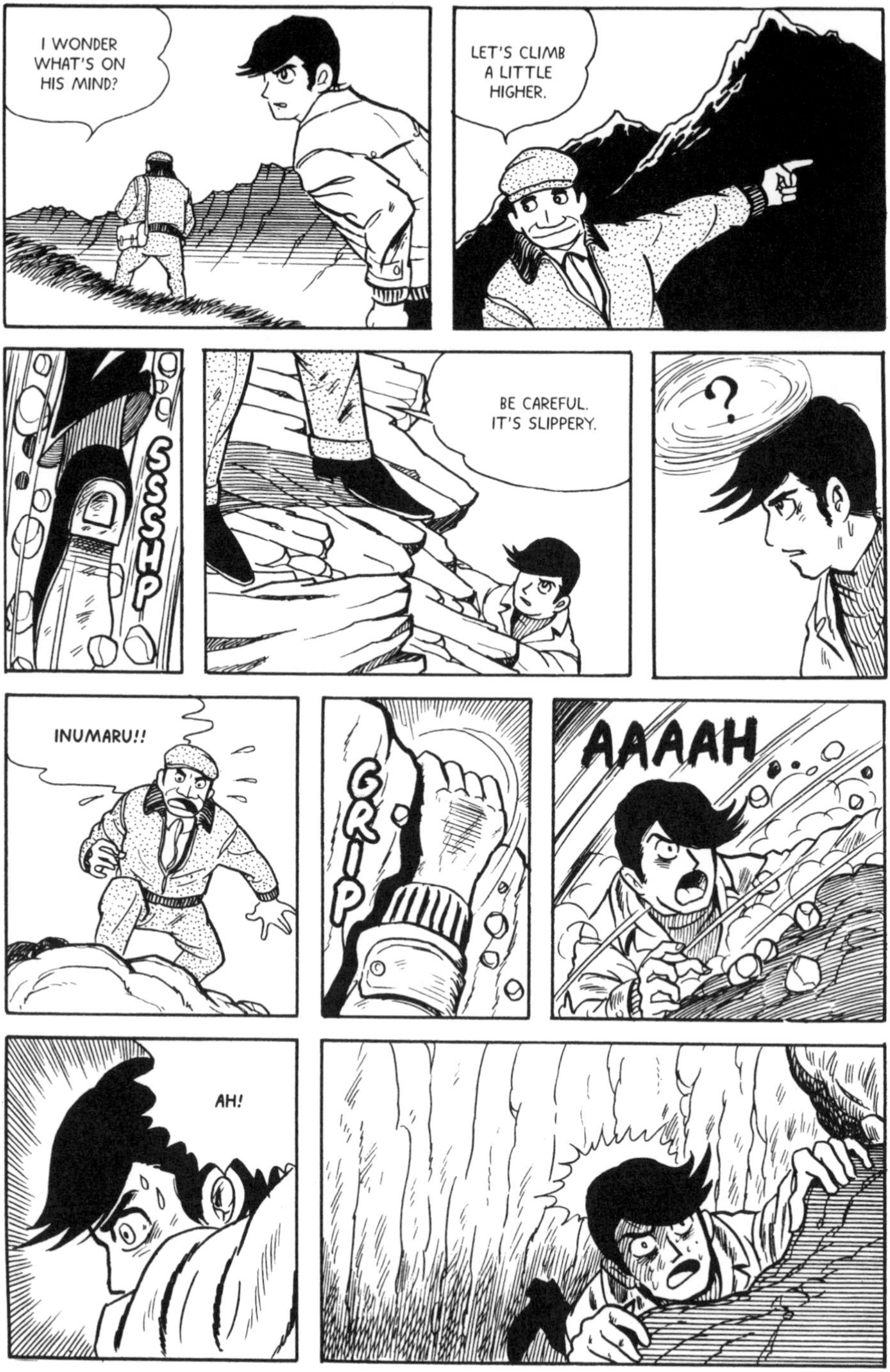
LET'S CLIMB A LITTLE HIGHER.
I WONDER WHAT'S ON HIS MIND?
?
BE CAREFUL. IT'S SLIPPERY.
SSSHP
AAAAH
GRIP
INUMARU!!
AH!

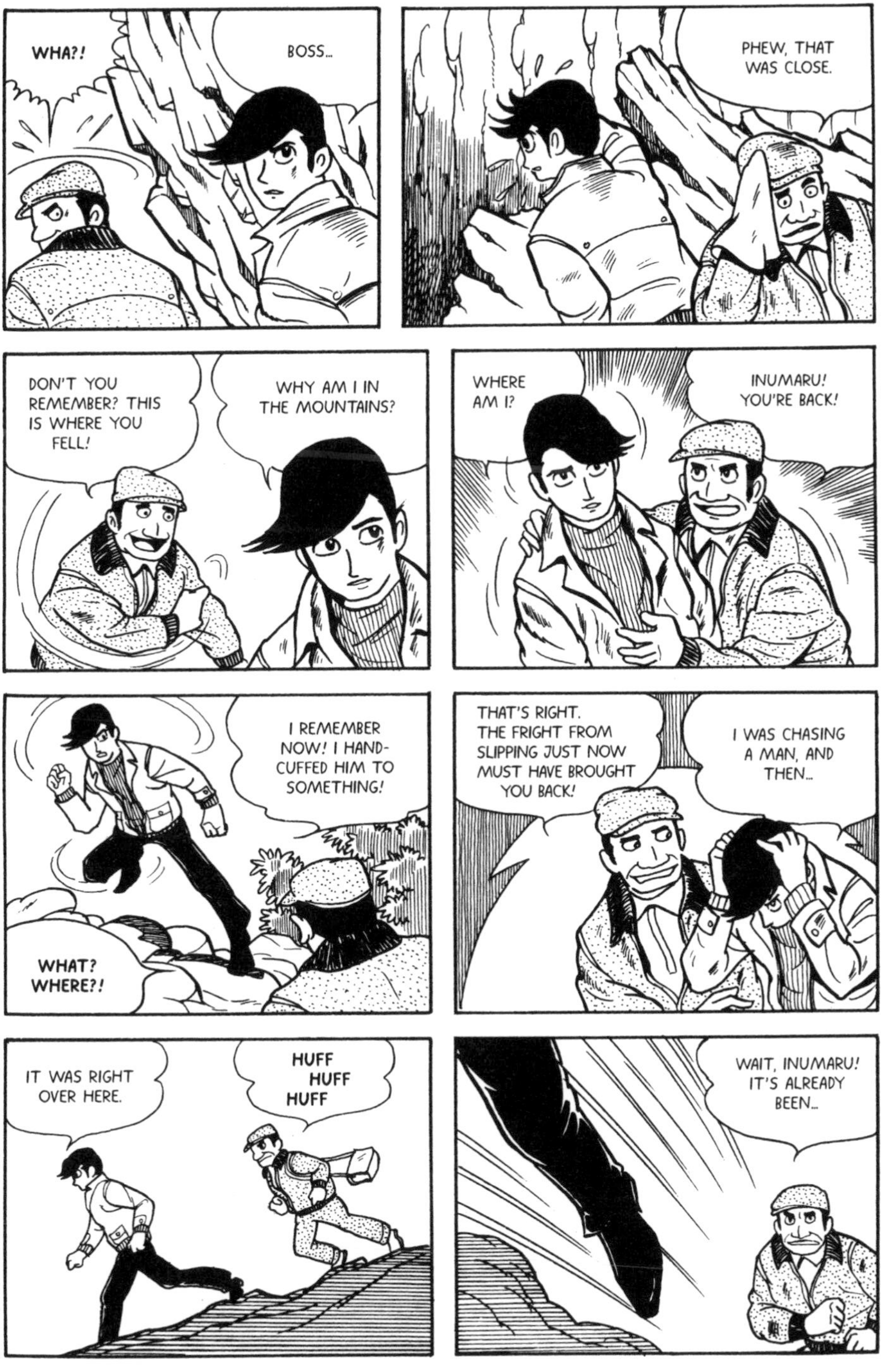
PHEW, THAT WAS CLOSE.
BOSS...
WHA?!
INUMARU! YOU'RE BACK!
WHERE AM I?
WHY AM I IN THE MOUNTAINS?
DON'T YOU REMEMBER? THIS IS WHERE YOU FELL!
I WAS CHASING A MAN, AND THEN...
THAT'S RIGHT. THE FRIGHT FROM SLIPPING JUST NOW MUST HAVE BROUGHT YOU BACK!
I REMEMBER NOW! I HAND-CUFFED HIM TO SOMETHING!
WHAT? WHERE?!
WAIT, INUMARU! IT'S ALREADY BEEN...
HUFF HUFF HUFF
IT WAS RIGHT OVER HERE.

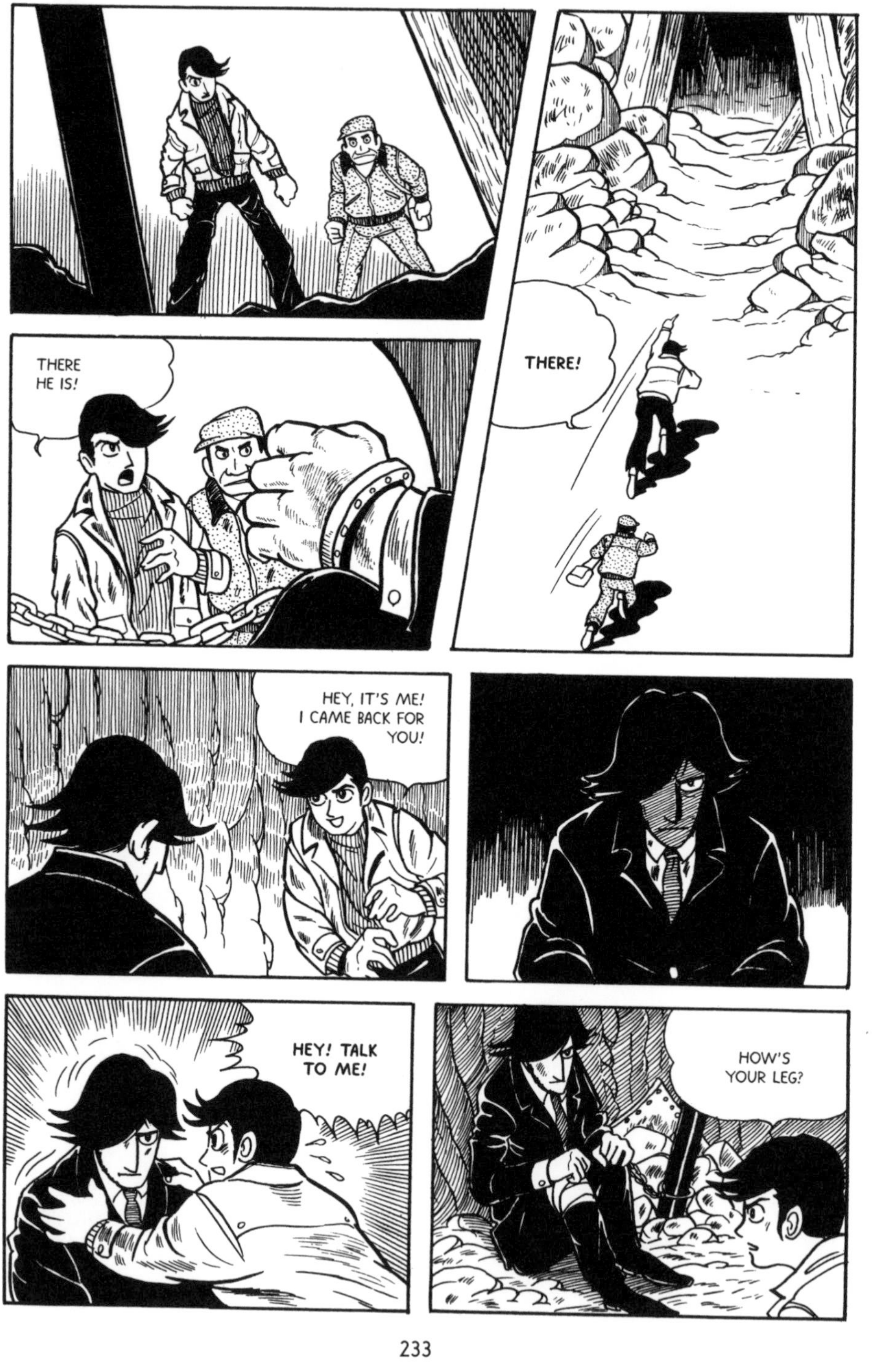
THERE!
THERE HE IS!
HEY, IT'S ME! I CAME BACK FOR YOU!
HOW'S YOUR LEG?
HEY! TALK TO ME!

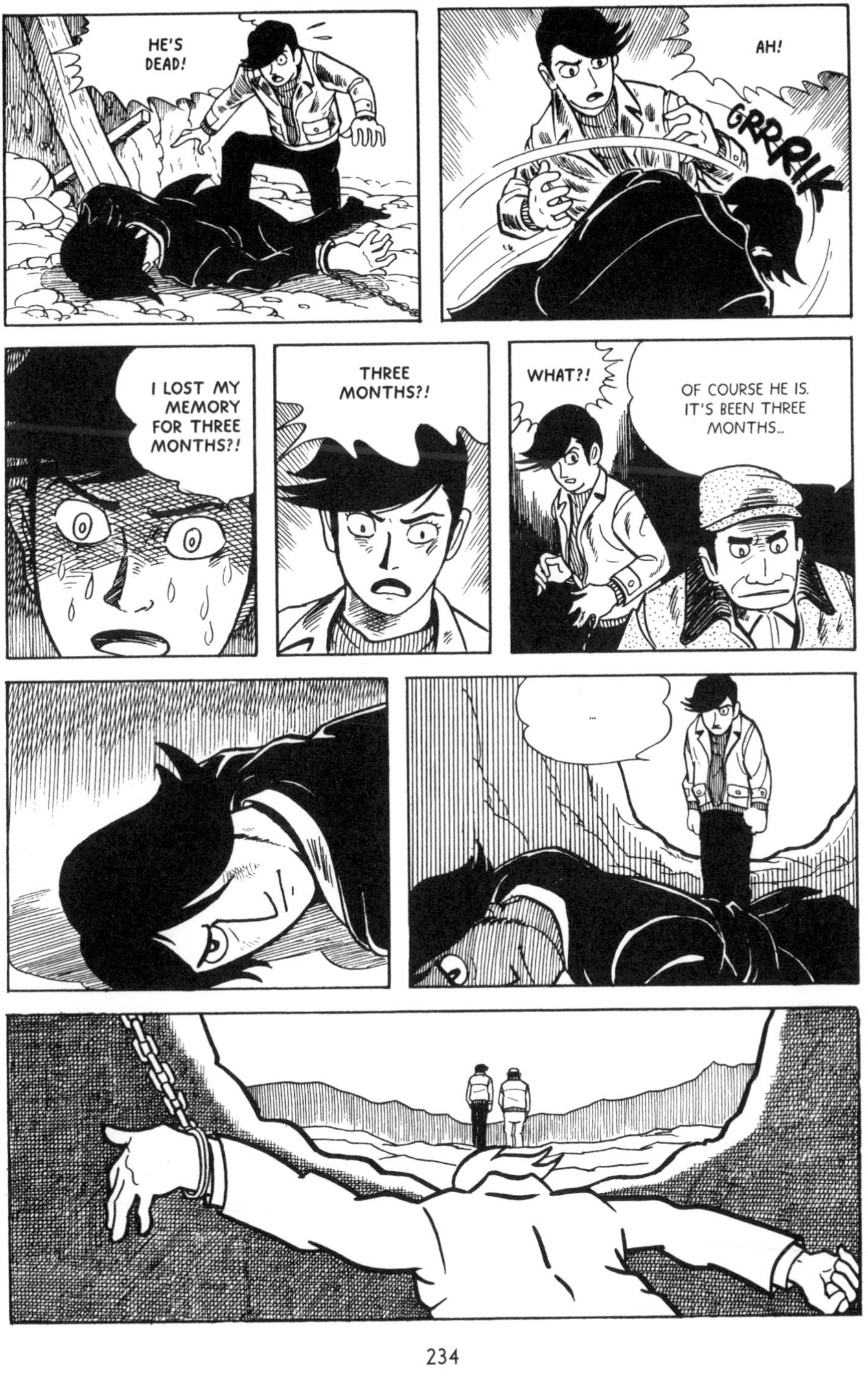
AH!
GRRRRIK
HE'S DEAD!
WHAT?!
OF COURSE HE IS. IT'S BEEN THREE MONTHS...
THREE MONTHS?!
I LOST MY MEMORY FOR THREE MONTHS?!
...

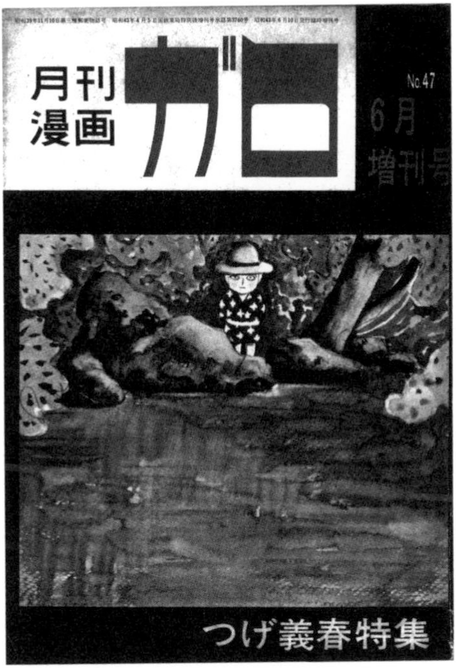
月刊
漫画
ガロ
No.47
6月
増刊号
つげ義春特集
Cover for *Garo* no. 47 (June 1968), special Tsuge issue

Then came "Nejishiki" (June 1968), published in a special supplemental issue of *Garo* dedicated to the artist's work. The response was immense. Based on a dream, it features a young man who wanders through a seaside town in search of a doctor after being injured by a mysteriously named "me-me jellyfish." Such is the basic story, although the exact connections between one scene and the next are unclear. Considering also the creepy way in which the characters are drawn, and a story world which seems to be a recreation of the unconscious, it is often said that "Nejishiki" represents the first expression of surrealist tendencies in manga. Some readers dismissed the work saying that it didn't make any sense. But many more responded with the highest praise, including not just manga fans, but also poets, playwrights, graphic designers, psychologists, and various other intellectuals, each offering their own interpretation of this strange work. With "Nejishiki," a wide variety of artists and thinkers began following Tsuge. And though he was never as prolific as he was during his kashihon years, and there were stretches when he published nothing, he continued drawing one masterpiece after another, gaining more admirers, and generating more critical interpretations than any other cartoonist in Japan. Tsuge turns 83 this year and hasn't drawn any manga since 1987, and yet his legacy remains as strong as ever.

This essay is based on one the author originally wrote for Sai Comics (South Korea, 2006), first published in Japanese in the Yoshiharu Tsuge issue of Spectator vol. 41 *(2018). The author would like to thank the translator Ryan Holmberg for suggesting ways to expand and flesh out the essay for the present volume.*

NOTES

1 Endō Masaharu, "Soshite, itsushika futari wa shōgyōshugi ni se o muketa," *Comic Box* special edition (April 2004), p. 47–48.

2 Tsuge Yoshiharu, "Maegaki: jisaku kaidai," *Natsu no omoide* (Tokyo: Chūō kōronsha, 1988), p. 5–6.

3 Tsuge Yoshiharu, "Kaisetsu: memo Ōtaki," in *Furoku no furuoku*, pamphlet insert accompanying *Nanatsu no haka* (Tokyo: Hokutō shobō, June 1974), p. 31.

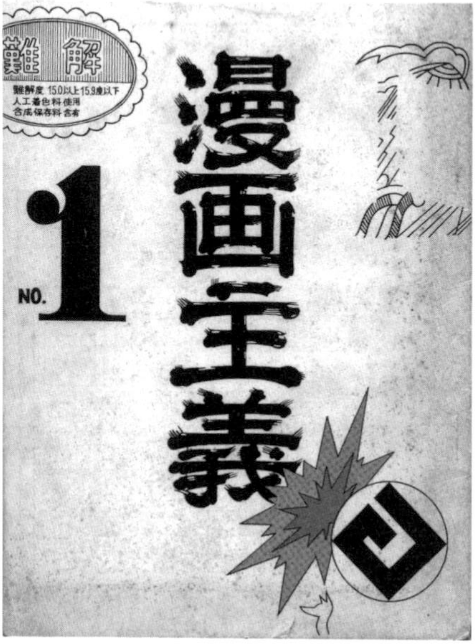
難 解
漫画主義
NO. 1

Manga-ism no. 1, cover by Genpei Akasegawa (March 1967)

He showed this work in a rough state to Yoshiharu to get his advice. Yoshiharu immediately recognized Tadao's nascent talents. But suffering from artist's block under a looming deadline, and enticed by the fact that the story was good and the artwork half completed, Yoshiharu asked Tadao, "Do you mind if I use this?" Thus, though Tadao has never been officially credited as the author of this story, it is possible to consider "Handcuffs" to be Tadao's debut work. Tadao also worked as Yoshiharu's assistant on some of his ninja and samurai stories in 1960–61, including *The Secret Ninja Scrolls* pictured earlier. He published a number of his own creepy mystery stories in kashihon venues before re-debuting in *Garo* in late 1968 with the story "Up on the Hilltop, Vincent van Gogh..." ("Oka no ue de, Vinsento van gohho wa..."), which is translated in the collection *Trash Market* from Drawn & Quarterly.

With both exciting new experiments and remastered oldies to his name, 1966 marked a major turning point in Tsuge's career. This was not just due to the strength of his work, however. Tsuge had been pushing manga in new directions since at least "Ghost Chimneys," but it was only now that readers were beginning to notice, partly because they were simply older. Born after the war ended in 1945, Japan's baby boomers were reaching their twenties in the mid-'60s. Though manga had been enjoyed by children since at least the '20s, what was special about baby boomers was that they kept reading manga into adulthood. One of the reasons for this is that Tsuge and other former kashihon gekiga artists were producing work that appealed to more mature tastes. Another is that the sheer number of children born after the war guaranteed a much larger and more diverse market. "The Swamp" was created right at this juncture, when a bigger, wider, and more mature audience put paid to long-standing beliefs that manga were just for kids. The initial reception of "The Swamp" and "Chirpy" may have been largely negative, but the fact that there was any feedback at all marked the mid-'60s as a fundamentally different era in manga culture.

Critical appraisal of "The Swamp" and "Chirpy" would come a little later. In March 1967, *Manga-ism* (*Manga shugi*), Japan and perhaps the world's first periodical devoted to comics criticism, published its first issue, focusing on Tsuge's work for *Garo*. As positive critical interest in his work increased, Tsuge was inspired to draw new works for *Garo* again. In the interim, however, he was traveling the Japanese countryside, visiting places off the beaten path, and falling in love with simple, rusticated, and sometimes outright poverty-stricken rural life and scenery. His stories based on these travels, capturing a Japan that had been left behind by postwar economic growth, were also warmly received. His motivations for drawing such stories might have been purely personal, but they also expressed an unease, shared by many of his readers, with the rapidity and ways in which things were changing in Japan. These stories will be collected in *Red Flowers*, volume two of the present Drawn & Quarterly series.

五十円
不思議な手紙
つげよしはる
女忍
つげ・義春 作画
手錠
つげよしはる

Left to Right: Original title pages for "The Secondhand Book," "A Strange Letter," "The Ninjess," and "Handcuffs"

Faced with the rapid decline of the kashihon market, Tatsumi, like a number of his peers, created his own publishing house, Dai-ichi Pro (No. 1 Productions), in 1963. Tsuge had previously contributed to Dai-ichi Pro's romance and science-fiction anthologies, and Tatsumi hoped to publish a standalone collection of Tsuge remakes. Ultimately, however, some of these remakes first appeared in *Garo*, and then were collected with additional stories in two books, *The Phony Warrior* (December 1966) and *The Antlion Pit* (*Arijigoku*, April 1967), both from Tōkōsha, run by Tatsumi's elder brother, Shōichi Sakurai. Presumably, the project was passed by Tatsumi directly to his brother. A sign of how close former kashihon artists were in these transitional years, *The Phony Warrior* includes a short afterword by Shirato, which begins as follows: "There are many kinds of cartoonists. The superman type, the businessman type, the craftsman type, and the scholar type, for example. Yoshiharu Tsuge is the epitome of the fine artist type." Shirato sums up Tsuge's approach with this memorable sentence: "Though he maintains his creativity by repeatedly disgorging his self, by doing so he inevitably puts himself in an increasingly unbearable position, as it entails taking personal, emotional responsibility for the value and reception of any one work. It is like perpetually holding your body in a forward-leaning posture poised for flight."

The four redrawn works in the present volume are as follows:

1. "The Secondhand Book" ("Furuhon to shōjo"): original version in *The Labyrinth* (*Meiro*, series 2) no. 2 (Wakagi Shobō, February 1960), remake first published in *Garo* (September 1966), but probably drawn many months earlier.
2. "A Strange Letter" ("Fushigina tegami"): original version in *The Labyrinth* (series 1) no. 4 (Wakagi Shobō, February 1959), remake first published in *The Phony Warrior* (Tōkōsha, December 1966).
3. "The Ninjess" ("Jonin"): original version in *Dragon and Tiger* (*Ryūko*) no. 14 (Tokyo Topsha, February 1961), remake first published in *The Phony Warrior*.
4. "Handcuffs" ("Tejō"): original version in *The Labyrinth* (series 1) no. 10 (Wakagi Shobō, August 1959), remake first published in *Garo* (December 1966), but drawn circa 1963.

While not a well-known work from this period, "Handcuffs" is significant because of the backstory of its production. Both the original version and the remake were published under the name Yoshiharu Tsuge, but in fact the original story and breakdown were by his younger brother, Tadao Tsuge (born 1941). Inspired by his older brother's example, Tadao aspired to become a cartoonist.

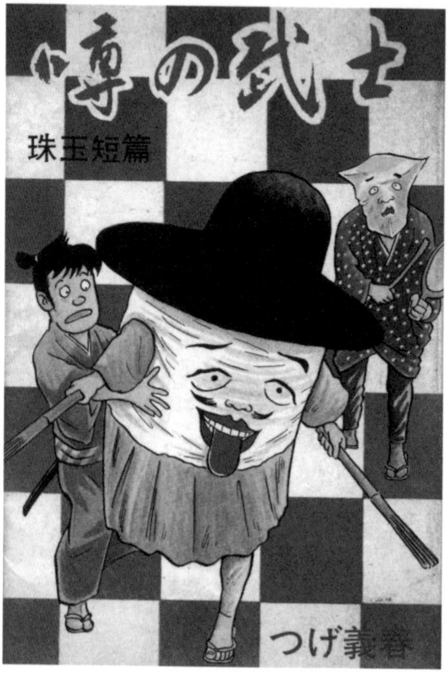
噂の武士
珠玉短篇
つげ義春

Tsuge, *The Phony Warrior* (Tōkōsha, December 1966)

himself. It is thus more appropriate to call Tsuge Mizuki's "helper" rather than "assistant," also considering that Tsuge was only called in when Mizuki was really crunched for time. Tsuge was mainly tasked with drawing a number of Mizuki's characters, including ones in the early installments of *Kitarō*. When Mizuki redrew his "Yokai Chess Necronomicon" ("Yōki shininchō) as "The Eerie Necronomicon" ("Kaiki shininchō") for the December 1966 issue of *Garo*, all of the backgrounds and characters were newly drawn by Tsuge.

The idea for "Mushroom Hunting" ("Hatsutake gari," *Garo* no. 20, April 1966), like that for "The Swamp," dates from Tsuge's time in Ōtaki. It was published in the same issue of *Garo* that carries Mizuki's "Namahage." Mizuki's story, about a bookish youth who is skeptical of folk superstitions and then cursed by having his face transformed into that of the northern Japanese demon Namahage, was supposed to have been sixteen pages. When Mizuki submitted only eight, Tsuge was asked to produce something quickly to make up the difference. The result was "Mushroom Hunting," drawn in just a few days. The setting is modeled on the Suehiro Inn in Ōtaki, which had a large clock similar to the one you see in the manga. While there, Shirato took Tsuge mushroom picking. And though Shirato (born 1932) was only five years older than Tsuge, the benevolence he expressed toward Tsuge seems to be reflected in the relationship between the old man and the boy in the manga.

Sharp-eyed readers will note a resemblance between the style of "Mushroom Hunting" and Mizuki's manga from these years. One of the reasons is that some of the backgrounds were drawn by Yoshikazu Kitagawa, one of Mizuki's assistants, who later published his own manga under the name Shōichi Kitagawa. The detailed linework, sharp tonal contrasts and deep shadows, and oversized sound effects also speak to the influence of Tsuge's time at Mizuki Pro. Likewise, Mizuki Pro kept a large collection of photographs clipped from magazines and organized in albums, sampled liberally in the creation of the classic Mizuki style of cartoony characters situated within highly detailed, photorealistic backgrounds. While the adoption of this style became an integral part of Tsuge's classic *Garo* period of the late '60s, its influence can already be perceived in the present volume in works like "The Secondhand Book" ("Furuhon to shōjo") and "A Strange Letter" ("Fushigina tegami"), which are also from 1966.

"Mushroom Hunting" was the last truly new story Tsuge published in 1966. Though an indispensable member of Mizuki Pro, Tsuge had lost confidence in his own abilities as an artist, and felt little desire to produce new work. Another colleague and admirer helped him through this slump: Yoshihiro Tatsumi. Unlike Shirato, who pushed him to create new stories, Tatsumi encouraged Tsuge to return to his roots and redraw some of his best kashihon works (a not uncommon practice among former kashihon artists at the time).

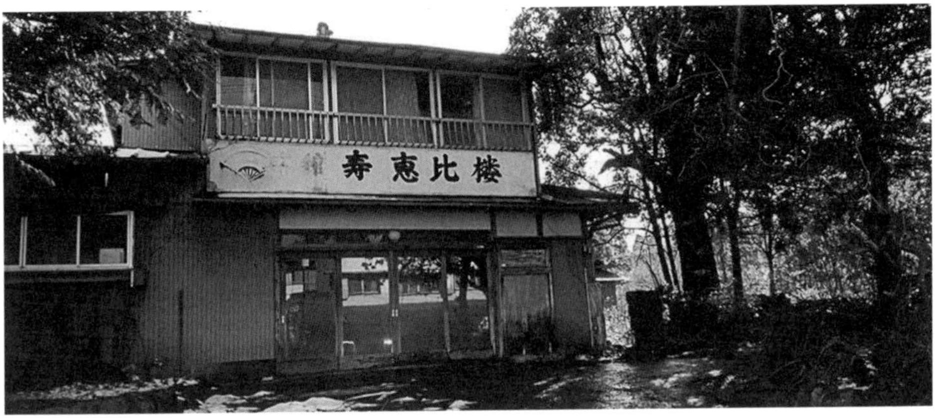
寿恵比楼

Suehiro Inn, Ōtaki; the inspiration for "Mushroom Hunting" and other stories in this volume
Photograph by Asakawa, January 2018

Though he was only there for a couple of weeks, Tsuge's time in Ōtaki provided him ideas for a number of future stories. Most important among them is "The Swamp" ("Numa," *Garo* no. 18, February 1966). With this conceptual story, Tsuge finally achieved a dramaturgy wholly his own. Here was the liberation from conventional storytelling that he had been fretting about for years. Upon completing it, Tsuge remembers thinking that the work was "perfect." The following issue of *Garo* featured "Chirpy" ("Chiiko," March 1966). Based on Tsuge's own private life, it marked the emergence in manga of a focus on the artist's daily life, something that had previously been the domain of prose literature and the "I-novel." Of course, past cartoonists, like Matsumoto, had drawn upon their immediate surroundings and people they knew. What differentiated these new stories by Tsuge was that, though fictional, they were based squarely on the artist's own personal experiences and were crafted in a way that made them seem at least partly autobiographical.

The response to "The Swamp" and "Chirpy" from readers and other cartoonists was not insignificant. Unfortunately, much of that response was negative. The dark, oppressive, and underlying erotic tone of "The Swamp," as well as the motif of the struggling cartoonist and the bar girl living together in "Chirpy"—both represent fairly early instances of the trials of young adulthood appearing unvarnished within manga. Many of Tsuge's contemporaries, however, simply found them "bleak" and "decadent," and said so. Disheartened, Tsuge once again considered quitting comics. He thought he might try to get a job working a factory night shift, and scheduled an interview at a printer in Ichigaya. But on the way, he stopped in at Seirindō, *Garo*'s publisher, located in Jinbochō, where publisher and head editor Katsuichi Nagai informed him that Shigeru Mizuki was looking for people to help him with his own work.

As a kashihon author, Mizuki had been fairly prolific but not very popular. Then, toward the end of 1965, he received the Children's Manga Prize from Kōdansha, one of the biggest publishing houses in Japan. Immediately, he began receiving commissions from major manga magazines, including a remake of his kashihon *Kitarō* series for Kōdansha's *Weekly Shōnen Magazine* (selections of which have been published in English translation by Drawn & Quarterly). Swamped and in dire need of help, Mizuki formally created Mizuki Pro in 1966. Though fifteen years younger than Mizuki (born 1922), Tsuge debuted as a cartoonist before Mizuki, and was established and respected

in touch with him. So they used the pages of the magazine: "Yoshiharu Tsuge, please contact us," it says in the margin of a page in the April 1965 issue. The missive found its mark. Tsuge soon began drawing for the magazine, with his first story for them, "The Phony Warrior" ("Uwasa no bushi"), appearing in the August 1965 issue.

Shirato's policy for *Garo* was to let artists draw what they wished without any editorial interference. This present volume—*The Swamp*—focuses on Tsuge's earliest contributions to the magazine. Markedly different from his classic *Garo* stories of the late '60s, much of what he drew in 1965–66 was an extension of the styles and themes of his previous kashihon work. For example, his first four contributions to *Garo*—"The Phony Warrior," "Watermelon Sake" ("Suika zake," *Garo* no. 14, October 1965), "Destiny" ("Unmei," *Garo* no. 16, December 1965), and "An Unusual Painting" ("Fushigi na e," *Garo* no. 17, January 1966)—revisited the historical

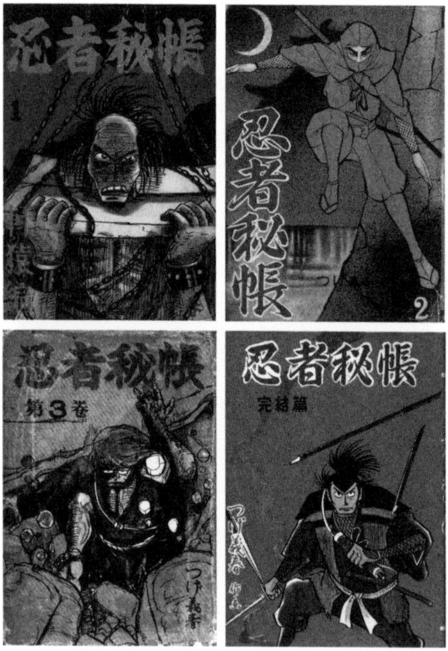

忍者秘帳
1
忍者秘帳
2
忍者秘帳
第3巻
忍者秘帳
完結篇

Tsuge, *The Secret Ninja Scrolls* vols. 1–4 (Wakagi Shobō, October 1960–May 1961)

settings and character types of the many samurai and ninja manga he had drawn since his debut. In the early '60s, Shirato's ninja titles were among the most popular kashihon manga, with the result that many artists, including Tsuge, were asked by their publishers to produce work in his style. It is perhaps possible to read the fake Musashi Miyamoto (c. 1584–1645) in "The Phony Warrior" as a stand-in for Tsuge as the "phony Sanpei Shirato." The lines in the second-to-last panel—"As Musashi, perhaps this man was a fake. But as himself, he was the real thing."—are colored by Tsuge's own pride as an artist. "Watermelon Sake" and "Destiny" also feature samurai, and similarly reflect the artist's personal life and dire economic situation.

In August 1965, Tsuge participated in an event in Tabata (north Tokyo) where readers could meet their favorite kashihon manga authors. Shirato and Shigeru Mizuki, both of whom Tsuge had previously met but never talked seriously with, were also guests. So that the struggling artist would have the time and space to polish his ideas for future stories for *Garo*, Shirato invited Tsuge to come stay with him at an inn he frequently used in rural Ōtaki, in the hills of the Bōsō Peninsula in Chiba Prefecture. Sympathetic to Tsuge's money troubles, Shirato even paid for Tsuge's room and board for the almost two weeks that he was there. "The time I spent in Ōtaki was truly purifying," recalled Tsuge in 1974 about the Suehiro Inn, located adjacent to the gentle Isumi River. "The sky, the mountains, the river, the rain, the inn, fishing—I really responded to the glimmering vividness of the natural world around me. Small birds, insects, dogs I passed on the road, simple rocks—it was hard to believe that I had barely noticed such things until just yesterday."[3] While there, Tsuge drew one work, "An Unusual Painting." Though the story itself is straightforward, by featuring an idiosyncratic artist who entertains himself by creating impenetrable pictures, the work seems to foreshadow Tsuge's own imminent break with comics orthodoxy.

established in *Four Crimes*. "The Ventriloquist" ("Fukuwajutsushi," March 1960) features Tatsumi-style characters. Works like "Black" ("Kuro," July 1959) and "Railroad" ("Tetsuro," September 1959) have much in common with Matsumoto's work. Tsuge's mastery of the medium was visibly growing in these years, but would soon be hamstrung by an outside factor: the shrinking of the kashihon market. With individual titles selling fewer copies, publishers attempted to stay afloat by publishing more titles at a faster pace, filled with whatever they could get their hands on. Though Tsuge was never prolific by Japanese standards, in 1960 he published twenty-three different works, totaling 1070 pages. Slave as he did, the page rate for kashihon manga was so low that he barely had enough money to support himself, let alone his girlfriend, who eventually left him. In 1962, a year in which he published no work, Tsuge attempted to kill himself with sleeping pills. Thankfully, he survived.

In 1963, Tsuge began drawing again, though still with the same resistance to producing mere entertainment. In the foreword for a collection of his work from 1988, Tsuge wrote the following:

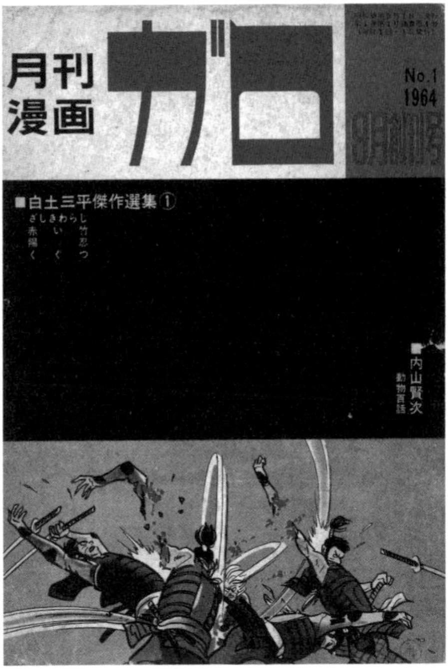

月刊
漫画
ガロ
No.1
1964
■白土三平傑作選集①
■内山賢次
動物百話

Garo no. 1, cover by Sanpei Shirato (Seirindō, September 1964)

The end of the kashihon era were the most difficult years for me. Not only was I having trouble making a living, but I simply could not bear the idea of drawing comics simply to entertain people. Being poorly read and poorly educated as I was, things like "high art" and "self-expression" were total mysteries to me. I didn't have any friends to talk about such ideas with either, so there was no question of me being directly influenced in that way. Still, that's the direction I naturally ended up heading, perhaps as a result of being opposed, emotionally and physically, to drawing just for entertainment's sake. Like some kind of writer's cramp, even drawing just a single panel made my hand shake and gave me the sweats. A ball of black anxiety would well up unpleasantly in my guts, and my head hurt so bad I thought it would crack open. I thought that maybe I could trick my body by just slapping out the first thing that came to me, but that only made things worse.[2]

Fortunately for Tsuge and other ambitious artists, Sanpei Shirato was about to team up with publisher Katsuichi Nagai, president of Seirindō, to create the now legendary magazine *Garo*. Fueled by Shirato's fame in the counterculture with the watershed kashihon series *The Legend of Kagemaru* (*Ninja bugeichō*, 1959–62), and backed financially by the artist's commercial success in mainstream manga magazines with juvenile titles like *Sasuke* (1961–66), *Garo* debuted in 1964 as an unrestrained platform for Shirato's new epic, *The Legend of Kamuy* (*Kamui-den*, 1964–71). Having been impressed by "Ghost Chimneys" when it was first published, Shirato hoped that Tsuge would be one of the magazine's regular contributors. However, as Tsuge rarely mixed with other cartoonists, no one at *Garo* knew how to get

at first he drew and painted the actual cards, once kamishibai's popularity among children began to decline, Shirato instead earned money by delivering card sets on his bicycle to storytellers across northern Tokyo. The Senjū Thermal Power Station, the model for the smokestacks in "Ghost Chimneys," was clearly visible on his delivery route. He was greatly moved by the fact that Tsuge had captured the life of the working poor against the backdrop of such familiar scenery. In general, however, it does not seem that "Ghost Chimneys" made much of an impression. Most readers probably just found the story drab and depressing. In retrospect, it is easy to perceive Tsuge's burgeoning talents and his uniqueness vis-à-vis his contemporaries. But at the time, only a precious few people appreciated how he was expanding the comics medium, leaving the artist unsure about how to go forward.

After "Ghost Chimneys," Tsuge mainly drew short stories for *The Labyrinth*. Much of this output appeared to stay within the style he had

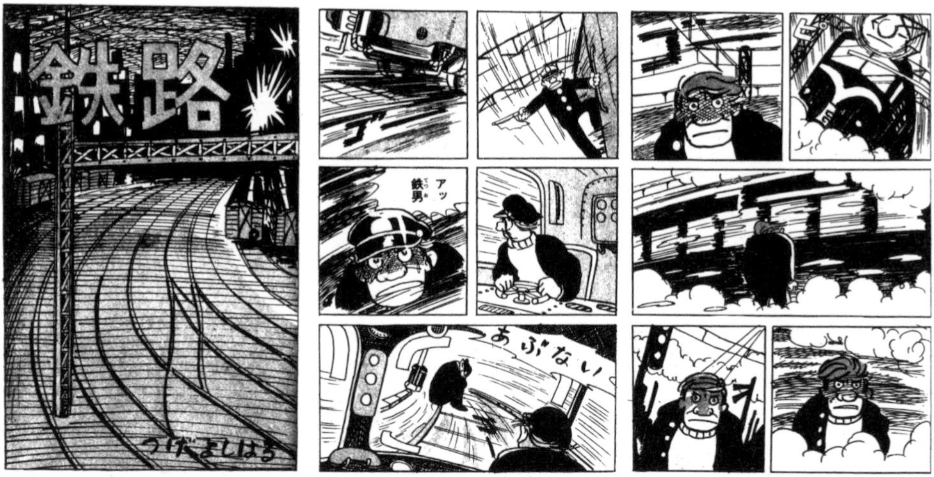
鉄路
アッ
鉄男
あぶない
つげよしはる

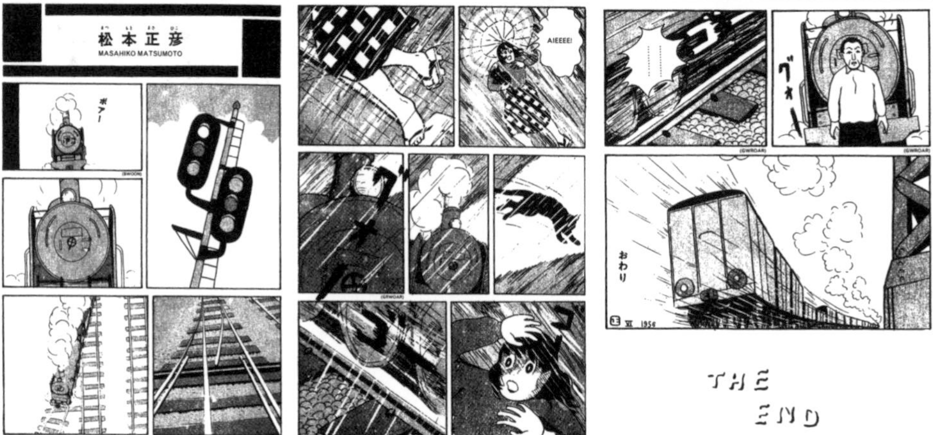
おわり
THE END
AIEEEE!
松本正彦
MASAHIKO MATSUMOTO
ボアー

Top: Tsuge, "Railroad," *The Labyrinth* no. 11 (Wakagi Shobō, September 1959); Bottom: Matsumoto, "The Cat and the Locomotive," *The Shadow* no. 9 (December 1956), as translated in *The Man Next Door* (Breakdown Press, 2014)

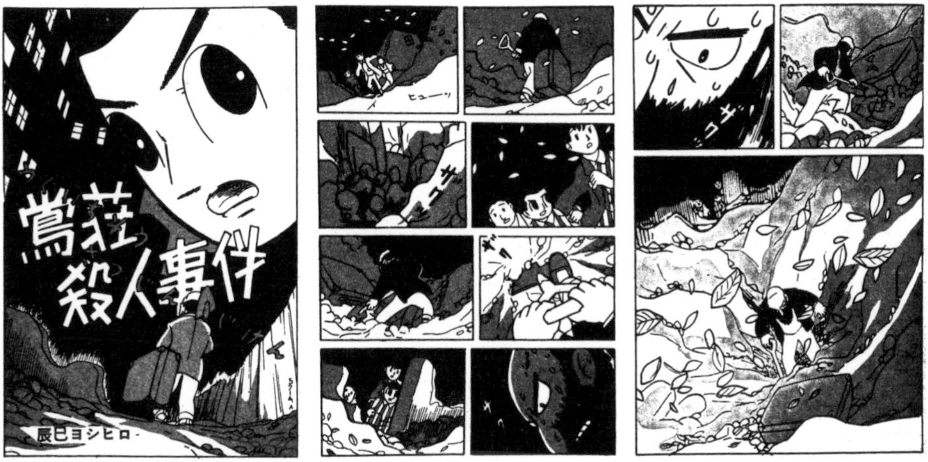
ヒューッ
鶯荘殺人事件
辰巳ヨシヒロ

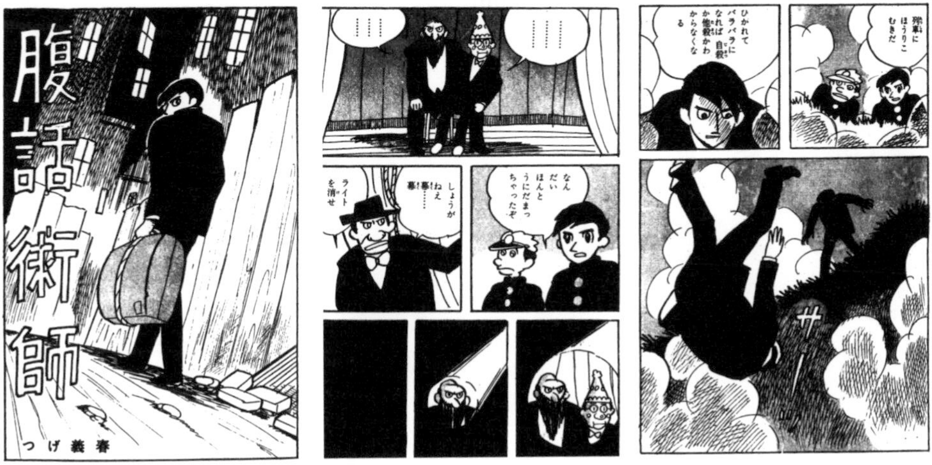
列車にほうりこむきだ
ひかれてバラバラになれば自殺か他殺かわからなくなる
なんだいほんとうにだまっちゃったぞ
しょうがねえ
幕!幕!……
ライトを消せ
腹話術師
つげ義春

Top: Tatsumi, "Murder at the Bush Warbler Apartments," *The City* no. 1 (Central Bunko, March 1957);
Bottom: Tsuge, "The Ventriloquist," *Meiro* no. 3 (March 1960)

and falls to his death, is irredeemably joyless. One might categorize this dark and heavy story as "neo-realist," in the vein of Vittorio De Sica's *Bicycle Thieves* (1948), one of Tsuge's favorite films, or perhaps as "proletarian manga." While "Ghost Chimneys" was not the exact overturning of storytelling tradition that Tsuge was pondering, its mood and open ending marked a break with conventions in kashihon manga. Like "Ghost Chimneys," many of the works that are regarded as turning points in Tsuge's career were produced spontaneously, without any real intention to create something different or groundbreaking. Rather than saying that Tsuge drew them, it almost feels more accurate to say that they drew themselves.

Fatefully, "Ghost Chimneys" caught the eye of Sanpei Shirato, the future founder of *Garo*, who was also drawing manga for kashihon publishers in Tokyo at the time. Between the late '40s and mid-'50s, before he started drawing comics, Shirato was involved with the picture card-based oral storytelling art form known as *kamishibai*. Though

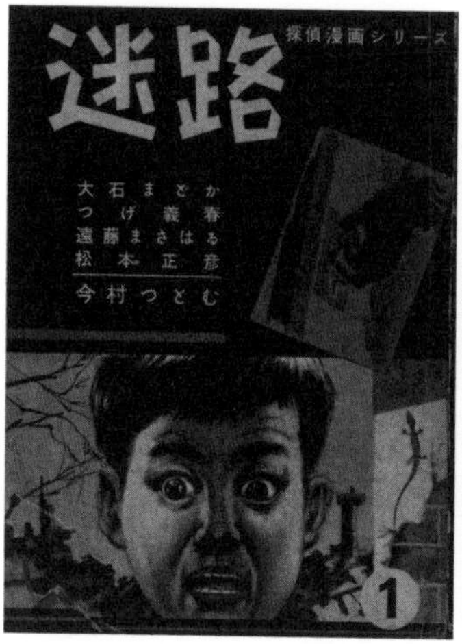
探偵漫画シリーズ
迷路
大石まどか
つげ義春
遠藤まさはる
松本正彦
今村つとむ
1

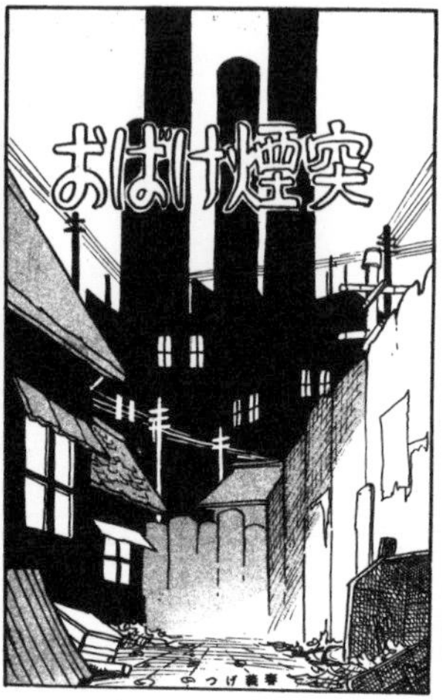
おばけ煙突
つげ義春

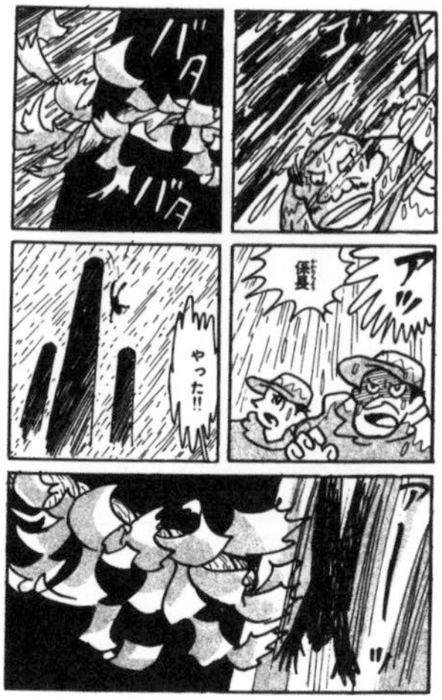
バタ
バタ
アッ
やった!!

Cover, *The Labyrinth* no. 1 (Wakagi Shobō, November 1958), containing Tsuge's "Ghost Chimneys," also above

Blondie, which had been popular in Japan since the Occupation and was being serialized at the time in *The Cartoon Reader* (*Manga dokuhon*), a popular monthly published by Bungei Shunjū that specialized in humor cartoons for adults. Of course, one also finds the aforementioned compositions and techniques from Tatsumi and Matsumoto. The emphasis on low angles is classic Matsumoto. Tsuge's settings typically resemble actual environments in Japan, as they do in Tatsumi's and Matsumoto's work. Here and there, Tsuge renders the details of his backgrounds so realistically that they almost look like lithographs. Such images, it turns out, are based on the work of illustrator Mitsuo Mutsu'ura. By combining these divergent influences, Tsuge was able to achieve a novel mélange: an everyday realism that one does not find in Tezuka, and an urban chicness that is absent in the work of his kashihon gekiga peers.

A few hundred miles away in Osaka, Tatsumi and Matsumoto were reading Tsuge's work in return, and have recalled being impressed by his creative adaptation of their own techniques and styles. However, due to being unsure how to transcend traditional story structure, Tsuge was approaching a creative impasse. Cartoonist Masaharu Endō, a friend of Tsuge's through Wakagi Shobō, recalled the following conversation: "Wait, so you mean to tell me that you have no need for entertainment, no need for usual storytelling, and no need even for logical dramatic principles (*kishōtenketsu*)? That such things just cloud pure art, is that what you're saying?" asked Endō. To which Tsuge responded, "No, I don't have the courage to take things that far. But I have this idea to break up and rearrange the various parts of dramatic composition, like by drawing just the climax and folding the other elements into it. I was thinking that something like that might be possible."[1] That said, kashihon manga remained committed to captivating readers with fairly clear-cut plots and panel-to-panel relationships to the end. No one was interested in manga without stories—at least not yet.

Tsuge was stuck. The work that resulted was "Ghost Chimneys" ("Obake entotsu"), published in the first volume of *The Labyrinth* (*Meiro*, November 1958), a kashihon mystery anthology from Wakagi Shobō modeled on *The Shadow* and similar titles coming out of Osaka. The protagonist, a poor, middle-aged chimney sweep, needs money to take his son to the hospital. Despite a furious storm, he accepts a standing offer of a large monetary reward to clean a tall, dangerous smokestack that no one dares climb. The finale, when he slips

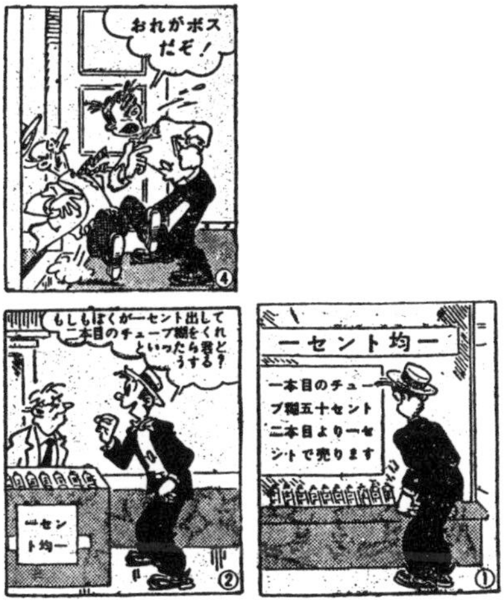
一セント均一
一本目のチューブ糊五十セント二本目より一セントで売ります
もしもぼくが一セント出して二本目のチューブ糊をくれといったら君どうする?
一セント均一
おれがボスだぞ!

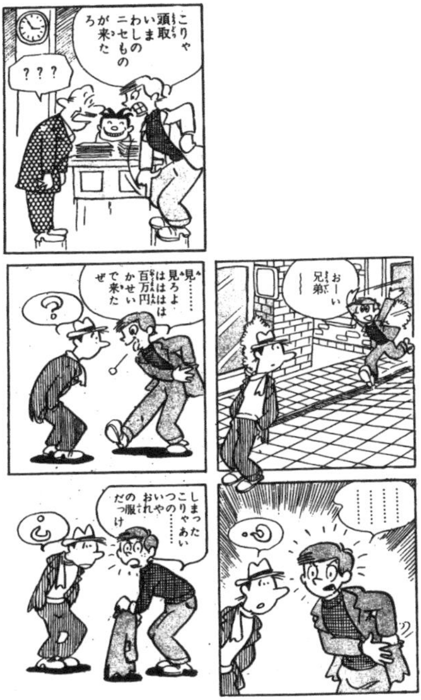
こりゃ頭取 いまわしのニセものが来たろ
???
おーい兄弟〜
見…… 見ろよ はははは 百万円かせいで来たぜ
?
……
しまった こりゃあいつの…… いや おれの服だっけ
?

Top: Chic Young, *Blondie, The Cartoon Reader* no. 13 (November 1956); Bottom: Tsuge, *An Invitation to Hell* (Wakagi Shobō, February 1957)

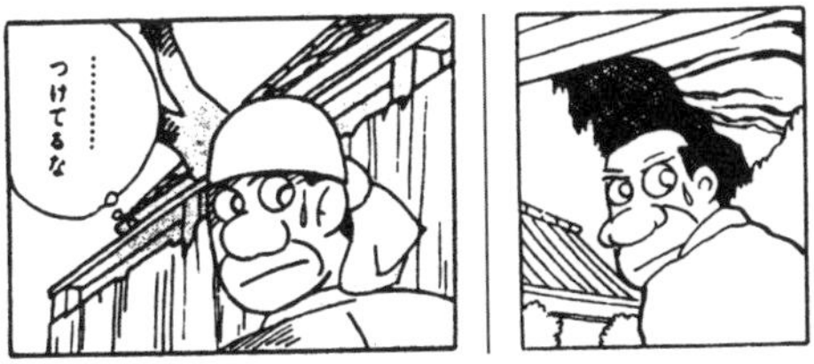
……つけてるな

Left: Yoshihiro Tatsumi, "It Happened One Night," *The Shadow* no. 4 (July 1956); Right: Tsuge, *The Living Ghost* (November 1956)

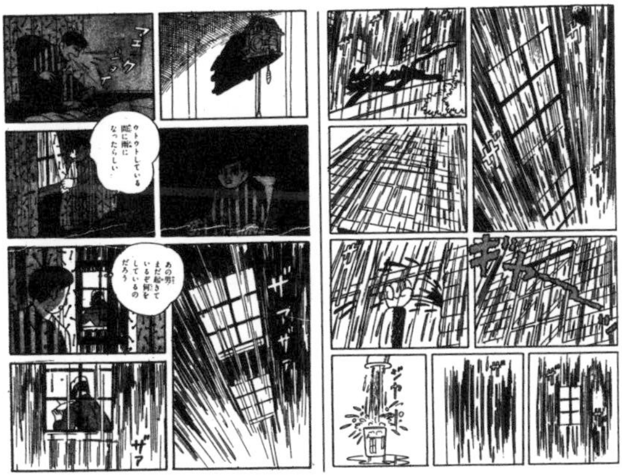
ウトウトしている間に雨になったらしい
あの男まだ起きているぞ何をしているのだろう
ザァザァ
ザァ

Left: Tatsumi, "The Mystery of the Black Cat Apartments," *The Shadow* no. 6 (September 1956); Right: Tsuge, *Four Crimes* (Wakagi Shobō, June 1957)

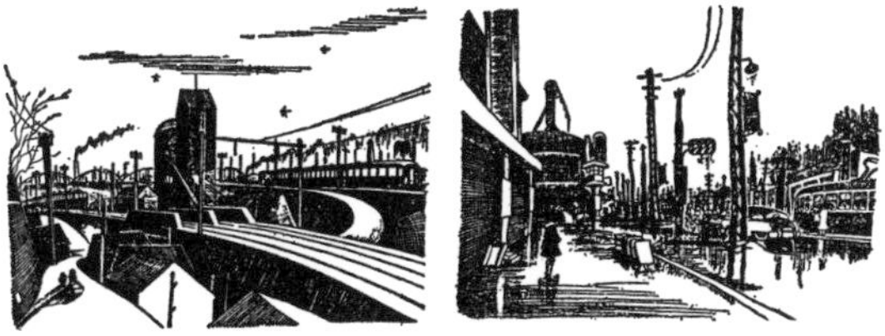

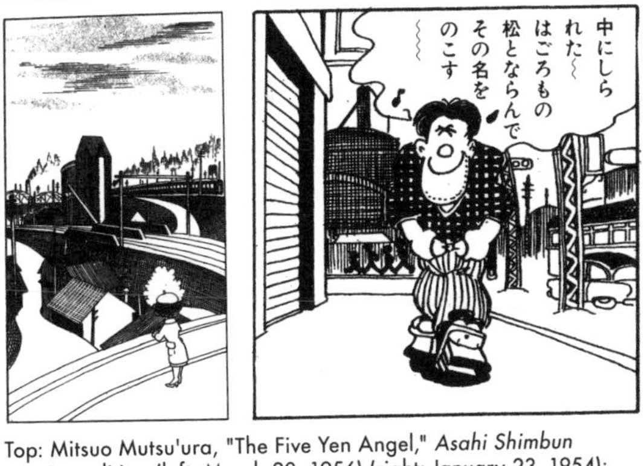
中にしられた〜 はごろもの松とならんでその名をのこす〜〜

Top: Mitsuo Mutsu'ura, "The Five Yen Angel," *Asahi Shimbun* evening edition (left; March 20, 1956) (right; January 23, 1954); Bottom: Tsuge, *Four Crimes* (Wakagi Shobō, June 1957)

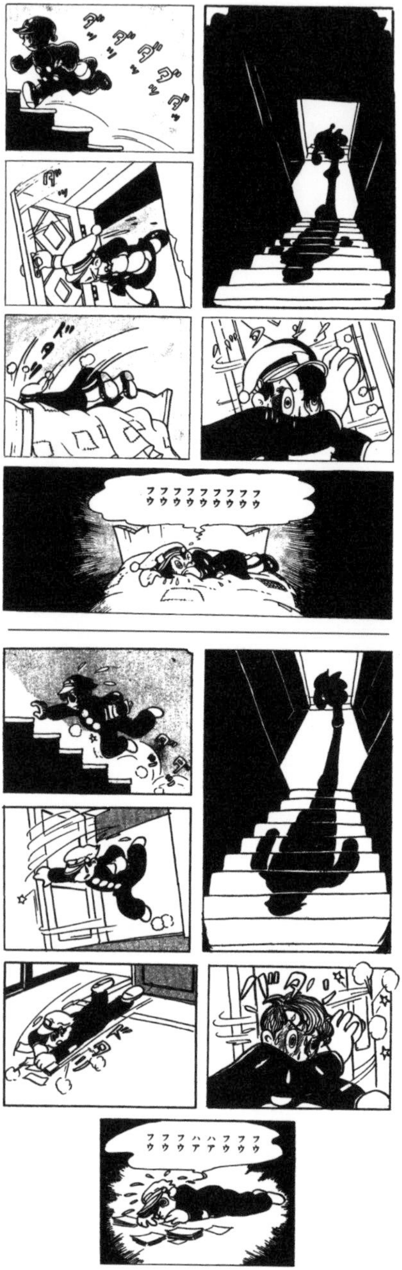
フウフウフウフウフウフウフウフウフウ
フウフウハアハアフウフウフウ

Top: Osamu Tezuka, *Crime and Punishment* (Tōkōdō, November 1953); Bottom: Tsuge, *The Living Ghost* (November 1956)

home was incinerated by American firebombs. He recalled jumping over charred bodies while escaping the sea of fire. Such experiences surely underpinned the dark settings and ambiguous moral situations in his early manga. Like many kashihon cartoonists, Matsumoto did not subscribe to an absolute dichotomy between good and evil, and was sympathetic to the fact that there is often a logical explanation for criminal behavior. To be sure, it is hard to call such manga edifying in the narrowest sense, and it is not surprising that these stories were criticized for corrupting young readers. On the other hand, given common experiences of death and destruction during the war, and the persistence of the war's legacy in the form of widespread poverty, personal and family trauma, and visible traces of physical ruins during the years kashihon manga flourished, such manga were arguably presenting to young readers a world they already knew and urging them to think about that world more critically. At any rate, Matsumoto's stories certainly expanded the possibilities of the medium, with Tsuge being just one of many artists who followed his lead.

Unsatisfied with how manga were made for mainstream retail publications, Tsuge started employing Matsumoto's and Tatsumi's techniques not long after his debut, as seen in *The Living Ghost* (*Ikiteita yūrei*, November 1956) and *Four Crimes* (*Yottsu no hanzai*, June 1957), both published by Wakagi Shobō. In both works, however, one can still sense the influence of Tezuka in the way characters are modeled. In *The Living Ghost*, Tsuge even appropriated an entire page from Tezuka's *Crime and Punishment* (*Tsumi to batsu*, November 1953). It's not unreasonable to read such overt copying as an intentional homage to an artist Tsuge had avidly read since he was young and a fond farewell before striking out in new directions.

The stylistic experiments in these works derived from various sources. For example, while sticking with a basic Tezuka style, Tsuge incorporated the way characters stand and move from Chic Young's

panel breakdowns in Matsumoto's. Because kashihon books were often read and circulated until they fell apart, and the few copies that have survived are kept in private collections, it is hard to conduct a thorough comparison of the three artists' work. Nonetheless, even a limited sample reveals that Tsuge learned much from his peers in the Osaka area.

Take Matsumoto, for example. Though Tsuge's drawing style differed from Matsumoto's irregular but gentle linework, Tsuge found inspiration in the realism of his stories, which featured protagonists that one might actually meet on the street, something rarely found in manga from the '50s. Using motifs derived from everyday life, Matsumoto produced many works in the detective genre foregrounding psychological suspense. Some of his characters are addicted to drugs or alcohol, some are mentally ill, others are homeless. These afflictions are often explained as the result of misfortunes during the war and/or the hardships of poverty thereafter. In Matsumoto's early masterpiece, "The Man Next Door" ("Rinshitsu no otoko," April 1956), one of the main characters, Niichi, spends his days drinking by himself in his room. He doesn't even greet his neighbors when he passes them in the hallway. According to the story, Niichi lost his mother and sister in the air raids, and drinks to drive away that painful memory. "It's all because of that war, that horrible war!" he yells while drunk and alone. Though such characters and settings constitute a relatively small percentage of Matsumoto's output, their uniqueness and power guaranteed his importance and influence.

Matsumoto was born in 1934 in Osaka. He lost his father in 1943. Twice during the war, his

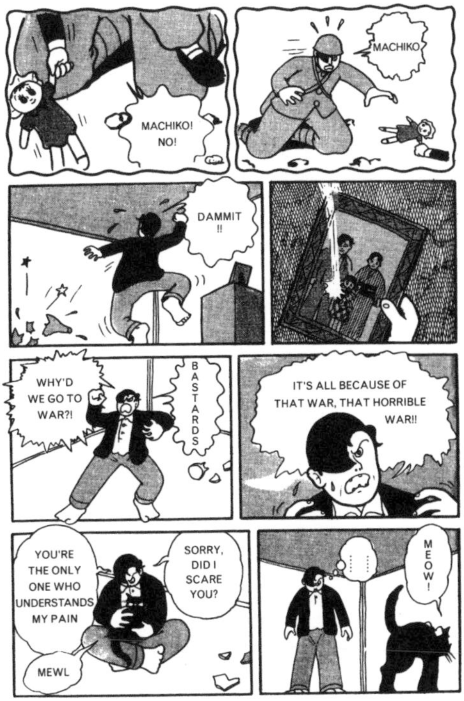
MACHIKO
MACHIKO! NO!
DAMMIT !!
IT'S ALL BECAUSE OF THAT WAR, THAT HORRIBLE WAR!!
BASTARDS
WHY'D WE GO TO WAR?!
MEOW!
SORRY, DID I SCARE YOU?
YOU'RE THE ONLY ONE WHO UNDERSTANDS MY PAIN
MEWL

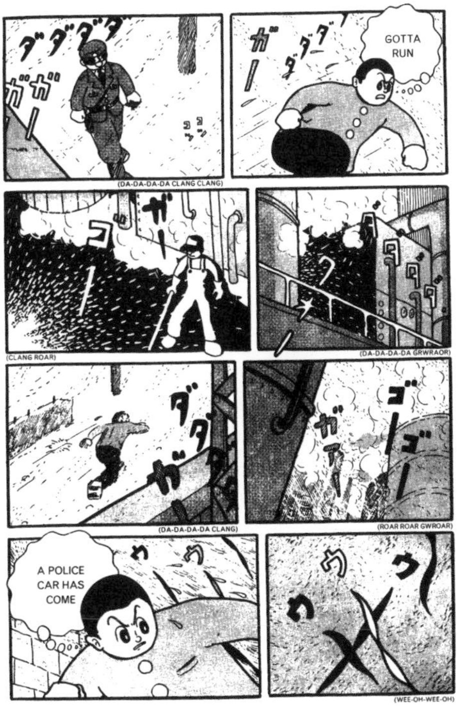
GOTTA RUN
(DA-DA-DA-DA CLANG CLANG)
(DA-DA-DA-DA GRWRAOR)
(CLANG ROAR)
(ROAR ROAR GWROAR)
(DA-DA-DA-DA CLANG)
(WEE-OH-WEE-OH)
A POLICE CAR HAS COME

Left: Masahiko Matsumoto, "Thick Fog," *The Shadow* no. 2 (May 1955); Right: Matsumoto, "The Man Next Door," *The Shadow* no. 1 (April 1956), as translated in *The Man Next Door* (Breakdown Press, 2014)

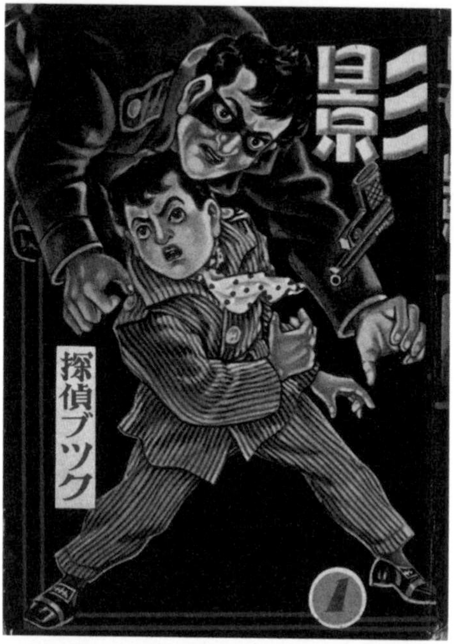
影
探偵ブック
1

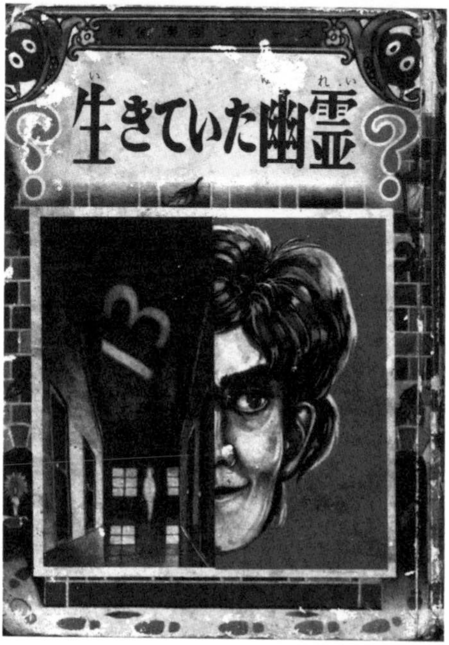
生きていた幽霊

Top: *The Shadow* no. 1, cover by Masami Kuroda (Hinomaru Bunko, April 1956); Bottom: Cover for *The Living Ghost* (Wakagi Shobō, November 1956)

of modern Japanese culture, Tokyo was home to many large publishing houses. These publishers, which produced books and magazines for retail sale across the country, typically paid many times more than the kashihon outfits. Their presence in Tokyo convinced many aspiring artists to move to the capital from the countryside and smaller cities. They also, however, routinely dictated content, requesting that artists soften their stories or art out of consideration for the juvenile market. This was the main reason Tsuge rarely worked with them, and one of the reasons he had a hard time identifying with other cartoonists.

For example, west of the Tokyo neighborhood of Ikebukuro is the former site of the Tokiwa-sō Apartments. Here, a number of young cartoonists lived collectively with the hope of breaking into the industry and be close to their hero, Osamu Tezuka, who had relocated to Tokyo from Osaka in the early '50s. Some of these artists, including Shōtarō Ishinomori, Fujio Akatsuka, and the Fujiko Fujio duo, would go on to become best-selling creators within mainstream manga and Japanese children's entertainment. Having befriended Akatsuka, Tsuge visited Tokiwa-sō. But their friendship did not last long as Tsuge could not identify with the Tokiwa-sō commitment to making manga that were "good" for children. Tsuge had not yet fully worked out his own artistic philosophy, yet it was clear to him that the potential for comics was larger than children's entertainment, and that artistic creation had to be based, first of all, on his own understanding of what "reality" meant.

The inaugural issue of the kashihon periodical *The Shadow* (*Kage*) was published by the Osaka publisher Hinomaru Bunko in April 1956. It was just a matter of months before Tsuge began incorporating the innovative techniques being used there by artists like Masahiko Matsumoto and Yoshihiro Tatsumi. He was particularly drawn to the characters, drawing style, and overall mood of Tatsumi's manga, and the everyday settings and

GEKIGA'S NEW FRONTIER:
THE UNEASY RISE OF YOSHIHARU TSUGE

Mitsuhiro Asakawa

Yoshiharu Tsuge's contributions to the development of gekiga and manga are immense. Tsuge was not only the first manga artist who used his personal life as story material, he was also the first to make his characters' internal conflicts the center of his stories. Previously these techniques had been limited to literature and the "I-novel"—a type of autobiographical fiction popular in Japan since the early 20th century. Against the mad rush of Westernization of Japanese daily life after World War II, Tsuge also employed comics to revisit and find new value in native Japanese customs and modes of living, and without lapsing into nostalgia. Furthermore, with works like "Nejishiki" (June 1968), Tsuge abandoned what had been considered one of the bare minimum requirements of the comics medium—storytelling—by exploring the possibilities of the irrational and the surreal. His work did nothing less than redefine the comics medium for readers, creators, and the world of Japanese manga.

Tsuge was born in 1937 in Tokyo, the second of five children. His father died when he was young, leaving his mother to raise the children alone. As it was a time of widespread poverty and turmoil in Japan, Tsuge had to get a job after finishing elementary school. Tsuge was introverted and demonstrated skill in drawing from an early age. He started reading manga soon after the war, and decided he wanted to become a cartoonist after falling in love with Osamu Tezuka's work. Though his first published manga were four-panel strips for the magazine *Thrilling Book* (*Tsūkai bukku*), a mixed comics and prose fiction monthly for boys published by Hōbunsha, in 1954, his true debut as a professional cartoonist dates to the following year with the release of *The White-Masked Demon* (*Hakumen yasha*, May 1955), a 128-page book from the Tokyo *kashihon* (rental book) publisher Wakagi Shobō. Tezuka's influence is strong in Tsuge's earliest works, with additional influences from fellow Wakagi artists Shinji Nagashima and Masaharu Endō. At the time, Tsuge was only eighteen years old.

Tsuge spent the next ten years working primarily with kashihon publishers. As the center

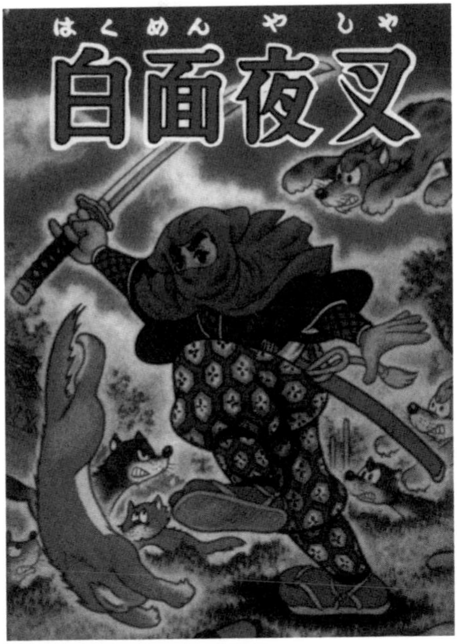
はくめんやしや
白面夜叉

Yoshiharu Tsuge, *The White-Masked Demon*, (Wakagi Shobō, May 1955)

YOSHIHARU TSUGE was born in Tokyo in 1937. Influenced by the adventure comics of Osamu Tezuka and the gritty mystery manga of Yoshihiro Tatsumi and Masahiko Matsumoto, he began making his own comics in the mid '50s. He was also briefly recruited to assist Shigeru Mizuki during his explosion of popularity in the '60s. In 1968, Tsuge published the groundbreaking, surrealistic story "Nejishiki" in the legendary alternative manga magazine *Garo*. This story established Tsuge as not only an influential *manga-ka* but also a major figure within Japan's counterculture and art world at large. He is considered the originator and greatest practitioner of the semi-autobiographical "I-novel" genre of comics-making. In 2005, Tsuge was nominated for the Best Album Award at Angoulême International, and in 2017 a survey of his work, *A World of Dreams and Travel*, won the Japan Cartoonists Association Grand Award.

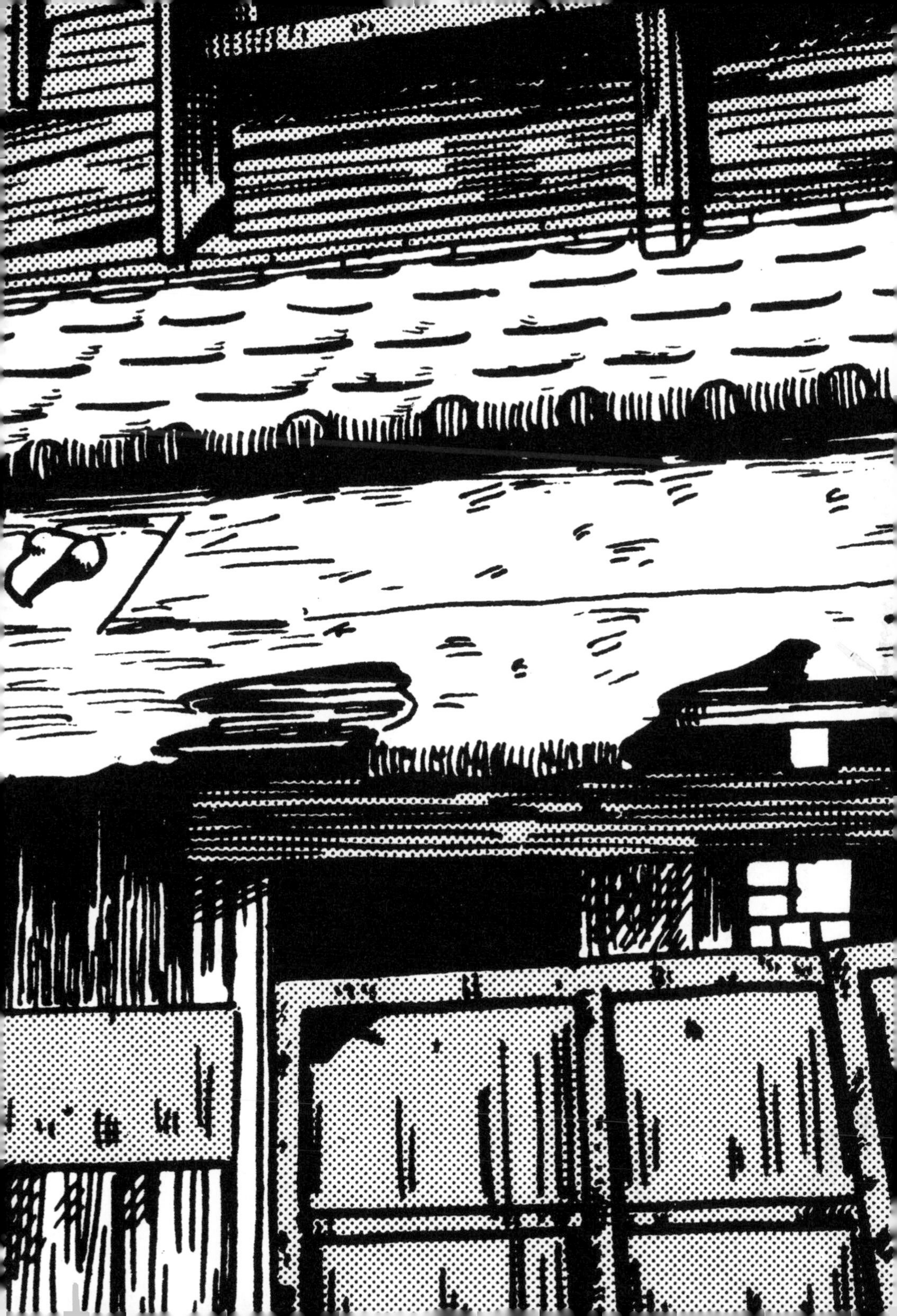

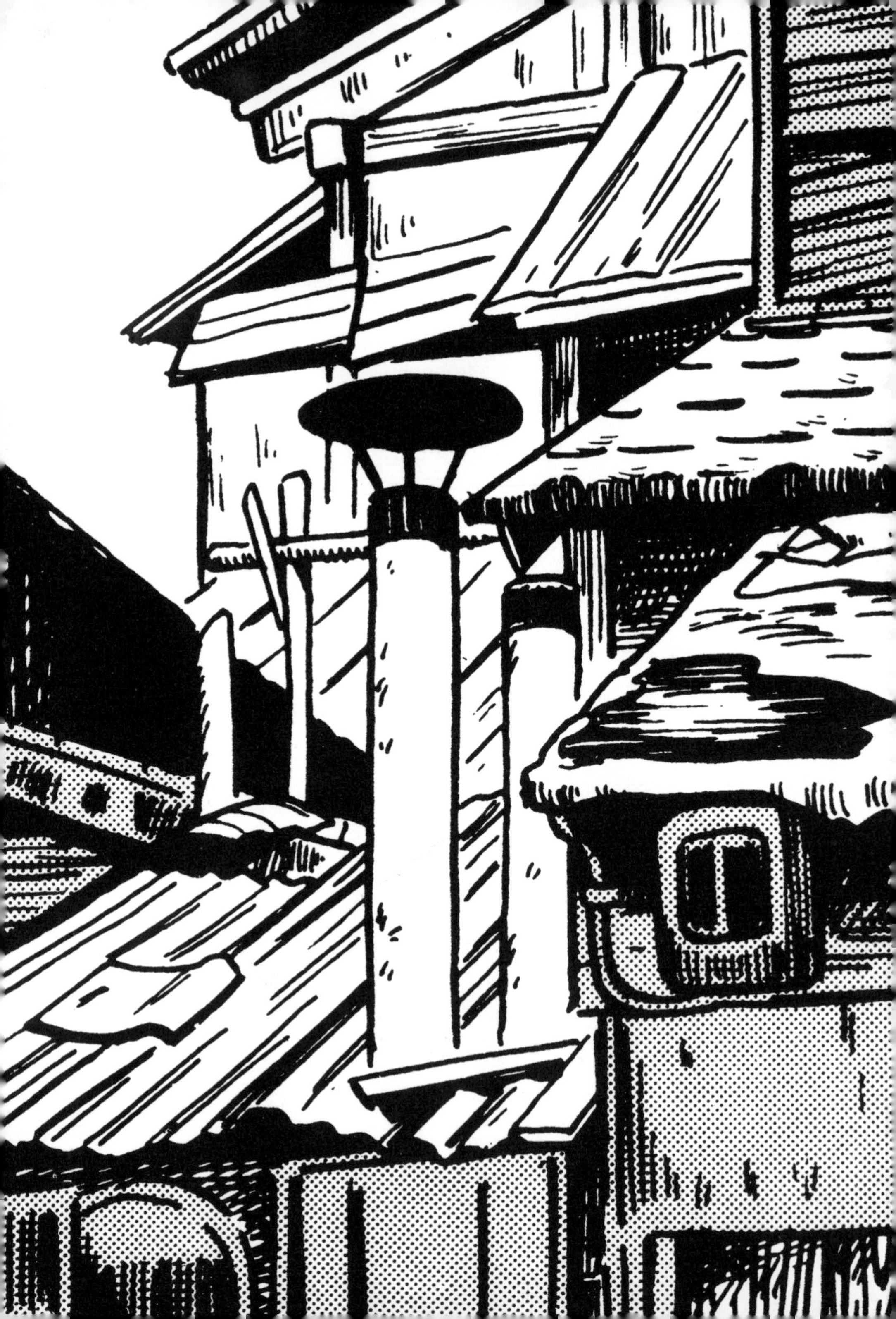

This book is presented in the traditional Japanese manner and is meant to be read from right to left. The cover at the opposite end is considered the front of the book.

To begin reading the manga, please flip the book over and start at the other end. For the historical essay, turn this page and read from left to right.

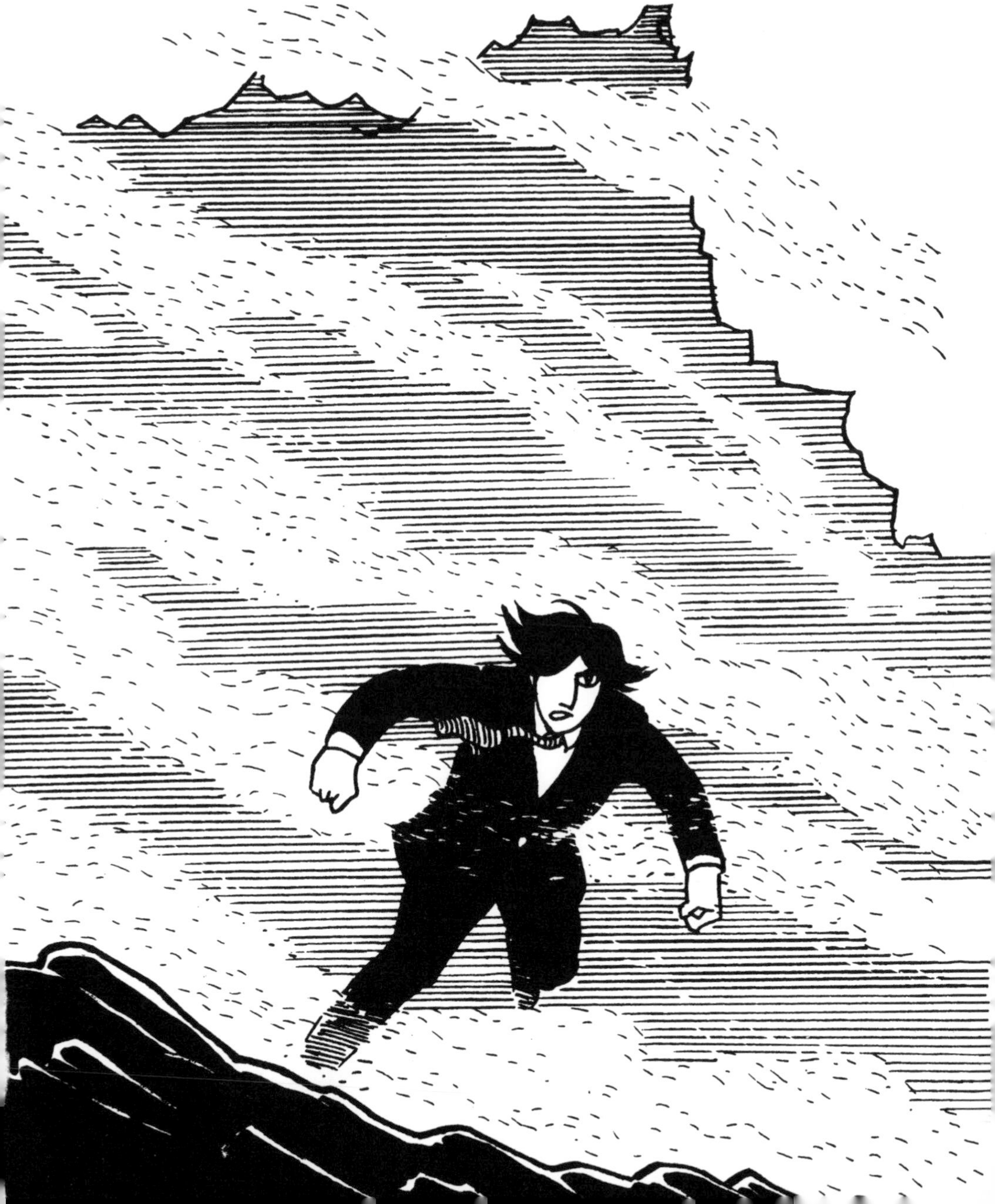

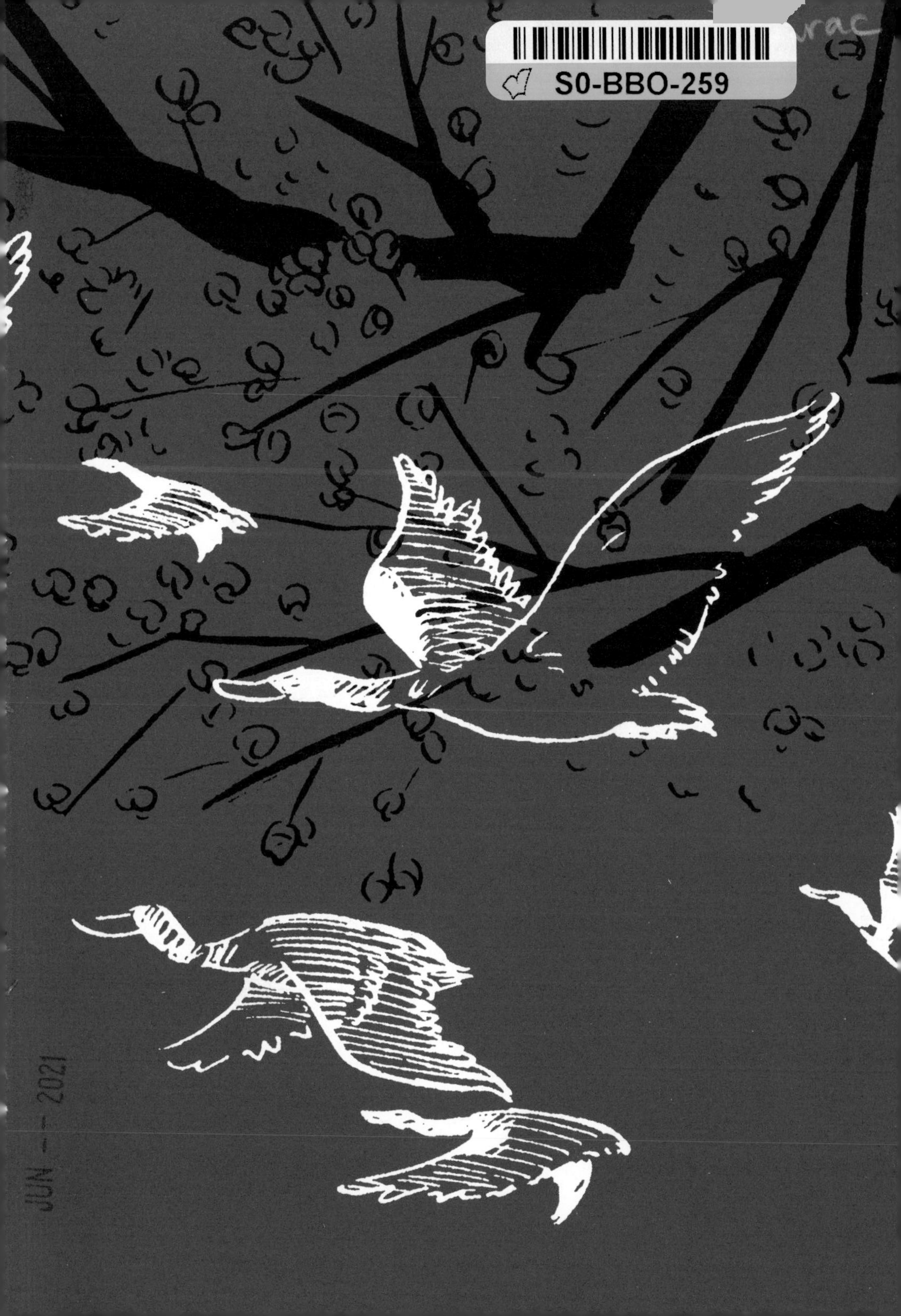